P9-EDC-338

TERTELING LIBRARY
THE COLLEGE OF IDAHO
CALDWELL, IDAHO

PS
3545
R815
Z664
110113

RICHARD WRIGHT
Ordeal of a Native Son

TERTELING LIBRARY
THE COLLEGE OF IDAHO
CALDWELL, IDAHO

RICHARD WRIGHT
Ordeal of a Native Son

Addison Gayle

ANCHOR PRESS/DOUBLEDAY
GARDEN CITY, NEW YORK
1980

110113

PS3545
R815
Z664

No copyright is claimed on the U. S. Government
material contained throughout this book.

ISBN: 0-385-08877-9
Library of Congress Catalog Card Number 77-12854
Copyright © 1980 by Addison Gayle
ALL RIGHTS RESERVED
PRINTED IN THE UNITED STATES OF AMERICA
FIRST EDITION

Grateful acknowledgment is made to the following for permission to use copyrighted
material:

Quotations from *The Unfinished Quest of Richard Wright*, by Michel Fabre,
copyright © 1973 by William Morrow & Company, Inc., by permission of the publishers.

Quotations from *Black Boy*, by Richard Wright, copyright 1937, 1942, 1944,
1945, by Richard Wright; from *American Hunger*, by Richard Wright, copyright
1944 by Richard Wright; from *The Outsider*, by Richard Wright, copyright 1953
by Richard Wright; from *Native Son*, by Richard Wright, copyright 1940 by Richard
Wright; all by permission of Harper & Row, Publishers, Inc.

Quotations from *Black Power*, by Richard Wright, copyright 1954 by Richard
Wright, by permission of Paul Reynolds, Inc.

Quotations from *The Quality of Hurt*, Vol. 1, by Chester Himes, copyright 1972
by Chester Himes; from *My Life of Absurdity*, by Chester Himes, copyright 1976 by
Chester Himes; both by permission of Doubleday & Company, Inc.

110113

In memoriam

For Loretta Gayle Carter
and Reginald A. Gayle
and for Yvonne and Dot, Mary and Debbie.

TERTELING LIBRARY
THE COLLEGE OF IDAHO
CALDWELL, IDAHO

"His interest in the problems of the Negro
was almost an obsession."

Agent (name deleted)
Federal Bureau of Investigation
Bureau File #100-157464
February 26, 1945

INTRODUCTION

To paraphrase Michel Fabre, the distinguished biographer of Richard Wright, to Americans of the nineteen seventies Richard Wright remains unknown and unread. This was true of the late sixties and early seventies despite the fact that from 1940, the publication date of *Native Son*, until his sudden death in Paris in 1960, he was the most famous black writer in the world. His books have been translated into many languages, and millions throughout Asia, Africa, Europe, and the Middle East have shared, vicariously, the experiences of a Mississippi black boy. Yet his reputation did decline in the early nineteen sixties, and this may be attributable to a number of factors. Among them were a rising militancy and determination to achieve human rights in America, which led to a search for political, not literary, writers; the popularity of such younger writers as James Baldwin and Ralph Ellison, whose works in comparison to those of Wright appeared moderate in tone and theme; subtle efforts by magazines and critics, with an impetus by the government, to render Wright's attacks on American foreign policy and racism negligible by diminishing his reputation; a self-imposed exile that kept him out of the country and away from the ferment generated during the civil rights crusade; and the reluctance of college and high school teachers to deal with the explosive acts of racism contained in most of his works.

However, in the past five years there has been renewed interest in Wright and his works. A number of critical articles have been written about his books in prestigious journals. *American Hunger*, the last half of the autobiography *Black Boy*, published in 1945, has been released, and a revised edition of the stage adaptation of *Native Son* has played before New York audiences. A new play is slated for Broadway, at least one other biography is headed for publication, several doctors'

theses are in the development stage, and plans are under way to release
some of his as yet unpublished work. Black intellectuals who ignored
him in the sixties today eagerly search through his works, seeking answers as to why and how the civil rights revolution of the sixties went
astray; young college professors are inclined to honestly confront his
commentary on the debilitating effects of American racism and his
death-stilled criticism of the United States Government. Today, more
and more Americans are reading of his life and trials, of his ordeal as a
sensitive black intellectual in a racist society.

Those who read *Black Boy* confront the man shorn of the writer's
mask. They discover that by the time he was fifteen he had known of
the lynching of a stepuncle and the brother of a neighborhood friend;
that he had spent time in an orphanage, had known poverty and hunger; that he had witnessed the paralyzing of his mother, her being rendered an invalid for most of her life; that he had personally experienced
southern brutality. He joined the black migration heading North before
his twenty-first birthday, hoping, as he implied in the closing pages of
Black Boy, to discover the new Canaan. The relative freedom of the
North enabled him to become a writer, and he was to create some of
the most exciting literature in America. Yet Canaan was always to
elude him. Before his success as a writer, he encountered poverty and
hunger again, racism and exploitation northern style, and authoritarianism in the Communist Party. The pattern of his life seemed not
to have altered greatly in many respects even after the publication of
Native Son made him world famous. He was involved in an unsuccessful marriage and in frequent altercations with leaders of the Communist Party, and was harassed by agents of the Federal Bureau of Investigation. He divorced his first wife and married again in 1944, and in
1945 he broke publicly with the Party. In 1947, with his wife and
daughter, he went into self-imposed exile in France.

If again he sought Canaan, again he was disappointed. His exile
afforded some relief from racism, but his fierce sense of independence
and his well-earned reputation intensified the conflict between himself
and agencies of the American Government, which sought to force him
to mitigate his attacks upon American domestic and foreign policy and
to inform on old comrades and friends in the Communist Party. This
aspect of the government's campaign began even before he went into
exile, and one of the reasons for his so doing was to escape the pressure
brought upon him to be an informant. In France, on a passport granted
by the State Department, which had the power to rescind it at any moment, he underwent an ordeal as severe as that he had previously recorded in *Black Boy* and *American Hunger*. It may well have been the

strain and stress attending this ordeal which brought about his sudden death.

Rumors concerning his confrontation with agencies of the American Government fueled my own interest in Richard Wright. During a trip to Paris in 1972, one of Wright's close friends informed me that Wright had been a special target of the Central Intelligence Agency and the Federal Bureau of Investigation. These agencies, the friend remarked, were responsible for his death. Such rumors were rife on the Left Bank, both among black expatriates and French intellectuals, but, at the time, I gave little credence to them, simply because I could not believe that a writer was important enough to incur the wrath of the government. But, as the biographies of Wright began to appear—by John A. Williams, Constance Webb, and Michel Fabre—each of whom spoke of government harassment, the rumors took on for me some semblance of credibility. Later, reading Chester Himes's comments in *Amistad One* and his autobiography, and reading Wright's private papers and letters (housed at the Beinecke Rare Book and Manuscript Library, at Yale, and at the Schomburg library in New York), I was then disposed to think of the rumors as having some validity.

If they did, then here was unexplored terrain, an ordeal undergone by Wright as severe and intense as any before, a dimension of his life that might serve to place his life and works in a new perspective. At the least, some of the intriguing yet unanswered questions concerning his relationship with the Communist Party and African nationalists abroad might be clarified, as well as the extent and nature of his involvement with the government. Fortunately, in undertaking this assignment, I had a research tool not available to past students of Wright: investigative files from government agencies interested in his activities.

The Congress of the United States passed the Freedom Of Information Act in 1966 and the Privacy Act in 1974. The former allowed access to previously classified documents compiled on American citizens by various government agencies, and the latter allowed American citizens access to their own files, if any existed. On July 7, 1976, I wrote the Department of Justice requesting theretofore classified documents pertaining to Richard Wright. This request triggered a response by other agencies, and in December of 1977, I received the first document from the Department of State. In April, I received a substantial number of documents from the FBI, and in June, two documents from the CIA. The largest number of documents—187 pages out of a possible 227—came from the FBI. These reflect the fact that information concerning Wright, as well as actions to be taken against him, were forwarded to the FBI. Thus in these files were found documents from the

United States Information Service, the military intelligence units of the Army and the Navy, and the Foreign Liaison Service, which supplied security agencies of other governments with data.

The documents are unusually legible, though deletions of names and information are frequent. Of the total number of pages in the FBI file, thirty-nine have been deleted according to provisions contained in the Freedom Of Information Act, which range from the interests of national security to the desire to protect agents and informers. Deletions of entire paragraphs and sometimes a number of pages occur in some documents, making clarification of certain events almost impossible. This is particularly true of documents originating with the Foreign Service and forwarded to FBI Headquarters in Washington from Paris during the last years of Wright's life.

Access to this new research tool forced the realization that none of my college training had prepared me to analyze the material at my disposal. I was taught to examine old and obscure tracts, to balance the thesis of one critic against that of another, to gather evidence for or against one set of postulates and to enunciate findings supported by the proper number of authorities and an abundance of footnote material. My graduate training had taught me to look at the works and lives of men and women as if they existed in a social and political vacuum. This methodology served well in work done in graduate school on eighteenth-century British literature. If Henry Fielding and Samuel Richardson were objects of interest to their government, I had no way of knowing. But the modern American writer, if outspoken and radical or an advocate of unpopular causes, is very likely to be a subject of investigation by some agencies of the government. The fruits of such investigation may be indispensable to understanding certain nuances of his life, which may well have influenced his work.

To my knowledge, Freedom Of Information Act material has not been applied to research on American writers; certainly none has been applied to black writers. Thus I was involved in setting a precedent, having no guidelines to follow. The material before me could only be understood if I understood as well the historical context of the forties and fifties, during which the adversary relationship between Wright and the government existed. The contours of the study I had planned was changed: I would need to analyze the period of American concentration upon subversives and the "Communist conspiracy," in the hope that light might be shed on some of the people named in the documents, on some of the events concerning Wright's most important undertakings, and on certain actions proposed against him. Thus, books on history were indispensable; so, too, in attempting to understand many of the codes and much of the terminology contained in the documents, were books on such governmental agencies as the CIA and the FBI.

The absence of guidelines, however, presented the greatest difficulty in another area: how was the material to be presented? The documents lend themselves to dramatic and sensationalistic treatment; here is the material of which good drama and fiction are made. There are portraits of cool, calculating agents, of comical ones whose ineptness is blatant, of paid and volunteer informants, black and white, including one labeled by an agent as "a psychopath." There are intrigue and suspense, and the drama of good and evil is well stocked with heroes and villains. To treat the material in a theatrical way was tempting; in my judgment, however, to do so would have been erroneous.

First, the story was one-sided, coming from the very agencies that had harassed Wright during his lifetime. Second, some of the material was damaging to Wright's reputation and had to be corroborated as much as possible from his private papers and from interviews with his friends. Finally, there were my apprehension and suspicion, heightened by some of the material, of possible governmental action against the late writer. In two instances, the documents suggest an attempt by the legal representative of the FBI in Paris to make the Baldwin-Wright literary controversy into a political one and pit one black writer against the other. I was forced then to confront the possibility that the vendetta waged by the State Department against Wright in the last days of his life might persist still among old and unforgiving bureaucrats, and that this writer might be used to impugn Wright's reputation. This concern led to my decision to present the data from the documents in as objective a manner as possible. The documents would speak for themselves. I would editorialize little, analyze and evaluate material only when there were adequate collaborative data from Wright's works, from previous studies, or from his own private papers. Looking at Wright and the documents concerning him from a historical perspective allowed me to place the material in chronological order, in accord with various stages of his life. Presented in this way, the documents assume an overwhelming importance in Wright's career, particularly the last years of his exile.

Even without emendation, the documents provide answers to questions heretofore unresolved by Richard Wright scholars. The 1958 document, for instance, reveals that Wright's sudden break with the Communist Party, after debating with himself about such action for a number of years, came about as the result of a personal altercation between him and Benjamin Davis. The document of 1944, consisting of logs of wiretaps on the phones of important party officials, reveals the concern of the Party over Wright's defection and outlines the campaign eventually waged against him. The documents reveal that problems concerning his passport did not originate in 1945, but began in 1940, when his passport was taken by immigration officials at the Mexican border. The document of 1943 reveals that the initial interest in Wright on a full scale occurred as a result of a memo, from the office of Secretary of War Henry Stimson to the director of the FBI, suggesting that Wright may be guilty of sedition—an offense punishable by imprisonment. Other documents reveal the nature of the operations of the Bureau, including the use of informers, questioning of neighbors, and mail openings. The documents of 1958–60 reveal that the major agency interested in Wright's activities abroad was not, as had been suspected, the FBI or the CIA, but the Department of State. In a letter written to his friend and translator Margrit de Sablonière, Wright corroborated this fact by pointing to the Department of State as his major adversary. If this is so, then assumptions that the CIA and the FBI were solely responsible for his early death might have to be reassessed.

The documents of 1956 and 1958 suggest that the State Department may have been engaged in blackmail concerning Wright. He was forced to sign statements and to answer questions regarding "the Communist conspiracy" before his passport was renewed. In letters to friends, in private conversations, in notations contained in the works of his biographers are revealed his anxieties about returning to the United States. Had he done so, he would have had to face the investigative committees of the Congress, and possibly, courtroom trials. Acquaintances such as Langston Hughes, W. E. B. Du Bois, Paul Robeson, and Canada Lee had undergone terrible ordeals with the House Un-American Activities Committee. Robeson and Du Bois had their passports revoked and their means of livelihood ended. Lee and Hughes were forced to disavow past "subversive affiliations." Wright's treatment, were he to be forced back to America, would have probably surpassed that of Robeson and Du Bois. He did not, like the other two men, have the support of progressives and the members of the Communist Party. Thus he would have had to undergo his ordeal alone.

The documents pertaining to renewal of his passport assume major importance. To Wright's applications were affixed questions pertaining to knowledge that he may have had of former Communists. In the presence of the passport chief and the legal representative, if the files are correct, he produced a statement denying recent Communist affiliation of his own and answered questions corroborating information concerning Communists of his knowledge. At the same time, therefore, when the documents suggest coercion by the government, they also suggest some degree of cooperation by Wright. Other documents also suggest such cooperation, but the most damaging document in this respect, the document of 1956, pertains to the conference of black and African writers sponsored by the magazine *Présence Africaine*. "On his own initiative," reads the document of 1956, "Mr. Wright called at the embassy to express certain concern over the leftist tendencies of the Executive Committee for the [*Présence Africaine*] Congress. He believed the members of the committee were liberal thinkers and he thought there was a distinct danger that the communists might exploit the congress to their ends." This act allied him with the CIA and the security forces of every colonialist nation, whose interest in the conference was pronounced.

If the motives for his cooperation, either reacting to threats of blackmail or attempting to curry favor with the government in his own interest, are indicated in the document, the degree to which such cooperation occurred is not. Nor are the reasons clear as to why, despite his seeming cooperation, the government agencies never trusted him and continued their harassment. The 1956 document seems to be a watershed for both Wright and the government; afterward, he would announce to friends both in conversation and in print that he was on the attack against the government of the United States. By the time of his death, in 1960, these attacks had intensified.

The temptation to draw conclusions in line with those who believe that the FBI and the CIA were directly involved in Wright's sudden death are great. To do so, however, based upon the facts of the documents, would be wrong. I did not find, nor did I expect to find, evidence to support this assertion, held by a great many of the writer's friends. What I found was a pattern of harassment by agencies of the United States Government, resembling at times a personal vendetta more so than an intelligence-gathering investigation. I discovered that the government was guilty of producing anxiety and stressful situations, which would have produced severe hypertension in most men, let alone one so sensitive as Wright. But I discovered nothing to convince me of FBI and CIA culpability in his death. In fact, late documents show the FBI attempting to call off the investigation.

The role of the State Department, however, is another matter, for it was here that the seeming vendetta occurred. The only document that supposedly originated with the State Department casts Wright in an unfavorable position. Documents filtered through the State Department to the FBI show an inordinate amount of activity on the part of the Foreign Service during the last months of Wright's life. Most of the documents are heavily deleted, so their content is difficult to comprehend clearly. Whether there is any connection between this activity and Wright's death may be known only if the deleted sections of the documents are released.

My own observation, however, is that Wright's death, by heart attack, was caused not by cloak-and-dagger assassins but, as Fabre concluded in *The Unfinished Quest of Richard Wright*, by the constant pressure and tension-ridden situations induced by the ordeal to which his government subjected him. In retrospect, this may well have been a crime of the magnitude of assassination. For nowhere in the documents prepared by the government is there evidence that Wright was engaged in subversive activity, that he attempted to undermine the security of the United States, or that he aided and abetted others in doing so. He was a humanist and writer, a man of principle and independent ideas, a black man who insisted on speaking out against the assault by governments left and right against the sanctity of the human spirit. He was, as Hoyt Fuller wrote, ". . . an American tugging at the conscience and the submerged sense of reason of America, and America should be proud to have produced him. His going into exile was a gesture of affirmation, testimony to his belief in the preciousness of human dignity and freedom."

RICHARD WRIGHT
Ordeal of a Native Son

CHAPTER ONE

Mississippi is a land of contradictions. For many, its most telling metaphors are those of oppression and intimidation, its most accepted images those of gnarled, hate-ridden men and women, of gasoline-soaked oak twisted into a Christian cross. To think of Mississippi is to think of tobacco-dripping sheriffs, guns hung recklessly about their waists; burning homes and mutilated black bodies. More than any American state, it symbolizes anarchy, is the universal graveyard for the rebellious, the resting place of the apostles of freedom and dignity, for Mack Parker, Medgar Evers, and Schwerner, Chaney, and Goodman. And yet, in contrast, there are the words of a black civil rights pioneer: "Always, without fail, regardless of the number of times I enter Mississippi, it creates within me feelings that are felt at no other time. There is the feeling of joy . . . because I have once again lived to enter the land of my fathers. . . . At the same time, there is a feeling of sadness. Sadness because I am immediately aware of the special subhuman role that I must play because I am a Negro, or die. . . ." Yet, ". . . there is the feeling of love. Love of the land. To me Mississippi is the most beautiful country in the world, during all seasons. In the spring all is green and fresh, the air is clean and sweet. . . ."[1]

The beauty, like the character, of this southern state borders upon the gothic. The Mississippi River seems particularly brutal when the periods of incessant rain cause it to overflow its banks, to bring ruin and devastation to entire communities. On the other hand, the river has helped to form the majestic loess- and lime-covered hills of the Natchez district, has fertilized the narrow, haunting ridges and valleys of the North Central Hills, and painted in dark tones the continuing strip of loam-covered hills around "the western edge of the Delta." The terrifyingly grotesque, yet beautiful, swamps and vast forests known mainly for the presence of twisted vegetation, contorted into weird, unnatural shapes, and the black soil of the black belt, named both for the land and its people, are, too, gifts of the mighty river. Thus the state, which repels and at one and the same time attracts, holds a stunning fascination even for some of its most passionate detractors.

In his later years, Richard Wright, while still recalling experiences of brutality, could speak of Mississippi in pastoral, poetic terms: it was a land of red, brown, and black clay, of fresh, tantalizing smells coming from the palm and pine trees, of rolling hills and swampy valleys of falling red and brown leaves, of full-grown cotton, of cane transformed into sugary molasses; of winter and long days of rain, and swollen creeks joining hundreds of "rivers that wash across the land . . . and occasionally . . . leap their banks and leave new thick layers of silt to enrich the earth, and then the look of the land is garish, bleak, suffused with a first day stillness, strangeness, and awe."[2]

He wrote these words in 1944, after publication of *Native Son*. The success of this novel earned him a reputation as an astute observer of the urban scene. Nevertheless, his descriptions of the South Side of Chicago lack the poetry and imagination of those concerning Mississippi. Like the civil rights pioneer quoted above, he maintained an affinity and affection for the state in which he was born, despite the ordeal that he underwent there. He was born on September 4, 1908, on a plantation near Natchez, Mississippi, and named after his grandfathers, Nathaniel Wright and Richard Wilson—two ex-slaves.

Nathaniel was said to have been an extremely dark man, though with the blood of both whites and Indians flowing in his veins. In the aftermath of the Civil War, he was not only accorded his freedom, but under the terms of the reconstruction program of the victorious Union forces, he was awarded "the plot of land which he had worked as a slave."[3] In Stanton, near Natchez, one of the more virulent outposts of Confederate resistance and racial animosities, possession of his small farm made Nathaniel an object of respect and admiration to blacks and an object of envy and hatred to whites. That a black man should be awarded land belonging to his former masters was one thing; that he would hold onto it with such tenacity was another. Strong, independent, "surly," he thwarted the efforts and schemes of whites to secure his farm. From the little that is known of this presumably exceptional man, he may well have been a model of strength and resistance for his grandson. Yet, in 1943, when Wright began making notes for his autobiography, he wrote little about the paternal side of his lineage. Because most of his early years were spent with his mother's family, he may have forgotten the Wrights, even strong old Nathaniel; but it may also be that later, ambivalent feelings toward his father caused him, psychologically, to blot out this branch of the family.

He remembered much more and wrote abundantly about the maternal side. At the age of eighteen, Richard Wilson made his leap to freedom. He had also been born on a plantation, the property of John Charles Alexander, on March 21, 1847, near Woodville, Mississippi. Together with a group of runaways from this and other plantations, he made his way through Confederate forces, intent on joining the Union Army. He was allowed, instead, to enlist in the Navy and served "in the Mississippi Flotilla from April 22 to July 27 as a Landsman on the U.S.S. General Lyons."[4] After a stay in a Memphis hospital, he was honorably discharged, and returned to Wilkinson County. In 1894, he settled in Natchez in ill health and constant agitation over what he considered the ingratitude of the United States Government. He had served his government well, had aided in the victorious campaign of the Union forces. He believed that the veteran's pension, awarded men who had performed such service, was his due. Yet, bureaucratic confusion had made him an invisible man to his government. During the discharge process, the name Richard Vincent was substituted for Richard Wilson, and thus no record of service by the old war veteran existed. His campaign to prove to his government that he did, indeed, exist, that he had been patriotic, courageous, and resourceful, was determined, insistent: "For decades a long correspondence took place between Grandpa and the War Department: in letter after letter Grandpa would recount events and conversations . . . he would name persons long dead, citing their ages and descriptions, reconstructing battles in which he had fought, naming towns, rivers, creeks, roads, cities, villages, citing the names and numbers of regiments and companies with which he had fought, giving the exact day and hour of the day of certain occurrences, and send it all to the War Department in Washington."[5] The quixotic campaign availed nothing. Richard Wilson remained, for the rest of his life, an angry man, convinced that the Confederates had conspired to cheat him of his claim.

The old veteran's war with his government meant that the responsibility for running the household and establishing the rules of moral conduct for his large family fell upon the resourceful shoulders of his wife, Margaret Bolden Wilson. A photograph of this dominant personality, whom Richard Wilson had married in 1871 and who bore him nine children, shows the matriarch past middle age, yet still strong in presence and bearing. The eyes are focused, squinting, the face angular, the chin jutting, giving her face an aura of proud defiance. The starched collar with dickey protruding, decorating a gown of somber-hued cloth, gives her the appearance of an Anglican divine. There is

something in her posture of the *grandes dames* of Tolstoy and Che-
khov, and the pasty-white hue of her skin belies her African heritage.
She was born around 1853–54, in Woodville, Mississippi, the illegiti-
mate child of a union between a white man of Irish-Scottish ancestry
and a black African woman. One of the more fortunate in the slave hierarchy, she was as close to being white, her grandson would later describe
her, as one could be without being white, which "meant that she was
white."

Status and skin color afforded her opportunities not open to other
blacks. After emancipation, she embarked upon a career as a midwife
and nurse. Later, in 1875, after marriage to Richard, she served as a
nurse to a white doctor in race-torn Natchez. Proud, defiant, and somewhat overbearing, her ancestry, coupled with her strong presence, won
her the approval and envy of her black neighbors, even as these traits
served to distance her from them. For such a sensitive, bright, and prin-
cipled young woman, the moral dilemma posed as a result of such
knowledge may have accounted for the air of superiority that, intentionally or not, she showed to other blacks. It may have been the reason
also that, early in life, she embarked upon a crusade, as intense and consistent as that waged by Richard Wilson, against the evildoers, the immoral, the godless—in short, all who were not counted among the followers of Christ.

The vehicle for this crusade was the Seventh-Day Adventist Church.
The Baptist Church, the abode of her black and white neighbors, where
she sojourned initially, seemed ill prepared to undertake such a mission.
The Adventist faith was different. Here was a creed that sought to divorce the individual from the world outside. The path to the Adventist
heaven was negotiable only if one became an outsider, and devoted oneself to a regimen of strict obedience: four or five prayer meetings a
week; a stricture against work on the Sabbath, which, for the Ad-
ventists, meant Saturday; no contact with books, magazines, or other
worldly media. The day began with the rise of the sun and ended with
its setting, and in between were tasks designed to combat sin and the
sinful. What her grandson was eventually to describe as her tyrannical
exercise of authority stemmed from her conversion to the Adventist
faith, to visions of a heaven alive with the immediacy of hope and salvation, of the soon-to-come dawn of the new day. Yet her belief in and
adherence to her doctrine of faith seems no less startling than her
grandson's conversion, at another time, to another faith: communism.
He, too, saw visions of apocalypse; became aware of the sanctity of a
religion that issued its own doctrines concerning man's damnation and
eventual salvation, that painted its own portraits of fiery hells and endless dark holes, of crystal-clear streams and bountiful green earth. Her

influence upon him was as great as, if not greater than, that of his mother, Ella Wilson.

Ella was the fourth of Richard and Margaret Wilson's nine children, four of whom were females. Born in June 1883, she grew up in the black middle-class environs of Woodville and Natchez, enjoying the privileges of a slight education and stern moral tutelage, before the family entered into a period of economic decline. She became a country schoolteacher and, like her mother, a stern moralist, though less zealous than Margaret Wilson. She found her place in the sanctuary of the Methodist Church, and this influence may have accounted for her sense of decorum. Her husband, throughout their marriage, was always "Mr. Wright" to her, and she, in turn, at least to one group of her many neighbors, was "a high-toned bitch." The derogatory epithet was occasioned partly by her complexion—light olive-colored—and by her seemingly puritanical disposition. If Margaret Wilson saw the devil emblazoned in all of his demonic fury on the books and magazines that her young grandson would read, Ella saw a much more furious devil in the sexual inquisitiveness of her child. Her later reprimand of him for gazing at the half-exposed legs of an appealing young woman and her diatribe against her landlady in Memphis, who ran a bawdy house—"you shouldn't have that in your house"—almost belie her moral pretentiousness. Was there, behind her supercilious façade, devils that had to be exorcised?

If not, then how does one explain the quick marriage to Nathan Wright, an illiterate laborer? Self-made man his father might have been, determined and strong in addition, but the son was also dark in color and had no qualities that Ella's mulatto middle class would have found acceptable. Yet Nathan was tall, handsome, sensual. Born in the Delta, presumably in 1880, he left home as soon as he was old enough to assume the duties of a sharecropper. His true ambition seemed to lay, however, in the ministry; and he waited in vain for the sign, the call, that would ordain him as one of the chosen. Such hopes may have accounted for his association with the Cranfield Methodist Church, where he met Ella Wilson, who was a fine catch for an illiterate, dark-skinned laborer. The objections of her family notwithstanding, one month later Ella Wilson became Mrs. Nathan Wright; a year later, she gave birth to their first child, whom they christened with the first names of both grandfathers, Richard Nathaniel Wright. A second son, born two years later, was christened Leon Allan.

Was Ella's family correct in their expectations for Nathan Wright? Certainly the first, trying years of the young couple's life seemed to bear out prophecies of Nathan's failure. The new couple settled down to sharecropping on a farm near Natchez, but the uncompromising weather and the excessive burden placed by white landowners on share-croppers black and white made the venture unsuccessful and unprofitable. The rapid arrival of the children meant that Ella had to leave her teaching job, forcing them all upon the largesse of the Wilson family. In 1911, surrendering his ambition to be a successful farmer for the time being, Nathan became an itinerant laborer going to the city to work in a sawmill while his small family went to live with Ella's parents. Young Richard's most vivid recollections were of times spent with the Wilsons in their well-kept, black middle-class home. He only dimly remembered having lived in a sharecropper's shack. . . .

It was during a sojourn at the Wilsons that he experienced the first of many traumas: He set fire to their home and was severely beaten, by his mother, for the act. Why had he set the fire? Was it simply accidental, the result of childish inquisitiveness; or was it an early test of dominance over his younger brother? He was an inquisitive child, and his mother encouraged that inquisitiveness. In the early years of his life, before the arrival of Leon Allan, she had been his prized possession, his sole possession. But the birth of his brother meant that affection had to be shared. Was an accidental fire the way to restore, at the age of five, the exclusive love he had had until the age of three? "All morning," he recalled when writing about that day, "my mother had been scolding me, telling me to keep still. . . . I was angry, fretful, and impatient."[6] The two brothers played alone, silently, in the large room, near a fireplace. Grandmother Wilson lay ill in bed. The elder boy stood transfixed by the flames. What would happen if one threw something into the flames? Would they rise, geyserlike, to the ceiling? He found a broom in the closet, began to throw hunks of straw into the fire. More smoke than flames erupted. His brother protested, and he threatened him. Over by the window were white, fluffy curtains. Richard moved toward them, burning straw clutched in his hands; the "Naw" issued instantly by his brother arrived too late. Quickly the flames danced up the curtains, gained in intensity until they met the ceiling, and suddenly the room was one big ball of smoke and fire.

The magnitude of his crime became more pronounced as the flames roared on. Fear drove him from the burning house. Confusion and bewilderment caused him to seek refuge beneath it. Ella Wright appeared, near hysteria. Her first thought was that her child was caught in the fire. She ran about wildly, shouting his name; and fear made him unable to respond. Somehow Nathan divined that his son had escaped the burning house. Instinctively he began to search for him. He found him cowering; Richard ignored his father's admonitions to come from beneath the burning structure. Punishment, Wright knew, awaited him; he did not know how to calculate the damage. What had happened to his grandmother, his brother? He retreated farther into the shadows. Finally, Nathan crawled under the house, seized one of the boy's legs, and despite fierce resistance, dragged him to safety. He surrendered hopelessly as Ella pulled the leaves from a thick, ominous-looking tree branch.

Propelled by hysteria, her fury fueled by the love of her elder child and the exasperation occasioned by the thought that she might have lost him, she lashed him severely, battering his body into colors of burnished red, purple, and black, thundering down blow after blow, until, as if in total resignation, the boy slipped into unconsciousness. He had sought renewed affection from his mother. Instead he received punishment and pain. Having been beaten into insensibility, he dreamed the dreams of the anguished. Somewhere, suspended in space and time, "huge wobbly white bags, like the full udders of cows" hung above him. They were filled with a liquid, indescribable, horrible. They threatened to burst, to spew their frightening contents over him. He filled the rooms with screams. He begged his mother and father to remove the bags. Day and night they hung there. Finally they were gone; so were the dreams. Only the memories remained, and chief among these was the knowledge that his mother had "come close to killing" him.

Youthful inquisitiveness led up to this first trauma, but the consequences did nothing to stifle its recurrence. After recovery, he ventured into the Mississippi countryside to discover the magical world of animals and plants, of trees and swamps. He learned to recognize the sounds of cracking leaves, the scent of ripe hickory, the terror of the butchering of hogs. He thirsted for sights, sounds, images to stimulate the sensuous and growing sensibility of adolescence.

He could not know, however, that difficult days lay ahead. His father failed once more. Economic depression ended his job as an itinerant laborer. Unable to find work in Mississippi, he decided to take his family to the big city, to Memphis, following the path of other desperate, migratory blacks, similarly affected by the depression.

Memphis was Nathan's Rubicon. It was the last gambit, an anxious attempt to salvage his self-esteem and his family. The past years were difficult ones. He had struggled against the weather, the racism in Mississippi, and perhaps even his wife's background. With the exception of Ella Wright, most of Margaret Wilson's children had fared well. On the surface at least, accomplishment was taken for granted. Not so for Nathan, to whom success was a wary antagonist. Status that would place him on a par with Ella's brothers and sisters was unattainable for a man of limited education—unless he received the call.

A preacher was a respected individual in the black community, his

importance measured in terms of the numbers, zeal, and enthusiasm of
his parishioners. Nathan still clung to the belief that he was cut of min-
isterial cloth. To preach the gospel was his destiny, and the tenor of
this obsession filled Ella and her children with anxiety. For Nathan
would not preach unless he was summoned, and the summons never
came. No star appeared directing him to the pulpit; no prayers were
strong enough to move the intractable heavenly host. Shortly after settling in Memphis, he became morose, more domineering, quicker to
anger. His job as a night porter in a Beale Street drugstore offered little
compensation for his dashed ambitions. He criticized his wife, abused
her for trivial things. Quarrels were frequent. The sensitive young boy
became attuned to the father's moods and changes. He seemed "endowed with a godlike quality."[7]

But Nathan was a man, and soon his elder son discovered signs of his
mortality: ". . . he ate long and heavily, sighed, belched, closed his eyes
to nod on a stuffed belly. He was quite fat and his bloated stomach always lapped over his belt."[8] Richard had known his father, briefly, during better times, as a man who brought him presents and who took him
on trips. Now, as pressures mounted upon Nathan in the city, this big,
violent, unpredictable man became in the boy's eyes "a stranger . . .
alien and remote." He became the tyrant whose absolute rule must not
be questioned, particularly when word was handed down that his two
sons should make no noise while he slept in the daytime.

On the morning of confrontation between Wright and his authoritarian father, the two brothers played in a small corner of the narrow
apartment. The kitten kept up a steady stream of noise, finally bringing
Nathan, half clad, from his bed, to issue dire warnings. The kitten must
be quieted, the noise abated. When Wright placed sole responsibility
for the noise on the hapless kitten, Nathan angrily insisted, "Kill that
damn' thing." He added, "Do anything, but get it away from here." His
boy, however, concentrated only on the first part of the demand. Here
was a chance to combat the moral authority assumed by his father. He
knew that his words were not to be taken literally. Yet in the small universe of the young boy, his father was the symbol of injustice. Not only
did Nathan scold him, but he was also the major competitor for Ella's
affections, demanding, receiving uncontested attention. Leon Allan was
quiet, noncompetitive. He was easily bullied by his elder brother and
seldom disposed to compete with him. Cunningly, Richard moved to
challenge the authority of his father. He secured a piece of rope,
stretched one end over a rusty, half-bent nail, and the other around the
kitten's neck. The kitten clawed, grasped, kicked at the air around him.
Its body shook like the ground beneath a roller coaster, and the tight-
ened rope, pulled ever tighter about the neck, stopped its cries.

The challenge to his father was successful. Nathan could not take retributive action without denying the power of his own request. "I had made him feel," the son wrote later, "that if he whipped me for the kitten, I would never give serious weight to his words again." Still, he was not to escape punishment. His father may have been caught up in the dilemma of limited power, but his mother was not. Ella's power stemmed from her own, unquestionable code of morality, buttressed by the lessons of Christianity: Thou shalt not kill. Her son had broken the Judeo-Christian law. He would have to be taught a lesson. Thus, at night, when his imagination opened like a fresh wound, conjuring up images of ghosts and dreaded apparitions, he was ordered to bury the victim of his violence.

The contempt from his elder and perhaps his younger son as well was probably the least of Nathan Wright's difficulties. There would never, it seemed, be enough money to ease the family's plight; their home was destined to be one ramshackle apartment after another, in some black ghetto like Memphis's. He could never provide for them as Richard Wilson had provided for his family. Ella's family had in fact been right; they had assumed Nathan would amount to little. Even his God had made him feel unworthy. Thus what had once been a responsibility loomed now as a burden. For relief, he took to the streets of Memphis.

There in the honky-tonks and bars, amid the soft, sometimes raucous, music, Nathan found an easier, more carefree world, where dreams were unlimited and burdens lighter. And there were women in that world, less pious and less stringently moral than the one at home. If initially there were feelings of guilt, they were soon abated. And one day, Nathan didn't come home at all. His sons seemed not to miss him. They were free to play without fear of rebuke, to make as much noise as they wished. For Ella, though, the missing Nathan constituted a calamity. Her worst fears were suddenly realized: She was already in her thirties, alone with two children to feed and care for in a difficult, cruel city. How would she survive?

And what part had she played in her husband's desertion? Was there some quirk in her character, some act committed, some word said or not said, that brought on the calamity? Might Nathan not return? As days, nights, and then weeks moved swiftly by and Nathan did not reappear, the hunger of her children made her increasingly aware of the terror of her new responsibilities.

To young Richard Wright, hunger brought home the full impact and consequences of the absence of the father he had grown to hate. For the first time in his life, the pain of hunger became constant, overpowering. It was unexplainable, frustrating, nerve-wracking. Whole days passed with scarcely more than bread and tea. The ability to play freely left him. He grew tense, nervous, morose. Whatever his feelings toward his father before, they intensified now: The man whom he hated as a rival, an injudicious lawgiver, he now hated with a biological bitterness. The fact that he now had undisputed access to his mother was little compensation. Deserted by her husband and beset with feelings of guilt and fear of an unknown future, Ella grew possessive of her elder son. "Poor lost woman," the boy was to write many years after the event, describing the mother of Cross Damon in the novel *The Outsider*, "clinging for salvation to a son whom she knew was as lost as she was."

The children sensed the feelings of dread and insecurity that now became dominant in the personality of their mother. She prayed more often to her God now, they noticed, and her moral dictums became more pronounced. Later, the elder son was able to analyze her predicament during this period of her life. In Mississippi, her primary education enabled her to teach school, but in Memphis her skills were unmarketable. The only work available for a black woman with limited education was in the kitchens of white people. Ella found such a job, washing pots and pans, and was forced to spend long hours away from her children. The fact of Nathan's desertion and her own forced absence intensified her anxieties concerning the fate of her sons. Thus her lectures on moral responsibility expanded to include teachings on independence and self-reliance. She frequently told them of the necessity of learning to care for themselves, of being able to protect themselves, of the difficulties of being fatherless children. She did not tell them, perhaps because she was not far enough removed from the event, that their status as fatherless children was due to the fact that Nathan had gone to live with another woman. For Richard, in addition to the teachings of his mother, there were other, easier lessons to learn in Memphis: the lessons of living as a child.

From a man who delivered coal Wright learned to count to one hundred, and Ella taught him to read, acquainting him with the magic and meaning of words. Other things, he learned on his own. His mother away at work, the backyards and streets of Memphis his for exploration, he discovered the world that had claimed Nathan, the Memphis of honky-tonk clubs, of willing, enticing women, of bright lights and paved streets, of the throaty, bosomy wails of jazz and blues. From Howard Institute, the first of many schools he was to attend, he learned the most popular obscenities, and there, too, among other boys and girls who were abandoned by their fathers, he learned the value of companionship.

And he learned something of people called white. When word circulated in the black neighborhood that "a black boy had been severely beaten by a 'white man,'" he did not understand his neighbors' reactions. Most of his family were white-looking, and he assumed that the man was the boy's father, ordained by right of parentage to beat his son. When he discovered that the man was not the boy's father, he was puzzled. Now concern about white people began, and would grow through the years. He learned something about the way they lived when he went with his mother one day to her job. Their homes were neat, well kept, far away from the shacks and shantytowns, the honky-tonks and nightclubs of his environment; they had tables laden with food, were indifferent to the poverty and hunger that were his lot.

He also learned something of their disdain for those like himself, through Ella's meager, insufficient wages. Not only did two rapidly growing boys need food and clothing beyond what she was able to afford, but she was determined that they should complete their schooling. Alone, however, this seemed impossible. Again and again she appealed to Nathan for financial support, all to no avail. Reluctantly, she was forced to seek redress from the courts. "When I awakened one morning," Wright wrote later, "my mother told me that we were going to see a judge who would make my father support me and my brother."[9] In the courtroom, presided over by a white judge, he sat with his mother and brother and stared across the room at his father, who sat "smiling confident." He remembered that his mother had warned him not to "be fooled" by his "father's friendly manner," and when his eyes met Nathan's, he turned his head abruptly. The proceedings outraged him as much as the condescending mannerisms of his father. Nathan was being asked to help feed him. He was hungry, had, even then, pangs in his stomach. Yet he did not want his father to feed him. He wanted to forget that he had a father.

Finally, Ella was called to face the court. Remembrances of anguish past and dire present momentarily immobilized her. When she regained her voice, she told of Nathan's desertion, of the children's hunger, of her feeble attempts to raise them alone. Tears came as she finished, and Nathan was called before the judge. He strode jauntily toward the rostrum, tried to kiss his wife. He looked at his children, spoke obsequiously before the white judge. He pleaded hard times and the desperation of his circumstances. He was, he told the judge, doing all that he was able under the circumstances to do. The contrast between his mother and father pained the elder son. Ella's crying and remorse made her pathetic, hopeless, weak in contrast to the grinning self-assurance of her husband. Still, her pathos and visible need meant nothing to a white-male-dominated court. Nathan's word was accepted. There would be no help.

Shortly after the trial, Ella became ill and was unable to work. Hunger became more prevalent. The family was forced upon the largesse of neighbors, who sometimes helped out with food or money. Grandmother Wilson contributed also, sending what little money she could afford. Much of the money went to purchase coal to warm the drafty flat in the cold winter months. Wright's schooling was interrupted briefly when he stopped going in order to care for his mother. He resumed his studies when Grandmother Wilson came to care for her daughter. During her visit, he learned for the first time the true reason for his father's desertion. He listened to "long, angrily whispered conversations" between the two women protesting Ella's situation. Nathan, it seemed, had left his family for another woman. "That woman," averred Grandmother Wilson, "ought to be killed for breaking up a home." To Richard, this meant absolving Nathan of responsibility, placing the blame for his actions upon the "other woman." To him, however, blame rested solely upon the shoulders of his father. "If someone had suggested that my father be killed, I would perhaps have been interested; if someone had suggested that his name never be mentioned, I would no doubt have agreed. . . ."

Margaret Wilson eventually returned to Mississippi, and the money she left her daughter was soon gone. Ella's health did not vastly improve. Emotionally and physically, she was a beaten woman. Pride was slowly cast aside, and she began seeking out charitable institutions. Finally, she found an orphanage that would assume custody of her sons until she recovered her strength and was able to work more frequently. The trauma of separation was severe for mother and children. What was good in Ella's marriage, what was worth salvaging, was the children. She wanted to bring them up assured and confident, with the education she herself had not had, so that they could take advantage of the limited opportunities for black males. Now, in order to save them, she was forced, for a while, to abandon them.

And her elder, more sensitive son? He was not yet six, and first his father, now his mother was abandoning him. Often she had turned to him emotionally; and though he could not act as the surrogate Nathan, he had drawn extremely close to her, had felt her dread, longing, anxiety, as if they were his very own. Long ago, it seemed, he had wished the father gone. Now he *was* gone, and his mother was without protection, because he, the son, was unable to protect her, or his brother. On the first day in the orphanage, Richard Wright came to sense the overwhelming defeat of the powerless: ". . . I began to wonder," he revealed later in his autobiography, "if she, too, like my father had disappeared into the unknown. I was rapidly learning to distrust everything and everybody."

The orphanage was an unimpressive two-story building situated in a wide field of overgrown grass. Inside were the abandoned, the unwanted, the forgotten. Starved for affection, the children were a community of the vanquished, each searching for his or her own gratification. They were hostile and vindictive toward one another; they preyed upon each other, informed upon each other, fought one another. Here, too, food was in short supply, and fights often arose over a slice of bread. The children were assigned the chores of pulling the tall grass from around the orphanage, but, weakened by hunger, some, like the Wrights, were barely equal to the task. At first, Ella came often to visit her sons, which made them hopeful. But all at once she stopped coming, just as she had been advised by the director of the orphanage.

That was Miss Simon; tall, gaunt, mulatto. She had a wart on her chin, which added an aura of the gothic to her face. A spinster who was domineering and possessive, she immediately began to pursue Richard. She assigned him the task of helping her in the office. She invited him to eat lunch with her; she broached the subject of adopting him, touched him regularly, drew close to him. The child might fare better, she told Ella, if the mother did not come to visit; and with Ella out of the way, she persisted after him, terrorizing him. Once, long before, he had touched his cousin's vagina at her insistence. His mother had severely chastised him. He had not known the threat of sexuality at that time. He was not really aware of the ramifications even now. But Miss Simon's pursuit of him was the pursuit of the sexually aroused, awakening in him the moral strictures of his mother, transforming the world about him into one of perversion and confusion, "feeling most of the time," he later wrote, "that I was suspended over a void."

When he spurned her offers, she became angry, and this perplexed him even more. Without the aid of his mother, he could not defend himself in this adult world. Instead, one night he ran away. He had gone a short distance before he was found by a white policeman. Here again, there was little precedent by which he might predict the outcome of a situation. What little he knew of white people was stereotypic. In his mind they were evil phantoms, like that white man who had beaten a black boy. He was afraid of the white policemen, but at the station the officers displayed kindness toward him. They fed him, asked him questions, teased him; they were warm, considerate. His first real personal confrontation with white people was reassuring. In later years, perhaps this would enable him to view them in terms of individuals, not as categories.

When the policemen returned him to the orphanage, he was beaten by Miss Simon. He vowed silently to run away again, but his every movement was now watched. Ella came to visit, and chastised him for having run away. She reminded him of his unique status—a child without a father—told him that she was working hard to support him and his brother and that having to worry about him imposed extra difficulties upon her. Finally she presented him with equally objectionable options: she wanted to move to Elaine, Arkansas, where her sister, Margaret, and her husband, Silas Hoskins, lived. There, in a new environment, she might be able to find suitable work and to raise her children properly. She needed money for the trip, however, and she wanted her son to accompany her to demand it from his father. He was called upon to weigh the hatred for his father against his hatred for the orphanage. After some hesitation, he decided to go with his mother.

They found Nathan in a scantily furnished apartment, sitting with a "strange woman" before a bright fireplace. Mother and son stood some distance from the couple, as though to move closer would violate some unwritten pact. Nathan laughed, mockingly. What images did the spectacle of his wife in this setting conjure up for him, and what satisfaction was derived from her humiliation? Were the whispered innuendoes from the lips of her family echoing now, in the present? He may have felt a sense of glee that the wife he had been unable to care for, to whom he perhaps attributed part of his own failure, now stood before him almost prideless, begging. He turned down her pleas. He had no money, he said heartily. The strange woman beckoned to the boy, implored Nathan to give him "a nickel. He's cute," she murmured.

Ella turned her moral indignation upon the woman. She ought to be ashamed, she burst out in tears, for depriving her children of food. Nathan laughed again, stretched his big long body, implored the women, teasingly, not to fight. His manner was much too offensive for his son. Watching the humiliation of his mother, unable to protect her or even help, absorbing her shame, he lashed out at his father: "I'll take that poker and hit you." Ella chided him; he should not say such things. Nathan laughed even louder. The woman put her arms around his shoulder. He promised food if the boy would come to live with him. Wright vehemently refused. Nathan offered him a nickel, which Ella forbade him from taking, and they left.

The boy was less impressed by his father's refusal to help them than by the spectacle of Nathan and the strange woman. There, in that apartment illuminated by flames, sex seemed a viable, tangible thing. And Ella's moral assault upon the other woman had added to the aura of sexuality. She had been unwilling or unable to discuss the reasons for Nathan's leaving, before. Now the boy surmised the motivations for himself. The spectacle of the woman and his father continued to haunt him; he was both repulsed and excited by the scene he had watched. "I had the feeling," he later confided, "that I had had to do with something unclean." Yet, in the same paragraph, he wrote that, years distant, the image of the couple erupted, volcano-like, in his imagination, seemingly possessing some vital meaning that he could not grasp.[10]

CHAPTER TWO

In the Civil War, in 1863, the troops of Union General William Te-
cumseh Sherman captured Jackson, Mississippi. The town was burned
so badly by the victorious army that for a long time afterward it was referred to as Chimney-ville. Later, during the civil rights revolt of the
nineteen fifties and sixties, Jackson's black citizens referred to the town
as "Jimcrow-ville." However, when Ella brought her children to live in
the newly purchased house of Grandmother Wilson in 1916, the dismal
slums, dank gray buildings, and industrial plants had not yet appeared.
There were homes, gardens of overripe magnolias, and the singsong of
hordes of multicolored bees, bringing back to the older boy, after the
depressing atmosphere of Memphis, the arcadia he remembered of Natchez.

Securing money for the trip to Elaine probably from Margaret Wilson, Ella decided to visit her parents en route. Now in her sixties,
white-haired, diminutive, Margaret was intent upon keeping the house
that was purchased for her and her husband by her son Clark as clean
of sin as it was of dirt. Dirt she found little of; sin she found in abundance, personified in Eloise Crawford, a boarder taken in to supplement
the stipends given by her children. Eloise was a teacher and avid reader,
studious and somewhat romantic. Novels were her favorites, while, for
Margaret Wilson, novels reeked of sin. To six-year-old Richard Wright,
they were objects of curiosity. He begged the young teacher to tell him
about the novels she read, presenting her with a dilemma. Eloise feared
to risk the ethical outrage of Margaret Wilson at the same time that
she admired the child's inquisitiveness and wanted to encourage it.
When he persisted, she finally consented to "whisper the story of Blue-
beard and His Seven Wives." Here was love and violence, intrigue and
suspicion, and he became consumed with a sensibility he had never

known before. The hero loved, married, and killed seven wives. Here was a universe in which things happened, violence was enacted—a magical universe where people did strange things, where men and women appeared surrealistically, embodied against a background of awe and madness. As Eloise whispered each new episode, he gave himself over to an ecstatic vision of the unreal.

He was so absorbed that he did not notice his grandmother appear suddenly. Margaret Wilson stood, flesh quivering, eyelids drooped in anger; her sense of outrage sparked: "You stop that, you evil gal. . . . I want none of that Devil stuff in my house." Eloise protested: The boy had cajoled her, pestered her; he wanted to know. The old woman was not consoled. It was her responsibility to keep her spiritual house in order, to assure her own passage to the promised land, and she would not be deterred by the antics of "a foolish child."

Still, the imagination of the child was aroused. Before Eloise Crawford was dismissed from his grandmother's house, he stole into her room, took books, tried to read them. He pondered the strange words and became frustrated by his inability to understand them. He vowed secretly that, when he was older, he would read all the novels he could find. That this intention would bring him into a headlong collision with his grandmother sometime in the future, he was no doubt aware. Yet there was already growing within him a feel for violence, a sense of the strange and forbidden. This might be more readily satiated by fiction than by the confused, frustrating actions of the adults around him, who seemed, somehow, to stand as impediments to his natural feelings; his mother tried to still his passions; his grandmother would quiet his imagination. The creation of his identity meant rebelling first and most vigorously against those he loved.

After several months in Jackson, Ella and her sons set out to take up residence with Margaret Wilson Hoskins and her husband, Silas, a prosperous saloonkeeper. Margaret was three years younger than her sister; she was robust, energetic, yet lacking in their mother's moral authoritarianism. To the young Wright, she was "Aunt Maggie," his favorite aunt, and his affable uncle was a respected man in the black community. Signs of his success were everywhere: a small bungalow close to town, surrounded by a garden; a horse and buggy; a table laden with food at all times. And equally as important, "a big shiny revolver" that he carried to work each day. So successful was his business that it was coveted by whites, who tried to buy it. When he refused to sell, they resorted to threats and intimidation.

Silas took the boys for long rides in his buggy and made his home congenial to them. For the first time in recent memory, they had enough to eat, but the elder boy could not believe his good fortune.

Hungry days and nights had made him cautious, apprehensive, and so he secreted bread from the heavily laden table, hiding it in his pants pockets. When his mother discovered what he was doing and reproached him, he did not stop. He hid it "about the house, in corners, behind dressers." As time passed and he grew more confident that food would remain a constant, he gave up the habit. It was too soon. The family-like atmosphere, along with the food, were approaching an end. Silas Hoskins was a marked man.

"During my visit at Granny's a sense of the two races had been born in me with a sharp concreteness that would never die until I died,"[1] he wrote later. He had begun to notice small, seemingly insignificant details, to formulate in his own mind the nagging question: what were white people? His grandmother was whiter than some Jackson people: Why was she not white? Or was she? If so, why did she live with him? The rule was that whites and blacks were separated as if by some natural, preordained boundary line. He knew this from his own, brief experiences in Memphis.

These two groups of people, who lived "side by side," came together only during times of violence. On the train ride to Elaine, he was conscious that he and other blacks were shuffled off to one section of the train, the whites to the other. He wanted to go and look at them, to see how they looked in their own part of the train.

His curiosity concerning white folks intensified one morning when Hoskins, who worked at his saloon at night, failed to return. It was fueled by the anxiety in the faces of his mother and aunt. The atmosphere in the house was one of silent, desperate waiting. Food was kept hot on the stove. Each sound inside and outside the house rang with deafening clarity. The two sisters took turns peering into the early mist. Sometime later, they were called to attention by a knock on the door. It was not Silas' knock. It was the knock of the dreaded messenger, one of the unsung blacks who historically, sometimes in the dark of night or the early morning, surreptitiously delivered messages of disaster. This one was short, precise: Hoskins had been killed by white men. His family was to stay away from town. There were to be no final rites.

Between night and morning, Hoskins ceased to exist. Immediately after entertaining the messenger, the family, taking only what was portable, fled to the distant town of West Helena. Days passed before either sister ventured out in daylight.

For the young boy, it was his first experience with what in later years he labeled "the white terror." At nine years of age, it was his most traumatic experience, and he had had no preparation for it! Was this the reason that, later, the mature man of letters introduced Fishbelly, the antagonist of *The Long Dream*, to the unpredictable world of white people? Frightened by a small group of white men, Fishbelly stumbles upon a dead dog. He begins to cut into its flesh, deep into bone and tissue, casting aside heart, entrails, muscles. It is a mock castration, turned into a baptismal ritual; afterward, nothing that white people could do would shock, surprise, astound him.

The young Wright, however, was not so readied. He was unnerved by the rapidity of events, angered and frightened by the sudden murder of his uncle, and somewhat contemptuous that Ella and Aunt Maggie were too cowardly to confront those responsible. Flight was the only possible reaction if more violence was to be averted.

They settled in the small industrial town of West Helena, among its large black population. The neighborhood into which they moved was populated with rats, cats, dogs, fortunetellers, cripples, blind men, prostitutes. Children constituted one of the larger groupings. Nearby was a locomotive repair house, where railroad engines were cleaned and repaired, and the neighborhood reeked always of coal and tar.

A sewage ditch, littered with bottles, tin cans, rubber tires, and sometimes the carcasses of animals, served, with the railroad repair yard, as a playground for the children. The two women were soon at work in the homes of whites, and the two boys joined the bands of roaming neighborhood children. From them, the elder Wright learned a great deal. A girl not much older than himself pointed out that the other half of the double apartment house in which he lived was one of the centers of prostitution in the area. From others, he learned anti-Semitic slogans, folk ditties, cruel bits of doggerel, all part of the defensive armory of the poverty-stricken, the powerless. And again, events added to his growing knowledge of whites.

A short time after they had settled in West Helena, Maggie, the more flamboyant of the sisters, began an affair with a man known to the boy as Professor Mathews. So named because of his sartorial appearance, Mathews was a kindly suitor, appearing at night and often leaving small gifts for the children. But he was also involved in an affair with a white woman! Attempts to sever the relationship had produced threats from the woman, and Mathews was aware of the potential danger of such threats. The number of black men lynched and castrated for severing relationships with old paramours was legend. The white woman had only to cry rape or molestation to endanger him. Unable to extricate himself, Mathews murdered the woman and set fire to her house. Now in fear of his life, he was running away and taking Maggie with him. The boy now knew enough about "the white terror" to understand Mathews' predicament. But his favorite aunt was leaving, and this saddened him. However, when officials inquired at his home about the mysterious Mathews, the boy all too readily heeded his mother's advice to remain silent.

"The dread of white people," he later wrote, "now came to live permanently in my feelings and imagination. . . ." It was 1920, the close of the First World War, when this "dread" was felt by entire black communities. In southern communities, defiant and not-so-defiant blacks were maimed, beaten, or murdered. Returning soldiers were often the major targets. Away from the kitchens and factories of whites, where they were somewhat immune from terror, the blacks of West Helena retreated in the evening to their porches or their yards, bewailing their plight, admitting their powerlessness, knowing that they might become the victims of violence at any time. They passed this sense of dread and impotence, hate and virulent anger on to their children: "I had never in my life been abused by whites," Wright would record, "but I had already become as conditioned to their existence as though I had been the victim of a thousand lynchings."

The camaraderie of children his own age and in a similar condition offered some solace. Then, too, Ella was still intent that he receive an education. When she secured a job in a doctor's office at five dollars a week, she enrolled her boys in school for the first time since Memphis. For Wright, school was an ordeal. Older and much taller, gawkier, and thinner than other boys and girls, having been absent for a long time, he was shy and hesitant. Called upon to pronounce his name, he was unable to do so; nor could he spell or write it, not from lack of ability, but from shyness. Before long, however, he was accepted among his classmates, welcomed into the fraternity of the dislocated. Acceptance was based upon his willingness to subscribe "to certain racial sentiments." He was expected to be hostile to whites and to honor and value race. Girls were to be disdained, conversations were patterned after those of adults: centering upon sex, machines, sports, war. To retain respect and membership, he was expected to join the others in fighting with white boys of similar age.

These battles between blacks and whites were fought on equal ground. Similar weapons were available to each: rocks, pieces of coal, broken bottles, twisted sticks of iron. Allied by the shared necessity to protect their turf, the blacks spilled their fair share of white blood. On one such occasion, Wright was hurt by a missile thrown by one of the whites. Ella was terrified at sight of his wound. She was even more terrified at the fact that he had been fighting whites. He was beaten. Here was another lesson to be learned. Once, in Memphis, Ella had sent him to buy groceries and he had been beset by a group of black boys who took his money. He'd retreated to the house, but Ella had driven him back outside: He had to learn to fight, to stand up for himself. Evidently, the same was not true when whites were involved. Ella begged him not to engage in any more scuffles with them. He promised but had no intention of keeping his promise. Fighting the whites offered him status in the fraternity, a respite from alienation and loneliness; the gangs were life itself.

But the days of boyhood comradery were numbered. The stress, strain, and tension of the past years took their toll upon his mother. Her strength waned; she grew gradually weaker. When she became too sick to work, Wright was forced to find odd jobs in the neighborhood. Poverty reappeared like an avenging phantom, and the family was forced to move three times because they couldn't pay the rent. Meanwhile his mother now became as much of a physical as an emotional burden upon her elder son. Her mind became preoccupied with visions of death and dying. He noticed a "halting, lisping quality" in her voice now, the sudden seizures of pain that wracked her body. It was difficult for him to look at her, to watch her suffering; he knew his mother was deathly ill. Again the universe had become purposeless, irrational, disordered. Chaos loomed always overhead and he was as impotent in the face of the unexpected as he was in the face of man-made dangers. Day after day, he came home from work to find his mother's condition unchanged; at night he lay awake, twisting, turning, trying to drown out her agonizing screams of pain. One morning, he awoke after fitful sleep to the anguished cries of his brother. Rushing to his mother's bedside, he joined Leon Allan in shaking her, trying to rouse her; Ella did not respond. Neighbors were hastily summoned. One of them pronounced the word "paralysis." The doctor who was summoned validated the opinion. Ella had been paralyzed by a stroke!

The boy was numbed, his senses battered. He brooded, despaired, refused acts of charity from the neighbors who came each day to tend Ella and to look after her children. He was beset by guilt and shame. Again he had failed his mother. Grandma Wilson came to take charge. She barked out orders that the boy followed mechanically, like an automaton. He wrote letters summoning the rest of the family to Jackson, helped pack his mother's few belongings, assisted in helping her into the ambulance that transported them back to the Wilsons' home. One by one, Ella's brothers and sisters gathered in the house on Lynch Street. Even Aunt Maggie journeyed from Detroit. Once together in the living room of their mother's home, they pondered and decided the fate of Ella's children. Leon Allan was to go and live with Maggie in Detroit; Richard, with Clark Wilson in Greenwood.

But the strain was too much for Wright. His dreams became nightmares; constantly, he awoke to the sound of his own screams. The pain of seeing his mother in her prostrate condition kept him away from her room. In Greenwood, Mississippi, he was unable to appreciate fully the hospitality of his uncle and aunt. He began to walk in his sleep. Finally he was allowed to go back to Jackson, to his mother. During his absence, Ella had recovered slightly. The family was optimistic; a Jackson doctor suggested an operation and there was hope of complete recovery. The boy did not share such hopes! For too long his life had been colored by the treachery of unfilled expectations. A sense of despair and impending doom enveloped him and made him a stranger to the wishes and expectations of those around him.

Still, accompanied by an uncle, he boarded the train with his mother en route to Clarksdale for her operation. He waited patiently in the Jim Crow section of the doctor's office, where the operation was performed because white hospitals would not minister to black patients. He went with her to the boarding house where she was to recuperate, noting along the way that she lay, eyes closed, dressed in virginal white. And he knew instinctively that his mother would never be well again. She was taken, finally, back to Jackson in the baggage car of a train.

The operation had not worked. A blood clot had formed on her brain and she suffered another stroke. The pain was almost unbearable. Day after day he sat by her side, obsessed with her suffering. The pain that tore at her tore also at him; her screams stood also at ready-point in his own throat. And then, one night, unexpectedly, unceremoniously, as he would later relate, his feelings became frozen, solidified: "I ceased to react to my mother. . . ."

The numerous incidents, occurring so fast in his adolescence, steeled him against unexpected, catastrophic occurrences. Each of them—the desertion by his father, the orphanage, Silas Hoskins' murder, the endless days of hunger—had impacted upon his sensibility. His mother's illness did even more: it provided him with a deeper insight into living and suffering and the hopelessness of hope, the chaos inherent in the daily lives of everyone. Together, these incidents caused his skepticism, his almost pathological interest in suffering, his thirst for the violent and unusual, his ambivalence about the sincerity of human relationships. They offered, too, the unconscious motivation of his life and later his fiction: to attempt to structure, if only in the imagination, the only orderly universe that he had ever known, by the words and images of books. At the age of twelve, clutching the hand of his paralyzed mother, he was catapulted beyond her anguish and despair. But he did not turn to religion, as Margaret Wilson believed he should. His mother's illness, she believed, should have forced him to his knees to beg for divine intervention. Instead, he was recalcitrant, a sinner, and thus threatened them all. Was it not true, as her religion taught, that one sinner in a household could doom the entire household? Was it not possible that even Ella's sickness meant that she was punished by the transgressions of her son?

In his already demoralized state concerning his mother's illness, such beliefs only disturbed him more. His vision of the dismal state of the human family was similar to that of his grandmother. Like her, he believed also that mankind was damned, doomed to suffering and pain. He believed that the universe was chaotic, despairing. But Margaret believed that those who accepted Christ could achieve salvation, could be relieved of suffering and pain. Their universe might be stabilized, despair dissipated. He did not believe this. His mother was religious, believed in and accepted the redeemer, and yet her life was filled with misfortune. There were few people on earth who believed more fervently than blacks, and yet their lives had been a continuum of disaster and turmoil. No, whatever the cause of the chaos in the universe, it was not some ethereal power, who, in his own good time and at his own fiat, would reinstitute order. Yet, with his mother ill, he came under the tutelage and direction of his grandmother. Margaret persisted, however, in trying to move him toward accepting Christ and in this endeavor found a willing ally. Addie, the youngest of the Wilson children, not much older than Wright himself, was as devout as her mother, and would begin in the fall as an Adventist teacher. Yet she seemed to the young boy marked by characteristics that he attributed to himself: a certain stubborn aggressiveness, a penchant for violence. Wright's status as a sinner perhaps rankled Addie more than it did her mother. Not only did her sister lie ill, but the financial situation of her once-proud family had shrunk from middle to lower-middle class. The recalcitrant, she argued, should be sent to her school when the fall term began. ". . . if the family was compassionate enough to feed me," he later recorded Addie's argument, "then the least I could do was to follow its guidance."

Addie's other students knew that her nephew was in attendance. She had to demonstrate unmistakably that she showed no preference. For the other students, however, these demonstrations were hardly necessary. Unaggressive and nonchallenging, they were passive accepters of the doctrine of Christian salvation. To Wright, they seemed, in contrast to his previous schoolmates, to be will-less, ". . . their personalities devoid of anger, hope, laughter, enthusiasm, passion, or despair." His mannerisms and language gleaned from "the big city" shocked them, as did the tenets of his moral code, which forbade "squealing" and which led to a confrontation once between himself and his aunt.

One of his classmates had been eating walnuts. The empty shells were clustered around his seat. Nostrils flaring, Addie strode to his seat, ruler in hand. "You know better than that," she shouted, rapping him fiercely across the knuckles.

He turned astonished eyes to the teacher. The walnut shells were not his. His walnuts were uneaten, in his pocket. He protested, and in his excitement he inadvertently addressed her as Aunt Addie instead of Miss Wilson. She stopped short; her hostility became more pronounced. She marched him to the center of the room, forcing him to face the class. She replaced the ruler with a green switch, and hit blow after blow upon his outstretched palm again and again as it turned varying shades of blue and black. He absorbed his punishment, refusing to cry out, though the switch smarted and stung. He simply stared at her with defiance and disapproval. When she finished, he held his hands forward still, "indicating to her that her blows could never really reach me, my eyes fixed and unblinking upon her face."[2]

It may have been his taunting suggestion that her punishment did not matter, or that he did not supplicate her. Whatever the reason, when Addie reached home, switch in hand she ordered him into the kitchen. But Margaret Wilson's home was not really her turf. Here her authority was minimal, and in an attempt to stave off his aunt, he shouted out the name of the boy who had committed the offense. It did not work. Addie was adamant. It was not only his behavior at school; it was his behavior everywhere: defiant, recalcitrant. Someone had to teach him a lesson. She swung at him with the switch, forcing him into a corner. Then she advanced, lashing his face. He maneuvered out of the corner, out of range. Screaming, he rushed past her, to the kitchen table. He snatched out a knife, positioned himself. She called upon him to drop the weapon. He refused. She paused momentarily, calculating this threat to her authority. Finally, she leaped upon him, bearing him to the floor. She was bigger and stronger, and this gave her an advantage. Across the floor, locked, like two lovers in an embrace, clawing, kicking, biting, screaming, they rolled, the woman fighting to wrest the knife, the boy, to hold onto it. Summoned by the noises, Grandmother Wilson dashed to the kitchen. Ella, limping, followed her.

The combatants separated, turning their attention upon the spectators. Addie demanded that Wright put down the knife. He refused. Grandfather Wilson was called. He was an old man, now senile, whom the boy no longer feared. But, in deference to him, Wright lied: said he had thrown the knife away. He was castigated by his mother and grandmother, both threatening that he would come to a bad end. He was distraught. Having rebelled upon a point of principle, he refused to submit to punishment for something he had not done. Three women were attempting to control his words, deeds, thoughts, to make acquiescence the price of acceptance by them. Instead, independence seemed increasingly attractive to him.

For his aunt, he became almost a nonperson. He continued in her school, but communication between them was almost nonexistent. Now and then, she flared up at him, but a dash to the kitchen to retrieve the knife brought an abrupt end to her threats. His mother remained a sometime ally, encouraging him in his schooling, to try to improve himself. Margaret Wilson was moved by his act of defiance. It meant that her nephew possessed a soul in moral terror and agony, that he was already too much of this godless world, yet might, by some miracle, still be redeemed. She began an intensified campaign of prayer and church service to redeem him.

Grudgingly, he accompanied the old woman to church. He sat, sometimes throughout the night, squirming on the hard wooden benches, moved by the images and symbols of Christendom, impressed by people who scorned life and acquiesced to death, haunted by hymns that suggested future paradise. Occasionally he regretted that he could not be a part of all of this, that he could not see with these women's eyes, hear with their ears, believe with their hearts. Perhaps his grandmother was right; he had lived too long in a different world. "If laying down my life," he later said, "could stop the suffering in the world, I'd do it. But I don't believe anything can stop it. . . ."[3]

Margaret Wilson was not deterred. Frequently she fell to her knees and asked the master of all masters to aid her in her difficult task. "God," the boy remembered, "was suddenly everywhere in the home, even in Aunt Addie's scowling and brooding face. It began to weigh on me." Though he thought more frequently now of running away, he was reluctant to act. So he tried diplomacy. He told his grandmother that he could believe if he ever saw an angel. The old woman was so obsessed that she concluded that he meant he *had* seen an angel. It pained him to shatter her illusions, but while he did, he also acquiesced to her plea that he pray harder.

When he used the time allotted for prayer to examine the rich prose of the Bible, images, metaphors, details stimulated his imagination. He wrote a story about an Indian girl. It was plotless, lacking in conflict or theme, a character sketch of a lonely being "keeping some vow she could never describe." To end the story, he subjected his heroine to a romantic death: ". . . and at last the darkness of the night descended and softly kissed the surface of the watery grave and the only sound was the lonely rustle of ancient trees." Now, from the holy book itself, coupled no doubt with remembrances of the strange stories told by Eloise Crawford, he created something out of his own fantasies. Yet he knew his family would disapprove.

His imagination was fueled; his religious ardor was not. Margaret Wilson finally realized that he was lost. Speaking on the family's behalf, she declared that those who dwelled in the outer world were dead to *them*. This was expulsion, the fate accorded Spinozas from time immemorial, and for the young boy, it meant separation from those he loved despite all. But the separation was not absolute. He was cut off from congeniality and kindness; yet he still had to face the recriminations and vengeance of his grandmother. The old woman waged a vendetta against him as intense as the campaign to save his soul. She refused to allow him to bring "worldly books" into her home. She refused him the money to purchase textbooks. He was ordered to wash and iron his own clothes and forbidden to work on Saturday, the Adventist Sabbath. Thus he was unable to earn money for basic necessities and was restricted to the household diet of starch, lard, and greens. When he entered the Jim Hill Public School, he felt shame in the face of his more prosperous classmates. They had relative freedom at home. They worked on Saturdays. They bought sweets, wore neat clothing while his was tattered, faded.

Yet his grandmother's anger had one positive result: He was let alone. Dead to his family, he was free to remain away from home for endless stretches of time. Once he had trounced the school bully at Jim Hill, he was welcomed by a "gang" of boys and girls that included Essie Lee Ward, Joe Brown, and Jim Learer, who remained lifelong friends. Day after day, he disdained the supper meal of greens, knowing that to return home meant that he would not be allowed out again. Instead, he fled with his friends into adventure and exploration. Or else he trekked alone, down the banks of rivers and creeks, through dew-moistened green fields, noting the beauty of this city of so much violence. In later years he became the novelist of the urban milieu, able to focus on stark details with the versatility of the naturalist. Yet, for sheer vitality and energy of the felt experience, such descriptions were inferior to those from his childhood memory of luminous green countrysides, semidark nights and wondrous, harmonious sounds. In nature, he felt a sense of freedom that "would lift me beyond hunger, would enable me to discipline the sensations of my body to the extent that I could temporarily forget."

Reading produced similar sensations. He hungered for things to read. Knowing this and of his constant need for money, a classmate suggested a way he might satisfy both wishes. He could sell one of the local Chicago papers, earning money while reading such lurid, sensationalistic stories as *Riders of the Purple Sage*. He decided to try, and as he began building up a string of customers, he read the installments each week, emblazoning them with his own imagination. His grandmother, who was unable to read, was oblivious of the paper's content, and so did not interfere with the venture: He was on his own, earning money, though little. Perhaps, just perhaps, he was not totally beyond redemption.

There were others in the neighborhood, however, who could and did read the paper. One of these, a friend of the family, was a man who burned with racial pride and with interest in seeing young blacks get ahead. After he received his first issue of the paper, he wanted to speak to Wright. Was the boy selling the paper at the behest of white people or the Ku Klux Klan? he wondered. Was he aware of the contents of the paper? He confronted Wright. He showed him the cartoons depicting helpless, inferior blacks, and the violent language, calling for death to the black race. Wright was astonished. He had never read anything but the supplement containing the stories. Now he looked for the first time, finding a cartoon figure of a big black man, thick lips, long cigar, above a caption that read: "The only dream of a nigger is to be president and to sleep with white women! Americans do we want this in our fair land? Organize and save white womanhood." The paper was in fact an organ of the Ku Klux Klan. The boy was mortified. He thanked the neighbor and threw away the rest of his papers. He contented himself with castaway copies of *Flynn's Detective Weekly* and *The Argosy All Story Magazine.*

At the end of the school term, when his classmates went off to summer jobs, he remained idle, prohibited from working on Saturdays. Then, suddenly, he found a change of luck. Brother Mance, who lived next door to the Wilsons, had become an insurance salesman. But he could neither read nor write. Thus he commissioned the boy to accompany him on his rounds to the Delta, to serve as his agent for a salary of five dollars a week.

If the plantation system did not originate in the Yazoo-Mississippi Delta, it was there that the model was perfected. Rich alluvial deposits, formed from the delayed conjunction of the Mississippi and Ohio rivers, created the basin, flat lands of swamp and forest. The clearing of the forests and the draining of the swamps occurred during Reconstruction and after the First World War, and offered up suitable land for cotton planting. Here the plantation system grew and flourished. It was a system structured upon white supremacy, white control, and black servitude. Blacks in the Delta were not only disfranchised; they were also forbidden access to education. They lived, for the most part, entire families in one-room structures in which sleeping, eating, and other essentials were carried on. The days, even those of the very young, were spent in the cotton fields. The people themselves were mostly illiterate, gullible, possessed of simple honesty and trust. Though Wright was barely literate himself and not much older than some of the children, parents pointed him out as a model for their youngsters. For him, on the other hand, they constituted "a bare bleak pool of black life." Here were children who had never had a book to read, who would grow up knowing little but the exigencies of the body, whose lives were inexplicably bound to cotton and land barons, people who all their lives would have to contend with the very real threat of physical harm. He had thought while gazing upon the stricken body of his mother that he had become inured to suffering. Now he realized that he had not. Here in the Delta he found unmistakable evidence of the human spirit crushed, of the desire for freedom not dormant but nonexistent—and he hated it.

Brother Mance died during the winter, and Richard was once again among the unemployed. He advanced to the seventh grade, and again asked his grandmother to be allowed to work on Saturdays. Again she refused. He dreamed once more of running away from home, but before he could act, the death of Grandfather Wilson and the funeral preparations stilled, for a while, his restlessness. Soon, however, the daily routine of his life resumed: ". . . sleep, mush, greens, school, loneliness, yearning, and then sleep again." And too, there was the inevitable comparison between himself and his classmates. There would have to be another confrontation, again with the old matriarch herself.

One day, he followed her from room to room, pressing his case very hard. He told her of his desire to work, of the necessity to do so. She punctuated each appeal with a raspy no. He persisted. He retreated to threats. He would quit school. The answer was still no. Then he would, he announced, leave home. Margaret Wilson paused, looked at her grandson. This time she pondered before issuing another no. He had made the threat and he knew the consequences of not following through. He would lose forever his chance at freedom, at self-assertion. He was penniless and he had nowhere to go. Still, he dashed wildly away from his grandmother, ran to his room. He threw his shabby clothes into a suitcase and moments later bolted for the door.

He found Margaret Wilson blocking his path. She snatched the suitcase from his hand. She relented, angrily, but not before predicting dire consequences: "All right"—he remembered their conversation—"if you want to go to hell, then go. But God'll know that it was not my fault. He'll forgive me, but he won't forgive you."[4] Her humanity had triumphed over her fear.

Having won entree into the world of work, which meant the world of white people, how would he fare? Could he decipher, let alone contend with, the strange codes erected by white people? These codes told blacks that they had no human rights that white men were obligated to

respect, and that any tendency toward rebellion had to be tempered
lest some impulsive action precipitate violence. Here white children
were to be addressed as Mr. and Miss, and blacks of whatever age as boy
and girl. Here, too, whites demanded to know the most intimate of
one's secrets and ambitions, in order to negate them. When he
confessed to one white woman that he wanted to be a writer, she responded: "Whoever put such a fool idea about becoming a writer into
your head?" He had difficulty on his first few jobs. One woman wanted
to serve him moldy molasses and mildewed bread for lunch. While
working as a water boy in a brickyard, he was bitten by a dog belonging
to the boss. The gash was deep and painful. The boss dismissed the incident. He was sure that a dog bite could not "hurt a nigger."

For the first time, he had to confront the white world alone. He
could not depend upon parental guidance or protection by the black
community, and thus he came face to face with the signposts that
would plague his future. The white South declared emphatically that
he and his kind were niggers. The term denoted inferiority, and spelled
out precise codes of conduct, violation of which meant death or other
violence. Acceptance, however, meant death of another kind; it meant a
life as bleak and meaningless as he had witnessed on his trip to the
Delta, as empty and void of purpose as the lives of many of his friends
and neighbors. It meant that "tension would become a habitual condition, contained and controlled by reflex." But was this a natural order-
ing of things? Were black men and women ordained by heavenly de-
cree to acquiesce in the destruction of their own individuality, their
own personalities? No, because he was certain even then that such
would not be his fate: "I was," he writes, "always to be conscious of it,
brood over it, carry it in my heart, live with it, sleep with it, fight it."[5]

CHAPTER THREE

At the age of fifteen, Richard's universe had assumed the existential complexity of a Kafka novel. To live at peace with his environment and his family meant to accept the irrational, to disavow the laws of logic. He was set upon by a host of antagonists, and he had no idea what he had done to warrant their continual assaults. Nothing that he had done was criminal. Except during these times of assault, he was not unkind to his family. He kept mostly to himself and harmed no one. Why, then, did his very presence seem to invite censure? His family, on the other hand, had little difficulty in understanding his criminality. All the women—his mother, grandmother, and aunt—were lonely and frightened in a universe even more complex to them than to him. Their moral pretensions and religion were their way of combatting complexity. By refusing to sanction the way in which they lived, he cast aspersion upon it; and the narrow walls of parochialism within which they had taken refuge were not strong enough to sustain such aspersion.

And what of his environment? Here were whites who were as frightened, perhaps more so, than the blacks who accepted the iron rule of arbitrary laws without rebellion. To these also his manner was threatening. Rebellion had become a mainstay of his personality. Honesty of emotions was natural to him. He could not turn off his feelings at will. Yet, to live, he had to curb his natural instincts. He had either to do this or leave. The only other options were death and insanity. His awareness of this and of his own character only heightened his tensions. He became more afraid now of the things that he might do to bring down destruction upon himself. What unthoughtful action or word, innocent in meaning and doing, might be misconstrued?

Not too long before, he had had such an encounter. Uncle Tom Wilson, a retired schoolteacher, had brought his family to live at the Wilson home in order to help with expenses. He was authoritarian and became antagonistic toward his young nephew. Yet he was also old, feeble, suffering from Parkinson's disease;[1] and his power over his family waning, he perhaps saw the recalcitrant boy as a test; to subdue him, to break his rebellious spirit, was to reassemble the shattered image of his own manhood. Or perhaps, having lived in Mississippi all of his life, privy to the dangers that confronted the rebellious, he was intent on saving his nephew by curbing his tendency toward revolt. Whatever the motivation, he early one morning accosted the boy. He aroused him from a sound sleep and demanded the time. The boy, half shocked into wakefulness, responded. Tom considered the response inadequate, impudent. "This day," he announced rancorously, "I'm going to give you the whipping some man ought to have given you long ago."

Tom bounded from the room, furious, determined. He vaulted into the backyard, tore a switch from one of Grandmother Wilson's elm trees. Hurriedly, the boy slid into his clothes. He was confused, bitter. Again, accompanied by no warning signs, he was threatened with physical abuse. And there was no cause! A strange "uncle" whom he did not really know was about to punish him for not being polite enough. But more; the uncle wanted him to lie, to become subservient, broken, like the children in the Delta. He would not be beaten like them. He rushed to the drawers standing some distance from the bed, removed two razor blades, concealed one in each hand, waited.

Tom returned and summoned him to the kitchen. Obediently, the boy went inside. "You need a lesson," the older man remarked, "in how to live with people." Again, as with his aunt before, the boy realized that diplomacy was impossible. The older man moved forward; the boy opened his palms, revealing the razor blades. Tom halted. He read the danger signals in the eyes of his nephew, calculated. He advanced, pushed by remembrances of his one-time authority, demanded the razors. The boy threw up his arms; his eyes blared, his hands waved menacingly, his voice was tinged with hysteria: "I'll cut you! I'll cut you!" Tom came to a complete stop. The confrontation was over. He attempted to salvage something of his wounded pride by resorting to clichés: "You'll end on the gallows." Cruelly, the boy would not allow him even this compensation. When the old man cried that he had wanted to serve as an example for him, the boy threw cold words upon this dashed ambition: ". . . you're not an example; . . . you're a warning." Another altercation with a member of his family had once again left him emotionally drained. Over time, he regained his emotional balance, but the frequent altercations between himself and his family and his environment in these formative years must have contributed to the shaping of his personality, causing friends at a later time to reflect upon his "strange" mannerisms. A Communist leader remembered the author in his maturity, after he had struggled to fame and faced various kinds of confrontations: "I met him in 1929, when International Publishers were about to bring out *Uncle Tom's Children*. I remember that he just sat, nervously, tense, like he was watching, waiting for some calamity to happen." "Hell," a friend remarked, "Dick was paranoid as hell; you know any black folks from Mississippi who ain't?"[2] He would admit in later years that his environment was shaping his character despite his attempts, through revolt, to prevent it. But his sensibilities and perceptions were being shaped as well. There were times, even in Jackson, when the days were not all bleak and dark. At school, his teachers often praised him for his intelligence. For the same reason, he was accepted by classmates and elevated to leadership of a small group of young people. Such occurrences there were, though they did not negate the differences between himself and his family. His brother returned from Detroit, and Wright had hopes that Leon Allan might side with him in the family dispute. But his brother, perhaps moved by Margaret Wilson's protestations, joined other members of the family against him. Given the difficulties with his family, however, here, too, actuality was less dire than his perceptions. His mother continued to encourage him and, now and then, even Grandmother Wilson had a kind word for him.

His evaluation of the whites of Jackson was sound, though the Walls, the white family he began working for in 1923, differed from the others. Mr. Wall was the foreman of a sawmill, his wife was a homemaker, and his mother-in-law a former teacher. Richard worked intermittently for the Walls for a period of almost two years, and the family succeeded in winning his confidence. They respected his aspirations, were kind to him, and encouraged him to study. Such interest, generosity, and kindness were seldom granted blacks by whites, and to him the Walls seemed not to think or act like white people.

On one occasion, when he was bringing firewood into the house, he inadvertently entered the bedroom of Mrs. Wall. The woman was scantily clothed. The incident was charged with emotion. The bedrooms of white women, he knew, were sacred, off limits forever, upon pain of death, for blacks. The woman, however, did not cry out. She sharply reprimanded him for the intrusion. Ashamedly, he retreated from the bedroom. It was the first time that he had ever looked directly at an almost nude white woman, and the incident remained with him. The pristine bedroom, the pretty young white woman, even the sexually aroused black male, were all to be ingredients, years later, in the novel *Native Son*.[3]

The Walls opened receptive ears to his plans and hopes and offered the security missing in his tense relationships with his family. The male image he lacked in his father and his uncle, he discovered anew in the young husband. He discovered also that order and stability were attainable, that people might and did live free of dread and tension.

Despite the good days and good people in Jackson, the irrational character of his universe did not, in later years, allow him to write of them. They were ancillary to the pattern of his life, exceptions, and though they enabled him to maintain some sense of perspective, of a rational universe beyond his experiences, they would not allow him to sweep off into abstraction, to create a mythical world wherein things were better than, in actuality, they were. His association with the Walls, however, may have enabled him to make invidious comparisons between his white family and his black one, and indirectly between the black community and the white.

"After I had outlived the shocks of childhood," he later wrote, ". . . I used to mull over the strange absence of real kindness in Negroes, how unstable was our tenderness, how lacking in genuine passion we were, how void of great hope, how timid our joy, how bare our traditions . . . how lacking we were in those intangible sentiments that bind man to man, and how shallow was even our despair."⁴ The image was close to what he thought he had perceived in the people in the Delta. It was an image for which he had both sorrow and hate, and from which he was determined to flee. The Walls personified a world toward which flight, though difficult, might be rewarding.

Again, concern about possible exile stirred his imagination anew. Beyond the Southland was opportunity, the chance to discover identity and purpose. A place, perhaps, where rebellion was not prohibited by lynch law. A place, even, where a black man might become a writer. The intention began gestating in his mind after he wrote and published "The Voodoo of Hell's Half Acre," his first accepted work, published in a black paper, *The Southern Register*, in 1924. It was a potpourri of personal experiences and included a character sketch of his next-door neighbor, James Biggy Thomas. Biggy was a bully. He dominated the other children, including Wright, through the threat of physical violence. He defied adults, blacks and whites alike.

Through flattery, Wright managed to make his peace with Biggy. But the young rebel signified even then the defiant, rebellious black, who was determined to preserve self-respect and human dignity even unto death. And over the years, this image became a constant, a phantom of Wright's creative unconscious, hungering to be free, to be transformed from apparition to dreaded symbol of twentieth-century urban man. He identified with this image, and the sketch of Biggy was more meaningful than "the plot" of the story, which involved "a villain who wanted a widow's home."

The story was spread across three editions of the paper. He was proud. He had done something, something that "a bad boy" was not expected to do. Yet, it did not endear him to his family or to his environment. For Margaret Wilson, the story was one more bit of evidence justifying her previous opinions that his was a soul stricken by moral cancer. Anyone who wrote lies—her definition of fiction—was unregenerate. Addie condemned the story because the word hell was used in the title. Uncle Tom argued, with some justification, that the story had neither a discernible point nor enduring message. Even his mother worried that his chances of getting a good job in Jackson would be seriously impaired by publication of the story: writing indicated frivolity and weakness of mind. His friends' opinions were close to those of Ella. Why would someone want to write something like that? Why would one want to be a writer at all? Why was he so strange?

Outside of the newspaper editor and the Walls, he received no encouragement from his community. He had broken with its currents. Writing had no practical value. A writer was a dreamer, unnatural, a freak, probably a misfit. The criticism only tempered his determination both to flee and to write. He had not expected wholesale approval for his venture; he had not expected universal condemnation, either. Somewhere in that community of depressed, alienated men and women should have been souls kindred to his that would understand. His environment was their environment; his pain should have been theirs. It was not; and it intensified his dreams of going North, now not only to flee the brutality of the South, but to write books, novels. In the meantime, he had to prepare for graduation from Smith Robinson School.

The school, providing education for black children up to the ninth grade, could technically be called a junior high school. In reality it was little more than an elementary school, offering only the rudiments of education. Educating blacks was not a priority among the white politicians of the city; and though Smith Robinson possessed a minimum number of qualified teachers, in the main the teaching staff was barely more educated than the students it served. Yet several teachers recognized Wright's talents: his penchant for answering questions correctly and the overall superiority of his work. On the strength of his achievement, he was selected class valedictorian and chosen to give one of the speeches on graduation night.

Again, the "bad boy" astounded his antagonists. His family was surprised, proud, and admiring. The boy was also proud of his accomplishment. Nervous, shy, he prepared for his speech. He practiced and chose his words carefully. His theme was "The Attributes of Life," which he would use to attack the southern school system, to point out its failures in relationship to blacks. When he received the summons to appear in the office of the principal, W. H. Lanier, he had no idea of the agenda for the meeting. When he found out, he was astounded. The principal wanted him to deliver a prepared speech, one written by adults.

Lanier's position was perilous. For years, he had walked the slippery tightrope of black-white relations in the South. In Jackson, he had so ingratiated himself with the mayor that he was allowed to open a school for blacks beyond the ninth grade. As compensation for his diplomacy, the school graduation for the first time would be held in a white institution and would be attended by whites and blacks. Political expediency was a must. Things that white people did not want to hear should not be said. Only adults, those who had had long years of dealing with whites, could define these things adequately. Wright was asked to acknowledge the situation and to make the speech written for him. He refused. He had little respect for the principal's situation. Lanier, in his eyes, like others who should have been role models, were simply weak men of little courage, cowering before white interests.

Wright's rebuff astonished the principal. The others had accepted his speech without contest. Was this boy being supported by whites in an attempt to ruin him? The principal offered inducements. The boy was under consideration, he announced, for a teaching position at Smith Robinson upon graduation. Wright refused to relent. The principal resorted—timidly, feeling his way—to threats. He may not allow the boy to graduate at all. Wright's position remained unchanged. Not even Lanier's plea of desperation, "You can't afford to just say anything before those white people that night," moved him from his position. In fact, the fearful antics of the principal only increased his resentment and his determination. Because of men like Lanier, who were willing to sacrifice principle as a result of fear, the monstrous machinery of white racism rolled, smoothly, unimpeded, over the lives of black people. He would make the speech he had written. It may not be a good speech; it may not be educationally sound or scholarly; but he wrote it and he would deliver it.

Lanier was not without allies. Uncle Tom, who forbade his daughters to have contact with Wright, came forward as an advocate. He read both speeches and pronounced the principal's the better one. Wright's mother argued that he was trying to go too fast, that he was jeopardizing whatever future he might have in Jackson. These words were echoed by his classmates. Others accepted Lanier's speech; why didn't he? Why did he insist on "throwing away his future"? He held firm against them; Lanier, still suspicious that Wright might have white support, silenced his allies. He realized that a greater danger might result from publicity surrounding the event if the boy did not participate than if he delivered his own speech. In the meantime, pressure began to take its toll on the boy's emotions. The barrage against him forced him to compromise. He would deliver his own speech, but Lanier could edit out, upon mutual agreement, overly offensive material. Borrowing money from the Walls to buy his first suit with long pants, he delivered his valedictory address to polite applause on May 25, 1925. He was not yet seventeen years of age.

Except for a brief stint as a student at Mr. Lanier's new school, recently constructed by the city, his school days were behind him. His need for money far outweighed his ability to continue his education. His situation with his family was worse, now that he was neither in school nor gainfully employed and had thrown away what they thought was an opportunity by opposing the principal. His mother recovered partially and continued to regard him with affection, and this alone prevented his alienation from everyone in the house. Still, living among people who openly displayed hostility toward him was difficult, sometimes unbearable. And the anxieties that arose as a result were intensified out in the white world, where his situation was, if possible, worse. Since his altercation with Uncle Tom, the actions of his family were almost predictable; he had forewarning of altercations: a rebuke, a biting, sarcastic comment; there was no longer concern of physical violence enacted against him.

Outside, in the white world, none of this held true. He discovered that the actions of whites were often precipitous; altercations with them might occur spontaneously, for seemingly illogical reasons or none at all. Among his earliest jobs was one as a porter in a clothing store owned by two white men, father and son. Both sported reputations for maltreatment of blacks. He witnessed several beatings and slappings of blacks who fell behind in their payments. One of the most despicable concerned a black woman. Unable to pay her bill, she was dragged into the store by the two men and herded toward the back room, where she was pummeled and kicked. Afterward, in a state of semiconsciousness, she was shoved out into the street. A white policeman appeared as if on call, stared contemptuously at the dazed woman, then arrested her for drunkenness. The two men washed their hands, gazed benevolently at Wright. One offered him a cigarette. He took it reluctantly, fearing not to do so. It was their way of assuring him that he need not fear similar treatment.

Part of his job involved making deliveries to the nearby suburbs surrounding Jackson. One day, after delivering a parcel, the bicycle he rode developed a flat tire, and he began walking back to town, maneuvering the bicycle along the dirt road. A group of young white men, jovial, loud, pulled alongside him, offered a ride. He climbed aboard, seated himself. One of them offered him a drink from the bottle they bandied among them. "Oh, no," he refused, matter-of-factly. "The words," he later recalled, "were barely out of my mouth before I felt something hard and cold smash me between the eyes." He did not see the bottle coming, did not see the arm swing in his direction. The blow caused him to reel in momentary blackness. He fell from the car. When consciousness came slowly back, he saw men hovering over him, threatening: "Nigger," asked one of the group, ". . . ain't you learned to say sir to a white man yet?" He did not reply. He looked at them out of numbed, teary eyes. When they offered to continue to ride him into town, he refused, thus salvaging something of his hurt pride. They threw the bicycle out after him, told him that he was lucky he had not encountered some other white men: if so, by now he might be dead; and sped off.

He did not take their threats about murder lightly. The example of Bob, brother of one of his classmates, was too recent. Bob, who worked in a hotel frequented by white prostitutes, was rumored to have been involved with one of them. Some white folks warned him to end the relationship. For whatever reason, he did not do so and was lynched. When his classmate had rendered the episode to him, Wright had been moved by his friend's grief; but he had felt, too, something of the anxiety and fear that the act of murder produced in the entire black community. Such actions were designed to control behavior and to stem the desire for rebellion among blacks. But his own actions were not precipitated by a conscious desire to rebel; no, it was, a friend told him, that he acted "around white people as if he didn't know that they were white." There was nothing aggressive in his behavior; he simply had difficulty following norms of behavior alien to his personality. In his guts, where the threats of white men could not reach, was a sensitive, rational being that made it impossible for him to allow the South to make him into a "nigger." To thwart such attempts, he steeled himself against his environment, as previously he had steeled himself against the recriminations of his family. But his efforts to mask his true feelings, by feigning respect and acceptance of white superiority, were unsuccessful. His own attempt and failure were analogous to that which, years later, he would ascribe to Fishbelly in the novel *The Long Dream*. Fishbelly said all the right words of obeisance and obedience, but still, the whites sensed his disapproval of them; were able to discern his contempt, his violent animosity.

Wright was fortunate enough to escape serious violence due to his attitude—perhaps because whites were not able to confirm their suspicions of his recalcitrance—but it was difficult for him to keep a job. He was abruptly dismissed from his porter's job because he "did not laugh and talk like the other" blacks. "I don't like your looks, nigger," one of the men shouted at him. "Now, get!" He lost other jobs because of his attitude, his manner of speaking. Even, he wrote later, "the look in my eyes." He came to realize, with the aid of a friend, that if he was ever to keep a job long enough to save money to leave, he would have to make a greater attempt at dissimulating. He would have to master the stratagems necessary to survive in a world of white people. When his friend helped him to secure a job at the American Optical Company, he was determined to obey the codes of his environment, to live by the norms established by people for whom he had contempt. The firm was run by a Mr. Crane, a Northerner who was only vaguely familiar with the mores of the region. He told the young employee that in addition to cleaning the shop and making deliveries, he would be able to learn the optical trade. Two lens technicians were already in the employ of the company, Reynolds and Pease, both white. Presumably, they would be his instructors.

He got on well with them. He tried to be affable, to act around white people as though he respected the fact that they were white. But he was not being taught the optical trade, a skill that would enable him to survive up North. Remembering the promises of his employer, he broached the subject to Reynolds, asked the white machinist to tell him about the work; he inquired as to when instruction would begin. Reynolds recoiled as if struck by a rifle shot. "What are you trying to do," he snarled, "get smart, nigger?" Wright misunderstood, thinking that Reynolds simply did not want to teach him. He approached Pease, who was even more vehement. Punctuating his tirade with epithets and invectives, he told Wright that the optical trade was white man's work. "Nigger," he bellowed, "you think you're white don't you?"

He did not know that job status demarcated black inferiority and white supremacy. Verbally the men in the shop assaulted him daily; called him names, cursed him. He thought of going to the manager of the shop. But this might bring about harm. It was the old dilemma faced by blacks around him, and now it was his. The question was how to fight and for what ends? Where could he mark out in his own mind that point beyond which he would risk death for self-respect and dignity?

The two men continued to harass him. One day, when the manager and his secretary were gone, Pease summoned Wright from his duties. Suddenly he found himself hemmed in between the white men in a narrow corridor. Pease glanced at him, winked at Reynolds, standing a short distance away. The machines were off. The two white men measured him with hostile eyes. "Reynolds, here," Pease drawled, "tells me that you called me Pease." Reynolds moved to the other end of the bench, blocking off the exit route. He was trapped. Blacks had been beaten for not calling white men mister, and to deny to Pease that he had not done so was to call Reynolds a liar; for which blacks were also killed. In panic his mind groped for a solution. He could fall back upon the strategy of dumbness. He could contort his face into a mask of bewilderment, bring his hand slowly to the side of his head in a gesture of confusion, stammer about, searching for words and, unable to find suitable ones, throw himself upon the mercy of the two men, appeal to their superior sense of whiteness to accept his dumbness as indication of his respect.

He knew he could not pull it off. "I had begun coping with the white world too late," he wrote later. "I could not make subservience an automatic part of my behavior. . . . While standing before a white man I had to figure out how to perform each act and how to say each word. I could not help it. I could not grin. . . . I could not react as the world in which I lived expected me to; that world was too baffling, too uncertain."[5]

So he tried diplomacy. "I don't remember calling you Pease, Mr. Pease," he said slowly, "and if I did, I sure didn't mean—" A slap stifled his words in mid sentence. The blow knocked him against the bench. Before he could recover, the men were upon him. He realized what they wanted: he volunteered to quit. "It was," he recalled, "as if I had been slapped out of the human race."

He began his campaign to leave Jackson in earnest. He drifted from one job to another. He mingled only with blacks. One of his jobs was as a hallboy in the same hotel in which the brother of his classmate had been lynched. There, for the first time, he became privy to the locker-room discussions among blacks his age and older. The discussions seemed aimless, pointless, almost frivolous. They centered upon sex, women, sports, and . . . the perfidy of whites. The conversations were placebos, ways of working off hostility and easing tension. But, to him, they were further evidence of how impotent the men were in controlling their own lives. In their fantasies, white men were conquered, vanquished, while, in reality, the situation was altogether different. He was an outsider among these men also, because he could not live on two planes simultaneously, the fantasy and the real. For him, reality always thrust itself upon his consciousness.

One night, as he left the hotel after work, he spotted a woman who lived nearby. She worked as a maid in the hotel. He caught up with her as she approached the gate, intent upon accompanying her home. As they walked through the gate, guarded by a white nightwatchman, the guard slapped the woman on the buttocks. She threw her head in the air unconcernedly and walked on. Wright froze in his tracks. He stared malevolently at the white man. Conflicts of race and morality fused inside of him. One did not do such things to women. Black men would be killed for doing such things to white women. The white watchman stared back in surprise, unaccustomed, perhaps, to the questioning malevolence in the black man's eyes. He undid the holster of his gun, dropped his right hand to the handle, sneered: "Nigger, you look like you don't like what I did." Wright looked at the gun and at the half-inviting smile of the watchman. He mumbled something barely audible. Immediately, the gun was out of the holster. The black man did not answer affirmatively enough. Sensing danger, Wright shouted with as much enthusiasm as he could muster, "Oh, yes sir." The gun slid back into the holster; satisfied, the watchman turned away. Wright walked on, past the girl.

He felt ashamed. Again he was unable to protect a black woman. The girl caught up with him. She seemed undisturbed by the incident. Why? White men did that all the time, she said matter-of-factly. They did not go further unless the women wanted them to. "I wanted," he said despairingly, "to do something." He could not explain, perhaps, that here was a devastating blow to his growing concept of manhood. He lived in a region of the country attuned still to the romanticism of Walter Scott. Here as in days bygone, men rushed to the defense of women, sacrificing all for the sake of virtue and innocence. For a brief second, he was torn between the natural inclination to do something and to suffer humiliation. "You woulda been a fool," the woman said, "if you had."

Her seemingly nonchalant attitude dismayed him, but the incident reminded him again that his life was in danger as long as he remained in Jackson. Carefully, he appraised and reappraised his initial estimate of the money necessary to leave. He would need, he calculated finally, at least a hundred dollars to resettle elsewhere. Because much of his salary went into the household of his grandmother, accumulating such a sum would be difficult unless he resorted to illegal means. Despite the urgency to leave, the thought of this means of augmenting his income brought about feelings of moral guilt. Stealing was wrong. And yet, was this no more an absolute than anything else in the world of men? White people stole more from blacks than money, and perhaps stealing money from whites was a form of black rebellion, allowing blacks to live lives they secretly hated. It was chancy revenge: but, for those who concluded that whites had no laws that blacks should respect, such actions were psychologically rewarding. Such anodynes did not motivate him. He would steal, but for the most practical, pragmatic of reasons.

Freedom was a real necessity. If he stole, he would achieve freedom more quickly.

With this objective firmly in mind, he stole a gun from a neighbor's house and pawned it. With the help of friends, he stole canned food from the basement of a black college and sold that also. Finally, he secured a job at a movie house, where he could earn extra money by scalping tickets. In the course of one week, he earned fifty dollars, half of what he needed to leave. The next week, he earned the other half.

Having reached his long-sought objective, the following Saturday he sent notice to the movie house that he was sick and could not come to work. Margaret Wilson and Addie were at church. Uncle Tom was upstairs, and his brother was asleep. Ella sat in "her rocking chair humming to herself." After packing his bags, he went to his mother. He was leaving, he told her. Her first reaction was one of alarm. He was fleeing from danger. He had done something to bring the wrath of whites upon him. He reassured her. No, it was not that. He could no longer live as he was forced to. He was going voluntarily. He had to go. She embraced him, holding him long, hugging him hard. She whispered words of confidence, warnings. "And send for me quickly," she admonished him, "I'm not happy here." He broke from her embrace, only partially able to stifle his tears. He walked out into the cool southern night and purchased a train ticket to Memphis, Tennessee. It was his first journey alone. He was leaving Mississippi, destined for what, he did not know. The burdens and tensions of the past seemed to ease somewhat from his mind as the train sped away. He felt an overwhelming sense of exhaustion. He was tired, drained, but freer than ever before in his young life.

CHAPTER FOUR

In 1834, Memphis, Tennessee, ranked along with Montgomery, Alabama, and New Orleans, Louisiana, as the principle trading posts in the South. Its history as a bastion of segregation and white-supremacist attitudes predates the Civil War, and the legacy of the old days extended far into the twentieth century. It was among the last cities to desegregate public facilities in the nineteen sixties, the last to make public libraries available to blacks and whites alike, and the city in which Martin Luther King was gunned down. "There are but two estates—the white and the black," according to one editorial in 1890. "Race makes and marks the dividing line, and this must always be the case so long as the superior stand in presence of the inferior race. There is a law of being, of existence, of blood, superior to all written law, which impels the whites to this position. . . ."[1]

To this city, Richard Wright, almost eighteen years of age, returned in 1926. Old memories abounded. Here occurred Ella's illness; here were the first days of hunger and fear. The orphan home to which he was once exiled was here, and it was here that his father disappeared with another woman. As he sauntered down notorious Beale Street, looking for a place to live, he looked about, nervously, suspiciously. His mother had warned him to beware the underclass of Memphis: the pickpockets, prostitutes, and common robbers. His money was taped, inside of his clothes, on his body. He stared simultaneously at the tall buildings and the windows of the quaint one-family houses, searching for "For Rent" signs. He found one and dragged his suitcase up the stairs. At the top of the porch, he paused and reflected. Then a woman opened the door. Seeing her, he almost moved back down the stairs. She looked like a prostitute. This was a bordello.

Mrs. Moss looked from the apprehensive young man to the worn suitcase in his hand. She laughed, loud, heartily. The look on his face amused her. He thought she ran a bawdy house. He was obviously a country boy, afraid, unsure. She laughed again and ushered him in. Something about her laugh enticed him. It was real, deep-bottom, black folks laughter, tinged with warmth and sincerity. He followed her into the house, which was neat and unpretentious, just as she was. Her husband worked in a bakery; and she had a daughter for whom she was saving the house, as soon as she found a suitable husband. She brought her daughter, Bess, in and introduced her, leaving Wright astonished. He had never known people or such warmth before. "Later, after I had grown to understand the peasant mentality of Bess and her mother," he recalled, "I learned the full degree to which my life at home had cut me off, not only from white people but from Negroes as well. . . . The main value in their lives was simple, good clean living and when they thought they had found these qualities in one of their race, they instinctively embraced him, liked him, and asked no questions. But such simple unaffected trust flabbergasted me. It was impossible."[2]

Living accommodations secure, he walked into the streets of Memphis, seeking employment, all the while mulling over the antics of this strange family. They had known him only a few hours and already the mother was boosting him as a possible husband for her daughter. Bess, his age and attractive, displayed an immediate interest in him. She was friendly, overtly so; she leaned her head upon his shoulder, instinctively pushing her young body against his. Her attentions were both flattering and threatening. He struggled to clear his mind of old moral and ethical strictures, to give in to the energy and desire that could easily envelop him. But, in her very simplicity of manner, echoes of Ella Wright and Margaret Wilson made him timid. What could such a girl possibly know about his world? Could he ever discuss his sensations and feelings with her? No. She could offer him sexual gratification, but little else. He walked on, past the drugstore in which Nathan had worked as a night porter, turned onto Beale Street, and stopping at a cafe, noted the sign: DISHWASHER WANTED. He went in and was hired for the job.

His early success at finding employment quickly endeared him to Mrs. Moss. He was not only intelligent and well mannered, he was also ambitious. He seemed a suitable son-in-law, someone she could leave her house and daugher to. She did all she could to encourage a relationship between them. Often, she left them alone. Wright tried to talk to Bess, but her answers were punctuated with laughter and repeated declarations that she wanted to be married. She combed his hair. She leaned over and kissed him. His body came abruptly alive. He returned her kiss, petted her. Her body was warm, soft, maneuverable. She enfolded him in her arms, wrapped her legs about him. He glanced about at the doorway leading into the room. Where was Mrs. Moss? "Let's go to my room," he said.

She said no, and this jolted him. What kind of crazy woman was this? Here, in this room, where her mother might walk in at any moment, she was willing to allow anything to happen. But she would not go with him to the privacy of his room. Finally, they untangled on the sofa. He lit a cigarette. "I love you," the girl said, and he tensed. He had never been so completely accepted before by another human being. He had never known such faith, belief, hope, springing from one person to another. His environment had taught him that acceptance had to be fought for, struggled for; that he was a miscreant cast out of the society of both man and God; and here, on supposedly sophisticated Beale Street, the humanity in him had been recognized by another. But it was too late. His feelings were armored against trust and affection that were simply given. His legacy was one of suspiciousness, watchfulness, wariness. His universe was a complex mosaic of chaotic designs and structures, filled with labyrinthine corridors, and to understand the designs and structures, to walk the labyrinthine corridors, meant to keep honed at all times a well-chiseled, rational intellect. The world of Bess and her mother coasted always on smooth, easy, rolling currents; his on savage, heaving, churning waves. He felt he would have to put a stop to the machinations of both mother and daughter. He did not want to hurt them, but he could not lead them on. He threatened to leave the household, and both discontinued their pursuit of him.

He set himself to the task of earning enough money to bring his mother and brother to Memphis. Jobs in cafeterias enabled him to save money, because he received meals in addition to his salary. But his savings accumulated slowly. He began to think of other options. He had worked in an optical company before. Perhaps there was a branch, here in Memphis. He searched through the telephone directory, confirmed his beliefs, and went to seek employment. During the interview, he spoke frankly about his past difficulties at the optical company in Jackson, and he was hired at a salary of eight dollars a week. There would be no opportunity, he was told, to learn the optical trade: his job consisted merely of running errands, washing glass lenses, and general light service work for the company employees. On his first day at work, he discovered something of the character of his fellow workers. There were twelve men in all, white, whose political and social philosophies ranged from "Ku Klux Klanners to Jews, from theosophists to just plain whites." Race hatred permeated the atmosphere, but it was buried under pretensions of urban smugness, covert, rendered more often through symbolic actions rather than overt ones. Common discourse concerning many matters was prohibited, particularly those calling for "positive knowledge or manly self-assertion on the part of the Negro."[3] His duties clearly defined, unlike the situation in Jackson, he was no threat to the men and got on fairly well with them.

He ate selectively and lived sparingly, and soon, counting salary and tips, he amassed a small but considerable savings; more money, in fact, than he had ever had in his life. With the extra money, he bought used periodicals, *Harper's Magazine, Atlantic Monthly,* and the *American Mercury,* from a bookstore. The Memphis *Commercial Appeal,* one of the city's leading papers, he read almost daily, despite its segregationist stance. He was coming into contact with strange, new ideas, different ways of looking at old ones, and he longed for someone to discuss them with. The blacks who worked in the area, however, were interested in more mundane pursuits. Only Shorty, the elevator operator, seemed interested in books and things of the intellect.

Shorty attracted and repulsed him at the same time. On the one hand, he was a man of intense racial pride and feeling. On the other, seemingly without remorse, he played the role of the "happy darky" that whites had come to expect of blacks. In Wright's presence one day, Shorty stopped his elevator to pick up a white passenger. Jocularly, he refused to move the elevator, demanding a quarter for doing so. The white man laughed; what, he asked, would the black man be willing to do for a quarter? Shorty turned, bent down, offered his rump. The white man grinned, lifted his right foot from the floor, planted it squarely on the backside of the other man. Wright was disgusted. What motivated one to accept such indignities? When he chastised the elevator operator, Shorty responded, "My ass is tough, but quarters are scarce." The rationale did not mollify Wright. It was not just powerlessness and fear that provoked such behavior from blacks; it was obeisance to an alien system of values, one typically American, based upon materialism. "If a white man had sought to keep us from obtaining a job or enjoying the rights of citizenship," he later wrote, "we would have bowed silently to his power. But if he had sought to deprive us of a dime, blood might have been spilt."[4]

Nevertheless, Shorty did read books, if only the popular fare of the day. He became something of a literary guide and confidant for Wright, one with whom ideas about writing and writers might be shared. Every free hour, Wright spent either in writing, reading, or browsing through bookstores. In a newly purchased pocket dictionary, he looked up unfamiliar and foreign words. As he put down crude ideas of his own on paper, he became more assured that beyond the world of books and the creative imagination lay another, one where the individual might impose some sense of order upon chaos. "When I get older," he had vowed to Margaret Wilson years before, "I'm going to read all the novels I can." It was an avowal of freedom, as much as a childhood fantasy concerning books. Now he was free for the first time in his life, and not only to read, but to indulge the natural curiosity of youth. Thus he began to grow, to strengthen some of the impressions of youth and to gain others through new experiences.

What was not new was the incidence of white action and black reaction; he discovered that it was seemingly universal.

But he was learning more about this superstructure and the kinds of reactions white America caused in him. One day, he delivered a pair of glasses to "a Yankee," a man of liberal persuasion. Looking at his gaunt, thin body, the man inquired if he was hungry. Hungry? Yes, he was. He was doing without food, scrimping, saving, raising enough money to bring his family to Memphis, and afterward to perhaps set out for someplace unknown. But these were things that he could not tell the white man. His life, like that of black people in general, depended upon how well he could hide his true thoughts, sensations, from whites. He wanted the dollar the man proffered, but he could not take it. He could not leave himself vulnerable by letting it be known that he was hungry. Fear, paranoia, and suspiciousness had already become so deeply imbedded in him that he would never be able to exorcise them. Nor was he able to completely understand his feelings. Thus far, the things that he read had not emotionally affected him. He was interested in the technique, the style, the mechanics of the writer.

One morning before work, he paused, as was his custom, to read the Memphis *Commercial Appeal* in the lobby of the building. An editorial attacking H. L. Mencken, the *American Mercury* editor, drew his attention. He read the concluding sentence over again: "one hot, short sentence: 'Mencken is a fool.'" The language denouncing Mencken was the same as that used to denounce blacks. But Mencken was not black. Evidentally, he had criticized the South, and the paper was retaliating by writing of him in language reserved for blacks. But Mencken must have done or said more to so enrage the whites of Memphis? Were there other white people like Mencken, opposed to the mores and traditions of the South? Outside of the Walls, he recalled few others, and none so defiant as to provoke the kind of reaction that Mencken had. Immediately, he identified with this writer. He wanted to know more about him, to read for himself what Mencken might have said.

He wondered how he could do this. The public libraries would not be open to blacks until 1960, and the only black library was a library in name alone; there would be no books by Mencken there. He could manipulate his way into the segregated library in Memphis if one of the men at the shop could be induced to let him use his library card. To ask the wrong man would, however, place him in immediate jeopardy.

Upstairs, he canvassed his fellow workers, his mind cataloguing the personality traits of each. Some were rejected as being openly, avowedly racist. One, a Jew, was rejected because his own perilous position made him identify with the more virulent racists. He settled upon an Irish Catholic, also the object of southern racism but a quiet, unassuming man, often seen reading books. Still, this, too, was a white man. Yet Wright wanted the books and there was no other way. With trepidation he approached him.

The machinist was amazed. He maneuvered the younger man farther out of earshot of the others. He wanted to read books by Mencken. The machinist did not think that Mencken was such a great choice, but he was impressed by Wright's eagerness. Wright outlined his plan. He would write a forged note to the librarian. With that and the man's library card, the librarian would give him the books. The advantage was that since white people believed blacks were dumb, they wouldn't imagine that the books might be for him. The white man smiled, and then relented. The library card in one hand, Wright later handed a note to the woman behind the desk in the Public Library of Memphis. It read: *"Dear Madam: Will you please let this nigger boy . . . have some books by H. L. Mencken."* The librarian studied him momentarily and asked a reflex question: "You're not using these books, are you?"[5] She handed him Mencken's *Prejudices* and *A Book of Prefaces.*

A few blocks from the library, he quickly began riffling the pages of *A Book of Prefaces.* He had difficulty in pronouncing the word prefaces. Names of unknown writers sped by as he flipped page after page, and he had difficulty with names such as Tolstoy, Balzac, Dostoyevsky, Zola. He turned to the other book, the title of which caused him momentary apprehension. Had he been taken in again, like the time he sold the Klan papers in Jackson? Was he mistaken about Mencken; was he really a man with prejudices and therefore numbered among the enemies? He closed the book and hurried back to the shop, slipping the white man his card, gesturing toward his prizes. Later that night, a can of pork and beans warming in hot water in the sink, he sat in his room and began *The Book of Prefaces.* Often, he turned to his dictionary, but his difficulty with many of the words did not prevent him from recognizing the writer's style, the clear, clean, sweeping sentences. How, he wondered, was it possible to write like that? What kind of man could be so demonic in denouncing America and praising Europe, in mocking weakness and laughing at the foibles of authority, the concept of God?

Here was a man engaged in warfare, a man fighting, and he was doing it with words. They were his weapons, his clubs! He read on, discovering new names, new writers: Sherwood Anderson, George Moore, Mark Twain, T. S. Eliot, Baudelaire, Stendhal, Turgenev. The beans

were cooling in the water in the sink. The noises of Memphis were raucous in the darkened streets. He read on. Here was a world immune to
the manipulations of whites and outside the impotent urgings of the
blacks. In Jackson he had told an imperious white woman that he
wanted to be a writer. The thought had not then assumed the force of
an urge, an obsession. But now, reading phrases, sentences of revolt, the
obsession was born. He later registered both his hopes and his anxieties:
"Perhaps, I could use [words] as a weapon? No. It frightened me."

Still, his life came to resemble a religious ritual. He would go to
work, come back to his room in the evening, take out pencil and paper,
and try to write. Later he would read, sometimes way into the night,
another book that he secured on the library card of the shop workman.
Among the books mentioned by Mencken, he read first the fiction of
naturalism: Theodore Dreiser's *Jennie Gerhardt* and *Sister Carrie*. Here
was the fiction of the brooding, the despondent, impotent, and powerless. Here was the tragedy of all human endeavors, the omnipotence of
unknown forces, the assertion that suffering was germane to all, dia-
gramed in words that paralleled the teachings of the church. The books
were not about black people, but the ambiance of the universe in which
Dreiser's people lived was familiar to him. "I no longer *felt*," he wrote
later, "that the world about me was hostile, killing; I knew it."[6]

Reading Mencken intensified efforts to leave the South entirely. If it
was possible for him to become a writer, it was not possible in the
killing atmosphere of the South. Shortly after his discovery of
Mencken, he accumulated enough money to send for his mother and
brother. The three were soon joined by Aunt Maggie, who had been
deserted by Professor Mathews; given her situation, she was not anxious
to return home to her mother. Once in Memphis, she joined the discussions about the possible trip North. Leon Allan and Ella had no real
preferences about where they would go. Wright only wanted out. One
aunt, Cleo, was already settled in the North, in Chicago, and rumor had
it that she was doing well. Therefore they decided on Chicago, where
they would go in waves of two; Wright and Maggie first, in order to
secure living accommodations and work, Leon Allan and Ella later.

They would have to leave quickly. To think too long or hard about
the plan might produce doubt and result in a decision not to go, particularly because the stories of migrants who had gone to the cities away
from the South and had failed were legion. Ironically, the South that so
repelled him seemed now to attract him, and part of this attraction, he
would later realize, was due to the fear that living in the region had produced in him, in them all. It was fear, above all, of the unknown, a paralyzing fear that prohibited adventure, questioning, trial by experience.

Yet he knew that he was not yet the "nigger" that every institution in the South tried to make him believe that he was, and for that reason he could down his fear. He would leave, quickly. The decision now irrevocable, he waited almost until the day of departure to break the news to his employer, and then formulated a strategy for doing so. There would have to be a believable excuse. Black men leaving the South to go North inspired violence in white men or, at the very least, harsh words and painful confrontation. He wanted to avoid both. "I would pose as an innocent boy," he later explained; "I would tell them that my aunt was taking me and my paralyzed mother to Chicago." The lie only impelled the foreman and the others to debate the fine points of leaving: The only place for black people was the South, they told him. He would change up North. "Would you," they wanted to know, "speak to a white girl up there?" To their questions he feigned naïveté, piled lie upon lie. "As I talked," he wrote later, "I felt that I was acting out a dream. I did not want to lie, yet I had to conceal what I felt. A white censor was standing over me and, like dreams forming a curtain for the safety of sleep, so did my lies form a screen of safety for my living moments."[7]

The next day, aboard a train bound for Chicago, he considered the strange, bewildering culture that he was leaving. He was not yet aware that it had given him the background and culture to write fiction; shown him an assortment of men and women black and white, a spiritual quality that would make him always uncomfortable in the big city, and a longing that would enable him to give substance to the marginal men. But also, through its unstinting attempts at dehumanization, the South had produced in him a tremendous concern for the humanity of others, which he felt more deeply than most. And in all of this, he would later maintain, he was southern: "Yet, deep down, I knew that I could never really leave the South, for my feelings had already been formed by the South, for there had been slowly instilled into my personality and consciousness, black though I was, the culture of the South."[8]

CHAPTER FIVE

The train sped from Memphis to Chicago, and he sat silent, thoughtful, his attention drawn to the scenery outside. Despite the quickened pace of the train, everything seemed motionless, the atmosphere permeated by stillness. He turned briefly from the window, glanced at his aunt sitting, eyes closed, head resting against the back of the seat, then returned to silent contemplation. In the forefront of his mind was the ambition to be a writer, but his major preoccupation now was finding a job. He wanted to work, to earn money to be able to end his hunger once and for all. He wanted the things of comfort and security, and he wanted to achieve them without having to sacrifice his dignity. He was nineteen years old, and he had lived a lifetime of mostly fear and dread, which he wanted finally to put behind him. Chicago might enable him to do this. But more, it might allow him to find his identity, so that in knowing himself, he might be able to breach that incomprehensible barrier that separated him from others. "In all my life," he wrote later, describing his hopes for Chicago, "though surrounded by many people —I had not had a single satisfying sustained relationship with another human being and, not having had any I did not miss it. I made no demands whatever upon others."[1]

His first glimpse of Chicago did little to fuel his hopes. The bitter-cold winds riding the waves of Lake Michigan seemed paradigmatic of the big city itself. His eyes roamed around the depot from which he embarked, and discovered no signs reserving seats, places for blacks, whites. The two races moved about as if in total disregard of the presence of each other. His sensitive antennae picked up no racial fear. On the trolley bearing himself and Maggie to the South Side, he stared as blacks and whites sat beside each other, and sensed, without knowing exactly why, as he recorded later, that Chicago was "the promised land, the longed for Mecca."

The two travelers reached their destination, disembarked from the streetcar, and made their way up a number of depressing-looking streets in the heart of the black ghetto to Aunt Cleo's. A onetime school-teacher, Cleopatra was Margaret's eldest daughter. She had come to Chicago with her husband shortly before World War I. Wright remembered that she was present during the time of Ella's illness, but his own devastated emotional state had prevented him from observing her too carefully. Now he noted a woman who was tired and dejected, battered by one catastrophe after another. Her husband, like his father, was a "peasant" who came to the city and was crushed because he could not function in a strange, new environment. He had deserted her as Nathan had deserted his mother, and the fact of such desertions led him to speculate upon the urban environment, to question what factors in it led to the breakup of black families. He felt more empathy for the women than for the men, and in time he would come to see them as symbolic of multitudes. In Aunt Cleo's face were mirrored the many "stricken black faces trying vainly to cope with a civilization that they did not understand." They had come from the backwaters of the South and were unable to walk naked into this new world; they had brought the survival equipment of old, which in the North left them vanquished and alone, trapped in the crime and squalor of Chicago's South Side. Here, in a rooming house, not, as he had believed, in a large, spacious apartment, Cleo waited out the last days of her life. Ruminating on the plight of his aunt, he became somewhat dejected, and the euphoria of the first hours in Chicago dissipated. Now he wondered how much like the Nathans of the world he was, and whether he could survive where they had not. Had he "fled one insecurity" and "embraced another?"

He rented a room in the same apartment house as Cleo, while Maggie moved in with her sister, and the next morning, lightly clad, he went out in subzero weather, boarded a streetcar, "and rode South, rode until I could see no more black faces on the sidewalks." He rode in search of a job, and he found one in a family delicatessen owned by a Jewish couple. He learned later that the Hoffmans were foreigners, migrants like himself. Their English was heavily dialectical, almost incomprehensible. Yet, he noted, they were able to own a store in a neighborhood across the boundary line of the black belt, away from the dirt and grime, in this neighborhood from which he was barred from living. He became envious and contemptuous of them and attributed their good fortune to the whiteness of their skin. Automatically, intuitively, he was beginning to interpret his new environment by signals derived from the old.

Still, Chicago was neither Jackson nor Memphis, and day by day he began to experience a new kind of freedom. Curiosity drove him to explore his new neighborhood, and he moved through streets filled with more excitement and people than any that Memphis had offered up. Honky-tonks and liquor stores, owned usually by whites and filled to overflowing with predominantly black customers, were the most prevalent businesses on each street. At night the streets were populated by prostitutes, pimps, and panhandlers. Youth gangs roamed the streets night and day, their faces already displaying the marked hostility of angry, rejected adults. He was even bemused by the places where Chicago's black inhabitants lived; apartment buildings from which whites had fled, now sliced up into efficiencies, one room and a box-sized kitchen containing a stove, sink, perhaps small refrigerator and nothing else, home sometimes for three or four people. Acquaintances from his old school days began arriving in Chicago, and when they met, they would discuss the contrast between the North and the South. These constituted his most sustained social contacts. Still shy and wary of strangers, he made few friends, one exception being the black owner of a small bookstore near his home. Like Shorty before, he became something of a literary guide and intellectual conversant. Aside from his explorations, he spent most of his time reading and working, adding to his savings, anticipating the time when he would be able to bring his mother and brother to Chicago.

At work, the Hoffmans were kind, friendly, and they treated him well. He appeared shy and reserved to them, but they knew something of the South and attributed his attitude to his having lived there. He was a good worker. He kept the store clean, ran errands, made deliveries, and stocked the shelves. He did not complain. He appreciated their kindness and regretted that he had once sung folk ditties and told the obscene jokes about Jews. Still, he could not trust the Hoffmans. Jews or no, they were still white people and they had a measure of control over his life. To believe that they were different from the whites of his past would have been emotionally rewarding, but he could not do that. Until he wanted time off to apply for a better job, however, he was unaware of how prevalent, how corrosive, his fear of them was. He learned the post office was offering examinations for clerks. The job carried a certain prestige for blacks; the work was easier and the pay better than most; and a worker could gain certain long-term job security. He filed for the position and began studying for the coming examination, reading the exam booklets, scanning maps of Chicago and its environs, practicing routing by shelving bits of paper into homemade cubicles. As the date of the examination grew near, a resurgence of old tensions and anxieties almost immobilized him. How could he take time off from work to take the examination? In the South, black men did not dare

ask white men for time off to seek other employment. Such an act
would be met with immediate dismissal if not physical violence. If one
wanted time off, one lied; it was part of the mutually agreed-upon code
of behavior.

Whatever lie he could tell the Hoffmans, it would have to be one
that would strike at the base of their sympathies. He might feign illness, but that did not work well in the South, as sickness was not a
strong enough reason for blacks to remain away from work. In leaving
Memphis, he had lied about his mother, knowing that the sense of dedication to motherhood was universal. The white men may not have
believed him, but even the most bigoted could conjure up a certain
measure of sympathy. As northern whites, the Hoffmans were impon-
derables: perhaps something more dramatic was needed. He decided
to take off for three days, abruptly, giving no notice at all. This would
allow time for study and taking the exam. He would return to work and
tell them that his mother had died suddenly, that he had had to travel
to Memphis to bury her.

After his three days' absence, he returned to face the Hoffmans. They
assumed that he had quit. He stood, nervously, ashamed, angry with
himself. He did not want to lie. He wanted to blurt out the truth,
openly; yet he needed the job and he was afraid. He told his lie and
they immediately rejected it. Why, they countered, had he not spoken
of his mother's illness before? Why had he or someone not telephoned
them? They insisted he was lying and that they knew the reason. In the
South, they told him, he had to lie, but here he did not. Tell the truth,
they implored him. as he looked from one to the other, realizing he
hated them because they made him feel naked, more insecure. To their
objections concerning his first lie, he added others, wondering whether
they knew that he abhorred his own lies, that he did not want to lie,
that he considered it even a more debilitating mark of his inferiority
than they ever could. They could not know, and thus their chas-
tisement of him was worse than the beating he might have received
from an employer in the South for telling the truth. Yet they meant
well, and while he needed the job, he knew that he could no longer
remain in their employ. To face them daily would be to face that self
which he secretly despised. His only recourse was to flee, not only the
Hoffmans but his old self, to try to unlearn all that he had learned, to
search for new and different modes of living. At the basic core of his
personality, he remained the black boy of Mississippi and Tennessee.
He learned that he did not really know white people, all of whom he
regarded as part of the same vast superstructure, dominating, controlling the lives of blacks. Unlike in the South, whites and blacks in
Chicago met on all levels of confrontation and were thus forced to be

ever cognizant of each other. And yet, he sensed a distance between the races as pronounced here as in the South. Each group mistrusted and feared the other, and like other blacks, he viewed whites in terms of the stereotypes shaped out of the group experience. He wondered if he would ever be able to look at whites differently.

He passed the post office examination and, while waiting to be called to work, accepted a job as dishwasher in a recently opened cafe on the North Side. The predominantly white staff was friendly and acted kindly toward him. The white waitresses did not shrink from close contact with him, put no distance between him and them, even asked at times that he tie their aprons, appraise their appearance, and he thought back to Mississippi and Tennessee and what such natural human gestures would have meant in terms of physical danger, if not for the waitresses then certainly for himself. His employer noted one morning that "the colored dishwasher reads the *American Mercury*," and he reacted with surprise and admiration.

One day, veering from the sink in the direction of Tillie the cook, who was a Finnish woman, he stopped suddenly to see her spitting into the food, into a big vat of soup, vapors rising ceilingward. He had feasted on this food time and time again, and the thought sickened him. Who would possibly believe what he had seen? Yet the white employer had to be told; he could not work there otherwise. Still, he hesitated. He told a black coworker, and the two kept watch. Together, they informed the boss. She was stunned. They told her that either Tillie would have to go or they would. Faced with such determination, the employer observed the cook, who, as if on cue, continued to spit into the food. The cook was immediately dismissed, but Wright's nausea lingered for days. So, too, did remembrances of the cook herself, causing him to reflect anew upon the white people of Chicago. These were either strange white people or, perhaps, simply human beings much like himself and the boundary line theretofore erected between them and him had prevented him from realizing this. The Hoffmans, Tillie, his employer, and the friendly waitresses were individuals, seemingly each with his or her own idiosyncracies, each preoccupied with his or her own demons. Southern segregation denied him the opportunity to observe whites from close up, and now that he was able to do so, he was mentally filing away strange acts, curious behavioral patterns, much as he had begun doing for blacks.

In June 1928 he was hired as a clerk in the Central Post Office at a salary of sixty-five cents an hour. This was two times what he earned at the restaurant, and more money than he had ever earned before. Now he could save more quickly, with money left over to eat as well as he wanted and to purchase books and magazines. The job was only temporary, however, and in order to continue working he had to pass a physical examination. He had done remarkably well on the written test, scoring in the high nineties. But he knew that he would fail the physical exam. The ravages of too many days without food or with the nutrition-poor meals served by Margaret Wilson had left him a body that was small, with long thin arms and legs. To pass the physical, he would have to weigh one hundred and twenty-five pounds, and though he gorged himself up till the day of the exam, feasting on milk, steak, eggs, and bread, he remained underweight. His job would end with the summer and he would be confronted once again with unemployment or going back to the restaurant, which meant a reduction in salary.

The arrival of Leon Allan and his mother, though he was glad to welcome them, presented problems. Aunt Maggie had rented her own apartment, and when his family arrived, at the beginning of the summer, the three occupied a single room and shared the kitchen with Maggie. In this small, windowless room, the situation was somewhat reminiscent of the early days in Memphis, shortly after Nathan's desertion of his family, when the elder son was forced into the position of protecting them all. Wright had been ambivalent about his role then; he was not so now. He had become in many respects father to his brother, husband to his mother, protector and provider for them both. Unknowingly, Maggie, too, was destined to become the ward of her nephew, in those not too distant years of his fame. But, in the summer of 1928, Maggie was unable to accept his reasons for failure to secure a permanent position with the post office. She believed that he had not tried hard enough, that he spent too much time reading. She once asked him if he was "reading for the law" and was angered by his short, quick answer: No, he had responded, he read because he liked to. "The emotional atmosphere," he recalled later, "in the cramped quarters became tense, ugly, petty bickering." His own volatile personality undoubtedly also contributed to the tense days and weeks. In such an emotionally charged atmosphere, therefore, reading and writing became therapeutic as well as instructional.

After reading Gertrude Stein's *Three Lives*, he was haunted by the virtuosic display of language, the grating, abstract, yet telling images. In Proust, he sensed weariness, futility, a sense of his own mortality. He doubted that he could ever match such lyricism, that he could ever describe his environment, silhouette in words the people whom he knew, envelop them and situations and events in so much serenity and power. Mencken's *Book of Prefaces* remained his literary bible, and there he encountered more apostles of the craft, adding to his reading list Tolstoy, Eugene O'Neill, Galsworthy, Dumas, Conrad, Poe, D. H. Lawrence—grim ferrymen all, pilots on the River Styx of the creative imagination. Reading and writing might serve somewhat to ameliorate the effects of his aunt's torrential outbursts, but he was nevertheless disturbed by them. When he was offered his old job in the restaurant, he accepted it and moved his family out of his aunt's apartment, to a larger, though by no means a more comfortable, one. The place was filled with vermin and heavy odors; yet there he could read and write at will! Another physical examination was scheduled at the post office for the coming spring, and Wright began a long, sometimes arduous campaign to condition his body for it. Food seemed to replace books as an obsession in his life, as he tried to gain weight. This time, he passed and was hired as a substitute clerk, a more permanent position, and one that was less demanding than the former. He was assigned to the night shift, on which he worked as a mail sorter and where he came into contact with a group of young educated men—black and white—many attending college during the day. Tim McAuliffe, Abraham Aaron, Len Mallette, and Dan Burley shared his love for books and were interested in ideas.[2] They were men with whom he felt comfortable, and in addition to this advantage of his new position, he was assured of a steady income, which enabled him to move his family into a still larger apartment. There was enough space for him to have his own room, to satiate his need for privacy. Heartened by the change in his living conditions and inspired by the men with whom he worked, he began to move away from attempts to emulate the "old masters," searching instead for ways to portray people in the black community.

"Perhaps," he wrote years afterward, "my writing was more an attempt at understanding than self-expression. A need that I did not comprehend made me use words to create religious types, criminal types, the warped, the lost, the baffled; my pages were full of tension, frantic poverty, and death."[3] He was attempting to write his first novel, to be entitled, after completion in final form years later, *Lawd Today* but now tentatively called *Cesspool*; but the undertaking demonstrated how isolated he was, not only from the white society but from the black as well. He insisted upon viewing the black community not on its own terms but in terms of its relationship to the outside world. Because he viewed his own relationship to that world from the perspective of a victim, an outsider, not by choice but by predetermined laws and mores, so, he concluded, did all blacks. And thus his yardstick for the black community was all too often to be discovered in the perceptions of liberal whites. He saw blacks as those prevented from grasping the energy and vitality of Western civilization, and who suffered immeasurably as a consequence. They were the angst bearers of the world, members of the clan of the vanquished and defeated, lacking the initiative to fight for their own dignity and freedom, and yet, paradoxically, men and women whose rage and anger, once roused, might make them the vanguard of the new revolution. Of the varied dimensions of their lives, he knew little; of their overwhelming ability to shape pain and disappointment into weapons, he remained oblivious.

His own, introverted nature prevented him from achieving a balanced understanding, a more realistic perception. He knew only a few blacks and none intimately. No black writers were included in the vast reading list he established for himself. Of the Harlem Renaissance, then drawing to a close, he knew nothing, and he was equally ignorant of black history. Much of his own ambivalence concerning the black community and his place in it had been articulated for the sensitive, intellectual black by W. E. B. Du Bois, but of Du Bois and his writings he knew nothing. Thus, he discovered little in the black community to nourish him, to sustain him. On those few occasions when he sought such nourishment and sustenance, always he was repulsed for one reason or another. He became acquainted with a Negro literary group on the South Side. Young men and women of middle-class background, they appeared to be dissimulators, intent upon aping white people and their values, trying to appear as little black as possible. He contrasted his sincerity and his dedication with their triviality and superficiality. Literary interest among them was, in reality, emotional sickness, cloaking their sexually warped lives. They were literary bohemians, seeking to use literature to escape their empty, bleak lives. On the other hand, though he had not had half their education, their privileges, he was dedicated to learning his craft and "made much harder and more prolonged attempts at self-expression than any of them."[4]

The blanket condemnation covered them all. Not one was as dedicated or serious as himself; not one was able, as he was, to understand the warfare raging unceasingly between their environment and the world beyond. But if they repelled him with their pretensions, their superciliousness, another group, the Garveyites, both repelled and attracted him. Followers of the Jamaican-born Black Nationalist Marcus Aurelius Garvey, these men and women wearing the rich peacock-colored raiment of their order were members of the Universal Negro Improvement Association. Garvey organized the movement shortly after taking up residence in America, and at the height of its popularity, in the nineteen twenties, it numbered over a quarter of a million people. Its slogans, "Buy Black" and "Self Determination for the Black Man," along with its program for eventual repatriation of blacks to the African homeland, inspired far more blacks than the actual membership roles suggested. In 1925, Garvey was sent to jail as a result of the machinations of jealous political and social leaders, among them some of the most influential blacks, but the Jamaican's influence survived in the closely knit, leaderless remnant of the organization.

Men and women dreamed still of one day erecting the New Canaan on distant shores, of effecting vast changes and revolutions in the consciousness of black Americans. For the young Mississippian, they seemed, almost alone in the dismal slums and back alleys of Chicago, to adopt a black nationalist perspective that offered dignity and self-confidence, one that fueled his imagination. He and they were one in their denunciation of American racism, in fears and suspiciousness, bitterness and anxiety. They simplified the world in terms intelligible to most blacks, established a vocabulary free of pretentious words, grappled with the demons of their psyches, and declared their hatred and fear of whites as the oppressors of humankind. They proudly believed themselves to be outcasts, proudly lived and breathed for the day when, outside the physical and mental boundaries of America, they might establish a land of peace, order, security, and love—a land where there were no white people.

Such feelings stirred also within him, but he knew that he would have to temper the natural impulse to hate all whites, rid himself of the desire of the wretched of the earth, himself included, to combat the world, forgo being an outsider for all time, relinquish the belief that salvation on American shores was impossible. He did not accept their quixotic dream of a return to Africa; for him, this defined them as romantic rebels, bearers of the impossible dream, and this aspect of their program made him suspicious of Black Nationalism. Thus, poor, desperate, frustrated, wary of whites, engaged in his own impossible dream to become a writer, he denounced the ideas of the young Garveyites, the militant young people of the UNIA, as visionaries, and their ideas as illusions. "Blacks," he wrote, "were people of the West and would forever be until they either merged with the West or perished."[5]

The black Communists whom he encountered at about the same time appeared to him as visionaries of a different sort. They reminded him of the members of the group of South Side writers; they were middle-class, affected, and supercilious, though they practiced political instead of literary bohemianism. Their most common practice was mimicking the postures, speech, and gestures of their newly acquired revolutionary heroes. Fanatical adherents to a doctrine they did not understand, they spread their ignorance among a people whose real day-to-day struggles they papered over with Marxian rhetoric. They disdained black culture and mores; they castigated intellectuals; they inveighed against God, knowledge, rationality. Their inability to understand the true meaning of their Communist creed led them into excess when interpreting the Marxist bible. They affronted Wright's intelligence by their disdain of new ideas, truths, feelings, perceptions. The source of his discontent with the Garveyites was the message, which he was simply unwilling to allow a permanent place in his psyche. With the black Communists, it was the messengers that affronted him, those who took a philosophy of hope and promise and reduced it to farce.

After all, they had begun the journey along the road to revolution. Beneath their façade, when the blinders of superficiality were removed from their eyes, they saw the world as it was, became disenchanted, longed for a better one. They had no idea, however, how this could be achieved. Given the conditions of black life in America, the chances for development into whole personalities was negligible. But, as long as this was so, the nation, too, would be unable to develop to its full potential, to achieve humanity. Here was a dilemma solvable only through recognition of the fact that the problems confronting blacks were those which confronted all Americans. Blacks therefore were, by nature of their suffering and strivings, the redemptive ethos of the nation, who, by struggling to save themselves, would save America also, would resurrect ". . . a confused, materialistic nation from its drift toward self-destruction."

Though he could find no place for himself either among the writers, the Garveyites, or the Communists, he was learning from them constantly, slowly developing sophistication. He also prowled the streets of the South Side, talked to people with different, strange ideas, learned something of the inner workings and dynamics of his environment. Still, he persisted in viewing his new relationships, ephemeral as they were, in light of his own needs and the long-accumulated storehouse of stereotypes and boogeymen gleaned from the past. No one seemed as ready as he to catapult over the wall that contained them all. He was an outsider from the American society by force of law and tradition; he was an outsider from his community by choice and temperament. In the winter of 1929, however, an event he noted only in passing—headlined in the daily paper—struck with such alarming, devastating force that, almost overnight, he was forced to drastically change these perceptions.

In that year, the flimsy foundation upon which the American financial structure rested groaned, heaved, and finally, like an avalanche of rock, stone, and earth, hurtled suddenly down a precipitous incline. Banks folded, currency was depreciated, and the unemployed and those without any means of subsistence whatsoever suddenly numbered in the millions. The Great Depression would change the character of American society forever. For the more unstable, chronically problem-plagued, black community, the effect of the depression finds its closest analogy in the catastrophic fury of a cyclone, drawing everything into its central vortex, smashing all to pieces; the unemployed, those left destitute and homeless, the dispirited men lounging or walking aimlessly, children, abandoned by parents who had surrendered all hope, in old slum houses. In other cases, the houses, blasted by furious winds in winter, airless, vermin-ridden, served as abodes for hundreds of families.

But it was not only the destitute, the cynical, and the militants who felt the full fury of the hurricane. Those who had purchased, at a high price indeed, the mythology of the American dream, who lived by the precepts of the Protestant ethic, the Booker Washington disciples whose gospel had been hard work and sacrifice, now faced a future as dark and gloomy and uncertain as the others. The depression, perhaps more so for blacks than for any other group in the American society, was the great leveler. Black men, unable even in the best of times to offer more than minimum security to their families, were now unable to offer any at all. Jobs that were almost nonexistent for them became, in some instances, available for black women, whose labor demanded a lower salary. Young children also, who, like women, would work for longer hours and lower wages, were more employable than their fathers, leading in many cases to a serious and perhaps irreversible exchange of roles. And for the entire community, racism added to the plight of the inhabitants, creating an atmosphere ripe for the charlatan, the exploiter, the demagogue.

Wright was immediately caught up by the depression. Work at the post office slowed; his work time was cut from five to three days, then from three to two. By the beginning of summer 1930, he was terminated altogether. And the disasters multiplied. Aunt Cleo died of a heart attack. In the long years of continuing inner tension, Leon Allan developed stomach ulcers, making employment impossible even if such were to be found. Ella who had partially recovered, became ill once again, almost helpless. His role as protector of his family was severely jeopardized because of his inability to find work, and he was increasingly becoming aware that he could not meet, even in part, their minimal needs. The soup lines and private charities were now an indelible part of the landscape of the South Side, but he would partake of neither. Fierce pride and a belief in self-reliance prevented him. He found odd jobs, a day's work, enough to scrape together a less than nutritious diet. Finally, he succumbed to the suggestion of a cousin to become an agent of a burial society.

It was not work that he liked or of which he was proud. Operated by blacks, usually the leaders of the community, the societies were staples, one of the few solvent enterprises in this period of economic gloom and doom. In the past, they had grown and prospered as a result of the unwillingness of white insurance companies to insure blacks. For as little as a dime a week, applicants purchased the insurance that would entitle the applicant or his relatives to free burial. For most blacks, burial with dignity numbered first on the list of priorities. Yet this business, too, now suffered from the shocks of the depression. It was difficult for blacks even to scrape up the ten cents needed for the premium. The agents were paid fifteen dollars for every fifteen dollars sold in premiums, but, for every policy allowed to lapse, they were docked fifteen dollars. They barely averaged fifteen dollars a week. Though fifteen dollars now and then, in these desperate months, enabled him to fend off hunger, to postpone acceptance of public charity, he hated the job forced upon him, hated the more fraudulent, seamier side of the operation. When he had worked with Brother Mance, traveling into the Delta, he had come face to face with hopelessness and despair so severe that it had left an ineradicable impression upon him. Yet the agent had treated the people somewhat with dignity, had performed his task honestly, had not attempted to dupe destitute, ignorant blacks. Here, in Chicago, the burial companies practiced fraud; a policy might be and often was canceled for such infractions as missing a week's payment. Moving to another location in those times of forced mobility also meant discontinuance of a policy; in other cases, policies were issued with fine-print provisions that promised little or nothing toward actual burial expenses.

The agents were men, and illiterate housewives were a special kind of prey, blackmailed or seduced into sexual relations according to how strongly they wanted the policy and their premiums kept up. Women who would enter such relationships in order to secure a policy, by using their bodies in lieu of the dime they did not have, were threatened with cancellation when they wanted to end the illicit relationship. Among the black agents, black women were auctioned off and competed for. Wright himself did not mind reaping the spoils of his position, though he refused to practice blackmail or to threaten the women! The woman whom he would later identify only as "an illiterate black child with a baby whose father she did not know" attracted him. Like Bess, she appealed to him sexually, stirred the passion of growing youth. Ignorant, uneducated, she had only her body to offer, and though he took it willingly, guilt made him want to make amends. He wanted to teach her to read. She wanted him to take her to a circus.

She was illiterate, to be sure; yet, in mocking his efforts to educate her, she was telling him that in the real world in which she lived, education was the least important, indeed, ranked way below going to a circus, on her list of demands. She knew and knew well the limitations imposed upon her body by both her sex and her race; she had had to in order to survive. Her body was the currency that she used to make it through the nights and days, the life raft that bore her to safety in deep, dark waters; it was a weapon to disarm, a prize to grant or withhold, a resource that would render her impervious to total possession by any man. It was the magnet that drew him back time and time again. And for this he despised both her and himself. In his childhood, sex had always been the hidden taboo, the "act of darkness," numbered foremost among the world's unmentionable acts. The natural sexual curiosity that manifested itself in him was quickly dampened at every opportunity by the teachings of Ella, the sermons of Margaret. Yet, somehow, those passions of youth, stirred even more intently, became in adult life unextinguishable, and the psychological conundrum became manifest.

He was a rebel against the dreaded taboo; yet he could not slake the thirst of his desires, still the fire in his body. He was thrust into the purgatory between desire and duty, and the result of his dwelling there produced guilt and anxiety. He wanted a rationale other than sex for being attracted to her. He wanted to negate this demon from his consciousness. If he could educate her, he could deny somewhat the powerful attraction of her body. On a deeper level, the needs of old had been aroused in him. He wanted to possess her, to own her, to control her, to reduce her from powerful, alluring black woman to object, malleable, maneuverable. She resisted his attempt at every turn. She mocked his speech, his manners. She ridiculed his insistence upon teaching her to read. She wanted only two things from him, it seemed: her premiums paid and a trip to the circus. She preferred Jim, and in so many words, she told him so. " 'Who's Jim?' I asked, jealous," he wrote later. "I knew that she had other men, but I resented her mentioning them in my presence. . . . I hated her then, then hated myself for coming to her."[6]

To make him privy to the knowledge of other lovers moved her forever beyond total possession, made her impervious to any attempt to alter her personality. All that she could and would offer was sex, and not even this could be his and his alone, but must be shared with other men. Sex, he learned now, was, for some, not a dreaded taboo but a fact of life, one giving meaning to life, but the old taboos sprang quickly to challenge this new knowledge, and he felt humiliated, ridiculed: "I could kill you," he threatened. They were vile words, masking the violence within, and he was sorry for them. But, like black women before, she had roused conflicting emotions within him, forced him into that chamber of his psyche where he did not want to tread. Could he ever admit to himself that he feared them, their sexuality, their fierce independence, their power?

But there was new awareness to be gained even from this episode.

Speculating upon the young woman's life in terms of his own, he had, he recorded much later, asked himself what her life meant "in the scheme of things" and concluded, ". . . absolutely nothing. And neither did my life mean anything." Neither, it seemed, did the lives of any of those living in the black belt, and it was a conclusion arrived at grudgingly, painstakingly. The old lenses with which he had looked out at his environment, at its people, had to be discarded. The philosophy that stated that their misery was of their own making, their poverty the result of ignorance, laziness, was one to which he had been in part attuned: did not much of the affliction they suffered result from their inability to struggle? His job provided entree into the homes of the inhabitants of the South Side, and such thoughts soon dissipated. The people packed together in efficiencies carved out of the once-fashionable apartments occupied by whites could not have chosen such desperate conditions of their own accord. And the hopelessness, everywhere apparent in the bleak, sullen faces of people out of work, standing in the "soup lines" or scrounging about in almost-empty garbage cans for food—certainly their disaster was occasioned by an architect employed by forces greater than themselves.

No; the moral anger welled within him. The young girls barely out of puberty, and some not completely so, who offered themselves for sale for a nickel, a dime, and their younger brothers, who auctioned off their wares, the battered and bruised women, victims of men made callous by the exigencies of their plight—these were not able to control their destinies, to thwart the machinations of powerful events or the men who manipulated them. No, their lives meant nothing, absolutely nothing in the scheme of things; he knew that now, and he knew too that he was part of them, their misery mirrored in his own. These black and hungry faces by their sheer number called his attention to his own condition, made him realize that he was bound, perhaps irrevocably, to them, that in the backwater of misery and impotence, their lives and his were weighed equally on the value scale that registered zero. They had become for him symbols of human catastrophe on a cosmic scale.

Called upon to participate in a deliberate fraud upon a policyholder, he resigned his job with the burial society and was thrust back into the army of the unemployed. Periodically, he found odd jobs, including work in successive elections for both the Republican and the Democratic parties, but such work was not enough to provide for his family. Once again, the resurgence of memories threatened to assault his mind; visions of Elaine, Arkansas, remained on the edge of his consciousness. There were the grief-stricken mother, the inept younger brother, whom he was powerless to help, facing days of hunger. Seeking to hold back the inevitable, he sold most of his personal belongings and moved his family to a cheaper apartment. This one, too, stank of filth and vermin, reeked with the odor of despair and futility, and yet the inevitable followed him, cornered him, finally subdued him: "I sat for hours," he wrote later on that momentous day, "fighting hunger, avoiding my mother's eyes. Then I rose, put on my hat and coat, and went out. As I walked toward the Cook County Bureau of Public Welfare to plead for bread, I knew that I had come to the end of something."[7]

CHAPTER SIX

The day he was forced to beg for bread from public officials, he reached the dead end of innocence. At the relief station, he waited, sullen with shame to speak to the middle-class black woman behind one of the many desks. A sea of black faces were before him, standing, lounging about in the aisles, leaning against the walls. They had come, each with their individual terrors, and he discovered that their terrors were collective ones. In a short time they broke down the superficial barriers that had separated them and began talking one to another of their plight.

He sensed no revolution in the making, but he did sense a vitality, an energy, a reservoir of rebellion, quickly moving surfaceward. It was not only their individual lives that were meaningless; it was their collective lives that had been made so by forces they could not comprehend.

Eventually he was called before the clerk, who asked him questions about his family, his history. He, too, was regarded as livestock. He, too, belonged to this collective whole. He was condemned to be with them, to be of them, but what formula would now enable him to become a part of this multitude of potentially rebellious men and women, so much so that his being with them might enable him to derive answers not only to questions concerning the meaning of their lives but his very own?

Viewing them collectively, he came suddenly to the conclusion that his evaluation theretofore had been incorrect. He had been as blinded as the men who controlled the machinery of the superstructure. No, their lives were not meaningless; they were not inconsequential in the scheme of things. They were, instead, that vanguard, capable yet of moving out of the bleakness of their condition en masse, united by the poverty and suffering they shared to cleanse the earth; they constituted a multitude who had lost all hope in the system, who had surrendered the dream of the materialist paradise, who found strength and sustenance in each other. Individually, fear was a debilitating force; but, in unison with each other, it was transformed into driving energy, into a weapon as powerful and energizing as hatred. "I was slowly beginning to comprehend the meaning of my environment," he writes; "a sense of direction was beginning to emerge from the conditions of my life. I began to feel something more powerful than I could express. My speech and manner changed. My cynicisms slid from me. I grew open and questioning. I wanted to know."[1]

When he was called back for temporary work in the post office at Christmastime, he listened to his old friends with new ears, asked new questions. He was invited to their homes, where he participated in lengthy discussions and debates concerning the present crisis. Whites, he noticed, had begun looking at blacks with new eyes, divining a similarity between their conditions. Suffering was now the one constant in the lives of millions, and it was rapidly becoming for him the major metaphor of the human race, its symbolism almost everywhere. Later, while working as a porter at the Michael Reese Hospital, aiding a doctor in preparing a dog for experimentation, he held the animal tight as the doctor slit its vocal cords: "I held each dog as the doctor injected Nembutal into its veins to make it unconscious; then I held the dog's jaws open as the doctor inserted the scalpel and severed the vocal cords. Later, when the dogs came to, they would lift their heads to the ceiling and gape in a soundless wail. The sight became lodged in my imagination as a symbol of silent suffering."[2] His discussions with his friends convinced him that this symbol, once almost entirely racial, was universal. This awareness catapulted him in the direction of those who claimed to represent the oppressed throughout the world. Still, his primary concern was writing, and he devoted many of his waking hours developing as a writer. To his reading in literature, he added tracts of sociology and psychology. He worked consistently on his novel about postal workers, and he tried to forget the now seemingly absurd story that he had published in a black weekly, *Abbots Monthly Magazine*. The magazine catered to the black middle class, and "Superstition," Wright's offering, void of social or political commentary, was written primarily to make money. The story is slight, fantasy-ridden, with an all-too-predictable plot: A gathering of businessmen settle back comfortably after dinner and spin yarns. The main character tells about his visits to a small town, where he encounters a black family. He learns of the curse that hangs over them, in which each family reunion brings about the death of one of its members. Two such deaths occur on two successive reunions, enhancing the superstition and adding further intrigue to the story. In the denouement, however, both deaths are proved to be caused by natural, not supernatural, occurrences.[3]

The story was published in 1930, though Wright never received payment; the magazine became a casualty of the depression. The tone of the story was much different from the novel he continued to work on. The influences of Dreiser, Crane, and Farrell were noticeable in his social commentary. In the novel, Wright sought to place the experiences of the past three years of his life in perspective. His white friends from the post office were helping this as well. Some of them also were writers, and they implored him to come to meetings of the John Reed Club, a Communist front organization and haven for young aspiring writers.

He was ambivalent. He remembered the supercilious black Communists he had encountered in Washington Park and told his friends of them as examples of the weakness of the movement. His friends avowed that overzealousness may have pushed some initiates into superficial antics; but, for the most part, Communists were dedicated men, committed to struggle and sacrifice. He remained unconvinced, whether out of stubbornness or something deeper he wasn't sure. Certainly some of the black Communists he heard must have been seasoned veterans, men with oratorical skills. Not all could have been circus performers, lacking in knowledge of Marxist theory and fact. It was possible, then, that his antipathy toward them sprang from his inability to see black men as the practitioners of this alien ideology, that he could imagine black preachers but not black Communists.

One night, at a meeting in a South Side hotel, one of his friends made a startling announcement. One of his stories had been accepted by Jack Conroy, editor of *The Anvil*, and he, the writer, had joined the John Reed Club. Wright joined in congratulations, realizing that here was an outlet for young untested writers; his friend was an example of this. How much could they offer him in terms of development, new ideas, new insights? And what would be their price for such offerings? Perhaps they might try to cajole him into the Party, tell him how to write. How could white people, even Communists, be sincerely interested in black people? "I did not think," he writes, "that there existed many whites who, through intellectual effort, could lift themselves out of the traditions of their times and see the Negro objectively."

Yet he needed to learn more about writing, needed organization that would enhance his already fierce determination, hone his discipline; needed someone to serve as a sounding board for his words, his ideas. One Saturday night, not long after this last meeting, he sat at home bored and preoccupied. He thought again of his friend, the published writer, and of the John Reed Club. He could go there to look around, he decided.

Named in honor of the American writer John Reed whose book *Ten Days That Shook the World* chronicled the revolution that brought Lenin and the Communists to power in the Soviet Union, the organization was of national scope, with affiliates and regional offices throughout the country. Though the club was not avowedly Communist, its orientation and philosophy made it one of the Party's more successful front organizations. Political activity was not a requisite for membership in this cultural organization, but the Party hoped to attract radical artists and intellectuals, to engage them in the war against capital, by coordinating their activities. The Chicago John Reed Club was housed in a suite of rooms, a dingy walkup, east of the Loop. Wary of what he would discover, Wright paused at the doorway leading to a flight of stairs. He had not known what he expected the building to look like, but he did not expect it to be somewhat ramshackle, as if tottering on the brink of ruin. Through a window above where he stood, he made out imprints fashioned upon giant paintings on the walls. He breathed deeply, tensed, mounted the stairs, and entered. The room was in chaos, littered with papers and cigarette stubs. Wooden benches lined one area of the wall, somewhat set apart from the giant murals.

Close up, one mural captured his senses: it was a giant collage of colors, depicting the universe of man in vivid, bright tones of red, blue, gray, green, orange; a cataclysm of colors. Workers of all races and nationalities were depicted, their mouths stretched wide in anguished cries, their legs "sprawled over cities." He stared at it for some time, and his attention was diverted only when a man approached, smiled, beckoned to him. He told the man that he had come at the invitation of a friend, and was warmly received. No affairs were being held that night, the man told him. But he was welcome to sit in on one of the meetings in progress, the editorial meeting of the club publication, *Left Front*. He accepted hesitantly and was ushered into one of the offices, where, he was to write later, "I was meeting men and women whom I would know for decades to come, who were to form the first sustained relationships in my life."[4] They were men and women much like himself, talented artists at the beginning stages of their careers. Among them were Nelson Algren, Edith Margo, and Nucia Castle, the writers; Herbert Klein, stage and movie director; and the painter Morris Topschevsky, all contributors to *Left Front*.[5]

They welcomed him with polite enthusiasm but without condescension. He took a seat in the rear of the tiny office, close enough to observe the faces behind the flow of words uttered in debate. And old suspicions of the past, once again, rose to confront him. Were they treating him kindly because he was black? What degree of racism lay submerged behind quick smiles and gestures of friendship and camaraderie? After the meeting, he was introduced to "an Irish girl," an advertising employee, the wife of a university professor who was a social worker. Wright had worked for people like these in the capacity of a servant, and he had noticed no difference between them and other whites. He was given back copies of magazines, *New Masses* and *International Literature*, and invited back to the club. He was noncommittal. On his way home, he continued searching for some unrecognized act of condescension. He could think of none.

Back in his room, his mother and brother asleep, the noises muted down in the street below, he began to read the magazines. In later years he would think back upon this night, this essential moment in time, and embellish it with wonder, lending to it the same aura of instant discovery that he had given years earlier to his first reading of Mencken's *Book of Prefaces.* "I lay on my bed," he wrote, "and read the magazines and was amazed to find that there did exist in this world an organized search for the truth of the lives of the oppressed and the isolated. When I had begged bread from the officials, I had wondered dimly if the outcasts could become united in action, thought, and feeling. Now I knew it. It was being done in one-sixth of the earth already. The revolutionary words leaped from the printed page and struck me with tremendous force."[6] "I did not want to feel, like an animal in a jungle," he relates, "that the whole world was alien and hostile. I did not want to make individual war or individual peace." What he had always wanted was an end to isolation. But, before now, he had known of no institution or philosophy able to gather together the lame, the halt, the blind, the sick, as well as the angry, the isolated, and the oppressed.

At no time during his twenty-two years had the need and desire to belong so overwhelmed him. The desire had always been present; where would he go, by what would he be accepted? The Communist Party was the only organization that appealed to blacks across the board, the militant and the moderate, the poor and the petit bourgeois. It had learned a great deal from the mistakes of the Socialist Party in the early part of the century. The Socialists had advocated a plan based upon color blindness, one that refused to take into account the special status of blacks in the American society. As early as 1924, spurred on by the success of the Garvey movement and influenced by Stalin's plan for dispossessed minorities in the Soviet Union, the Communist Party embarked upon a program designed to highlight the specific status of black Americans, to recognize color discrimination as one of the tools of oppression. One year before the depression, a party spokesman declared: ". . . the Negro question assumes ever growing importance. The especially intense exploitation and heavy oppression to which the millions of Negroes in America are subject make it imperative for the Party to devote its best energies and its maximum resources towards becoming the recognized leader and champion of the interests of Negroes as an oppressed people!"[7] As Wright wrote later, "It was not the economics of Communism, nor the great power of trade unions, nor the excitement of underground politics that claimed me; my attention was caught by the similarity of the experiences of workers in other lands, by the possibility of uniting scattered but kindred people into a whole."[8]

As he read on, he began to believe that he could become a part of this movement, that he might even contribute to it. The party organs were magazines through which he might speak "to listening ears." The creative impulse swelled within him, gradually, slowly, then exploded: ". . . I swung from the bed and inserted paper into the typewriter. . . . I wrote a wild crude poem in free verse; coining images of black hands playing, working, holding bayonets, stiffening finally in death. . . ."

I Have Seen Black Hands is one of several poems composed during this period of conversion. Though crude in composition, the poem suggests that the long nights spent in reading and intense studying were not wasted, that the days of working and reworking words and sentences would pay rich dividends. The influence of Sandburg and Eliot is discernible in the style, that of Gertrude Stein in the attempt at word juxtaposition. The overwhelming ponderousness of images piled upon images, of heavy-laden sentences, bear the imprint of Dreiser and the naturalists. Still, as a technical construct, the work is a failure. He has not yet assimilated the various styles, nor developed the talent for creating sharp, clear images and metaphors that are the forte of his literary mentors. But, as a tribute to his newfound awareness, *I Have Seen Black Hands* succeeds very well.

The poem begins and ends with images of birth. The narrative moves from the singular birth of millions of tiny hands to the multibirth of millions of workers, who, side by side, raise fists skyward in revolt, welcoming the advent of a new, red day now visible across the horizon. Equally as important is the rebirth of the narrator, the author himself, after so many years of doubt and confusion, prepared now to accept an identity that allies him with the wretched of the earth. The refrain, "I am black and I have seen black hands," beginning the first stanza of the poem, represents an attempt to achieve immediacy. For him, it is the first real, unashamed identification with a people whose lives, heretofore, he has viewed from a white perspective. The literary conceits of the past are missing: the images of sensationalism and atavism, the stereotypes of laughing, brutal, ignorant darkies so much a part of the machinery of both black and white writers of the past. The images instead are those of black workers confronting a world of racism, oppression, and exploitation from the cradle to the grave. They are forced into poverty and into the nation's wars; they are brutalized, maimed, and sometimes lynched. Yet out of these images of degradation and catastrophe are derived the metaphors of men and women whose lives are pregnant with meaning, whose examples inspire and move millions.[9] *I Have Seen Black Hands* is a tribute to suffering, to struggle, to sacrifice, to the coming revolution: "And some day—and it is only this which sustains me— / Some day there shall be millions and millions of them / On some red day in a burst of fists on a new horizon."

Encouraged by his friends, he submitted this poem, along with others, for publication. Some went to *Left Front*, others to *The Anvil*; *I Have Seen Black Hands* to *New Masses*. He admonished the editor of *Left Front* not to publish the poems if he did not think they were good enough. He would be a member of the club now; he would work with kindred spirits. The club was involved in a number of projects. It demanded jobs for artists from the government, put on art exhibits, sent proselytizers to public rostrums, trade-union meetings, and community gatherings. It sponsored discussions and debates on the great issues facing humankind, on poverty and want, war and peace, illiteracy and education. It sponsored lectures and forums devoted to books and ideas, invited radical authors to talk about craft and technique. In no time at all, he was completely absorbed into the life of the John Reed Club. Outside of his job at the Michael Reese Hospital, his spare hours were spent in the Loop or at some meeting or lecture offered by the club elsewhere.

The club, however, was not free from inner turmoil. As he became more closely involved with the members on varying levels, he became more aware of the almost open warfare that had been waged for some time between the two factions of the club, the artists and the writers. The artists were predominantly Communists and had assumed leadership positions. They were the more vocal group and often pushed through resolutions by the sheer weight of their argument and numbers. They controlled access to the funds of the organization, which meant that *Left Front*, the writers' publication and club organ, was always in jeopardy. The writers wanted to wrest control from the artists, and to do so they had to secure more influence over funds in order to ensure the continued publication of the magazine. But first they had to oust the leadership by running one of their own members for a club officer slot in the forthcoming election. The best way to capture this prestigious and important office was to run the newest member. He had important assets. He was bright; he had proved during his short time in the club that he was congenial, energetic, straightforward; most important, he was black.

Here was a dilemma that no Communist would evade. At that very moment, party cadres were circulating in the black belt, preaching the Party's dedication to equal rights and fair treatment. None, therefore, would dare vote against a black candidate. The candidate himself was not unaware of the machinations of the writers. He did not want to be involved in the schism, did not want to be executive secretary. But he wanted *Left Front* to continue. The magazine was important to untested writers like himself. Because he wanted to be able to develop new ideas, to offer new programs, he realized the best way to do this was by being among the club leaders. He would be fair, would side with no faction, would work to bring writers and artists together. The writers were not, perhaps, enthused with his declaration of neutrality, but he remained their sole hope. He was nominated for executive secretary and unanimously elected.

True to his pledge, he managed to lessen some of the hostility between the two factions. He began to insinuate some of his ideas into the club's programs: his lecture entitled "Negro Culture in a Marxist Perspective" inaugurated the series of lectures offered by the club; he initiated the Saturday lecture program, in which such progressive intellectuals as John Strachey and Melville Herskovits participated.[10] He took to the lecture circuit himself, speaking on black revolutionary poetry to various branches of the club. After his own poems *A Red Love Note* and *Rest for the Weary* were published in *Left Front*, he became a member of the editorial board. Despite the energy, enthusiasm, and diplomacy he brought to his position, he was not able to stifle the dissension between the Communist and the non-Communist members of the club. Part of this was due to the fact that "local party authorities made excessive demands upon the club for money, speakers, and poster painters. . . ." A Communist front organization, these officials believed, should serve the bona fide interests of the Party.

Thus the club magazine was threatened anew. The Party demanded that publication cease. The writers angrily rejected the demand. The executive secretary, somewhat apprehensively, went to plead the writers' cause before party officials. "Feelings," he related, "waxed violent and bitter. . . ." The officials used the occasion of his visit to cajole him into joining the Party. He was a bright, rising star. He was articulate. The Party needed such blacks as himself. To continue as a club secretary, they informed him, he would have to become a member. To do so in fact as well as in spirit presented no obstacle for him. Yet he had come on behalf of writers, and he was intent on pressing his/their case. Again, he did not want to see *Left Front* discontinued. He favored, he told the party officials, "a policy that allowed for the development of writers and artists." The policy was accepted and, he later wrote, "I signed the membership card." He returned to his mediation efforts. One remaining point of hostility between party and nonparty factions of the club was the demand of the party faction that copies of the *Daily Worker* and *New Masses*, the Party's official organs, be offered for sale at all meetings. The nonparty group believed that such actions would limit club membership only to avowed Communists, that other radicals and progressives might shy away from a club that appeared so blatantly a part of the party apparatus. His compromise was to withdraw the *Daily Worker* but to continue the sale of *New Masses*. Still, he was a man caught between two opposing forces, able to completely satisfy neither. The future of the club itself was in danger because of the internecine warfare, and he knew that none of the members stood to lose as much as he from its dissolution. "The club," he wrote later, "was my first contact with the modern world. I had lived so utterly isolated a life that the club filled for me a need that could not be imagined by the white members who were becoming disgusted with it, whose normal living had given them what I was so desperately trying to get."[11]

As a member of the Communist Party, he was assigned to a local unit, or "cell." Due to his work with the John Reed Club, however, the unit allowed him to continue with the club, freeing him from cell programs and meetings; the stipulation was that he come to the cell meetings occasionally to give reports concerning his party work. He had been a member for some time, therefore, before he first appeared at a cell meeting in the black belt of the South Side. He had published little up till that time; yet his reputation had preceded him. "Welcome, comrade . . . ," he was greeted condescendingly by a grinning, seemingly pompous black man, "we're glad to have a writer with us." He managed a sheepish smile. The immobile, seemingly passive faces of black men and women stared out at him. They were those whose loyalty predated his own, whose need for the Party and its apparatus matched if it did not exceed his. Downtown, in the Loop, among whites, he had rank and advantage as a black man who had been ardently sought by the Party. He could pull no such rank on them. The Party had gone to great lengths to recruit them also. They measured him skeptically. Nervously, he issued his report. He told them of his work at the John Reed Club, spoke of his attempts at writing. He was devoted, he said, and he wanted to make whatever contribution to the Party that he could. In talking to comrades, he believed, despite their passivity, that his enthusiasm could find rapport with their own.

His report drew derisive laughter. From somewhere in the back of the room, a smothered giggle; then another. He looked at the organizer seated to his left. The giggle, half suppressed, formed on his face also. The others, noticing that the organizer was amused, suddenly broke out laughing. Wright fought to contain his anger. Embarrassment riveted him to the floor. Not since the days of Memphis and Jackson could he recall feeling so ashamed or so enraged. But the laughter did not concern the report. Few of them heard it, really, or understood what they heard. The object of laughter was Wright himself. Three years before, he had encountered people like these in Washington Park, and he had been repulsed by their speech, their dress, their manner. Now these same attributes, paraded by him, drew forth their resentment. The miracle of communism had not eradicated their prejudices or insecurities. They had lived all of their lives in an environment that had taught them to revere the superficialities; symbols mattered more than actual things; they were less frightened of dealing with people in terms of abstractions than they were in confronting them on a deeper level of feeling and understanding. His clothes, gestures, mannerisms, speech differed from theirs. He was a writer, a manipulator of words. How could they measure his dedication, his devotion, since he was a writer and intellectual: had not Lenin declared that intellectuals were dangerous to the Party?

"These black people who meet here," he later wrote of a party cell in Harlem, "are hungry in more than one sense. They love this Communist Party which is the only organization caring enough for them to give them [a] world view of things."[12] He tried to understand what the party rhetoric concerning bourgeois intellectuals had to do with him. Had it prevented them from seeing with their own eyes, from being able to recognize the similarities between himself and them? He was, after all, a worker, who wanted to write. His job at the hospital ended, he now swept the streets of Chicago for a living. His family was on public assistance; he had not finished the eighth grade. His fears, anxieties, hatreds, even enemies, were the same as theirs. Still, he threatened them, frightened them.

Only David Poindexter seemed different. A southern migrant who had come to Chicago, he joined the Party and distinguished himself as an orator and organizer. Though dedicated to the party program, he refused to surrender his deeply felt racial hostilities. He had been drawn to communism by its advocacy of the separate-development program, and when the organization shifted ideologically from its position, Poindexter disobeyed party orders to do likewise. He continued to adhere to the precepts of the program, which followed closely one of the planks of the Garvey movement. The Party, however, modified the separate-development proposal, substituting its own brand of black nationalism.

It declared that blacks in the southern states were an oppressed minority along the lines Lenin defined for minorities in the Soviet Union. Centuries of exploitation, the Communists argued, had given blacks a separate culture and a separate way of viewing the world. Thus, in order to achieve full equality, they must be allowed to develop separate cultural, political, and economic institutions. Communists like Poindexter had been called upon to defend the program against such Negro leaders as Walter White, Channing Tobias, and W. E. B. Du Bois, who strenuously opposed it. Poindexter was a valiant defender, arguing in support of the Marxist program from one speaker's rostrum after another. However, in 1934, without prior warning, he was admonished to stop his defense. In that year, the International League of Workers, directed from Moscow, began the "Popular Front," a program designed to reach out to moderate, conservative organizations. Poindexter finally came to realize that the separate-development program was being shelved, and he took his stand against a party directive.

Though his defiance caused grumbling among his comrades and whispers that he was a Trotskyite, his valuable work as an organizer prevented the leadership, for the moment, from taking corrective action against him. Moreover, he was under indictment for inciting to riot by the Chicago courts and defended by Oliver Law, "the south side representative for the International Labor Defense." The leadership may have been hesitant to damage his case by actions of its own. Poindexter's predicament and his fierce stand for principle appealed to Wright. He saw the organizer as a peasant who had come North and not withered away in the urban jungle. He was a black militant who had adopted an ideology still unpalatable to most blacks. The example of such men, he believed, would mean a great deal to the Party and even more to blacks in general. Most blacks had no conception of what a Communist was, outside the descriptions given in the media, and few understood what a black Communist was. Most blacks retained negative concepts of them. He remembered that his mother, for one, had been repulsed by the abstract portrait of a worker dressed in tattered overalls on one of the John Reed Club magazines. The fault was not altogether his mother's, nor that of black people. The Communists did not know how to appeal to such simple people. They "had oversimplified the experience of those whom they sought to lead." Here was an area in which he might make a contribution. He knew these people, knew something of their pragmatic perceptions about the world: "I would make voyages, discoveries, explorations with words and try to put some of that meaning back. I would address my words to two groups: I would tell Communists how common people felt and I would tell common people of the self-sacrifice of the Communists who strove for unity among them."[13] One way of doing this was to write about exceptional men like Poindexter, and so he conceived the idea of writing a series of biographical sketches. He would entitle the series "Heroes, Red and Black" and offer the lives of these men as proof of the redemptive powers of Marxism. Poindexter agreed to the project and hoped to enlist other friends in the venture.

Word spread quickly through the party apparatus concerning the project, and questions arose anew as to Wright's identity, his real purpose, and how much influence he could bring to bear on Poindexter. He received a late-night visit from a "quiet black Communist" who spoke to him openly about the Party's growing suspicion. "Intellectuals don't fit well into the Party . . . ," the man told him. He nevertheless continued his interviews with Poindexter, arriving in the early-morning hours, taking notes. On one such morning as he sat talking to his subject, scribbling away on his note pad, the doorbell rang. The man ushered into Poindexter's living room was Oliver Law. Abrasive, demanding, and doctrinaire, Law had little respect for intellectuals and less for creative writers. His military background gave him a fierce pragmatism and an abrasive, dictatorial manner. He did not bother to take the seat offered by Poindexter's wife but instead began a sharp, accusatory interrogation of Wright. He demanded to know what the interviews were for, whom Wright worked for, to whom the material would be shown.

Wright answered Law's questions. He knew that Poindexter was under indictment, but he made no connection between his project and Poindexter's troubles. He knew, too, that Poindexter was in ideological trouble because of his opposition to the Popular Front program, although this dispute had nothing to do with him. But Law's manner offended him. The man was insulting, accusatory, hostile. Abruptly he ended his questioning of Wright and beckoned to Poindexter. The two men went into another room and when, shortly after, they returned, Law shot a hostile glance at Wright, turned, and left. "He's wondering what you're doing with this material," said Poindexter. Wright paused, eyes opened wide. Doubt and fear began to fill out the lines in Poindexter's face. He was becoming cautious. Wright tried to reassure him. He repeated his earlier request that Poindexter need only tell what he wanted to. His wife rushed to explain that Law was afraid Poindexter had offered up some incriminating statement that might be used against him in court. Law must have thought that Wright was an informer, a plant. But, while Poindexter knew better, the sense of trust that permeated their talk before Law's arrival now vanished. Poindexter seemed to view him as a possible, if not actual, enemy. "We two black men," he wrote, "sat in the same room looking at each other in fear.

Both of us were hungry. Both of us depended upon public charity to eat and for a place to sleep. Yet we had more doubt in our hearts of each other than of the men who had cast the mold of our lives." Shortly after, he gave up the attempt to write "Heroes, Red and Black," but a painful process of reevaluation was begun. The nature of the party members puzzled him. "I had embraced their aims," he confessed, "with the freest impulse I had ever known. I, the chary cynic, the man who had felt that no idea on earth was worthy of self-sacrifice, had publicly identified myself with them, and now their suspicion of me hit me with a terrific impact, froze me within. I groped in the noon day sun."

The intellectual and creative efforts that provoked such discontent among the black comrades of his local unit were applauded down in the Loop and among his increasing number of white friends and readers both inside and outside of the Party. The Popular Front campaign of the Party made the John Reed Clubs expendable, and they were voted out of existence at a meeting in which he voiced strong protest against the move. Yet, during the one year left in the life of the club, he spearheaded its activities, functioning as official greeter, in which capacity he met and welcomed party bosses Earl Browder and Mike Gold; he also initiated and took part in lectures and discussions. More and more, he was called upon to lecture at other party units, and on one such occasion he delivered a lecture "tracing the career of Langston Hughes from *The Weary Blues* up to *The Ways of White Folks*," at the Indianapolis club.[14] His own poems were appearing regularly in party publications. *Rise and Live* and *Obsession* appeared in the first issue of the publication *Midland Left* in 1935. In the April issue of *International Literature* for the same year, *A Red Slogan* was published, and *Red Leaves of Red Books* was published in *New Masses* in January 1936. Though he retained good relationships with black friends from his old Jackson days now residing in Chicago—Essie Ward, Joe Brown, and Dick Jordan—his most influential friends, those who guided him toward literary models, were white. Joyce Gourfain and her husband, Ed, progressives though non-Communists, debated the high points of literature with him, listened to his readings of his own writings. Mrs. Gourfain guided him toward Henry James, to *Daisy Miller, Portrait of a Lady*, and *Roderick Hudson*.[15] In the Newtons, Jane and Herbert, he discovered another set of intellectual companions. Mrs. Newton was a white woman, "a member of a socially prominent Chicago family that had attempted to have her declared insane for marrying a black man. . . ."[16] "She showed me the poems she wrote . . . ," Henrietta Weigel, who later met Wright in New York, remembered; "she said her forefathers had fought in the Civil War for freedom, and she was carrying on their tradition by marrying a black man. When I told this to Dick, he re-

sponded angrily, saying that Mrs. Newton thought so little of herself
that only a black man could be her husband—then, at least, she could
feel superior to someone."¹⁷ Herbert, the black man in question, was
one of the party leaders, a friend of Poindexter's who, after the defiant
Marxist was condemned for his stand against the Popular Front, advised Wright to stay away from him.

His new friends introduced him to new forms of literature, and the
works of E. E. Cummings, Joyce, Faulkner, and Eliot were added to his
reading list. By the time he met Margaret Walker, in February of 1936,
he was able to recommend such nonliterary works as *Ten Days That
Shook the World, Das Kapital,* Strachey's *The Coming Struggle for
Power, The Complete Philosophy of Nietzsche,* and Adam Smith's *The
Wealth of Nations.* "If there were two literary books that were Wright's
bible they were Henry James' *Collected Prefaces on the Art of the
Novel* and Joseph Warren Beach's *Twentieth Century Novel,*" wrote
Ms. Walker.¹⁸

Among the intellectual readers of the party organs, his reputation
continued to grow; condescendingly, he was referred to in some quarters as another Langston Hughes. Editors who later admitted to the
crudity of his work accepted it nonetheless because the writer was
black. His name had appeared along with those of such established
writers as Dreiser, Erskine Caldwell, Lincoln Steffens, and Langston
Hughes in the January 1935 call by Granville Hicks for an American
Writers Conference, to be held in New York.

Such honors, condescending or no, compensated somewhat for the
continuing harassment he suffered at the hands of his party cell, and
the growing friction between himself and his family. He had moved, in
the past years, from hospital porter to street sweeper, and finally to
counselor at a South Side boys' club. Out of his salary the family
budget was set. Leon Allan continued his malingering, working only
sporadically. Ella remained ill, undergoing one semicrisis after another,
which may have occasioned her more intensive moral lectures and ti-
rades against his newfound friends the Communists. Perhaps she sensed
that her elder son was slipping away, growing up in a world ruled by
new and strange ideas. In 1934 Grandmother Wilson had arrived to live
with the family, and Wright had moved them again to larger quarters.
But he was doubtful now that he could ever truly satisfy them.

His job at the boys' club was a welcome diversion from both the family and the Party. Mrs. Mary Wirth, the social worker and wife of sociologist Louis Wirth, had secured the temporary position for him, in
which he worked with the impoverished youngsters of the black belt.
He was later to write that these young boys were, "a wild and homeless
lot, culturally lost, spiritually disinherited, candidates for the clinics,
morgues, prisons, reformatories, and the electric chair of the state's

death house." He felt a kinship to them since he had once been regarded as just such a youth. His sympathies therefore lay with them
and not with the authorities. He differed from them now only because
he had found a vehicle that could move him away from, or help him
win against, his environment. These boys had no such instruments;
theirs were crude: the violent act here, the antisocial act there. The authorities sought to divert their behavior by offering them games; ping
pong and tennis, checkers and marbles. "I would work hard with
[them]," he later wrote, "and when it would come time for me to go
home I'd say to myself, under my breath . . . 'Go to it, boys! Prove to
the bastards that gave you these games that life is stronger than ping-
pong . . . !"[19]

In the meanwhile, Poindexter's defiance of the Popular Front program had reached the stage where the Party had to take remedial action. The program was important to the Soviet Union; a wave of Nazi
hysteria was beginning to sweep the European continent; the enemies
of Russia abounded. Common cause with other progressives was necessary for the Communist parties throughout the world. Already, Wright
had been affected by this new policy. At the National John Reed Club
Congress held in the summer of 1934, where he had opposed, single-
handed, the order to close the clubs, that order was promulgated by the
new policy: ". . . I was informed that the People's Front Policy was
now the correct vision of life," he later wrote, "and that the clubs could
no longer exist." He despaired, seeing, in a personal sense, the loss of
party publication organs to new and unknown writers like himself. Yet
he had not really opposed the new policy, only the dismantling of the
clubs.

But Poindexter's actions were considered traitorous to the party command: He was charged with "anti-leadership tendencies, class collabo-
rationist attitudes," and "ideological factionalism." His friends were advised to keep away from him; he was to be cut off. This suggestion
ruffled Wright, who did not believe in turning his back on a friend. It
was, he was informed, a party decision, handed down with absolute authority. He was to stay away from Poindexter! He parried their suggestion. He did not like being told with whom to associate. His past life in
Memphis and Jackson had been filled with such orders, handed down
by men who made no pretense of respect for human dignity. "It was
not courage," he wrote, "that made me oppose the Party. I simply did
not know any better. It was inconceivable to me, though bred in the lap
of southern hate, that a man could not have his say. . . ."[20] The best
policy, he surmised, was to shun the comrades from the South Side.
After all, he was not a politician; he was a writer; at least, he was trying
his damnedest to be one.

CHAPTER SEVEN

An effusive Earl Browder looked down from the rostrum at Carnegie Hall at the gathering of writers, party members, fellow travelers, and the curious. The occasion was the historic American Writers Conference and Browder greeted the gathering: "We are all soldiers, each in our own place, in a common cause. Let our efforts be united in fraternal solidarity."[1] He had great cause to be ebullient. The Party had succeeded in gathering under one roof some of the most prestigious writers in the nation: Erskine Caldwell, John Howard Lawson, John Dos Passos, and Kenneth Burke were there; also present were Theodore Dreiser, James T. Farrell, Langston Hughes, Meridel Le Sueur, and Malcolm Cowley. His comrade writer Mike Gold was introduced as "the best-loved American revolutionary writer" and spoke of "the deepening cultural influence of the Communist Party." Lecture sessions and workshops were to be held, both at the New School for Social Research and at Carnegie Hall under the directorship and staging of Alexander Trachtenberg, head of International Publishers. The Comintern, the ruling body of international communism, had issued directives to close ranks and unite progressives in the Popular Front. This was being carried out with consummate skill. It was a great day for world communism, and the next two days should be equally successful.

Wright listened to the enthusiastic commentary from one speaker after another with mixed emotions. He was in New York City for the first time, and like a magnet, the vibrancy and pulsating energy of the great metropolis attracted him. Further, he was one of those writers, of whom Browder, Gold, and Freeman had spoken. Later he would hear himself praised as a new, fast-rising star on the literary horizon and would be publicly ranked with the older writer Langston Hughes. These were men and women like himself, writers and revolutionaries,

and his name was linked with theirs, as well as with writers throughout
the world: André Malraux, André Gide, Albert Camus, Arthur
Koestler. The American League of Writers was founded at the conclusion of the conference. Wright was honored by being chosen a member
of the National Council. How different all this was from the atmosphere in Chicago. The national party leaders did not shun writers, indeed went out of their way to stress that the writer must aid the cause
in the way he knew best: by using words as weapons. Sitting here
among other writers, he felt a sense of power, a sense of belonging;
these were his kinsmen, these were writers.

The momentary euphoria captured him, somewhat shielded him
from reviewing the tension-filled hours before the conference, those
hours in which, looking back on the event years later, he would ask,
". . . Could a Negro ever live halfway like a human being in this goddamn country?" The words were caused by an altercation with his comrades, whites whom party idealism had supposedly washed clean of
racism. He arrived in New York to discover that no housing had been
secured for him. He had had no idea that such would be the case; he
had come, after all, as a delegate, not as a Negro. He had been turning
over and over in his mind what he might do to aid the plight of "young
left-wing writers" now that the John Reed Clubs were dissolved. The
New York Communists charged with securing housing looked from one
to the other, then away from him. They were ashamed that none had
thought of housing for *him!* "Goddamn, I cursed under my breath," he
related later. "Several people standing nearby observed the white communists trying to find a black communist a place to sleep. I burned
with shame."[2]

Finally, someone gave him the address of a place in Greenwich Village. Though tired and needing a bath, his spirits lifted somewhat. He
made his way through the winding streets, found the house, paused,
knocked. A white man opened the door, stared at him defensively, told
him that the party he sought was not in, and abruptly shut the door in
his face. He returned to the convention hall, and finally was offered a
room for the night by a white woman and her husband. Now, seated in
this enormous hall, he realized that he had no place to go, that he still
had to find accommodations for the remaining days. "As I listened to
the militant speeches," he wrote, "I found myself wondering why in
hell I had come." His mind was preoccupied with the coming night,
with finding a place to live, so the speakers' fine words seemed ironic.
After the evening session, he made his way to Harlem, New York City's
black belt, a world far removed from Carnegie Hall and The New
School, one filled with restless energy, vibrant smells, and different

noises, a strange kind of oasis, set down in the jungle of the metropolis, where, he believed, one might find respite.

Again, initially, he was rebuffed. The flowing black life of Harlem notwithstanding, the streets upon streets of black faces, the curious pungent odors wafting from restaurants, from the open-windowed kitchens of black homes—despite all such concrete evidence that Harlem was a place reserved specifically for blacks—there were no hotels for blacks there. He was forced to rent a room at the Negro Young Men's Christian Association, where, after bathing and falling into a sound sleep, he awoke to reflect upon the events of the past days.

The symbolism and irony of his situation were clearly apparent. He had begun his journey away from the black belt seven years ago, expended much energy and time to remove himself psychologically from what he believed to be the hopelessness of his environment. He had made a superhuman effort to down the suspicions of the past and to accept whites as equals, to see them as victims of institutions and corrupt governments. He had risen rapidly in the literary heaven, from obscurity to recognition of a sort, and now was being accorded a place among the most respected, a writer among other writers. Still, all of this had led him, unceremoniously, to Harlem's black belt. Of all the blows thus far delivered by the Party, this was the worst. Other disputes involved not race but politics, but the inability of white Communists to find him room in a city in which he was a stranger was racial as well as an act of personal betrayal. It reminded him that he was still a man alone, with no support outside of himself. "I lay in bed thinking," he wrote, "I've got to go it alone. . . . I've got to learn how again. . . ."[3] This he knew would be difficult. Marxism had not only given him a sense of self, offered a forum for his writing, but it had also enabled him to see blacks as abstractions, as part of a mass of humanity, and in this regard, he was of the Communists, with them. But on the purely pragmatic, concrete level, though he had fought to rid himself of the feeling, there was a certain measure of contempt for them. "I sometimes wonder," wrote Margaret Walker, "if it is malicious to think he would have been happier if he had been born white than he was as a black man. He seemed to feel and believe that all his troubles stemmed from being black. Unlike Langston Hughes, who loved all mankind and especially his black brothers, Wright often said that there was no kind of cruelty worse than black people could inflict on their own people."[4] And in words destined to provoke censure from blacks in the coming years, he wrote in *Black Boy* in 1945: "Whenever I thought of the essential bleakness of black life in America, I knew that Negroes had never been allowed to catch the full spirit of Western civilization, that they lived somehow in it but not of it. And when I brooded upon the cultural barrenness of black life, I wondered if clean, positive tenderness, love, honor, loyalty, and the capacity to remember were native with man. . . ."⁵

At Carnegie Hall were those to whom he was drawn despite his disappointment with the Party. He had nowhere else to go, could desert it only to plunge feet first into waves of impotence and despair. The Party offered him a haven, even though sometimes it brought him anguish.

The next morning, he journeyed back downtown. His spirits lifted as he participated in the life of the Congress. He sat in on workshops, listened to lectures, continued to meet writers whom he had known only through their works: Dreiser, Farrell, Le Sueur. He spoke as a member of the Chicago delegation during the Sunday session, adding his voice to those who opposed narrowing the scope of literature. He also attended the Broadway theater and drank in the awe, mystery, and vibrancy of the city, the seemingly carefree banter of the people, the ceaseless hurrying. The city evoked images of freedom, that quality so necessary for a writer. As he headed back to Chicago after the conference, despite his disappointing episode there was a feeling of accomplishment, even of elation. He was selected for the National Council of the League of American Writers. Unknowingly, he was selected also for inquiry by the Federal Bureau of Investigation. Secreted away in the private files that the government was to maintain on him in the coming years was this appraisal of the conference by writer Eugene Lyons: "The remarkable fact is that an organization as frankly Muscovite should, within less than twelve months, dare to pretend to be independent and non partisan. Only one fact is more remarkable: that so many hundred of writers throughout the country should have believed the outrageous lie." Among those writers listed by Lyons, the FBI checked the name of Richard Wright.⁶

He returned to Chicago with growing self-confidence. When his job with the boys' club ended, Mrs. Wirth helped him secure a job with the Illinois Federal Writers Project, part of the Works Progress Administration, administered by Harry Hopkins basically to employ out-of-work artists and writers during the hard times of the depression. Wright was hired to work on a project researching the history of the state, a job that allowed him a great deal of leisure time, which he used to further his writing ambition. "The writer whom the Illinois project helped the most was Dick Wright," Nelson Algren, also a Federal Writers Project employee, has said. "He was more alert to its advantages and more diligent than most of us. He used the time it gave him to write 'Big Boy Leaves Home' and *Native Son*." Meanwhile, his doubts about the Party were renewed, as hostility continued between himself and the local Communists. The Party alone would not remove him from the black belt, so he wrote like a man in a frenzy, experimenting with poetry, short fiction, the novel, the essay.

He finished rewriting his novel *Cesspool* and sent it off to publishing houses. He worked on the short fiction that would soon constitute the volume *Uncle Tom's Children*. His first attempt at the journalistic essay, "Joe Louis Uncovers Dynamite," published in *New Masses* in 1935, brought him to the attention of black members of the Party's central command, the National Committee. Still, poetry remained the medium by which he was best known, and his recognition factor was enhanced by the poem published in *Partisan Review* in 1935 entitled *Between the World and Me*. It was about lynching and was based on his experiences in Mississippi and Memphis, where his actions regarding the white world were conditioned by the ever-present threat of the lynch mob. "The gin flask passed from mouth to mouth," wrote Wright, "cigars and cigarettes glowed, the whore smeared the lipstick red upon her lips / And a thousand faces swirled around me / clamoring that my life be burned."

He sought to heighten the dramatic intensity of the poem by allowing the narrator-victim to recount the tale of his own lynching. But the real vibrancy derives from his own bitter reactions to an event and its participants, and from the symbol of a nation that achieves gratification through murder imbued with the ardor of a religious ritual: "Then my blood was cooled mercifully, cooled by a baptism of gasoline / And in a blaze of red I leaped to the sky as pain rose like water boiling my limbs / Panting, begging I clutched childlike, clutched to the hot sides of death / Now I am dry bones and my face a stony skull staring in yellow surprise at the sun. . . ." In *Between the World and Me*, he was able to project one image of blacks, that of the Christ figure, the bearer of eternal angst. The Party had truly helped him "to see with new eyes," for this was an image fundamental to its own definition of black life in America. For him, however, it was an elusive, shifting image, colliding always with other images, those also gleaned from his own experiences. He wondered how much Christ was the architect of his own disaster; could he not have moved to save himself? And though the spectacle of the man hanging from the cross, head bowed, body nail-riven, evoked his sympathy, it also evoked contempt for the rebellion that did not occur.

Sympathy or contempt for blacks? Or both? "Perspective is that part of a poem, novel, or play which a writer never puts directly upon paper," he would write later. "It is that fixed point in intellectual space where a writer stands to view the struggles, hopes, and sufferings of his people. There are times when he may stand too close and the result is a blurred vision. Or he may stand too far away and the result is a neglect

of important things." Time and a new environment allowed him somewhat to distance himself from the material of poems like *Between the
World and Me,* to look back upon the experiences of his past with a
certain measure of detachment. But the novel *Cesspool,* which he
finished after many revisions, concerned time now. The present had to
be captured, frozen; thus he was forced to stand in close, too close,
proximity to the ongoing struggles around him, and his perceptions of
the blacks on Chicago's South Side were therefore blurred; ". . . black
people," wrote Margaret Walker, "were never his ideals. He championed the cause of the black man but he never idealized or glorified
him. His black men as characters were always seen as the victims of society, demeaned and destroyed and corrupted to animal status."[7] *Cesspool* was his first novel, and his ambivalence concerning his perception
of blacks probably contributed to the fact that, once his fame was assured, he ceased offering the book for publication; it was published, as
Lawd Today, in 1963, three years after his death.

Two creative concerns governed the composition of the novel. First,
it was a vehicle for experimentation. Stylistically and technically, he attempted to assimilate the art of writing as gleaned from the works of
those he admired and to move through the barrier their achievements
presented to find his own voice. For this reason, there are echoes in
Cesspool of Waldo Frank and Theodore Dreiser, of James Joyce and
Hart Crane. Page after page of the book is filled with naturalistic and
realistic paraphernalia: newsprint, advertisements, inscriptions, and the
haunting radio refrain cataloguing the life and times of Abraham Lincoln.

But he also wanted to examine the environment into which he had
recently come, to analyze its people. He would write a juvenile novel,
therefore, that for him would mean more than the genre usually meant
to first writers: it would be an instrument of understanding others as
well as himself.

He etched out the contours of Jake Jackson's life along lines parallel
to his own. This fictional hero of his first novel was a migrant who had
fled the South searching for new ways of living. He was lower-middle
class; he was uneducated, he was a postal worker, sharing many of
Wright's experiences and characteristics. Only, Jake Jackson's future
could not be his. Thus, in the course of the novel, his perspective on
Jackson shifted from the individual to the general. Jackson was a para-
digm of blacks stunted in their growth and mired in poverty and hopelessness. "As he mounted the steps," he describes Jackson in one telling episode, "he wondered if he would have to go on this way, year
after year, until he died. Was this *all?* Deep in him was a dumb yearning for something else; somewhere or other for him. But where? How?

All he could see right now was an endless stretch of black postal days; and all he could feel was the agony of standing on his feet till they ached and sweated, of breathing dust till he spat black, of jerking his body when a voice yelled."[8]

Throughout the years, the author revised his manuscript. Yet the overriding symbol of the novel remained pointless. Nothing that happens in that single, Joycean day in the life of Jake Jackson is important: At the end of the novel, he is as blind to the meaning of his own existence as he was at the beginning. His search for the materialist's heaven is pointless; his attempts to achieve manhood through his sensationalistic exploits or possession of his wife are pointless; his desire to satiate his hunger for an identity is pointless; in short, as for others in his environment, life itself is pointless. Having set Jake down in cold print, looked at him with the eyes of a clinician, Wright knew now the shadow he had to outdistance. Unlike the Jake Jacksons of his imagination, he traveled the high road of struggle and sacrifice; fiction like *Cesspool* served to warn him that under no circumstances could he afford to detour. But there was now enough distance between himself and the Jake Jacksons of the ghetto to allow him to discern the differences among members of the community. There were other blacks, serious, dedicated, determined to struggle their way out of the morass in which their environment had mired them. Part of this new perspective was occasioned by party rhetoric and part by the experience his position with the John Reed Clubs granted, plus his growing reputation as a writer. He would meet Arna Bontemps, Frank Yerby, Frank Marshall Davis, Claude McKay, Willard Motley, and Ralph Ellison. Along with other black writers, he helped to form the South Side Writers Group, a loosely knit organization of aspiring writers that included poets Fenton Johnson and Margaret Walker and playwright Theodore Ward. ". . . I read a group of my poems," Margaret Walker wrote of one meeting. "I was surprised to see that they did not cut me down. Ted Ward and Dick Wright were kind in their praise."[9] Here were men and women of talent and ideas, as dedicated to the art of writing as Wright was himself. They were equally as strident against racism, exploitation, and oppression, and they sought to cultivate a literature that would counteract the stereotypes of blacks already prevalent. He attended other literary gatherings during his time with the South Side Writers Group, gatherings comprising mostly white intellectuals and writers, and he learned from those also.

Yet there was a world view held by black writers that must be forever missing among whites, no matter how progressive or racially free. Thus he was more at ease among the members of the South Side Writers Group than among groupings of white writers and intellectuals.

"Wright was attractive," wrote Henrietta Weigel; "he alternated between sullenness, when he felt rejected by whites . . . and volatile
warmth when sensing kinship in spirit. . . . At parties Dick never
joined the groups of people dancing. He seemed like a deacon at those
times, silently condemning his people for being what he considered
court jesters in the white world."[10] "Dick," recalls a friend, "was a great
raconteur. He could tell 'darky' jokes with the best. No . . . he, nobody ever told these jokes around the white folks." At these weekly
meetings, he read his works aloud without feeling shame or guilt when
announcing some demeaning racial epithet; this was the Dick Wright
that he often kept hidden from others. "Dick," noted the friend previously mentioned, "was down inside all that paranoia, a Mississippi
boy . . . you know what that means . . . no sophistication, real country, overawed by all his fame and success."

These contradictory aspects of his personality surfaced in his writings.
In the article "Joe Louis Uncovers Dynamite," he articulated a new reservoir of passion and energy among the people of the South Side. Joe
Louis, the Brown Bomber, had captured his imagination as he had that
of blacks throughout the ghettoes of America. Swift, smooth, powered
by bursts of nervous energy, his thunderous right hand ignited the fantasy of those unable to confront the powerful whites in their daily lives.
Each time Louis sent a white man hurtling to the canvas, blacks were
pleased. The reaction was purely racial, and Wright, too, was caught up
in the symbolism. Nor was he oblivious to the example Louis set for
others. The mounting string of victories achieved by the boxer seemed
to uncover revolutionary intensity among the South Side residents. And
when Louis defeated Max Baer, they took to the streets, singing, shouting, greeting one another; they moved about the community as if it
were theirs, staring boldly, questioningly, into the faces of whites, walking strong, upright: "Something," Wright noted, "had happened that
night."

This was the race pride and communal spirit that produced in men,
women, and children the illusion that their lives might be different,
that they, too, might defeat their foes, that obstacles could be overcome. The spectacle impressed him first as a black man and secondly as
a Communist. If blacks were the vanguard of the coming revolution, the
sleeping giants of history, their revolutionary potential must be awakened, harnessed. Louis had done the first; the Party must now move
to do the second.

"Joe Louis Uncovers Dynamite" was a crude piece of propagandistic
writing, yet it caught the attention of the powerful Buddy Nealson
(Harry Haywood). Haywood had fought his way to the top leadership
of the Party, become a member of the Central Committee. With Wil-

liam L. Patterson, he traveled to Moscow and sat among the members of the Comintern itself. He was involved in the campaigns to free Sacco and Vanzetti and the Scottsboro Boys, and his ideas of a dedicated Marxist were formed from these campaigns. Such a Marxist was one who organized the masses, took part in demonstrations, confronted police and jails, became involved in rent strikes and acts of civil disobedience. He had little understanding or tolerance for writers, especially creative writers. "Harry Haywood," his old comrade Patterson recalled, "then top organizer on the Southside, did not exhibit the slightest appreciation that he was dealing with a sensitive, immature creative genius, i.e., Wright with whom it was necessary to exercise great patience. He criticized some of Wright's earlier characters sharply and tried to force him into a mold that was not to his liking. Name-calling resulted and Haywood used his political position to get a vote of censure against Wright, who thereupon resigned from the Party."[11]

He had had no intention then of resigning. He only wanted to stay clear of the South Side cell, of men like Haywood. His work was being published and read more widely now in the party organs than before. He was working on several pieces of fiction and some poetry. Therefore, when he was summoned to appear before Haywood, he made an appointment to see him despite some reluctance. "I . . . listened to him intently," he wrote of this meeting, "observed him minutely, for I knew that I was facing one of the leaders of World Communism." Haywood greeted the writer effusively. For him life was simple, blunt, direct. He believed that World War I was a Fascist war; hence he refused to be drafted and confronted jail instead. He was to be one of the prime architects of the Party's separate development program for the black belt. But the policy now was the Popular Front; the directive had been handed down, he would obey. He was to prepare and organize his cadres for the convention of The National Negro Congress, due to be held in Chicago in 1936.

The National Negro Congress was an outgrowth of the Joint Committee on National Recovery, organized during the early days of the New Deal by a group of "prominent Negroes." The aims of the Committee were to oversee the rights of blacks in the numerous governmental agencies created by the Roosevelt administration. The Committee was supported by black "religious, fraternal, labor, and political" organizations. In 1935 the Committee decided to establish a more widely representative organization, one that would involve all strata of the black population, in order to "give sharpness and unity to race organizations and arouse the Negro masses to effective political and economic action."[12] The mandate to The National Negro Congress was to set up such an organization on a permanent basis. From the outset, the

Communists sent their most effective black leaders with instructions not to take over the Congress at that time, but to "assist in building an overall Negro organization whose primary purpose would be the unification of varied Negro groups . . . around the general united Front program."[13]

The choice of Chicago as the host city meant that the local party apparatus was expected to perform well, and this meant, Haywood knew, increased activity in the black community in order to extend the Party's influence, support, and respect among the masses; diligence and perseverance had to be exercised to make sure that delegates from local organizations either controlled or influenced by the Party were present in large numbers; the Party, he knew, though it was not interested in direct control, wanted a program geared toward its own. Against such stalwart Negro leaders as A. Philip Randolph, Ralph Bunche, and Lester Granger, the black party leaders would need all the help they could get.

He told Wright, "We've got to defeat the fascists. . . . We discussed you and know your abilities. We want you to work with us. We've got to crash out of our narrow way of working, and get our message to the church people, students, club people, professionals, middle class. . . . We want you to organize a committee against the high cost of living. . . ."[14] He noted the look of apprehension that spread across the face of the other man. He did not want to do this, Haywood knew. He wanted to write. He explained he was already engaged in writing a novel; he could not do both. Haywood was unmoved. He knew something about men; he knew a great deal about black men. Those like Wright, like himself, like other black leaders now moving up in the party hierarchy, were in the Party because they had no place else to go. They had been exposed to progressive thought; they were bright and sensitive; racism prevented their progress as individuals in the society at large. Despite their ambivalent feeling about the Negro masses, deep down they wanted to reach out to them, spur them to action. The Party gathered such men to its bosom, gave them a sense of community, status, of being part of a worldwide effort to change the universe. For Wright, for all of them, there was nowhere else to go. "The Party," he told the writer, "has decided that you are to accept this task."

Wright shifted his eyes, reflectively. Haywood had issued a party directive; was he asking him whether he wanted to be a Communist or not? He wanted to be his "kind of Communist." But Haywood had made no such provisions. Fleetingly, he thought again of resigning: "Again," he wrote, "I urged myself to quit, but I could not do it." He would organize against the high cost of living. He would take part in the many nightly meetings, join fellow Communists in debating the

concerns of the community—housing, living conditions—angry and perturbed at having to tabulate "the daily value of pork chops," wanting to
be instead at home, at his makeshift desk, writing.

His perturbation notwithstanding, he performed well as an organizer,
so well in fact that he came to the attention of John P. Davis. To
Wright he seemed a vain, egotistical man, "Napoleon." To those in the
Party and out, however, John P. Davis was one of the Party's intellectual stalwarts. Shrewd, calculating, his forte was manipulation of
people and events. "Now, Davis," said a prominent black, a fierce anti-
Communist, "was a genius at maneuvering. He was quick, a master
strategist; he knew when to sit still; when to move in for the kill. That
guy knew where all the levers were and he knew when to pull each
one." Davis' assignment was to make sure that much of the party platform was adopted by The National Negro Congress and that the Party
had men placed in important positions in whatever permanent organization developed. And he would have to do this without giving the appearance that the Party was trying to control the Congress. It was a
diplomatic challenge worthy of his talents. The young Communist
writer standing before him, however, was not so much a challenge but a
problem.

Of all the black Marxists, Davis was intellectually astute enough to
assess his organization realistically; he knew that the claim of vast black
membership was false, that, indeed, recruitment among blacks had produced little in terms of numbers since the outbreak of the depression.
Black leaders, he knew, were at a premium. He may even have thought,
when canvassing the present black leadership of the Party, that new,
younger blood was needed. Wright was already known and respected by
white progressives for his leadership potential. Given the proper handling and staging, he could be a valuable asset to the organization.
Thus Davis offered him a chance to go abroad, to Switzerland and Russia, as a delegate of the Party.

The proposal came suddenly, and Wright had little time for reflection. He knew what such a move would mean. The way to party leadership for blacks was a sojourn to the Soviet Union. It was a route that
had been taken by Haywood, William Patterson, James Ford, Henry
Winston, and others. Such a trip gave the black member international
credentials and status. But he did not want to be a leader; he wanted to
write. Though most of the leading black Communists had authored
books or had them ghostwritten, none could be said to be writers. Being
a leader meant absolute devotion to world communism. Almost instinctively, he grasped hold of the rationale necessary to give him breathing space. Not only was he engaged in writing, he told the party boss,
but he was the main source of support for his family. He could not take

such a trip at the moment.[15] Seemingly, the rationale satisfied Davis.
He was assigned as a national delegate to The National Negro Congress
and presided over the "Writer's Section" of the convention.

The February 1936 issue of *New Masses* carried his report on the
Congress, entitled "Two Million Black Voices." Though he was careful
to give such party figures as Ford and Davis due recognition, he seemed
most admiring of the speech delivered by a delegate in the name of the
absent A. Philip Randolph. Randolph's speech demanded broadly
based militant action, and he foresaw the eventual alliance between
blacks of all classes first and secondly between blacks and whites. This
was a theme to which the Party adhered, but to the young writer who
had learned from party rhetoric of the past to disavow all black leadership that was not connected with the Party as bourgeois and reactionary, the words attributed to Randolph made a lasting impression.
He was impressed also by the unity of black men and women with the
problems that confronted them all, seeing them as "the vanguard of a
huge rising people, a section of a world wide army of toilers, driving towards liberation." The enthusiasm of Davis and the party leadership,
however, though Wright does not note this in his article, was less idealistic, more pragmatical. The Party had done well. Most of its program
was adopted. John P. Davis was named executive secretary of the permanent organization. Other important positions went to Marxists:
Ford, Benjamin Davis, Jr., Edward Strong, and Max Yergan. "The National Negro Congress," noted Ford, "recorded progress made by Communists and the many delegates who supported our program, in the increasing work we are carrying on in the various organizations of the
Negro people. Our modest successes are . . . just beginning."[16] The
Party was now in position to capture the Congress at the opportune
moment.

"Two Million Black Voices" was a clever piece of journalistic report-
age, somewhat in the vein of "Joe Louis Uncovers Dynamite," but he
was writing widely now, doing more experimenting. He published the
long poem *Transcontinental* in *International Literature* in January
1936. In the same month, his fictional piece "Big Boy Leaves Home"
was accepted in the anthology *The New Caravan*. He was revising *Cesspool* again, even as the novel was making the rounds of the publishers'
offices. In April of 1936, he reviewed Arna Bontemps' *Black Thunder*
under the title "A Tale of Folk Courage" for *Partisan Review*. Writing
of Bontemps' hero, Gabriel, he averred: "When considering Gabriel
solely as an isolated individual, he seems sustained by an extremely
foolish belief in himself; but when one remembers his slave state, when
one realizes the extent to which he has made the wrongs of his people
his wrongs, and the degree in which he has submerged his hopes in

their hopes . . . he appears logically and gloriously invincible."[17] The description was less true of the character of Bontemps' work than it was for those Wright wanted to project in his own fiction. But were these values—making "the wrongs of his people his wrongs," submerging his hopes in their hopes—were they also what he envisioned for himself? Was the individual glorious and invincible only when he became a metaphor for millions, when he ceased being the nothing that was the individual and became meaningful as "a vanguard of a huge rising people"? "Alone," he was to write much later, "a man is nothing." He was no longer alone, no longer the man who had come to Chicago afraid, nervous, tense, expectant, only nine years before.

He was constantly in touch with other people now, all kinds of people, and he was learning from them all. One of these was Margaret Walker, who knew him during his more productive years, and part of his growing awareness, no doubt, was attributable to his newfound relationships with blacks like Ms. Walker and the members of the South Side Writers group. What the aspiring poetess, soon to become an author in her own right, was able to add was a dimension lacking in his associations with the artists and intellectuals of the John Reed Clubs. With her he could discuss his own writing and other writers, and offer philosophical reflections upon the world, upon blacks, whites. The shield that he used to protect him from the world outside was somewhat lowered when the two "went to some of the same studio parties, read the same books, spent long evenings talking together, and often walked from the North Side where the Project was located on Erie Street, downtown to the public library, or rode the El to the Southside where we lived."[18]

But here, too, was an intellect equal to his own, a woman who disdained condescension, and he respected her ideas, her insights, was warmed by her encouragements. His trouble with the Party continued unabated; he was being pressured to become a party functionary; the members of his old cell still held him in contempt, still disparaged him as an intellectual. Concerns about the security of his family were somewhat mitigated, as his job on the Federal Writers Project enabled him to care for them, but his whirlwind round of activities, lectures, organizing affairs for the John Reed Club, writing, left him little time for reflection, for relaxation. Margaret offered a modicum of security; her friendship was a sanctuary from the harassment and quickness of his daily life. Since he was not formally educated, Margaret was able to help him improve his grammatical skills, just as her keen awareness of the plight of blacks in America's South Sides helped him to refine his own perceptions: ". . . you [have] done more than anyone I know to help me with my book." He was to write Miss Walker, after the publication of *Native Son:* ". . . each and everytime I sat down to write I wondered what I could say to let you know how deeply grateful I felt."[19]

He was deeply grateful also for the intellectual and moral support given him by Miss Walker and others, which enabled him to become somewhat less dependent upon the Party. His reputation continued to grow outside the party hierarchy, so that what once seemed his only avenue out of hopelessness and despair appeared so no longer; the organization that once constituted his only real family was no longer the sole institution from which he might gain intellectual nourishment. Yet if given the choice between being a Communist and a non-Communist, he would still choose to be a Communist. But he would not choose to be a Communist instead of a writer. He tried to impart something of this to Davis, when again the party boss implored him to travel, to widen his horizons, to gear himself for party leadership. "Much as I'd like to," he told the Marxist strategist, "I'm afraid I can't make it. . . . I simply cannot drop the writing I'm doing now."[20]

The smoke from Davis' cigarette curled silently ceilingward. The eyes, behind thin-rimmed glasses, half closed, opened; his hands were tense, displaying his impatience. He was offering Wright the chance of a lifetime to learn about the world, to become seasoned, sophisticated, polished. It was an opportunity offered few white men, let alone blacks. And he was recalcitrant! He would probably, if it came to that, disobey a party order. He had no sense of the gravity of world events, of his own trying position. He brought his eyes to bear upon the younger man, fixed him in his sights, stared for a long time, then, finally, said: "Wright, you're a fool!"

Wright sprang forward. He recalled the days in Mississippi, in Memphis, where a boy showed his mettle by his quickness to respond to insults and indignities with his fists. There he would have fought to the last, had a similar remark been made to him. Suddenly he recoiled. He was no longer in Mississippi; he was no longer a boy. He strove to gain some control over his emotions. He turned, picked up his hat, and quickly left the room. "This is good-by," he shouted.

Once outside, he walked aimlessly, thoughtfully. Two equally dreadful choices lay before him. He could sever all relationship with the Party or he could acquiesce to its orders and directives and lose his hard-fought-for and valued individuality. The first choice was difficult, because he believed in the Party's goals and aims. It was the only organization capable of welding so many diverse elements together in a holy crusade to cleanse the earth. Probably he did not make the connection, but the Party loomed as omnipresent and magisterial to him as Christianity did to his grandmother and his mother. All three had discovered the church militant, and though that church sometimes disappointed, sometimes angered, still it was the one church, man's one and only salvation. And despite his growing independence from it, despite his newly acquired arsenal of friends, he needed the Party in a way incomprehensible even to himself.

"Wright's philosophy," wrote Margaret Walker, "was that fundamentally all men are potentially evil. . . . Human nature and human society are determinants and, being what he is, man is merely a pawn caught between the worlds of necessity and freedom. . . . All that he has to use in his defense and direction of his existence are (1) his reason and (2) his will."[21] Given certain emendation, his views and the Party's concerning human possibilities were almost compatible. It was the job of the Communists to shape man's reason and thereby to bolster his will. This could be done only through an apparatus managed by men willing to use dictatorial, almost draconian measures; he knew this, and he somewhat admired the men capable of doing it. But there were pragmatic reasons as well: the Party not only demanded discipline, but it had a program; alone among the organizations fighting for the rights of blacks, it set a course toward freedom and dignity charted along rational lines. The Party made black men leaders as it heralded the plight of blacks before the whole world, confronted jail and faced violence on behalf of blacks. The Party's mettle was proven in many skirmishes and major battles; the fight to save Angelo Herndon and the Scottsboro Boys came readily to mind. "Richard Wright . . . ," wrote William Patterson, "came to the Communist Party and was inspired to begin his career as a writer. Although he was convinced that the political philosophy of Communism was correct, he did not see a book as a political weapon. He thought that the creative genius of a writer should be freed from all restrictions and restraints, especially those of a political nature, and that the writer should do as he pleased."[22]

Part of this was simply party rationale; but part of it was true, and highlighted the difficulty confronting the writer in making his second choice. When his friend had first suggested, aeons ago, it seemed, that he become associated with the John Reed Clubs, he had stated upon accepting the invitation that "no one" was going to tell him how to write or what to write about. He would have to write from the storehouse of his own experiences; of this he was even more sure after the dismal attempt to do otherwise in the sensationalized short story he had written for *Abbots Monthly Magazine*. He had not wanted the organization to tell him how to write; he wanted it to help him to organize his experiences, to give them body and form, to allow him to look at them rationally, objectively; the Party had done this. He might have groped toward his present status as a writer without its aid and assistance, but he could not have done so so soon, nor perhaps so well. And though he had known that, somewhere down the line, Mephistopheles-like, the Party would come to claim its compensation, he had always thought that he might forestall foreclosure on his soul, his individuality.

By the time he had reached his apartment, he knew what he had to do. He had to ask for a new compact between himself and the Party, one that would allow him to serve it while retaining his soul. "I attended the next unit meeting," he wrote, "and asked for a place on the agenda, which was readily granted. . . ." He had come prepared. Three of the Communist bosses, including Haywood and Ed Green, were there. From this very platform, some three years before, he remembered, he had confronted grinning, laughing faces; now they were impassive, attentive. Here and there he met a hostile stare, a cynical glance. He moved into his short speech. He had searched for a way out of the difficulty imposed upon both himself and the Party by his membership. He wanted his name dropped from the rolls. "No ideological differences," he pointed out, "impel me to say this. I simply do not want to be bound any longer by the Party's decision. I would like to retain my membership in those organizations in which the Party has influence, and I shall comply with the Party's program in those organizations."[23]

He resigned not from the Party but only from his local unit; and this distinction was not lost on such knowledgeable leaders as Haywood and Davis. He was, in essence, still theirs. He had not sought confrontation, but amelioration. "Immature," William Patterson would later call him. Had he made a speech denouncing them, attacking their policies, gone on the offensive, they would have had more respect for him. After all, he was not without resources. He had some influence among party intellectuals and among that most important group, which the Party was now wooing, the progressives. Thus far, no quarrels could be made on ideological grounds with his writings. What he had done was to pit his will against that of the Party, though feebly so, and for this, and this alone, he had to be punished.

The Party thus went on the offensive. They spied on him at parties and social and professional gatherings. They denounced him as a Trotskyite, a deviationist, a bourgeois reactionary. They spread rumors about him throughout the Chicago area, and if he is to be later believed, helped to instigate a revolt against him by other blacks, his coworkers on the Federal Theatre Project. Seeing itself as the collective patriarch ordained in the interests of struggling mankind to wield swiftly its ever-ready sword of vengeance, the local unit finally summoned him to one of its Trotskyite trials. Such trials were common among party cells in the thirties. Each unit could transform itself into a tribunal. It heard evidence for and against a recalcitrant member. It had the power to vote guilt or innocence collectively. When a party functionary informed Wright that he was to come and witness the trial of his old friend Poindexter, he hesitated. Suspiciously, he wondered if a trap had been set. Did they want to lure him there to put *him* on trial? Still, he had never witnessed such a procedure before. Curiosity won out over suspiciousness.

"And I became one with the dry bones," his speaker-victim remarked in *Between the World and Me*. He had written those words in an attempt to symbolize the merger between the poem's narrator and the victim of lynching, to dramatize the fact that they were one and the same. Now, as he sat among men and women whose hostility was more pronounced against *him* than the defendant on trial, he felt something of the sense of merger he had wished to portray to his audience, felt a close identification with another human soul in agony. The defiant Poindexter was defeated even before the trial began. His friends had been transformed into judge and jurors, but he knew that from nowhere among their ranks would there appear an Isaiah to ask if the judge of all the earth should not be just; no, there would be no intercessor between himself and his prosecutors. His seemed to be crimes against the whole of humankind, and his prosecutors moved hurriedly to establish this fact.

Poindexter's crime was defiance: he allied himself not with the vanquished but with their oppressors, not with world communism but with its enemies.

Wright followed the proceedings with great interest. His eyes flickered from the face and hands of the defendant to the faces of his accusers. Here was a masterful presentation of the drama between good and evil; all of the defendant's accusers evoked the Old Testament sentiment. Satan may have arisen heroically from the pages of John Milton's *Paradise Lost* and from the writings of the existentialists, but here, in this new guise, he stood condemned by the disciples of Lenin and Marx, condemned at home and abroad, condemned for the miserable conditions of blacks and workers, for the depression, for the unequal distribution of income, for poverty, for criminality. What man would rather rule with Satan in a capitalistic hell than die in mortal combat against him in order to bring about the Marxist heaven?

Certainly not the defendant. Under a steady barrage of facts, under stern and retributive symbolism, he began to crumble. The guilt showered upon him by his accusers, his friends, became as real to him as to them. He wanted to give way to that catharsis within, to cast the devil from his conscience. "Comrades," he shouted hysterically, prostrating himself before the Communist assemblage, "I'm guilty of all the charges, all of them. . . ."[24]

The final act of the drama overwhelmed Wright. The degree of empathy between himself and the accused was too great. He had witnessed power and authority adroitly, skillfully applied, and he admired it even as he disdained it. What had driven this powerful man, this rebel, to prostrate himself before men as mortal as he was, was fear; the fear of excommunication, of being thrust out into a confused and chaotic world alone, without Bible or commandments to guide him. Poindexter had found an identity within the Party, and once this was threatened, in danger of being taken away, he recanted his former sins, admitted to even those of which he was not guilty. The organization that could so shake men like Poindexter stood as omnipotent, invincible. The proceedings had shaken Wright also. "I could not stay until the end," he writes. "I was anxious to get out of the hall and into the streets and shake free from the gigantic tension that had hold of me." The trial had been meant as an example to him and he knew it.

In Poindexter's fate was mirrored his own. But the spectacle so appalled him that the example made the obverse impression. There was little choice now but to go it alone. They had demonstrated what was in store for him if he remained and held fast to his own principles. Still, he found himself unable to cut completely away. "I lay in bed that night and said to myself," he wrote, "I'll be for them, even though they are not for me." In a letter to his editor, written much later, in 1959, he summed up his intentions: "The American Communist Party tried strenuously to convince me that writing was not my forte and that I would serve better as an organizer. I refused to accept this and withdrew from the Communist Party. . . . Feeling that the Communist Party in New York was more liberal and intelligent, I left Chicago for New York in 1936, and upon arrival, I was reinstated into the Communist Party and given charge of the Harlem Bureau of the *Daily Worker*."[25]

CHAPTER EIGHT

In a letter dated March 1, 1938, two years after he had arrived in New York, he wrote his friend Joe Brown of his decision to leave Chicago. He did not offer his difficulties with the Party as the rationale for leaving. The trip had been germinating in his mind for some time. Chicago was flat, dull, and ugly; New York, in contrast, was compact, exciting, grand in the sense that he imagined the old cities of Europe to be grand. Chicago was the hub of American industry, but New York was the center for the arts, the home of publishing companies and magazines, the headquarters for the nation's intellectual enterprises. A writer in New York had opportunities to meet more established writers, to publish in more magazines, to make himself known among those who controlled the media. If one was ready to "click" as a writer, New York was the place.

But he had also become restless in Chicago, begun to think in terms of distance: distance between himself and his family, between his old self and what he hoped a newer self might be. His family was somewhat stable now. Grandmother Wilson had died, but he had made up with his aunt Maggie, who again became part of the household. Leon Allan had managed to find work, and Ella's health had improved. Still, he was emotionally tied to her in a way that often made him guilty and ashamed for defying her moral code. That day in Jackson when she suffered her second stroke and held his hand, fast, tight, remained etched in his memory. He had interpreted her gesture as a plea for help, for him to save her, and the fact that he could not do so brought forth feelings of impotence and dread. "He was aware," he would later write, putting his own ideas about his mother into the mind of his character Cross Damon, in *The Outsider*, "intimately and bitterly, that his dread had been his mother's first fateful gift to him. He had been born of her not only physically but emotionally too. . . . As her son, he was much too far from her and at the same time much too close, much too warm toward her and much too cold. To keep her life from crushing his own, he had slain the sense of her in his heart and at the same time had clung frantically to his memory of that sense."[1] Distance between her and him would not mean surrendering his responsibility toward her; it would simply allow him an opportunity to attempt to establish his life along moral and ethical lines peculiar to himself.

He wanted to go to New York and yet he hesitated, pondered. He had been called to permanent work at the post office, and this meant job security. There was no real promise of work in New York, though he had hopes of finding work on the Federal Writers Project there. He would be leaving with forty dollars in his pocket and no real promise of more to come. But, above all, he wanted to be a writer, and this was what his voyage entailed. Could he really make it as a black writer at a time when publishers were offering fewer and fewer books by blacks? Again he sought out Margaret Walker for encouragement: "Aren't you on your way to fame and fortune? You can't be making a mistake . . ." They were words that he needed to hear, echoes of his oft-repeated self-declaration: "I want my life to count for something. I don't want to waste it or throw it away. It's got to be worthwhile."[2]

He arrived in New York City in May of 1937, making the trip in a "dilapidated car" belonging to friends, a white couple who were also heading for the city. "Wright," remarked Ms. Henrietta Weigel, at whose house on Bleecker Street the trio first stopped on their arrival, "was sullen suspicious. . . . They were all tired and dusty, as well as hungry, after the long trip." The Weigels suggested that the trio "freshen up" and handed out bath towels: "Wright said, 'Me too?' " she wrote, "evidently wondering whether he was included in our hospitality."[3] He had moved to New York City accompanied by all the emotional baggage of old; the fear, suspiciousness, doubt, the longing for acceptance in the white world, coupled with the feeling that it would always reject him. The fear remained paramount. "We had travelled downtown by bus," Ms. Weigel recalled. "After I was seated, he retreated to the back of the bus, ignoring me. When we got out, he walked quite a distance behind me. He told me later that he had not wanted to disgrace me in the bus by letting me be seen with a black man. He had, furthermore, walked behind (not with) me in the street to save embarrassment."[4]

It was a different Richard Wright, however, who participated in the sessions of the Second American Writers Congress, which began near the end of May, 1937. He moved effusively among such other participants as Sylvia Warner, Dashiell Hammett, Christina Stead, Kenneth

Burke, and Malcolm Cowley. "This time," wrote Malcolm Cowley, comparing the first Congress with the present, ". . . there was more attention paid to strictly literary matters."⁵ The political situation, however, remained ominously in the background; German troops had begun the first offensive against Eastern Europe, and exiled writers were represented at the conference. Still, the participants were more concerned with craft, with securing a wider reading audience, with, as Cowley observed, the problems of writers. Henry G. Alsberg, director of the Federal Writers Project, whom Wright introduced at one of the sessions, told the assembled writers: "Now, if I can get a magazine, if I can get creative stuff published in a book, and if I can get the guidebooks, I can give some writers time to do their own creative writing."⁶ The project that Alsberg had in mind was publication of the anthology *American Stuff*, which would allow writers free time to do their own creative work at home and also to justify this activity to the overseers in the Roosevelt administration and the Congress. Thus Wright's job problem was resolved when he was allowed to transfer to the Federal Writers Project in New York, a transfer instigated by Alsberg. Here he worked along with John Cheever, Charlotte Wilder, William Rollins, Jr., and Anthony Netboy, on the New York City Guide.⁷ Already, however, Alsberg, the innovative, creative director, had the young writer in mind for work on *American Stuff*, and soon Wright, along with such more established writers on the Federal Writers Project as Maxwell Bodenheim, Willard Mass, Claude McKay, and Harry Kemp, were allowed, in addition, "to work at home on their own material, with the sole stipulation that they report to the Project office once a week with evidence of their work."⁸

New York was all that he assumed it would be. He was soon caught up in a maze of parties, social engagements, intellectual gatherings. He moved to Harlem, renting a furnished room after initially boarding with a friend. He dated women both black and white, married and unmarried. He met other black writers, Claude McKay, Willard Motley, Frank Yerby, and a young man at that time more interested in music than in writing, Ralph Ellison. Ellison had arrived in New York one year before Wright, after having received training in music at Tuskegee Institute. He was six years younger than Wright, but their friendship blossomed. "Wright persuaded him to write a review, which he accepted for *New Challenge*, a short lived magazine Wright was then editing; then in the Spring of 1938 he helped Ellison land a relief job on the New York City Project. . . . With Wright as his literary mentor, Ellison approached the art of writing in the same methodical fashion he studied music."⁹ Wright had been assigned to *New Challenge* by the affable, astute Benjamin J. Davis, one of the black titans of the

Party. Davis was impressive. Standing well over six feet, he dwarfed most of his contemporaries in intellectual stature as well as height. He was less doctrinaire than the almost intractable Harry Haywood, more confident and assured than James Ford. "A Party hack with a law degree," Wilson Record called him, but the descriptions nowhere befits the man. He was Harvard-educated; he was born of middle-class parentage in Dawson, Georgia, in 1903; his father was a Republican national committeeman from the state and the publisher of a black paper, *The Independent*. Returning to Atlanta to practice law, Davis was soon involved in the *Angelo Herndon* case. "It was," he later wrote, "a turning point of my life. In the course of trying that case I suffered some of the worst treatment along with my client, with the judge calling me nigger and darky and threatening to jail me."[10] The treatment accorded him by the court and his association with the radical Herndon pushed him into the arms of Herndon's adamant defenders, the Communist Party. In 1935 he arrived in New York to become editor of *The Negro Liberator*, and one year later, he became editor of the *Daily Worker*, the party organ. When he first encountered Wright in his Harlem office, he was organizer in the Harlem area and one of the fastest-rising Marxist stars.

His background as a journalist made him more charitable toward the young writer than other Communist leaders had been. The struggle against racism and oppression, he knew, was one requiring the unanimity of all, writers and workers alike. He had put his journalistic skills at the service of the Party. So, too, could the somewhat shy, yet arrogant, young man before him, whom careful handling might transform into one of the journalistic stars of the Party. An intellectual, Davis had no disdain for intellectuals. He wanted Wright's services as a writer, not as a leader, and he offered the young man a position as staff writer for the *Daily Worker*.

Wright at once felt a certain sense of ease with Davis that he had not experienced with other party bosses, black or white. Davis' solicitation of him as a writer was flattering. He was being accepted, it appeared, by the New York Communists, on his terms. There would be no bullying, no threats, no intimidation. He was being offered the opportunity to continue his writing with the sanction of the Party, to continue to gain valuable experience. He accepted the offer to write for the *Daily Worker*. Later he would join Marian Minus and Dorothy West in launching the magazine *New Challenge*.

From 1937 to 1941, he wrote assiduously for the paper, contributing articles and essays on a number of subjects, cultural and political. In such pieces as "New Negro Pamphlet Stresses Need for U.S. Peoples Front" and "Communist Party Leads Struggle for Freedom, Satchel Says," he advocated the Party's Popular Front line. In "Rank and File

Who Campaigned for Herndon and Scottsboro Boys Live in Harlem"
and "Scottsboro Boys on Stage Is Opposed," he espoused familiar party
propaganda concerning its relationship with the black belt. These four
pieces, written in 1937, along with others, including coverage of the
Louis-Schmeling fight of 1938, are not distinctive; they are works following and advocating the party program. They are works that demonstrate also that the older Communist's faith in him was well founded.
His dedication to the ideals of communism, his treatment at the hands
of Marxists in the past notwithstanding, remained as strong as ever—in
fact, under the new, more congenial climate of New York, had grown
even stronger. His relationship with members of the Party improved.
His economic situation was better than ever before, and he was involved in satisfying social engagements. He wrote more frequently and
consistently, and he began to grow as a writer and to sharpen his
awareness of the urban scene. But as he did this, as his own material
and work on the paper forced him into increasing contact with blacks
far less fortunate than himself, he was obligated to review his own position vis-à-vis the strong tendency toward Garveyism, toward black nationalism, which was as much a vestige of his heritage as that of poorer,
uneducated blacks. Black nationalism and its spokesman had always
fascinated him.

None of the speakers he had listened to in Chicago had impressed
him as much as the Black Nationalists. Their perception of the world
struck a responsive chord in his own mind. After all, if one discounted
the Garveyite dream of a return to Africa, how far different, in essential
details, was the Party's separate development program from that of the
followers of the exiled Jamaican? He had been accused by members of
the Chicago cell with being in sympathy with Poindexter's "deviationist views," his Black Nationalist perspective; he had denied the allegations. Yet, they were essentially true. And yet black nationalism, as
he was to write, was "cramping and warping." It was, he believed, parochial, defensive, maintaining the boundaries established by the society,
which precluded the growth and development of blacks. For this reason
he cast aspersion upon institutions of nationalism: black churches,
lodge halls, clubs, etc. He did not believe in an all-consuming fire that
would melt all racial characteristics away in one giant caldron, but he
believed, on the surface level of consciousness, in one people and one
world. Americans must be subsumed all under one cultural determinant, and the integrated society was a necessity, not so much for
whites as for blacks, for those still struggling to vault into the twentieth
century. Nationalism was the devil that had to be exorcised!

Yet how was this to be done with the least psychic damage to himself? Even in his writings, he had been unable to tame the nationalist

demon. In the *Daily Worker* of June 24, 1938, he wrote on Louis' victory over Schmeling. The articles view Louis' victory as a defeat for fascism and a victory for freedom: "What happened in Harlem Wednesday night marks in a certain sense the high tide of popular political enthusiasm ever witnessed among American Negroes. The Fascists, even though it was over a mere prize fight, had laid down a dare, and Joe Louis had answered it with his brawny fists. Harlem approved by reiterating a thousand times: 'Say, ain't you glad?' "[11] The same sense of ceremonial exuberance pervades the *New Masses* article: "They shouted, sang, laughed, yelled, blew paper horns, clasped hands, and formed weaving snake lines, whistled, sounded sirens, and honked auto horns." The theme and tone are reminiscent of an article, written by Davis, appearing on the same day as Wright's, for the *Daily Worker*: "Indescribable joy and unprecedented exuberance," wrote Davis, "swept through the world's largest Negro urban community Wednesday night and swelled into one of the most magnificent anti-fascist demonstrations that America has ever seen."[12] Nationalism is a felt force in the work of each man; yet Davis had learned to contain the demon within his psyche, to integrate the philosophy with ease into the structure of Marxist thought, so that his praise of the black community blends almost imperceptibly into praise for the working class as a whole: "There were parades, meetings, demonstrations, snake dances, speeches, Ethiopian and American flags, homemade confetti in which every strata of the Negro people took part. And there were not only Negroes. There were Jews, Spanish, Puerto Ricans. . . ."[13]

Wright could not so effectively sublimate his own nationalistic tendencies. In those articles written for the *Daily Worker*, in his short fiction, indeed even in his poetry, the theme of black-white unity appears almost as an afterthought, long after he has described and articulated a core of experiences common to blacks, after he has celebrated a group spirit. But if the nationalist devil could not be cast out of the psyche, how was it possible to deal with him? How had Davis, Ford, A. Philip Randolph, and others managed so well? Being black he believed was unimportant in itself, but how did one adhere to that belief in a society that made being black the most important determinant? "Negro writers," he wrote in 1937 in "Blueprint for Negro Writing," "must accept the Nationalist implications of their lives, not in order to encourage them, but in order to change and transcend them." Transcendence lay in Marxism: here was to be found a theory "about the structure, direction, and meaning of society." Here, then, was a rational solution to a very perplexing, ofttimes emotional, problem. To accept nationalism was not difficult; it meant to accept the realities of black existence in America. But to transcend and to change the nationalistic implications of one's life was to deny them viability, to deny their importance, the historical role they had played in a people's survival. It was a desperate attempt to convince himself that he had not been mesmerized, captured by nationalism, that he could move outside and beyond its influences.

Thus "Blueprint for Negro Writing" is a curious article. Ostensibly he purported to establish criteria for a body of literature with which he was unfamiliar. His knowledge of black literary history was scant, consisting of bits and pieces gleaned from research for an article and for book reviews on current black writers. The theme of his essay had already been pronounced by Eugene Gordon: ". . . There is little in recent Negro poetry," wrote Gordon, "that would lead one to believe that poets are conscious of the existence of the Negro masses. . . . They do not echo the lamentations of the downtrodden masses. Millions of blacks are suffering from poverty and cruelty, and the black poets shut their eyes."

Like Gordon, he also found black writers lacking. They were basically of the middle class and anxious to make their own deal with the ruling class. Thus they viewed blacks and portrayed them in their writings as complaisant and nonrevolutionary. But he was not altogether in agreement with Gordon that the masses yearned for freedom and liberty, though he was convinced that nationalism was rife among them. This the black middle-class writers ardently denied, and thus he was able to distance himself from them by identifying with the nationalistic impulse if not the Black Nationalist program. In this respect he believed himself to be far more progressive than other black writers, who "lagged sadly behind the black workers" and whose writings were little more than facile offerings to whites. The writers themselves he portrayed as "decorous ambassadors" who were afraid to portray the actualities of the lives of their people, who argued that blacks "had a life comparable to that of other people."

There was no intention in this essay, which despite certain points of departure, assigned such a messianic role to the Party, to curry favor with Davis, to repay his generosity. He had found a home, at last, in the Party, and he assumed, without question, that this home was the place for the sensitive, the rebellious, the radical. His own, limited views of blacks and their capabilities had ameliorated only under the world view promulgated by communism; for only Marxist rhetoric was so capable of making heroes out of men and women whose actions and antisocial acts provoked his disdain.

But his fiction began to take on a distinguishing pattern long before "Blueprint for Negro Writing," and it is probable that much of what he recommends there in terms of literary outlook for black writers he had resolved himself through the creative process. *Cesspool*, he would later become convinced, was not the kind of fiction that met his own standards, did not deal realistically with the masses, was too negatively one-dimensional. As a writer it was almost impossible for him to identify with Jake Jackson, whose life, in the scale of things, amounted to nothing. Rather, his identification must lie with the migrant Negroes, those outside the urban environment, of whom he knew still very little; this would enable him to make the leap back into the experiences of his past, painful though that may be. He was able to understand now, perhaps due to party association, perhaps due to knowledge of Angelo Herndon, that there was a courage, a heroism, dormant in those whom he had met in the Delta, who continually faced the darkest of the Mississippi nights.

He began to articulate such attributes in a short story published in *New Masses* in 1937. "Silt," a slight tale, almost plotless, begins with little drama. "At last the flood waters had receded. A black father, black mother, and black child tramped through muddy fields, leading a tired cow by a thin bit of rope."[14] Here he describes the eternal conflict between man and nature and, for blacks, the more pervasive one between themselves and both whites and the elements; over his black characters, these men and women of the Delta—a region long buffeted by wind and rain, overflowing rivers stampeding like frightened cattle onto the land and into the lives of the people, leaving, in its departure, vast alluvial deposits of loam and silt, moistened soil, soon to be browned, darkened and turned into powdery dust in the ensuing days of heat and drought—he spread an aura of strength and endurance that would always be lacking in his depiction of blacks in the metropolis. Like sharecroppers throughout Mississippi—like his father—Tom and May before the days of flood and silt are heavily in debt to the white landowner. The debt has increased year after year as the white man has continued to supply food and sustenance to Tom and his family and to keep his own, fraudulent records of the transactions. The land will never allow Tom, under the best of circumstances and the most honest landlord, to extricate himself, and his attempt to wring subsistence out of it and to free himself from the landowner is existential, reveals the Sisyphean struggle against impossible odds.

Was he once again, as in "Blueprint," working through the creative process toward some resolution of a personal dilemma? Outside the obvious similarities—both Tom and his father were poor, ignorant sharecroppers and were victimized by white men and the elements—did they also have in common a storehouse of courage, a reservoir of strength that he had been unable to understand before? And the image that he had taken away of the defeated, hopeless children in the Delta—was it possible to down this one by replacing it with another? A younger Tom, he knew, might have extricated himself by leaving the land; he could have braved the urban jungle rather than continue on in futility. But he did not see Tom in this way; he saw him as a man with few options, one whose days were regulated by the turn of the seasons, whose existence must ever be dictated by the whims and changes of nature and white men. He is destined to face each day, refusing to believe that the following will be like the last; he will forge from the racial past the optimism that allows him to believe even when disbelief is more pragmatic. And if the days before and the days now were not terrible enough in their intensity, he must now do battle with nature, must confront the aftermath of the great flood: "When the flood waters recede / the poor folk along the river / start from scratch."

The family returns from the hills after the water begins to trickle off into streams and lakes. They discover that all is gone: houses, livestock, trees, all except the "caky, yellow mud" that clings here, there, everywhere, but then the child makes an important symbolic discovery. In what remains of the shack, hidden in a shelf the waters could not reach, he finds, "High and dry, untouched by the floodwaters . . . a box of matches," and beside it "a half filled sack of Bull Durham tobacco." This is little compensation for the ravages of the flood; yet, for such as Tom, little compensations are enough to refuel the dying embers of optimism, to reestablish the belief that tomorrow will be better than today. And thus, lit by a spark of hope as feeble as that which ignites a pipe of tobacco, and encouraged by the rich legends and folklore of a people whose history taught perseverance, unending struggle against adversaries both human and nonhuman, Tom will go on, will accept more largesse from the landowner, become more deeply entrenched in debt, will go on like all poor people after the flood, to start from scratch.

The politics of Marxism fueled Wright's imagination, to be sure, but he managed to subsume ideology under the very human ordeal of black people. The essence of black life, he knew, was founded upon hope and endurance; there was about such people, even the most militant, like himself, an implicit faith that tomorrow might be a better day and the times of trial and struggle would pay dividends.

Tom's dream—that which sustains him—of being free may be an illusion, but Wright's own dreams were being fulfilled in the city of stone and steel. "In the fall of 1937," according to Margaret Walker, "he wrote that he was entering the WPA short story contest sponsored by *Story Magazine* and Harper's publishing house." If he was, indeed, ready to "click," now was the time to do so. The contest was open to all WPA members, and he knew that he would face stiff competition. Some of the soon-to-be-best writers in America, both black and white, among them Claude McKay and John Cheever, were members of the WPA. Success here would almost assure him a great career; at least, he would have one long leg up the ladder. He vacillated almost till the last moment, finally beating the deadline, to submit the four stories that constitute *Uncle Tom's Children*. The judges for the contest were Harry Scherman, president of the Book-of-the-Month Club; Sinclair Lewis, the novelist; and Lewis Gannett, the critic. Shortly before Christmas, he was informed that he had won first prize, five hundred dollars; "second prize was won by Meridel Le Sueur, who contributed a short novel, *The Horse*."

The sunshine days had begun! Hungry for heroes, the black press played up the award. Letters of congratulations poured in, some asking for money, some from black women proposing marriage. He made a gift to himself of a steak dinner and a new suit. Flushed with his success, he proposed marriage to a black "bourgeois girl he was dating." Certainly, winning the prize marked him out as a man of promise. Publishing houses were open to him now, agents and editors alike clamoring for his attention. The money awarded him was more than he had ever received for writing in his life, but this was a harbinger of more prosperous days to come. Certainly, he was marriage material. The girl thought so even though she knew little about the intricacies of writing and probably assumed the award meant that financial security was achieved. But her father knew better! Writing, prize or no prize, did not guarantee financial success. His own affluence had come through hard, steady work; writers were among the idle, the unpromising. He would not allow his daughter to marry Wright. ". . . on the wings of success," wrote Margaret Walker, "came the news that he was getting married. I hastened to congratulate him, and he denied the whole thing."

He felt, probably, the pain of rejection but little else. This situation was similar to a later one, when, again slated to marry a black woman, he discovered that his bride-to-be had congenital syphilis. He was not so much disheartened by the ruptures between himself and the women as he was by the circumstances that forced them: parental authority in one case, illness in the other. If his perceptions were undergoing serious alteration, his perceptions of black women remained on the whole unchanged. Somewhere between poles represented by his mother and grandmother; the universal victim against whom he had to develop intricate defense mechanisms to "keep her life from crushing his own" and the stern matriarch, lay the image with which he was most comfortable. This made it impossible for him to recognize black women—still—as other than abstractions. He was drawn to women who symbolized his mother. But psychologically he was unprepared as an adult to deal with black women whose characteristics bore resemblance to those of the grandmother he was forced to deal with as a child.

Whatever his disappointment, if any, over parental censorship of his marriage, the rewards and attentions attending his success more than compensated. He had only been in New York for approximately one year and already had achieved national recognition. He had been able to solicit as his agent Paul Reynolds, of the famous agency that had once handled the works of Paul Laurence Dunbar. The collection of short stories was accepted by Harper as a result of the arrangement with *Story Magazine*, and Reynolds successfully negotiated a contract for a future novel. "He remarked in a letter," wrote Margaret Walker, ". . . that he had set a goal for five years and one of those years was over. He wanted to write another book right away, a novel. . . . Then he wanted to go to Mexico and he wanted to go to Paris."[15]

Undoubtedly, he was exhilarated and felt somewhat vindicated at the response of the Party to his success. Now they openly and publicly avowed him as one of their own. He was proof positive that under the aegis of Marxism, a young black boy from the dust and swamps of Mississippi, from the masses, ignorant and untutored, through careful guidance by the Party, could achieve fame and recognition. His success, therefore, was twofold; for himself and for the Party as well, and in tribute, they celebrated his achievement with a party at the Suitcase Theatre, in Harlem. An informant called upon by the FBI in 1943 to supply data concerning Wright's career recalled the occasion: "I met Richard Wright at the Suitcase Theatre that was located on 135th Street between 8th and St. Nicholas Avenue, New York City. The affair was given in honor of Richard Wright. . . . It was attended by about 200 people, mostly Party members and sympathizers." Among those "who made speeches of tribute . . . were Benjamin Davis, Jr., Executive Secretary of the Upper Harlem Section, Samuel Patterson, National Executive Committee I.W.O. Columnist People's Voice. Abner W. Berry, former Executive Secretary Upper Harlem Section, Louise Thompson, Organizer I.W.O."[16] Such events marked the culmination of one career and the beginning of another. The days as a "revolutionary poet," as primarily a "party writer" whose works seemed destined only for publication in party organs and left-wing journals, were over. In his review of the newly published *Uncle Tom's Children*, in the March edition of *New Masses* in 1938, Granville Hicks made much the same observation: "You cannot read these stories without realizing that the literature of the left has been immeasurably strengthened. It is not only a fine piece of writing; it is the beginning of a distinguished career."

The four novellas constituting the original manuscript of *Uncle Tom's Children* were drawn from information supplied by Poindexter

during the time Wright was putting together sketches of Marxist ora-
tors for "Heroes, Red and Black" and his own wide-ranging southern
experience. The terrain of "Big Boy Leaves Home," "Down by the Riverside," "Long Black Song," and "Fire and Cloud" was his in the way
that Yoknapatawpha County was Faulkner's—places, people, and events
caught and frozen in creative time. The stories were written before he
left Chicago, but the same question pervades them all: What are the
values of courage and endurance that enable blacks to confront the terrors of the southern environment? It is as if he were looking beyond his
fictional creation, thundering the question to those like Poindexter,
Davis, and even himself. In "Big Boy Leaves Home," he attempts to
give form and structure to long-term concerns—about the nature of innocence and fear, the role of white women in the never-ending conflict
between black men and white, and the nature of the relationships
among blacks—that so bewildered and confused him as a child.

Big Boy, Buck, Bobo, and Lester are children much like those he had
known in Memphis and Jackson. On one particular day they decide to
play hooky from school to go swimming in a lake owned by a white
man whose antipathy to blacks is well known to the boys. In addition, a
sign warns of dangers to trespassers. Yet, innocence recognizes few barriers or dangers, is impervious to markers dividing one race of people
from another; the boys therefore strip naked and swim and frolic in the
water. Into this setting, instantaneously, without warning, walks a white
woman, more force than human. She accosts one naked boy and the
panic transforms them, making them ashamed of their nakedness, their
innocence. Her screams summon her companion, a soldier, who appears
with his gun at the ready.

As the boys fall over each other in an attempt to cover their nakedness, they try to appeal to the gunman, who unceremoniously shoots
one of them down. Big Boy manages to wrestle the gun from the soldier's hand. With Bobo nervously scurrying into his clothes, the older
boy holds the white man at bay. Yet the soldier's upbringing has taught
him that white womanhood must be protected and that blacks are ever
subservient to the will of those like himself. Thus he arrogantly demands that the boy return his weapon, refusing to believe that Big Boy
will not do so. The boy's warning to his antagonist is a plea for peace;
he wants only to leave the ground where his friend has been killed; still,
the white man advances. The scene is filled with dramatic tension as
much for the author as for his characters. If, Wright had once boasted
in his adolescence, white men tried to kill him, he would fight back.
Now he was able to re-create such a situation in his imagination. Fear
was as constant in his own life as it was in that of the young boy holding the gun against an advancing white man. "Fear," he would later

confide to a group of black friends, "is the most dominant emotion in Negro life. . . . We're all scared all the time. . . ."[17]

But fear was also a catalytic agent, leading to acts of courage, enabling the individual to tap reservoirs of strength heretofore undiscovered. It had happened in his case. There were times, moments, when he erected a boundary line beyond which he could not be pushed, the hour when fear drove him into rebellion. And now Big Boy erects his own monuments to fear and courage, hurls down his own stop sign, the line beyond which oppression must not advance. The shot that kills the soldier astonishes not only the white man, who dies in disbelief that the lessons of mythology are untrue to life, but to the black boy himself, who, through fear, had courageously become a rebel. Black rebellion galvanizes the black and white communities into action. In their desire for revenge, the whites capture the helpless Bobo, and in a ritualistic, cannibalistic orgy, gleefully torment him, lynch him, tear bits and pieces from his dead body, sacrificial relics attesting to their ability to exact total retribution. The black community unites to protect one of its own. Big Boy's act of defiance placed them all in jeopardy; the lust of the mob, they know, will be all-consuming. "Lucy," Big Boy's father agonizingly commands, "go t' Brother Sanders n tell im Ah said c'mere, n go to Brother Jenkins n tell im Ah said c'mere; no go to Elder Peters n tell im Ah said c'mere."[18]

The writer who heretofore perceived the black community as paralyzed by fear and inaction, who long believed that it was incapable of meeting challenges posed by antagonists, now looks at that community in a new light. Was this insight attributable to the Marxist experience of the past years, or did he still dream of organizing black men and women into a collective force to protect the individual? More likely, he was so enamored of his own success and accomplishments, achieved through struggle and courage, that he now began to believe that such was possible for others. Called together, the black community maps out a strategy of escape for the two boys: they are to hide in a kiln overnight and be ferried away the next morning by another black in a truck heading North. Bobo has fallen victim to the white mob, but Big Boy, the rebel, survives and, leaving innocence behind, heads toward Chicago and a new life.

"Big Boy Leaves Home" establishes the pattern for the stories to follow. This young boy, innocent no longer, having achieved adulthood through rebellion motivated by fear, stands as a metaphor for the characters in such stories as "Down by the Riverside," "Long Black Song," and "Fire and Cloud." It is as if Wright's own rebellious past has gained deeper meaning in the present, as if what once seemed, according to his family and his neighbors, a defect, was so no longer. They

had tried to stifle his rebellious sensibility in his youth; that they would
do this, caused him nervous anxiety and guilt. There was guilt no
longer. He himself might have written the words of Albert Camus, one
of his favorite writers, in *The Rebel:* "Rebellion cannot exist without
the feeling that somewhere and somehow, one is right. It is in this way
that the rebel says yes and no simultaneously. He affirms that there are
limits—and wishes to preserve—the existence of things this side of the
borderline. He demonstrates with obstinacy that there is something in
him which is worthwhile . . . and which must be taken into consideration. In a certain way, he confronts an order of things which oppress
him with the insistence on a kind of right not to be oppressed beyond
the limit he can tolerate."

Mann, the hero of "Down by the Riverside," arrives at this realization after the end of a long ordeal. During a recent flood, when the
banks of the Mississippi had overflowed, Mann, his pregnant wife,
Lucy, his brother, Bob, and his young son and grandmother, like many
others, black and white, were trapped by the waters of the swollen river.
Bob was dispatched to purchase a boat to rescue the family but, unable
to do so, he stole one instead from the white postmaster. Reluctantly,
Mann and his family set out for shore and, along the way, encounter
the postmaster and his family. The white man shouts obscenities at
Mann and fires upon the group. When Mann returns the fire, the postmaster is killed. Lucy dies also, from the arduous trek over angry waters
and an aborted pregnancy. Mann discovers the death of his wife when
soldiers who have come to fight the flood send his son and grandmother
to the hills and force him to aid in rescuing victims of the flood. In this
role, he is drawn back to the house of the white man whom he had
killed, and though given a chance to kill the remaining witnesses to his
crime, he rescues them instead. . . . Once ashore, the postman's family
point him out to the authorities, who take him into captivity. It is then
that his act of rebellion occurs, that he ends suffering and humiliation
by dashing away from his captors and forcing them to shoot him in the
back: "His fear subsided into a cold numbness. Yes, now. Yes, through
the trees? 'Right thu them trees. Gawd! They were going to kill him.
Yes, now he would die. He would die before he would let them kill
him. Ah'll die fo they kill me! Ah'll die. . . .' He ran straight to the
right, through the trees, in the direction of the water. He heard a
shot. . . ."[19]

Mann's predicament echoes Wright's experience. On that day in
Elaine, Arkansas, when Uncle Silas' family fled after his murder by
white men, a bewildered boy accosted his mother, asking the most important yet dreaded of questions for a black adult: why had we fled,
why had we not fought back? ". . . and the fear that was in her," he

wrote, "made her slap me into silence." But the question would not go away, and over the years as he saw incident after incident of white criminality occur, the question remained, why had we/I not fought back? The answer—fear of violence and death—was acceptable to the young boy; for the mature man, such an explanation no longer sufficed. Men and women were fighting back, and that fight began for them at the point at which it began for Mann, when violence was accepted as inevitable and necessary for retaining human dignity and freedom.

In the first two stories, "Big Boy Leaves Home" and "Down by the Riverside," he was able to delineate clearly his protagonists and antagonists. Big Boy and Mann pitted their feeble resources against other men and an environment "red in tooth and claw." He could make no such clear-cut distinction in the third story, "Long Black Song." The line between antagonist and protagonist here is blurred, and the reason may be that he is incapable of distancing himself emotionally from perceptions that continue to plague him concerning the relationship between black men and black women. Sarah, in "Long Black Song," finds herself joined in a conspiracy to bring about the death and destruction of her husband, Silas. Though married to Silas, a prosperous farmer who labored hard to own his land and to measure up to white people, she constantly daydreams of the past, fantasizes about her lover before Silas: "There had been laughter and eating and singing and the long gladness of green corn fields in Summer . . . always it had been like that. . . ." During one day of such fantasizing, a white salesman arrives, seduces her, and leaves not only telltale evidence in the bed but a clock, his wares.

From the moment of Sarah's seduction by the white salesman, Silas' death is preordained. Arriving home from his journey to secure more power and wealth, he finds evidence of the white man's presence: a hat, a pencil, a wad of cotton left in the bed. His howl is directed against the universe as well as against his wife: "From sunup to sundown Ah works mah guts out to pay them white trash bastards whut Ah owe em, n then Ah comes in fins they been in my house. Ah can't go into their houses, n yu know gawddam well Ah can't. They don have no mercy on no black folk; we jus like dirt under their feet. Fer ten years Ah slaves lika dog t git mah farm free, given every penny Ah kin t em, then Ah comes in fins they been in mah house. . . ." When the white salesman arrives with a companion the next day to collect payment for the clock, he confronts an enraged Silas. The farmer kills one of the men; the other escapes to bring back the mob. Silas reloads his gun, sends his wife and child to the hills, remains waiting for the inevitable. Silas thus joins Big Boy and Mann, becomes the romantic rebel, fighting till death out of that innate sense of courage, stubbornness, and pride that is his heritage; he awaits his ordeal, and dies more heroically than he has lived.

These, then, are Wright's alienated rebels, men who come to manhood through the existential struggle, who pay the price in terms of death or exile. Theirs, however, is a personal rebellion, their achievements nowhere calculated to cement a link between man and man, to validate the importance of the human community. At this point they are essentially un-Marxian heroes. Not so the men in "Fire and Cloud," the last story in the volume. Here he attempts to assimilate his Marxist ideology into fiction, to create a hero whose trials and struggles will be symbolic for the entire community. Two Communists—Green, who is black, and Hadley, white—come to a small southern town caught in a food crisis. They are to organize demonstrations for relief among blacks and poor whites. However, they know little of the mentality or people of the region, and they know nothing of the confused Negro leader Rev. Daniel Taylor, whose support is essential if such demonstrations are to succeed. Taylor must weigh his decision to support the demonstrations or not against the possible effect of his actions upon his congregation and upon the goodwill he has built among the town's white leaders. After he is kidnaped by a mob of whites and beaten, and after being assured of the support of his people, the minister explains his decision to lend his support to the demonstrators: "We gotta git wid the *people*. . . . Too long we done tried t do this thing our way n when we failed we wanted to pay off the white folks. We's too much alone this way. We's los when we's erlone! We's gonna be wid our folks. . . ." "Freedom," the minister proclaims as he joins whites and blacks who march and win concessions from the town's leaders, "belong to the strong." That the strong comprises blacks and whites together is obvious symbolism, manipulated by the author to coincide with the position of the Party in the People's Front campaign. Still, he could not believe in such men as Taylor. Big Boy, Silas, and Mann are more familiar to him. Alienated and alone for most of his life, rebellious since the early days of his childhood, he is joined as one not with the Taylors, who had to be goaded into revolution, but with those whose entire life had consisted of rebellion. Thus the Marxist influence must always be at war with his own, personal experiences.

It was therefore difficult for him to believe completely the statement he ascribes to his Marxist hero Johnny Boy, of "Bright and Morning Star": "Ah cain't see white n Ah cain't see black. . . . Ah sees rich men n Ah sees po men." The story was published in *New Masses* on May 10, 1938, and added to *Uncle Tom's Children* in later editions. For his source, he went back to a story he had heard in his youth involving an old black woman who, enraged over the treatment of her son by

white men, hid a gun in a sheet, went to the place where her son was being tortured, and managed to kill several of the torturers before suc-
cumbing herself. To this folktale, Wright added his own, Marxist em-
bellishment. Aunt Sue is the mother of two boys, Sug and Johnny Boy,
both Marxists and both eventually caught by the authorities. Though a
confidante of her sons and privy to their secrets, she retains her strong
belief in Christianity and her suspicion of white people. When a white
man, posing as a friend of the little band of Marxists, tricks her into
revealing the names of the local Communists, her suspicions are
justified. Later, after discovering her mistake, she plans to kill the informer before he can tell the secret to the sheriff. Johnny Boy, in the
meantime, is captured by the mob. Carrying a sheet for burial, she
knows that she can gain access to the place and scene of his ordeal.
Once there, she is forced to wait and watch as the sheriff and his men
break her son's legs and shatter his eardrums in an attempt to force *her*
to talk. She considers killing her son to spare him pain, but soon the informer arrives. She casts away the sheet, levels the gun, kills him, and is
killed herself, saying finally, "Yuh didn't git whut yuh wanted."

Experiences had taught Wright that those who did not live by the
sword would perish as quickly as those who did; the difference was that,
for those who shunned violence, death would be futile, meaningless.
Only in rebellion, only then, despite injury, banishment, or death,
would one be able to create a reason for having lived, would have attained a sense of dignity and humanity. "Yes," he would later record in
his journal, "there must be a lot of blood shed in this nation between
whites and blacks before it is over. Perhaps the killing may not be
directly between whites and blacks, but that will play a part. . . . The
Negro will be so spurred that some whites will welcome him into their
ranks for encouragement in what they are trying to do. Who will tap
this pit of red-hot lava?"[20]

But, in 1938, as more good reviews began to appear for this book,
thoughts of racial conflagration were far from his mind. He was at work
on his novel, which was already accepted for publication. The novel
was as yet unnamed, but the plot sequence was already formed. It
would be the story of an urban northern black. "During the first week
in June, 1938," wrote Margaret Walker, "I received in rapid succession
two airmail special delivery letters . . ." from Wright, who wrote: "I
have just learned of a case in Chicago that has broken there and is exactly like the story I am starting to write. See if you can get the newspaper clippings and send them to me."[21] The story involved a poor illiterate black, Robert Nixon, who had been accused of rape by the
Chicago police and the courts. Under police torture and coercion,
Nixon later confessed to other crimes of rape and burglary. Halfway

through his own novel at the time of the case, Wright laid his work aside and went to Chicago. There, in addition to looking in on his family and meeting with Margaret Walker and other friends, he reviewed the terrain of the setting for his own novel and talked to black lawyers involved in the *Nixon* case. Back in New York, "he made his full use of his free project time to work . . . on *Native Son.*" In discussions with Jane Newton and her husband, into whose house in Brooklyn he had moved, and with Ted Ward, his old friend from the Negro writers group in Chicago, recently arrived in New York, he talked of his novel, using them as a sounding board for the ideas and utterings of his characters.

With Ted Ward he also discussed the dilemma confronting him as he once again considered marriage. The choice was between two white women, Dhima Meadman and Ellen Poplar. "He was attracted to white women, and felt they were stronger than white men," Henrietta Weigel wrote. "He married two: the first a dancer; then Ellen."[22] Ellen Poplar, bright, attractive, was Jewish, of Polish extraction. She was a hardworking Marxist who performed her party duties with singular devotion. These consisted in part of picking up mail and instructions, ferreting through directives from the section offices, attending meetings of higher officers at district headquarters, attending school, and issuing reports. When she met the writer for the first time, she found him attractive, she told Constance Webb; but she was "all Party" and had little time "for romance." Still, a mutual attraction developed between the two on that first night. Ellen was desirable in almost every respect. She was intellectual, devoted, strong, and idealistic, and as concerned as he about oppression and exploitation. And yet . . . that singular devotion she had made to the Party, she was unable to make to him. At the moment, she was wrestling with the problem of breaking emotionally from her parents, who frowned upon her relationship with a black man.

His own inability to sever his emotional ties with his family notwithstanding, he did not understand Ellen. What he needed from a mate, especially a white one, was the strength and courage to withstand the hostilities of blacks and whites alike. The rebellious act of marrying Ellen would, he knew, pit him against most of America. But he also demanded total and complete loyalty. As a result, ". . . he wasn't going to fight my family," remarked Ellen, years later, "and he cut it off, just like that, neat, as he always did. . . ."[23] The cutting off was traumatic, because she *had* broken with her family. She had gone away on a vacation, considered her options, and decided in favor of Wright. She rented a hotel room and insisted on talking things over with him. She wanted to tell him of her decision and her actions. Instead, almost without warning, he announced that ". . . he had met the person with whom he wanted to spend the rest of his life."

That "person" was Dhima Rose Meadman. She was the daughter of a former actress who, the stage behind her, had turned organizer for the International Ladies' Garment Workers' Union. Few people seemed less capable of singular devotion than Dhima. She was a woman of various interests and pursuits. She was a ballet-trained modern dancer with a career of her own. She had traveled widely and maintained an interest in literature and the arts. She had been married previously, and the divorce had given her custody of her child. To Ted Ward, she seemed not ". . . a clinging vine type, but a robust woman who believed herself a match for any man." Dhima, remarked another of Wright's friends, was striking; "she had presence, sophistication, intelligence." But she also had a life-style that must have awed the young writer from Mississippi. She lived with her mother in a town house—spacious, elegant— and he brought his friends, among them Ward and Ellison, to this seemingly palatial estate, in which all were welcomed by Dhima's mother. Dhima was a prize for any man. But, too, she had the courage to join him in rebellion against the customs and taboos that both would face. Despite her varied interests, he sensed that she was as capable of singular devotion to him as she was to her son, her mother, or her profession. That she was "a match for any man" probably did not occur to him at this time, when his novel *Native Son* was being rushed into print. In August 1939, with Ralph Ellison as best man, Richard Wright and Dhima Meadman were married. Seven months later, in March 1940, Harper & Brothers published the first of many editions of the novel *Native Son*.

"That there is an identification between Bigger Thomas and his creator," wrote Dr. Frederic Wertham, "is evident."[24] Violence, Wertham concluded, was the objective correlative for the writer and his creation; around the concepts of violence and rebellion the perceptions of both men coalesced: ". . . the key scene in *Native Son*," wrote the psychiatrist, "is when Bigger Thomas unintentionally kills Mary Dalton in the presence of her blind mother."[25] Wertham's findings came as a surprise to Wright; the connection between Mary Dalton and the young Mrs. Wall, years before, and that between the blindness of Mrs. Dalton and his puritanical mother were unconscious thoughts buried deep. But feelings of rage and anger were always at conscious level, and it was not difficult to voice them through a young black in the ghetto. "Half the time," said Bigger, "I feel like I'm on the outside of the world peeping in through a knot-hole in the fence. . . ." Bigger lives behind that "knot-hole" with his mother, sister, and brother in one room, an efficiency carved out of a multifamily dwelling. His father has met death at the hands of a southern mob; his mother is on relief. He has been in and out of trouble and unable to keep a job for most of his life. His companions are young men much like himself, angry, idle, their situation bleak. Yet he differs from his friends, his family, almost everyone in his environment: he dreams of a better life, of making his life more meaningful. The author himself had once harbored such dreams, and it was this that had kept him from being imprisoned mentally as well as physically behind the ghetto fence. Whether running to outdistance the image of his failed father or the hopelessness of the children he had seen in the Delta, he had run fast and furiously, driven by the same demons that propel his fictional creation. He had been forced to create a new image of himself, and he had done this, over the years, through rebellion and violence. To portray Bigger as a young man of great sensitivity and feeling would be the most difficult task in writing the novel. "Wright," said James Baldwin, "was Black Boy; yes, but he was not Bigger." Or, as Ellison put it, "Richard Wright could imagine a Bigger Thomas, but a Bigger Thomas could never image a Richard Wright." These comments seem to testify to Wright's failure to portray his protagonist as a dreamer who, but for the accident of skin color and environment, might have established some meaning for himself through socially accepted channels. "They don't let us do *nothing*," Bigger remarks, referring to whites. ". . . I just can't get used to it. . . . I swear to God I can't. I know I oughtn't think about it, but I can't help it. Everytime I think about it I feel like somebody's poking a red-hot iron down my throat. Goddammit, look! We live here and they live there. We black and they white. They got things and we ain't. They do things and we can't."

But there were things, the writer remembered, that "they" would do for black youngsters like Bigger. Yet Wright knew that the job offered Bigger by the social worker was not, as Bigger's mother and Mrs. Dalton believed, a chance: Bigger wanted far more out of life and himself than a chauffeur's job.

The job brings him into contact, however, with the Daltons and as such with a totally strange world. But in this new environment, he was like a rat leaving its hole, and he did not know how to cope. Mr. Dalton owned the tenement in which he and his family lived, and his way of making restitution for extorting higher rents from blacks than whites was the tennis balls he sent to the boys' club and hiring such "wayward boys" as Bigger, whom his wife saw as another case history in a charitable ward who might be saved through Christian goodness. Their daughter Mary looked upon him as a social experiment, one of the downtrodden masses, everywhere her equal, who had to be blasted into revolutionary awareness.

Mary was pretty, flirtatious, and the ultimate taboo. She was also insensitive. On Bigger's first outing in his new job, she insisted that he drive her and her boyfriend, Jan, to the South Side; that Bigger sit beside her in the car; that he sing Negro spirituals. Later he would admit that "She acted and talked in a way that made me hate her. She made me feel like a dog. . . . All I knew was that they kill us for women like her. We live apart. And then she comes and acts like that to me." On the night that he was to be quickly vaulted into adulthood, both Mary and Jan acted toward him as if he were not black. Jan Erlone was a Marxist, supposedly more sensitive than most. Given his Marxist training, he looked upon such as Bigger as fellow human beings. But Wright knew better, knew that there were men and women in the Party like Erlone, who, believing that they were able to look beyond race and color, succeeded not in regarding all as equal but in regarding blacks as fantasies, images culled from the imagination. On that day in New York, when he had stood looking angrily into the faces of white Communists embarrassed because none had considered finding a black Communist a place to stay, he came face to face with the Party's reality as opposed to its pretensions. These Communists were blind toward him, just as Jan and the Dalton family were blind toward Bigger. Had there been one person in the Dalton household, he noted later, who recognized Bigger as a human being, the murder would have been solved immediately. But had there been any such person, the murder would not have occurred at all!

This young boy with a criminal record would not have been allowed to take Mary Dalton out alone on his first night at work. Ostensibly going to classes at the university, Mary instead has a rendezvous with Jan. After spending some time together riding through the park, going to the South Side, and forcing Bigger to eat with them in a black restaurant; after necking in the car, Mary becomes drunk, and unseeing Jan allows the black chauffeur to take her home. Bigger maneuvers the almost senseless girl to her room. He has scarcely finished laying her upon the bed when her mother enters, calls her name. He is a black man trapped in the bedroom of a white woman. It is not lust that pervades Mary Dalton's room but paralyzing fear. ". . . the white brutality that I had not seen," Wright later recorded, "was a more effective control of my behavior than that which I knew." Out of the fear of things unknown, Bigger Thomas moves instinctively to protect himself; he covers the girl's face with a pillow, presses hard, harder, until she can no longer breathe, until she lies dead.

After Mrs. Dalton leaves the room, he discovers the magnitude of his act. Again, his actions are predictable, given his fears. He must get rid of the body. Without it, there could be no proof of murder. He takes the dead girl down to the basement, to the furnace he is charged with stoking, hacks her body into small pieces, and burns it. Only later, after panic and fear subside, does he realize the significance of his act: "The thought of what he had done, the awful horror of it, the daring associated with such actions, formed for him for the first time in his fear-ridden life a barrier of protection between him and a world he feared. He had murdered and had created a new life for himself." A new, more aggressive Bigger Thomas is born; he enlists his girl friend Bessie in a plot to extort money from the Daltons by forging a note saying that the girl had been abducted; he manages to convince reporters and detectives alike that he is innocent, while placing blame for the girl's disappearance on Jan. After fragments of the body are discovered in the furnace and his guilt is revealed, he murders again out of a need for self-protection, this time his accomplice, Bessie. He holds the police department of Chicago at bay, managing to elude them by living in the destroyed tenement houses of the South Side. Once captured, he undergoes his trial with dignity, develops warm human feelings toward his lawyer, Boris Max, and Jan, who, having forgiven the murder of his fiancée, has tried to help him. When he goes to his death without remorse, without guilt, he faces his executioners bravely, having at long last attained manhood.

The world that was previously blind to Bigger and his kind was blind no longer. "I hope," Wright told a luncheon gathering at a New York club at which he was the guest speaker, "you will all have a chance to meet Bigger Thomas." He was speaking metaphorically of his hero, for Bigger's extra-literary qualities lay in his value as a shock symbol. American blindness could be cured, if at all, only through realization that Bigger Thomases walked the streets of the South Side and Harlem, that they were larger than the fictional creations of stereotypic literature. Everyone knew of the stereotype of "the bad nigger," but none could actually accept him in all of his complexities. "Multiply Bigger Thomas twelve million times, . . ." Wright has Boris Max say in defending Bigger, "and you have the psychology of the Negro people." The Negro middle class, Wright noted in the essay "How Bigger Was Born," "Negro doctors, lawyers, dentists, bankers, schoolteachers, social workers and businessmen . . . [have] narrowly escaped the Bigger Thomas reaction pattern themselves—indeed, still [retain] traces of it within the confines of their own timid personalities. . . ."[26] The Bigger Thomases were the nuclear conflagration waiting to happen, and they were not all black: "I made the discovery that Bigger Thomas was . . . white, too, and there were literally millions of him. . . . The extension of my sense of the personality of Bigger was the pivot of my life; it altered the complexion of my existence. I became conscious . . . of a vast muddied pool of human life in America."[27]

CHAPTER NINE

Native Son was published on March 1, 1940, and was an instantaneous success. The first novel by a black writer to be so chosen, it became a Book-of-the-Month Club selection. In three weeks, the novel sold over a quarter of a million copies. Magazines pursued the author for biographical sketches and interviews. Radio talk shows and lecture rostrums beckoned. His name was added to "The Wall of Fame" at the reopening of the New York World's Fair and letters poured in from across the country, many congratulatory, some venomous. Book reviews were, on the whole, filled with praise. Unbeknown to him, however, the personal file, concerning himself and his activities, kept by the Federal Bureau of Investigation, began to grow. The letters received by the Bureau were far from complimentary. On August 20, 1940, an irate citizen addressed a letter to J. Edgar Hoover, Department of Justice. "Please read David Cohn's article, 'The Negro Novel: Richard Wright' in May Atlantic Monthly . . . and more important read the author's answer to Mr. Cohn's article in the June issue, 'I Bite the Hand That Feeds Me. . . .'" Speaking of the novel itself, the writer informed the director, "This kind of literature subtle and inflammatory . . . can cause more harm than bombing squadrons. Our American public are gullible, curious [and] like sensations and will read and be influenced by such books as Native Son. . . . Can't the Fed. Bureau of Invest. be as subtle as the author of Native Son and Grapes of Wrath and expose them for what they are—agitators? . . . If our country ever falls," the letter concludes, "it will be from within led by a combination of . . . Native Son Sympathizers, C.L.O., W.P.A. . . . led by foreigners, college students . . . Professors. [Also] exiled German Jews make excellent subjects for communism." The Bureau was unprepared, at the moment, to initiate any action against Wright: the irate citizen thus received the usual Bureau form letter acknowledging receipt of the letter and expressing "appreciation for your courtesy and interest in writing me as you did."[1]

The review by David L. Cohn was one of two that provoked Wright's angriest reaction. "Justice or no justice," Cohn concluded his article, "the whites of America simply will not grant to Negroes at this time those things that Mr. Wright demands. The Negro problem in America is actually insoluble. . . . Hatred, and the preaching of hatred, and incitement to violence can only make a tolerable relationship intolerable."[2] By June 1940, when Wright's reply, "I Bite the Hand That Feeds Me," appeared in the same magazine as Cohn's article, he was in Cuernavaca, Mexico. "The Negro problem in America is not," he wrote, "beyond solution. (I write from a country—Mexico—where people of all races and colors live in harmony and without racial prejudices or theories of racial superiority. Whites and Indians live and work and die here, always resisting the attempts of Anglo-Saxon tourists and industrialists to introduce racial hate and discrimination . . . at no time in the history of American politics has a Negro stood for anything but the untrammeled rights of human personality, *his* and *others'*."[3]

Such criticism as Cohn's, and Burton Rascoe's, which appeared in the *American Mercury* in May, was irritating but hardly devastating. Reactionary whites of course would have strong personal reactions to his novel. But the critical appraisals he waited for were from the Party. In the interests of personal and emotional truth, he had, he knew, committed several "indiscretions" that would offend the more parochial Communists. "He really wanted the Party to like that book," remarked a friend; "I thought he paid too much attention to what they would say. But he was concerned." "Dick told me," Horace Cayton remarked later, "about the Party's reaction to *Native Son*. Since the book did not follow the orthodox Marxist line on the Negro question, the Communists were quite hostile. . . ."[4] The hostility, like the criticism, was slow in coming. Mike Gold and Samuel Sillen were complimentary in their appraisals of the book. Still, the review that he waited for most desperately was from the black leadership of the Party. A favorable word from Ford or Ben Davis would still all party criticism. Ford, however, might not acquiesce, as he was intractable. He had risen in the party ranks because of his skill at political compromise. Party law, for him, was doctrine. But Davis was different. He was an intellectual; he had lived in both worlds, that of the bourgeois blacks and that of the urban proletariat. He walked the streets of Harlem daily, was well known and respected among workers and the bourgeois alike. Certainly, he would recognize the truth and reality of Bigger Thomas. In April, writing in the New York Sunday *Worker*, Davis gave his long-awaited critical appraisal of *Native Son*.

He called the book an important achievement, "the most powerful and important novel of 1940." The writers' objectives, he thought, demanded congratulations: he wanted to demonstrate the degrading and oppressive nature of capitalism; to show that "the Communist Party is the only organization . . . interested in relieving the terrible plight of the Negro people." Yet, the book fell far short of its goal. ". . . every single Negro character," Davis wrote, sounding more now like a black man than a Marxist, "including Bigger's own family is pretty much beaten and desperate. . . . This is where the book falls into one of its most serious errors. Bigger is exaggerated into a symbol of the whole Negro people. . . ."5 Yet Bigger had little viability as metaphor for American blacks, his reaction to oppression not being that of the vast majority. There were other errors in the book, the depiction of members of the Party, Jan and Max, but the portrait of Bigger affronts the Marxist intellectual most of all: ". . . because no other character in the book portrays the Negro masses, the tendency becomes that the reader sees Bigger and no distinction whatever between him and the masses. . . ."

It was a terrible indictment, striking as severely at the writer's perception of black life in America as at his indiscretions regarding Marxist aesthetic canons. When Mike Gold wrote a favorable review of the book in the *Daily Worker* of April 29, 1940, the Marxist chief's efforts did not calm the angry author: "If I should follow Ben Davis' advice and write of Negroes through the lens of how the Party views them in terms of political theory," he wrote in a letter to Gold, "I'd abandon the Bigger Thomases. I'd be tacitly admitting that they are lost to us, that fascism will triumph because it alone can enlist the allegiance of those millions whom capitalism has crushed and maimed."6 Nor did personal intervention by Earl Browder in an attempt to somewhat placate this now even more valuable member of the Party assuage his anger: "Earl Browder, head of the American Communist Party, stated that he saw nothing wrong with *Native Son*," said Cayton, "but Dick did not accept this implied invitation to resume his activities in the Party." Still, he was no less committed to the aims of communism than before: "What does fasten my attention upon Communist action," he wrote at a time when party manipulations concerning Hitler and blacks were forcing others from its ranks, "is whether it overcomes settled and ready-made reality, whether it effectively pushes outward and extends the area of human feelings . . . (sometimes I find myself most deeply attracted to it when most people are repelled—that is for instance when the U.S.S.R. signed the pact with Nazi Germany). . . ."7

This sentiment, expressed in an unpublished essay found among his private papers, demonstrates the validity of Patterson's later charge, that Wright was "politically naïve." His letter to Mike Gold probably reinforced this conception among other high-ranking Communists like Davis. "It is still possible for a wave of nationalism to sweep the Negro people today," he warned. But, due to an important shift on "the Negro question," occasioned by the Pact, signed in August of 1939, the Party was now fully supporting the old separate-development program for blacks, a program in which nationalism was an accepted reality. In his review of *Native Son*, Davis skillfully forwarded the once discarded thesis: "There is little," Davis criticized *Native Son*, "that directly shows the power of the Negro people, although the book as a whole assumes the existence of the Negro masses. Yet that power is historically present and is evident today in political struggle . . . the failure of the book to bring forward clearly the psychology of the Negro masses will find the capitalist . . . trying to attribute Bigger's attitude to the whole Negro people."[8] When Wright, in his letter, was inveighing against the "Separate Development Thesis," which emphasized the "psychology of the Negro masses," Davis was well aware that the thesis was now once again party policy, having been necessitated by the Stalin-Hitler arrangement.

The Pact obligated the Russians to support German military action, short of committing its own forces, on German behalf, and when the Nazi march into Poland precipitated war between Germany and France and England, the Soviet Union, "In dutifully carrying out this end of the bargain . . . through the various sections of the Communist International . . . sowed the seeds of political confusion. . . ."[9] The American Communist Party was charged with preventing American entry into the war on the side of the French and the British. To accomplish this, the Party sought to appeal to the conservative element in the country, and thus old positions on the Negro question and the People's Front campaign were reviewed and amended. Separate development, a program that appealed to racists across the country, was substituted for progressive programs demanding integration in all areas of American life. The People's Front campaign, an attempt to foment an alliance between blacks and whites, was downgraded and eventually discontinued. Keenly aware that this new shift in policy would provoke opposition by progressive whites and black workers and lower-echelon party functionaries, the Marxists sent their most important black leaders on the lecture circuit. Their marching orders were to campaign against England on the colonial question, to depict the plight of American blacks as worse than that of the peoples of Eastern Europe under the Nazis, and by concentrating upon the evils of England and France, to shift emphasis away from the arrangement between the Soviet Union and Germany and its own turnabout on the Negro question. They made opposition to the war the essential issue and argued that because racism was all-pervasive in France and England, this was "not a black peoples war." Davis thundered in print and from rostrum alike: "Even if all discrimination were broken down, still Negro people are faced, along with other Americans, with the prospect of dying in a useless war. . . . There is a special duty upon the Communists to show that job discrimination is a phase of the war program, that Negro people are opposed to the imperialistic war. . . ."

The true black struggle, therefore, was to be against the war and for the "establishment" of a black republic in the South. But national black leaders were not taken in by the Party's subterfuge: they realized that the Marxists had retreated from their position on the Negro question, and they were not convinced that the British and the French posed greater threats to human rights than the Germans. When they began to attack the new party program, the party stalwarts assailed them as moderates, traitorous lackeys of the British colonialists, and sent their master strategists, such men as John P. Davis, to end the People's Front campaign and to take over such organizations as The National Negro Congress.

Nevertheless, the Hitler-Stalin Pact precipitated an exodus by black and white intellectuals from the Communist Party. These intellectuals, Malcolm Cowley noted, had earlier accepted Communist doctrines and wrote and acted on "their new beliefs." In the early forties, however, "most of these semi-converts" turned against "Party Policies; they had continued to attack Hitler and even to call for war against him at a time when good Communists were silent about Hitler and were saying that Churchill and Roosevelt were the great enemies of the revolution."[10] Wright was not among them. He was not entirely mollified by Browder's intervention on behalf of his novel; still, he was not yet ready to break, as so many others were doing, with Marxism. But the fast-moving events forced him to question his own convictions. "I do not believe," he wrote in "There are still men left," "that the aim and goal of human life is to be found in individual happiness, or an agitation of the senses, or in moral piety. . . . The most meaningful moments of experience I have gotten from this world have been in either making an attempt to change the limits of life under which men live, or in watching with *sympathy* the efforts of others to do the same. For that reason I am a card carrying Communist. . . . Communism to me is a way of life, a spectacle of life, an unusual mode of existence, an intense organic drama. . . . Millions, regardless of the tactics of the U.S.S.R., stand firm, for there is nothing to *go back to*."[11]

His growing international prominence made him more, not less, dependent upon the Party. He was estranged from the black masses be-

cause of his intellect and sensibility; and his radicalism and dedication
to revolutionary change distanced him from the black middle class. On
the other hand, the progressive-liberal left favored him in part, because
of his reputation in the Party. Unlike Cowley, Hicks, and Bates, those
who broke with the Party after the Nazi-Soviet Pact, he could not be
accepted as the prodigal-child-returned by a racist America. He needed
the protection of the only organization in America willing and able to
render that protection. The Party needed him, too, just as it needed
Ford, Yergan, Davis, et al., more than ever, with his international re-
nown. Though it might rebuke him, it could not afford to disenfranchise
him. For the time being, therefore, he set aside his personal feelings
concerning the attacks on his novel, even his reservations about the
Party's new stance, and adopted their new position. He attacked Negro
leaders from the rostrum and in print, including A. Philip Randolph,
whom he admired. Under the heading "Negroes Have No Stake in the
War," he argued that the war was being waged between the two racist
evils, Britain and Germany. He supported the Party's nominees, Ford
and Browder, in the presidential campaign of 1940, and used the occasion to reiterate opposition to the war: "With cold ruthlessness, they tell
us that we must fight or else. As fast as the days run, Congress grinds
out reactionary laws to repress and enslave those who dare to question
or protest. Today, even more than in the first World War is the time
for fearless, forthright leadership to protest and voice the fundamental
interests of the Negro people."[12]

His own life matched in tempo the rapid, accelerated pace of world
events on the international stage. He began work on a new novel, *Three
Sisters*; he accepted a proposal from a group headed by Orson Welles to
produce *Native Son* on stage; he was inundated still with requests for
lectures and speaking engagements. He worked on the text of *Twelve
Million Black Voices*, the collaborative effort between himself and photographer Edwin Rosskam. Horace Cayton recalled a trip to Chicago
that Wright had made in researching the book: "Do you know of any
Negro who has lost his job because of *Native Son*?" Wright had asked
the sociologist. While in Chicago, he purchased a home for his family
and made the round of parties held almost everywhere in his honor.
Arna Bontemps recalled first meeting Wright, along with Langston
Hughes, during his early days in Chicago: "Finally we met up with
Dick Wright at a party. . . . Dick was such a flaming young Communist at the time. He didn't have time to dance or anything like that,
though he liked girls and was just at the dancing age, but he had great
zeal only for his politics and his writings." A guest, however, recalled
Wright after *Native Son*: "He was shy, strange; there was a biting kind
of tone that came into his voice at times. I remember him telling me

that he could tell that I was a Negro [the guest, female, was part Negro], that he could always tell Negroes who were trying to pass." "What I remember about him," another acquaintance remarked, "is that he appeared fatigued; he, Trachty [Alexander Trachtenberg, head of International Publishers] and I were together, but he hardly said a word the whole night." He had probably been exhausted from his activity in Chicago, where he made frequent visits to refresh his memory for an article on the South Side for *Life* magazine. He saw his family and many old friends during his trips—but Margaret Walker was not among them.

"I sometimes ask myself," Ms. Walker later wrote, "if I had not made the trip to New York that June of 1939, would we have remained friends?" The trip she made at Wright's insistence turned into disaster for their friendship. "Some mutual 'friends,'" she later mentioned to Nikki Giovanni, "told him some kind of lie. They said that I had said something. I don't know what they told him, but he became inarticulate with rage."[13] He accused her of betraying him but refused to name the informers; he ordered her to give up her room at the Y and to leave New York. He refused to offer the help he had promised with her novel: "I'm not interested in your novel anymore . . . the relationship is over."

The incident occurred during a period of intense pressure. He was awaiting the publication of his first big novel; he had received a Guggenheim fellowship; his first book, *Uncle Tom's Children*, was being translated into many foreign languages; day by day, his fame and reputation grew. He became an object of interest to the Dies Committee. (The Dies Committee, named after Chairman Martin Dies, Democrat of Texas, more properly designated the Special Committee on Un-American Activities, was formed in the summer of 1938. One of its first tasks was to investigate Communist influence in the WPA in general and in the Writers Project in particular.) ". . . Richard Wright the Mississippi born writer was an alien who was kept on the project while veterans were being fired," the committee was told.[14] Speaking of Wright's article "The Ethics of Living Jim Crow," published in *American Stuff*, the Project's anthology, Dies commented, "That is the most filthy thing I have seen." And daily, Wright believed himself to be under increasing pressure from his comrades in the Party. Yet, Ellison told Constance Webb later, "he was aware of the hostility of . . . Party leaders from the beginning. . . . Nor did he ease it from his mind, rather he seemed to require opposition and dwelled upon the antagonism of fellows who were little more than newsboys who delivered the *Daily Worker*."[15] He was convinced, Ellison concluded, that because Ben Davis was a lawyer, the party chieftain "was an F.B.I. man."[16]

The intense pressures probably accounted for his treatment of Margaret Walker in the summer of 1939; and increased pressures also, much more severe, probably led to the breakup of his first marriage.

He had taken his vacation-honeymoon in Cuernavaca in the spring of 1940, in order to gain respite from pressure. The hectic schedule of Chicago over, he set out for the Mexican city, taking up residence along with his wife, her son, and her pianist in a ten-room house situated on the spacious grounds of a large estate.

Cuernavaca bears scant resemblance to idyllic, romantic Acapulco; it is not bounded and enclosed by a wealth of blue-black waves; it does not bear the impressive burden of history and legend of nearby Mexico City, and few natural treasures of long ago are to be unearthed there. What it has in common with other Mexican cities is a range of bold, impressive mountains, warm, congenial climate, and an ethnic population of bronze, tan, and black men and women, beautifully bearing the traits of all the races, Indians and blacks, Spaniards and Europeans. Wright was caught up by the interracial harmony and cooperation that he discovered there. For a young man who had spent the past fifteen years of his life in narrow, one-room apartments, the spacious grounds, enormous house—complete with gardens and a swimming pool—sunbright mornings and cool, moon-drenched nights appeared like some magic island imagined by romantic poets. With his wife, he entertained visitors from the States; he began Spanish and guitar lessons.[17] He completed work on the lecture "How Bigger Was Born," turning it into the essay that finally became part of the novel, and he joined Herbert Klein, his old friend from the John Reed Club days, who, along with John Steinbeck, the novelist, was filming *The Forgotten Village* in explorations around the countryside. A representative of Orson Welles and John Houseman, who were planning to stage *Native Son*, came down to talk with him about the adaptation and about the playwright, Paul Green.

He continued to support the Party from afar: In the *New Masses* of April 2, 1940, his name appeared, along with others, in an "Open Letter to President Roosevelt" protesting, among other things, activities of the Dies Committee. He defended Earl Browder, who was imprisoned by the government, and lent his name to a *New Masses* petition against American entry into the war.[18] And a letter from Ralph Ellison brought him the latest party news—one important item being the final takeover of The National Negro Congress by John P. Davis and the Communists. Ellison served as a correspondent for *New Masses* and watched firsthand as the Marxists skillfully executed the coup de grace on the concept of the United Negro Front. The objective was to force Randolph from the presidency of The National Negro Congress and make the Party's "anti-war" position that of the Congress. Among the delegates following Davis out, Ellison noted Ellen Poplar. He communicated to Wright the news that Ellen displayed concern about him.

The news was comforting. The very countryside itself now seemed oppressive, dismal. The most pervasive fact of the city, he wrote his agent, seemed to be death and crime. The most pervasive fact of his own life, however, appeared to be his troubling relationship with his wife. He told of Dhima's being bitten by a scorpion: "She was mean to me. At last she found a beast that stood up to her."[19] "Dhima," Ellison told Constance Webb, "didn't always understand Dick." Strong-willed, she was unable to subordinate her strength and interests to those of her husband. That fierce singularity of devotion and loyalty that he demanded of everyone, and which, at this particular time of inner turmoil and confusion, he needed so badly, was difficult for her to offer. Part of her loyalty belonged to her son, her mother, her profession. She refused to sympathize about the poor and deprived of Mexico, not out of insensitivity, but because she was less inclined than he to believe that their lives could be radically changed. These personality traits were not new discoveries; here in Cuernavaca, in this somewhat isolated setting, her strength and will to resist domination were dramatically revealed. Tensions increased between them and they separated. Dhima returned to New York, hoping that a reconciliation was possible. Wright prepared to make his first trip to the South since leaving, in 1927.

When he informed Klein and Steinbeck about his decision to go to the South, the two men tried to persuade him not to. Steinbeck feared the worst. Along with his personal belongings, the writer was taking his typewriter and copies of Lenin's, "What Is to Be Done?" and Marx's *Capital*. "I wouldn't do that if I were you," Steinbeck protested, conjuring up visions of the radical black writer being subjected to southern justice. Wright pretended to weigh the advice of his friends. But the dissolution of his marriage left him restless; his natural sense of curiosity and adventure was heightened at the prospect of returning "home" to test himself, to discover how much he had changed. The South, he thought, had such a profound impact upon the personalities of blacks that, long after they had left the region, they retained old patterns of action and reaction.

The only black passenger aboard the train across the Texas border, Wright was separated from the white passengers, ushered to a segregated area of the train. He reflected upon the homogeneous culture from which he had recently come, and moved on. The most dramatic confrontation occurred with the customs official. White, condescending, and officious, the man took one look at the writer's bag, glanced at his black face, smiled, and asked, "Well, boy, what you got there?" Wright's eyes grew hard, cold. He was a man of age and achievement, an internationally known writer; still, the man before him referred to him as a boy. He wondered how well he could compose himself. He breathed deeply, looked away from the man, mumbled, "Just baggage."

He had won a tactical victory over his own emotions, and this steeled him for the ordeal that followed. His typewriter and books were examined. The white man looked at him again, this time with deep introspection, inquired what he did for a living. "I write," the author replied. The white man's body stiffened. Negroes with books and typewriters were either preachers or teachers. He confronted the black man with more certainty, boomed again and again, "You're a teacher." ". . . I had," Wright wrote later, "walked into his world and had upset it. . . ." He gave the same answer, knowing that the black writer and the white Southerner "were struggling with each other over the possession of reality." For the official to relinquish it would bring down the foundation of his living as a white man. Again he looked penetratingly into the eyes of the writer. "Where were you born, boy . . . ?" His eyes brightened as Wright pronounced the word Mississippi. "I knew you was a southern nigger." He smiled affably. . . . "You niggers can travel all over the world, but when I see a southern nigger, I know it."

Wright flinched at the word "nigger," clenched his fists, tensed his muscles. The man walked abruptly away. Wright relaxed, reflected: "I had not been in the South for fifteen years," he later wrote, "and I had returned a different man; but I had successfully evaded violence in my first encounter with my traditional enemy, and I had saved my pride." He had, however, lost his passport. Passport number 614947, issued to him on May 1, 1940, for "travel to Mexico, England, and France for a visit of one year's duration for the purpose of study and writing . . . was taken from him by immigration authorities at the Mexican border on June 15, 1940."[20] There was apparently no explanation. Confused and somewhat angry, he continued his journey. At San Antonio, Texas, waiting to change trains for New Orleans, he was accosted by another white man, an invalid, whose posture in the wheelchair hid his true height. He wheeled himself over to Wright and, without warning, began inspecting the suit he wore. He demanded to know the price. Still confused and concerned about the loss of his passport, Wright realized that he would now have to exercise the maximum restraint. An altercation with a white man might have he did not know what consequences. Intuitively he calculated the cost of avoiding a confrontation. What price could he name that would not be beyond the means of a poor southern black? It would have to be one that the white man himself could afford. He halved the price of the suit, gave the man a figure, and escaped another possible incident. He was able to do the same on the train taking him on the last leg of his journey. He remained in his compartment, hungry and sullen throughout the morning and into the evening because a group of white sailors would not allow the black porter to take "a tray into the nigger coach."

On one level, at least, his experiment was a success. He managed, despite provocation and with superhuman effort, to control his violent emotions. In doing so, he proved to himself that nothing had changed in the South. On another level—the personal—his trip was excruciating. The psychological balancing act was more difficult now. The tensions and anxieties necessary for survival appeared now even more debilitating. "I was there when Wright arrived," John Houseman wrote of first meeting Wright in Paul Green's home, in Chapel Hill, North Carolina, "a surprisingly mild mannered, round faced, brown skinned young man with beautiful eyes. It was only later, when I came to know him better, that I began to sense the deep, almost morbid violence that lay skin deep below that gentle surface."[21]

At the end of this odyssey through the South was the confrontation with his father, Nathan, whom he had not seen in over twenty-five years. There had been violence in his heart toward this father on that long-gone day when Ella had begged Nathan for money. But now, in Natchez, on soil eroded by time and weather, amid squalor and filth, the violence and rage was transferred to other men and events. He measured his father with new eyes. Nathan became one with the image of those numberless black men who had left the South for the big city. Ill equipped in education and culture, they had been ground up in the vortex of the city, never allowed, because of racism and oppression, to reach manhood.

For Nathan, time had not stood still; it had been reversed. He left the land a poor, ignorant black peasant; he returned poor and ignorant, a peasant still. The only visible change was in his once powerful body; it was now aged and decrepit. There were the unmistakable signs of kinship between father and son, the angular cheekbones and furrowed forehead. But Nathan's skin was wrinkled, hardened, pulled taut by the chaos of the years. He inquired about his wife and other son, in a manner of a man inquiring about the weather. These were questions designed as conversation pieces, meant to fill in the thickened void between father and son, an attempt to establish means of communication despite the impossibility of doing so. The only bond between them, Wright knew, was a mystical one, formed in terms of kinship and accident of birth. He, the son, had outdistanced the father. Two peasants challenged the juggernaut of the strange city; only one, he, survived.

"Scalding experiences," he wrote later of the meeting, "that had swept me beyond his life and into an area of living that he could never know." What enabled him to survive? Nathan retired from the struggle too early! He surrendered any claim to a meaningful life by being unable to thwart the conditions and forces arrayed against him. Yet Wright was driven as much by the necessity to outdistance the father as by his own natural instincts for survival. Now standing under the hot, mosquito-laden sky, on the land from which both had begun their odysseys, he moved to fortify the image that he conjured up in his mind throughout the years: "I forgave him and pitied him as my eyes looked past him to the unpainted shack . . . my father was . . . a black peasant—whose life had been hopelessly snarled in the city, and who had at last fled the city—that same city which had lifted me in its burning arms and borne me toward alien and undreamed of shores of knowing."[22] Somewhat exhausted, thoughtful and perturbed, he went on to Chapel Hill for an exploratory meeting with Paul Green regarding the stage adaptation of *Native Son*, and returned to New York. Wright, Ellison told Constance Webb, had visited his father on the way back from Mexico, spent two weeks or a month in the South: ". . . he came back very disturbed."

His wife had moved into a house rented by the Ellisons. She knew that Wright, upon returning to the city, would visit his old friend. She hoped, by seeing him regularly, to effect a reconciliation. Wright, however, was open to no appeals. For him, the marriage was over. He went to Chicago for further research and work on the book *Twelve Million Black Voices*. "I've come to write a picture book," he confided to Horace Cayton; "I want to get into your files." From Chicago he went South once again, this time directly to Chapel Hill for a working session with Green and Houseman. "Among the books that were sent up to us in our retreat at Victorville, where Herman Mankiewicz and I were working on the script of *Citizen Kane*, was Richard Wright's *Native Son*," John Houseman wrote. "We both read it and decided immediately that we should adapt it to the stage." Houseman sent an emissary to Cuernavaca to consult with Wright and learned later that "arrangements had already been made for Paul Green to dramatize the work. I was disappointed . . ."[23]

Green had written the author after publication of *Native Son* and suggested collaboration on a stage adaptation. The playwright had impeccable credentials. He was a Southerner whose liberalism on the "Negro question" was secured by a number of plays involving sympathetic treatment of black life. Among them were *No Count Boy*, *In Abraham's Bosom*, and *Hymn to the Rising Sun*. Despite the racial climate of North Carolina, he invited the black novelist to share his home while work on the manuscript was being done. "Paul Green," Houseman wrote later, "was a man who sincerely believed himself free of racial prejudice. His action in inviting Wright to live in his home during their collaboration was an act of some courage. . . ."[24] Green also had his own idea of black life in America, his own definition of what being a black man meant: "The Negro," he wrote, speaking of his prizewinning play In Abraham's Bosom, "has borne the brunt of the brutal dirty work. . . . [My] chief concern is with the more tragic and uneasy side of Negro life as it has exhibited itself to my notice. . . ." The black character, he believed, should represent the race as a whole, a metaphorical Christ figure, sacrificed upon the altar of a society unjust to all men. Thus he refused to accept Wright's basic premise ". . . that only through an act of violence could a Negro like Bigger Thomas break through the massive and highly organized repressive structure by which he was surrounded . . . morally or artistically." He resented what he called Wright's "existentialism" and insisted that at the end of the play a priest's intonation, linking Bigger with Christianity and a race whose faith remained as strong as ever, be sounded: "I am the resurrection and the light . . . ," he wrote.

Green appeared, to Houseman, to be obstinate and set in these opinions, and thus a conflict developed between the two. The conflict centered around the views of both men concerning the reality of black existence in America. Houseman believed that his liberal credentials were as solid as Green's and that he therefore had as clear an insight into what the novelist was attempting in Native Son as the playwright. He had directed plays, including some of Green's, for a black theatrical company. He had also worked with such black actors as Canada Lee, whom he had portray blacks outside stereotypical roles. Houseman's interest in producing the best play possible, however, was motivated also by personal concerns. Along with Welles and Mankiewicz, he had formed a company, United Productions. The group was finishing work on Citizen Kane, and because of strained relationships between himself and Welles, Houseman had decided to end his role in the company after the production of Native Son. He wanted a play that would crown the partnership with success, and he believed that this could be accomplished if the play followed the story line of the novel very closely. He was aware that Welles was also interested in making the play a super hit, and thus the director quickly sided with Houseman against the playwright.

Wright, however, though disagreeing with Green, maintained neutrality. Part of the reason may be attributable to an agreement between himself and Green, which Green later revealed. The playwright wrote that he would "have freedom to invent new characters and make editorial story changes where necessary. . . . I could make the Communist slant in the book comic when I felt like it. . . ." In addition, the writing of the script was to be done entirely by himself, with discussions with Wright.[25] Part of his unwillingness to antagonize Green was due also to the fact that he sincerely liked him and respected his ability; but part was also due to the reason that he gave John Houseman: ". . . under no circumstances would he risk a public disagreement with a man like Paul Green. There were too many people on both sides anxious to enjoy a dogfight between a successful black intellectual and a white southern writer of progressive reputation—an avowed 'friend of the Negro people.' "[26] No less important was his ambivalence concerning his relationship with the Communist Party. If he quit the Party, he would need the aid of such progressives as Green; at the very least, the Party could make capital, against him, of any dispute between the two. He was relieved, therefore, to conclude the preliminary work on the play and go back to New York, because he would not have to take part in the continual infighting between the playwright and the producers concerning such details as thematic structure and the characterization of Bigger Thomas. Meanwhile, he had to put finishing touches on *Twelve Million Black Voices*, fulfill speaking engagements, and attempt to reassess his opinions of blacks, as well as reexamine his relationship to the Party. His journeys to the South had left him depressed about the desperate state of blacks and convinced him that they were so beaten, hopeless, and disillusioned that no rebellion, such as that he had predicted in his novel, would occur. And while he had once believed that the Party might offer hope for blacks, might ignite a spark of revolt, this belief was fast eroding. The Communists were too often willing to sacrifice the interests of blacks for political ends. These were the major reasons that he thought of severing his ties with the organization altogether. But, as "There are still men left" demonstrates, he was psychologically tied to it and the umbilical cord was difficult to sever. He managed, however, to curtail much of his activity on its behalf and to withdraw from all but the most mandatory functions. A Washington, D.C., Communist, an FBI informer, reported in May of 1941 that "the secretary of the local Communist Party had made a number of efforts to communicate with Richard Wright. . . ."[27] Though he avoided the Washington Communist's attempt to have him speak on the Party's behalf and though he was gradually beginning to withdraw from party functions, still, the FBI's list of his party endeavors for 1941 shows that he remained active.

His name was listed in the February issue of *New Masses*, along with "Earl Browder, Ben Gold and Joe North as one of the speakers" at the *Daily Worker*'s celebration of "Mike Gold's 25th anniversary in the labor movement." He was among the writers greeting Dreiser at a testimonial on March 1, a testimonial held "under the auspices of the American Council on Soviet Relations." In an issue of *New Masses*, March 19, he greeted William Foster, National Chairman of the Communist Party, on his sixtieth birthday, and on March 22, he agreed to serve on the Board of Honorary Chairmen of the May Day Committee. His name appeared on a "Call to the 4th Congress of the League of American Writers to be held in New York City . . . to discuss how best writers can resist the trend towards war. . . ." On April 21, he condemned the imprisonment of Earl Browder, and on June 9, his name appeared "among the American writers who pledged full support to Great Britain and the Soviet Union." In August, he was a member of a citizen's committee to free Earl Browder, and in November, "he protested against police brutality and general economic conditions existent in Harlem" along with A. M. Berry, Secretary of the Communist Party, Reverend Adam Clayton Powell, Jr., and Horace Marshall, Vice-President of The National Negro Congress.

Though engaged in these activities, he still found time to renew his relationship with Ellen Poplar. An informant told the FBI on March 1, 1942, "that Richard Wright about 1938 lived as man and wife with [name deleted], who was a member of the Communist Party." Like so much of the information supplied by informants, the dates and facts are wrong. When Wright moved back to New York, he once again took up residence with the Newtons. Ellen visited the family, and the two met for the first time since the abrupt termination of the relationship two years before. She did not know that he was back on that day when she visited her friends. Nor was she aware that her messages of continuing interest in him reached him in Cuernavaca and helped to raise his spirits during difficult times. Now, as he confronted difficult times again, thoughts of the bright, attractive young woman whom he had so abruptly rejected before, were constant. And she had thought often of him! She had broken with her parents and moved out on her own. She continued to devote her time and energy to the Party, but she hoped for a reconciliation with Wright. On the first night of reunion, therefore, the two rushed to embrace each other. And though aware that her family still opposed Wright, she later noted, ". . . there he was and I knew immediately that my family counted for nothing, where my feeling and interest lay. . . ." On March 10, 1941, the two were married in Coytesville, New Jersey: among the witnesses were Abraham Aaron and Benjamin Davis, Jr. Fifteen days later, *Native Son*, with Canada Lee featured as Bigger Thomas, opened on the Broadway stage to mixed reviews. Among the favorable comments concerning the stage adaptation, the FBI noted those of Burns Mantle and Brooks

Atkinson. "Brooks Atkinson, in the New York *Times*," the agent quoted, "had the following to say. . . . In the drama Mr. Green and Mr. Wright work in a more objective style. Without the subjective background their defense of Bigger Thomas' ghastly crime in the court scene sounds like generalized pleading. It lacks the stinging enlightenment of the last third of Mr. Wright's novel. But that completes this column's bill of exceptions to the biggest American drama of the season."

The author, however, was almost as preoccupied with beginning domestic life again as he was with the success or failure of the play. He and his wife took up residence in a small apartment on West 140th Street, near the Ellisons, before moving to a more comfortable one in Brooklyn. He settled down to family life: "he cooked, designed furniture for the home, and taught himself photography." His relationship with Ellen's mother remained strained. Ellen refused to see her mother until she would accept the fact that her daughter had married a black man. When Ellen became pregnant, in August, the prospect of being a grandmother somewhat mollified her mother. "But she and her son-in-law remained aloof," wrote Constance Webb. "She could never bring herself to speak to Richard frankly or even admit her prejudice."[28] The situation was frustrating for Wright. He knew the importance of a strong relationship between mother and child; he wanted his wife's family to accept him. He understood that they were immigrants who had imbibed American racism with the rest of American culture. His marriage to Ellen destroyed their concept of reality, shattered the peace and stability of their lives. He understood, but all about him was chaos and turmoil, and he needed peace above all else in his home. The hostility of his wife's family was only one of the irritants plaguing him; much more important were the actions of the government concerning his request for permission to travel abroad. On September 17, 1940, after his return from the South, he requested the return of his passport. He wanted, he told immigration authorities, to travel to the Soviet Union "as an invited guest of the League of Russian Writers." His request was denied. Then, two months after his marriage, he made another appeal. He wanted renewal of his passport in order to travel "to the Soviet Union and China . . . to write articles for the Associated Press." His intention was to take his wife with him. On June 24, the immigration officials denied his request, informing him that the State Department prohibited American journalists from going to Russia until the Russians acted in kind toward American journalists. He was being prohibited by the government from traveling abroad, and his political affiliation, he believed, had something to do with this. The reply to his latest request had come two days after German troops invaded the Soviet Union.[29]

"A change of attitude of Richard Wright and other writers is pointed out in that early in June they adopted a firm anti war program," wrote an FBI agent, "and in July they advocated full support to the Soviet Union. Further, that Germany declared war on Russia on June 22, 1941." Given the consternation caused by these events, he was in no mood to do battle with bigoted in-laws: ". . . in private," wrote Webb, he insisted that his wife "tell her mother to go home and stay there . . . either they come to the house and behave themselves or they stay away . . . there's peace and love in our home."

Among the leadership of the Communist Party in America, all pretensions of peace and fellowship dissipated under the repercussions following the German attack. Party chief Earl Browder demanded a cessation of the internecine warfare waged by the black leadership of the Party against each other. A new policy change was mandatory and a united effort required. The correct line was no longer "no war against the fascist enemy." The American people had to be convinced now that all-out war must be waged against the Germans—a war of national liberation for the preservation of humankind. Attacks upon Roosevelt, Negro leaders, those who supported war against Germany, and liberal progressives turned to phrases of praise and commendation. The old party positions on the Negro question and the Popular Front were reinstated. Ben Davis, Yergan, Patterson, and Ford were hastily ushered back onto platforms and into print to persuade black Americans that *this* was the Negroes' war. Only weeks before the German invasion, Ford had argued the opposite position with passion and authority. One week after the Soviet Union was invaded, the Communist leader argued equally as forcefully that "the struggle for the rights of the Negro people is an inseparable part of the struggle against fascism and reaction, for democracy and equality; it is an inseparable part of the international people's front to defeat and destroy Hitler."

On the Negro question, Ben Davis' about-face amounted to sheer cynicism: "Although the Jim Crow system is still in force in our country," claimed the party leader, "it is slowly—too slowly giving ground to vast new forces of labor and the people united in the cause of victory. . . . The movement for the full freedom of Negro Americans is today on the broad highway of victory. . . ." These were disciplined Marxists and their world view was predicated upon the ethics of power politics. All ends necessary to produce a Communist society were valid, and because of this view they were able to execute the shifts demanded by the Moscow Comintern, with no pangs of conscience, with no sense of violation of personal principles. For one so sensitive and—in spite of him-

self—idealistic as Wright, violation of principle was very difficult. He
followed the party leaders in reversing his own stand against the war,
under both pressure and humiliation. In the *New Masses* of June 17,
1941, he had written, in the essay "Not My People's War," that black
treatment in past wars, along with black discontent, refuted the claims
of the nation's leaders that the war was a democratic war." Other
writers wrote on "Why This Is Our War," and in July Wright, along
with other American writers, pledged all-out support to England and
Russia.

A November issue of the *Sunday Worker* noted that Wright "was
declared winner of the Spingarn medal for the writing of 'Native Son.'"
But neither the *Worker* nor the agent who filed this information revealed the details of Wright's acceptance. Established by Joel Spingarn, president of the NAACP, the medal was awarded to blacks who
had distinguished themselves. Since the author's relationship with the
NAACP was at best only polite, he had not spared the organization or
its leadership criticism either in public lectures or in print; the award
was made for his dedication to principle and his courage in speaking
out. The speech he had planned for the acceptance was close in theme
to "Not My People's War." He was forced, though, to change it at the
last moment, by party leaders, "into an appeal for Blacks to volunteer
to defend democracy."[30]

It was not only humiliation that the Party continued to heap upon
him. More important, he was forced into opportunism and cynicism; he
was being coerced into accepting values antithetical to his experiences,
that the ends of the strivings of world communism necessitated acceptance of unlimited authoritarianism. Though born in an environment of
southern hatred and oppression, he later wrote, he found it inconceivable that any man could be silenced. Yet Ellen Wright told Constance Webb that she had worked in Negro neighborhoods and saw
how the Party used Negroes. Her husband had begun to share her vision. The Party, caught up in the throes of its own vacillations, with
massive defections by blacks and whites, would not allow anyone his
say. When he had written of his respect for party discipline, this was
not what he had had in mind. In fact, in the past, he had been able at
least to air his own views; now he was being confronted with one party
directive after another. "Go back to your writing," Davis ordered him
after he contested one such directive, "and leave politics to the Party."

But his writing had begun to suffer, probably as a result of his politics. He was unable to complete *Little Sisters,* and the novel was laid
aside. He began work on two other novels, *Black Hope* and *The Man
Who Lived Underground.* "My own stuff comes pretty slow," he said.
"There are no fireworks in my life, just work day in and day out." The

spontaneous combustion of energy and desperation that produced *Native Son* no longer produced satisfying results. Time was needed to feed the creative mind to the point when he gained the perspective to put down in long fiction the daily eruptions of his life. He was more successful with documentary prose, the demands of which were pragmatic, calling for research, exploration, rational thought. In October 1941, Viking Press published what he called "a picture book, 12 Million Black Voices." "I explained to him," said Cayton, who helped with the research, "the idea of urban versus rural, of culture versus civilization, of a sacred versus a secular society." He also explained the differences between societies wherein folkways determined modes of conduct and those where such conduct was determined by a system of laws. From these conversations Wright concluded that there existed a superstructure governing the lives of blacks North and South and he created section titles to emphasize this. One such heading, "The Bosses of the Buildings," described the forces of the cold, impersonal cities of the North; another, "The Lords of the Land," symbolized "the rural, sacred society of the South."

In his text for this collaborative effort between himself and the photographer Rosskam, he worked much like a scientist in a giant laboratory. He wanted to place a race of people, as it were, under a microscope, and evolve theories in order to explain their ways of living to other Americans. They were, he postulated, a people born of "cultural devastation, slavery, physical suffering, unrequited longing, abrupt emancipation, disillusionment, bewilderment, joblessness, and insecurity—all enacted within a short space of *historical time*." He needed no research to help him arrive at this formulation. He knew such people. He had seen them in the Delta, on the South Side of Chicago, in New York's Harlem; their faces were as real to him as those of himself, his mother, his father, all of them mired upon a psychological island called "Negro." "If we had been allowed to participate in the vital processes of America's national growth," he asked on behalf of the collective Nathans, "what would have been the texture of our lives, the pattern of our traditions, the routine of our customs, the state of our arts . . . ?"[31] The Nathans would have emerged as different men; a race of people would have been stronger; America, greater.

In his review of *Native Son*, Davis chided the author for his mysticism, for not identifying clearly enough for the reader the negative forces acting against Bigger and the positive forces acting in his behalf. Wright would not make that mistake again. He could clearly identify and label the villains now and, in Marxian terminology, enunciate their enormous crimes. America was not what it might be because "The Lords of the Land" and "The Bosses of the Buildings" both had the same aim: the perpetuation of the feudal system that pitted poor whites against blacks and maintained the capitalist structure. Acting against this powerful combination were the progressive forces of America, black and white, dedicated to undoing the work of capitalists past and present. They realized that blacks were America's metaphor, that "if we black folk perish, America will perish."

But were these progressive forces essentially Marxist? Now on the verge of his psychological break with Marxism, he believed less in the possibility of a Marxist solution. However much he did believe, he thought a solution could be engendered without the Marxists. Certainly the kind of rebellion he foresaw in *Native Son* seemed unrealistic now. Oppression had sunk too deeply. Was the energetic positive denouement of the book attributable more to his wishes for black success and survival than to what he actually believed? His own faith in his ability to confront the world without Marxism, to go it alone, seemed shaky. How much more difficult was it for those like Nathan to continue the struggle alone? If in the fiction of *Uncle Tom's Children* and *Native Son* he had suggested that there were limits beyond which oppression would not be allowed to march, *Twelve Million Black Voices*, positive evidence to the contrary, suggests that oppression and racism will remain constant in American life.

Twelve Million Black Voices received "enthusiastic reviews" and occasioned its share of letters to the FBI. One such letter, written on July 25, 1942, stated that "Among the most dangerous of the secret Communist activities in America is its organizing 12,000,000 Negroes as shock troops of their Jewish overthrow of America at a moment when America has been weakened by sending its manpower to Europe. I suggest that you obtain a full report these channels offer to you of Negro crime from all large Negro centers in the U.S. . . ." Investigation of subversive activities by blacks, the writer noted, should "result in charges against one Richard Wright, author of *Native Son* and 12,-000,000 *Black Voices* and other vile publications by this Negro Communist. . . ." Quoting Wright's comments concerning the admiration of some blacks for the Japanese, the writer raised the question of sedition: ". . . that I charge is seditious and should warrant the arrest of Wright and confiscation of every copy of his books, especially 12,000,000 *Black Voices.*"

A more serious letter reached the offices of the director of the FBI. The letter was written on October 13, 1942, to Henry Stimson, Secretary of War. It was relayed to the Military Intelligence Service, and forwarded on November 2 to "Lt. Col. J. Edgar Hoover, Federal Bureau of Investigation, Department of Justice." "I beg to call to your attention," the writer began, "books by one Richard Wright designed to air racial dissension in America confining my charges to one entitled 12,000,000 *Black Voices*. Its entire contents are designed to destroy the morale of an important percent of American citizens under call to the armed forces of the United States." The writer noted page 143, whose contents concerned Japan, charging that such favorable assertions aid America's enemies. The "publication" had considerable distribution, noted the writer, among "colored people and other enemies within the United States. . . . Material of this character in the hands of the designing persons can lead to many forms of sabotage and result in a general breakdown of morals bound to be used to corrupt national unity. . . ."[32]

This letter did not receive the usual form reply expressing gratitude to the sender. Instead, on December 1, 1942, a directive was issued from the director of the FBI to the Special Agent in Charge (SAC) of the New York Field Office: "In view of [deletion] specific allegations as to certain writings [deletion] of subject, it is desired that your office make inquiries of sources available to you for the purpose of determining whether the book entitled '*Twelve Million Black Voices*' or other publications of subject are in fact given to the expression of statements having significance under the Sedition Statutes. If possible, you should secure a copy of this publication as well as other writings of subject and review the same for possible presence of such material.

"If your inquiry develops information of an affirmative nature, you should of course cause an investigation to be undertaken as to subject's background, inclinations, and current activities."[33]

CHAPTER TEN

The war clouds that had darkened the American sky for over three years burst on December 7, 1941, when the Japanese attacked Pearl Harbor. Roosevelt's decision to actively join the war against Germany and Italy as well as Japan made the party chieftains jubilant. Again the black party leaders took to the public rostrum and party organs, heaping praise upon Roosevelt and demanding black loyalty in the nation's fight against the Axis enemy. The Communists were to pay even greater attention, Ford averred, to the problems of the black middle class and black intellectuals, who embodied the cultural aspirations of their people and played "an important role in the struggle of the Negro people for democracy and for defense of the democratic institutions of our country."[1]

Again under party pressure, the author of *Native Son* lent his appeal to the party cause. In the Introduction to a condensed version of *Twelve Million Black Voices* slated for publication by *Coronet* magazine, he wrote, in December, that blacks were allied with the West. There were still many things wrong with the country, he admitted, but the wrongs of America ". . . *will not* and *cannot* be righted by Hitler, Mussolini, or Hirohito." In a letter that began "Dear Comrade Sender Garland," published in February 1942, he argued that "The Communist Party is the only political party in America vitally concerned about culture and its problems."[2] These tributes to the Party and its line masked the deep and growing schism between himself and the leadership. The question was no longer whether or not he would break with the Party but how to do so quietly, with a minimum of publicity. The circumstances surrounding the proposed "March on Washington movement," headed by A. Philip Randolph, had pushed him to an irrevocable decision. Early in 1940, Randolph, incensed at discrimination against blacks in defense programs, proposed a march of thousands of blacks to the nation's capital, at a time when the government had stepped up its defense production.

The proposed movement won the support of the major civil-rights organizations and captured the imaginations of millions of blacks, including Wright. He had long admired the energetic leader of the Brotherhood of Sleeping Car Porters. He had not protested Randolph's treatment by Communist delegates during the siege at The National Negro Congress, but he regarded the black leader as a man of principle and courage. The proposed March on Washington demonstrated courage and might provide the spark of hope necessary to weld black people together—a task that he had once believed the Party was capable of initiating. Moreover, the March, scheduled for June 14, was to enunciate one of his favorite themes: victory over fascism abroad and at home. He believed that the Party should be involved.

The Party, however, was even more adamantly opposed to the Randolph march than the Roosevelt government was. The new policy of all-out aid to the allies—now including the Soviet Union—against the Germans demanded unity of the American people. Randolph's actions would create disunity, would disrupt the defense effort at a time when Hitler's troops were advancing toward Stalingrad. The salvation of the motherland of world communism was preferable to demonstrations against segregated blood banks, discrimination in hiring, inequality in the armed forces, racism in daily life. The Party supported Roosevelt in his attempts to pressure Randolph to call off the protest. When Wright stood before Ben Davis and Ford, arguing his case for Randolph, he had vague notions that Davis might be persuaded to see his logic.[3] Ford, he knew, would not. Recalcitrant and dogmatic, he was openly antagonistic toward the writer, despite the glowing tribute to him in his book *The Negro and the Democratic Front*. "The alternative to support of the war and of Roosevelt is the support of reaction!" he thundered; "you're an obstinate, subjective fool."[4] Anger flooded Wright. With great difficulty, he fought to control himself. He looked to Davis for assistance. Davis moved to temper Ford, and when his comrade left the room, he placed a fatherly arm around Wright's shoulders, offering no response to the plea for support of Randolph. He could not. Opposition to the March was a party directive.

For the writer, it was one party directive too many. He had to get out now. He had once pledged, in Chicago, when seeking to break with his old cell, that he would still be faithful to the Party's aims and objectives; he did not want, he said then, to be an active Communist any longer. Now, seven years later, he arrived at the same conclusion. This time, however, intentions were different. He would, under pressure, participate in the Party's programs, lend his name to its efforts, as in the case of the letter to Sender Garland and petitions in support of Earl Browder and Harry Bridges. But his dedication to the American Communist Party, his faith in its goals and objectives, were gone. His relationship was no longer a spiritual one; it was based upon the cold, hard, pragmatic fact that he needed time to prepare himself "to go it alone."

In the early part of April 1942, his thoughts lay elsewhere. On the thirteenth, Ellen Wright entered Brooklyn Jewish Hospital to give birth to their first child. He was exuberant and anxious. Children were necessary to the stability of a family. And based upon his own experiences, he knew he would strive to be a caring, loving parent who would shield and protect his child, perhaps somehow atone for the lack of protection he had felt from his own parents. And yet, how much protection could he really offer? Julia, born on April 15, 1942, was categorized under American law as black. The nurses at the hospital made contemptuous remarks about "somebody who'd had a black baby." Not knowing that Ellen was the "somebody," they told her also. "And when they found out," said Benjamin Appel, "Mrs. Wright counted the days like a prisoner."[5]

For Wright, however, the white uniforms of the hostile, racist nurses came to symbolize all the terrors that he imagined might befall his child. ". . . there was no escaping them," Appel noted; "they came after him in his dreams, and after his child, guilty too because of color." The dreams were repetitious, of white men turned monsters: "Whiteness shook him awake and he would hurry into his child's room." Relieved, he discovered that "they" had not taken her away, ". . . not this time." She was safe! But for how long? "Often," as he told Appel, ". . . he would sleep in the same room, next to his baby."[6]

But, in reality, how much protection could he give? How could he prevent her from undergoing the scarring, searing experiences undergone by every black child in America? He could and would protect her from the more overt, physical onslaughts of racism. But how shield her from crass innuendos and derogatory remarks, from situations that might threaten her morally and spiritually? He moved from Harlem to Brooklyn in July of 1941, and after Julia was born, he moved again, into a house shared by George Davis and Carson McCullers, the novelist. The house, at Seven Middagh Street, became famous as a kind of artists colony. Poets, writers, musicians visited regularly. Wright had met Davis when, as editor of Harper's Bazaar, Davis had selected one of Wright's earliest stories, "Almos a Man," for publication, and a fast friendship had developed. Carson McCullers had been one of Wright's favorite writers ever since he favorably reviewed her novel The Heart Is a Lonely Hunter, for The New Republic. When he met her, he was even more impressed by "her tortured soul, her zest for the ordinary moments of life. . . ."[7] The group had strictures against people moving into the colony with children, but due to Davis' and Carson's affection for Wright, the rule was relaxed.

At Seven Middagh Street, he was immediately attracted to the debates, the camaraderie existing among artists. "He felt a sense of brotherhood with them. . . ." Like his comrades in the Party, they, too, were concerned with social events, were activists, men and women who spoke out against injustice. Still, racism again intervened. Upon discovering that the new tenants included a black man, a black servant told the landlord: "I'm not waitin on no nigger. . . ."[8] Ellen's child, an angry white neighbor told Appel, "had been tarred black." But the most serious threat to Julia's well-being, Wright believed, came from the atmosphere of the colony itself.

He came to believe that Carson was "a disruptive personality in the house. . . ." What he had seen as her "zest for the ordinary moments of life" were really the desperate strivings of a writer bordering upon severe neurosis. The talented writer was a compulsive talker and consumed far too much alcohol. Her frailness, constant illnesses, and emotional problems seemed designed for self-destruction. He feared for her health, he told friends, "not so much for Carson's own sake, but that she might collapse at the feet of his young daughter and inflict some deep psychic wound on her. . . ."[9] He had to move again.

He was less certain, however, concerning his future involvement in the war effort. He was willing to serve in the war against fascism, he told friends, but not as a foot soldier. He wanted an officer's commission to work in one of the Army's propaganda departments. He was registered with Selective Service Local Draft Board No. 178 and assigned "order No. 2025." Because of "collateral dependents," he was placed in "3-A classification" on May 28. In July 1942, the collateral dependency was eliminated and he was reclassified 1-A, but just as he was about to "be inducted into the Army," he asked for and was granted a ninety-day extension. On November 16, he received a 3-A classification "to permit him an opportunity to take Officer Candidate Training." He furnished a "list of his writings to the local Board," submitting *Uncle Tom's Children* along with his other works, and admitted that the work "was later translated into Russian by the U.S.S.R. and issued in international literature."[10] His gesture was an honest one, but his application for Officer Candidate School was rejected. Again he faced the prospect of being drafted into the Army. Already his friends were being drafted. Conscription had been stepped up, as the Allies suffered defeat after defeat in Asia, Europe, North Africa. He had to find some other way to participate in the war effort, and tried to maneuver his volunteer

work for the Office of War Information into an official position; all to
no avail.

Then, unexpectedly, he received an unusual party directive: ". . .
shortly after his introduction to [name deleted], he was approached and
asked to make a formal application to work for the Office of War Information." He was quizzical. He had wanted to work for the department
but had been consistently rebuffed. His Communist background, he
had thought, was against him.

Now his Marxist bosses were demanding that he make application.
To Max Yergan, James Ford, and Benjamin Davis, the three party chieftains, he told of his reservations. Davis, shrugging his shoulders, ". . .
informed him that the Communist Party knew exactly what it was
doing in asking him to make this move and that he should forthwith
get an application blank . . ."[11] He would, Davis said, help him fill it
out. Now curious as to whether or not the Party could place him, he
obtained the application, and he and Davis jointly filled it out.[12]
Wright noted that he was a member of the Communist Party and "ob-
jected to the linking of Communism with fascism"; he indicated that
he was "a patriotic person wishing to make a contribution to the war
effort." Before a notary public, he "swore to the truthfulness" of the application. Years after the event, when the legal attaché at the American
Embassy in Paris heard the author relate this part of the episode, he
could hardly retain his composure. This act, he later recorded, made
Wright at that time "perhaps, the only sworn Communist in the
United States."[13]

At the Office of War Information, he was greeted with hostility.
"You are really intransigent . . . ," he was told by one of the officials.
They read his application and consulted each other about it, out of
earshot. They advised him to go home, said that they would contact
him later. He waited anxiously for some days and then began to suspect
the agency never really turned in his request. He sought answers from
Davis. He looked straight at Wright. He had—he chose his words carefully—"no recollection of having helped [Wright] make out such an
application."

Wright was paralyzed with astonishment. He wasn't sure he had
heard right. Yet Davis denied the entire incident. Wright was not oblivious to the shenanigans that the Party was capable of pulling, but
this seemed beyond the bounds of imagination. There were, however,
witnesses to all that had actually transpired. Ford had been there, and
Yergan. Still, he wondered whether they would really contest Davis'
version of reality. It was possible that Davis was feeling nervous strain
and anxiety over his campaign for the City Council of New York;
Wright himself had been one of Davis' sponsors. But Davis had been as

steady as ever. No, he had been used again. This time, seemingly more treacherously used than before: He had been lied to. As he walked the Brooklyn streets, his rage increased with comprehension. ". . . he realized that the Communist Party had undoubtedly decided he was too well known as a Communist to be sponsored for work in the Office of War Information, and they had, therefore, chosen someone else less politically prominent to take the job he was supposed to have."[14]

The Party, he would later write, knew a great deal about politics, but little of the human heart. That was his province. But the Party also knew little of the human ego, and thus the party bosses had never really known him. The obstacles that he had overcome, the challenges that he had successfully met, had earned him the right to demand what was of the utmost importance to him: respect for the human being. The Party could offer no such respect. It was limited by its perceptions of men as little more than spokes and cogs in a giant piece of machinery. Davis' cynicism and dishonesty toward him were symbolic of this. This realization left him no options. When the party leaders had forced him into making embarrassingly abrupt changes concerning the war, Negro leadership, the Popular Front, even the Randolph affair, he had complied in the interest of party politics. Now he was wounded, realizing that the Party would use the Negro question as one more pawn in the political game.

But, even worse, he could not rationalize the party bosses' affront to his ego, to his sense of self, to his humanity. It was now clear that he must go it alone. There were no alternatives. "For God's sakes, let us quit," Ellen quoted her husband; "I have had it." Confronting Davis, he told the party leader "that he would no longer support him as councilman and would not campaign for him, and that he was through."[15] Davis remonstrated with him. He did not want to lose this bright star of the Party. Davis suspected Wright's reason concerned the Party's support of Roosevelt on the Randolph issue. That was certainly part of it. Davis' own indiscretions had been minor, and dictated by pragmatic considerations. The Party needed contacts in the Office of War Information. Wright had done volunteer work there, knew some of the important officials. He had seemed a logical choice. But he was too well known. The Party needed someone far less visible, whose usefulness could be maximized. There was nothing personal in the decision, in any party decision. The Party did not deal on the personal level. He tried to placate the younger man: he suggested that he not renounce his affiliation completely, that instead he "become a member-at-large of the Communist Party."

Wright rejected the proposal. The decision was made. The break would be clean, quick. He could not afford to be swayed by Davis' rhetoric. The psychological wounds were too raw. All he wanted, now that the decision was made, was distance between himself and the leadership. He recalled that the Party had once seemed to say to him and to those like him, if you bear the strength of your convictions and have the courage to speak out, come and be one of us. But it had proved to have few convictions of its own. The leaders were less capable of voicing their own beliefs than most men. None were as militant as he. He was leaving a corrupt and battle-scarred organization. "On October 14, 1942," an informer told the FBI, ". . . Richard Wright, a former known Communist Party member, had split with the Party because of his dissatisfaction with the way the Party handled the Negro question."

But who the hell was Richard Wright? The agent, perusing the directive handed to him, probably did not know. The directive to find out came from Headquarters, from the office of Hoover himself. And it was top priority. The case was catalogued under "Internal Security—Sedition." Something of a seditious nature had been written by "Subject, Richard Wright." If the articles, books, whatever, were truly seditious, the writer was subject to imprisonment. The Secretary of War was concerned. The memorandum had come from his office less than three months before. On December 2, 1942, the orders were passed on to E. E. Conroy, Special Agent in Charge of the New York Field Division. Now, only three days later, the agent was charged with evaluating the assertions made in the letter to Stimson. He did not have much to go on. As files go, the Wright file was slim. There were some data left over from the investigations of the Dies Committee, but these were mostly assertions, accusations. There were letters in the file from crackpots, but these were about the writings, not about the man. They were ofttimes so unintelligible and badly written that even their evaluation of the writings was suspect. Thus far, there was no cadre of informants assigned to report specifically on Wright, and his name cropped up now and then in conjunction with others. No, the agent would have to start from scratch, do legwork. Picking up the few documents at his disposal, he headed for "the Public Library of New York City, located at 5th Avenue and 42nd Street." He reviewed the indexes for biographical material, read articles about the subject, including one by M. B. Tolson written in the *Modern Quarterly* in 1939. He read criticism of the play *Native Son* by Burns Mantle and Brooks Atkinson, and he read *Twelve Million Black Voices*. He contacted an informant who ". . . advised that the subject had been employed by the W.P.A. on a Federal Writer's Project from January 3, 1938, to May 17, 1939, when he resigned to accept private employment."[16] He completed his research, wrote up the report, and handed it to the SAC, who would analyze it and propose courses of action. There were certain errors in Wright's bi-

ography that he had copied directly from Tolson: "Richard Wright
was born 'on a broken down plantation near Natchez, Mississippi. . . .
His family travelled from town to town like grub worms. His father got
tired of his poverty ravaged household and deserted the family. Paralysis struck his mother down and he entered an orphan asylum but ran
off at fifteen. . . . he bummed his way all over the country, fighting,
stealing, lying. . . .'" He went on to refer to correspondence from the
Secretary of War, which "reflected that on page 143 of [*Twelve Million
Black Voices*] there was material that appeared to be seditious in nature . . . for the benefit of the Bureau, the above mentioned page is
being quoted in full." Page 143 noted the movement of blacks from
previous servile conditions, the despair and hurt that prevented many
blacks from working "with whites," the return-to-Africa sentiment
among some. Included also was the statement that suggested an implicit admiration for the Japanese enemy: "There are others of us who
feel the need of protection of a strong nation so keenly that we admire
the harsh and imperialistic policies of Japan and ardently hope that the
Japanese will assume the leadership of the darker races." The agent also
included several quotes from the last page of the book, among which
were the following energetic lines: "The seasons of the plantations no
longer dictate the lives of many of us; hundreds of thousands of us are
moving into the sphere of conscious history."

Upon receiving the reference report, on March 3, 1943, SAC, New
York Field Office, sent a memorandum to the director: "In reference to
Bureau letter of January 20, 1943 (Bureau file 100-157464) requesting
the status of the above entitled matter, [Richard] Wright, Internal Security, Sedition this is to advise this case has been reassigned and placed
in line for immediate investigation."

The immediate investigation began in earnest. Agents were sent to
check out Wright's background. Party functionaries turned informers
were contacted; non-party-affiliated informers supplied the Bureau with
tidbits of gossip and erroneous information as well. "I was informed by
[name deleted]," said one informer, "that Wright is a member of the
Communist Party. This information was given to me today during a
conversation. . . . He is a University graduate. He attended North
Western University. . . ." When it was discovered that Wright had
once lived at Seven Middagh Street and later in Brooklyn's Columbia
Heights, agents invaded these old neighborhoods, questioning neighbors and associates, though this, reported one agent, "produced no information of value. . . ."[17] He was designated a "key figure in Communist activities" in the New York Field Division, "and his activities [were
to be followed]."

In relation to the Party, his activities were almost nonexistent. He avoided the party leadership, ignored the calls of Davis and Ford. When he encountered Max Yergan, shortly after the episode concerning the Office of War Information, he sought a fuller explanation. But Yergan would not contest Davis' account of the conversation. The Party was hoping for a rapprochement. When *Native Son* returned to the Broadway stage in the fall of 1942, the play ran up against a censorship movement by church groups and others, who argued that the play was immoral; though elements of the Party had attacked the play during its first run, the Party now came to its defense. Party officials from throughout the country continued to petition him for appearances, lectures. His inaccessibility was attributed to bouts of pique; he was still, they believed, one of them.

However, he began moving closer to non-Marxist progressives, black and white. He wrote introductions to books by two new writers: *No Day of Triumph*, by Saunders Redding, and *Black Metropolis*, by Horace Cayton and St. Clair Drake. He joined a special committee set up by the "Mayor of Harlem" following the riots of August 1, 1943, and helped to organize "The Citizens' Emergency Conference for Interracial Unity." He came to the defense of a white policeman charged with murdering "a Negro psychotic." He conceived the idea of a magazine "devoted to improving the understanding between Blacks and Whites," for which he sought financial backing from Marshall Field III, owner of the Chicago *Sun*, among others. He cultivated his relationships with the white progressives Dorothy Norman, of the New York *Post*, and Roger Pippett, book-review editor of *P.M. Magazine*. His interest in psychology and his awareness of the problems of youth led him to take an active role in the Wiltwyck School for juvenile delinquents and to aid Dr. Frederic Wertham in establishing a free psychiatric clinic in Harlem. On April 9, 1943, he appeared at Fisk, the largest black college in the Deep South.

The distinguished chairman of the Sociology Department, Charles S. Johnson, had invited Wright and Horace Cayton to the university that once counted Du Bois among its faculty. Wright decided to join Cayton in Chicago. From there the two would travel to Tennessee by train, as Wright was somewhat wary of air travel. After his first plane trip to Chicago, he confided to Jack Conroy that "he was swept by some sort of unreasoning terror." "Did you ever smell your blood?" he asked. ". . . Well I did. I smelt my own blood." He spent a week in Chicago going to parties, meeting people from the University of Chicago and members of the Institute for Psychoanalysis. When the two men boarded the train for Nashville, they were exhausted, and the first-class accommodations afforded them the opportunity to relax. The following morning, however, Wright insisted on going to the diner for breakfast, instead of eating in his compartment. ". . . I knew," Cayton wrote, "Dick would goad me into going to the diner; I knew he would persist, driven to a new experience in Jim Crow living which he knew would humiliate and infuriate him."[18]

The dangers of insult and humiliation were secondary. Wright's curiosity took precedence over his apprehension. Having traveled very little in the South, he wanted to know how blacks were segregated on the train. One way to find out was to use himself as a guinea pig. Over the protests of Cayton, the two men went into the diner. Cayton, who had worked as a waiter, knew something about the Jim Crow arrangements on trains. He explained them to Wright as the white steward seated white diners—late arrivals—ahead of them. The tables nearest the pantry, ". . . where the waiters set up their trays, call their orders, fill their water pitchers and coffee pots . . ." was the Jim Crow section. Finally Cayton and Wright were seated near the pantry. A curtain was strung around the table, almost shielding them from the sight of other diners. But what really startled him were the mannerisms of the black waiter. Wright compared the way he spoke to them with the way he spoke to the white steward: ". . . his voice went up two octaves and his testicles must have jumped two inches into his stomach," Wright told Cayton. His theory as to why the black man changed his voice when speaking to the white was that he emasculated himself, made himself "more feminine, less masculine, more acceptable to a white man."[19]

But how many black people were aware of this? How many suspected their personalities, voices, gestures, were affected by their proximity to whites and to the debilitating effects of racism? Because he felt that very few knew, he decided to tell the Fisk students, by way of his own experiences, the true-to-life story of a black man who had lived in the South: ". . . what I felt and thought about the world; what I remembered about my life, about being a Negro."

Thus, once on the rostrum before the largest crowd of blacks and whites he had ever addressed in the Deep South, he related something of his fears, hatreds, anxieties. He noticed that applause was scant; the audience was silent. Now and then "a hysterical, half repressed, tense kind of laughter" dented the silence. He felt somewhat embarrassed and uncomfortable, but angry also. No one, blacks or whites, wanted to hear about the race question, and certainly did not want to discuss it openly. "Everybody is expected in polite society to wrap the problem up in myth, legend, morality, folklore, niceties, and just plain lies. . . ."[20] "Goddam," one black educator told him, "you're the first man to tell the truth in this town." "You've brought the race problem to Nashville," a white man told him uneasily. The abundance of such comments convinced him that the problem everyone tried to avoid had

to be explored. Once before, he had thought of writing his autobiography. Now ". . . I resolved that night that I would stop writing my
novel and string my autobiographical notes, thoughts and memories together into a running narrative. I did. After much hesitation, I called
the book, 'Black Boy.' "21

He would become the scientist again, dissecting himself, placing his
ego under the microscope. He knew he was seen as a famous black
writer, among the most renowned and prestigious in America. Few
imagined that he harbored deep reservoirs of self-doubt, uncertainty,
and confusion. Fame and success had not isolated him from racism. On
the train ride back, he insisted on sitting through the night fully
clothed: "When I'm below the Mason-Dixon line," he told Cayton, "I
want more between me and white people than a curtain. I want iron
and steel." While the Party had afforded him protection, now, without
its cohesiveness, like the blacks in his audience, he was virtually alone,
forced to fall back upon his own resources. He hoped writing his autobiography would allow him to draw upon his past struggles under the
darkest of Mississippi's nights for strength to confront the future. It
was important, he noted, "to try to set down a simple, straight, honest,
clear record of how one black boy grew up in the South. . . ." To
speak of the things that went on within, he would discover, was more
difficult than "taking part in a revolution . . . writing like that is a kind
of war and revolution."

He had written autobiographical sketches before. But, except for the
unpublished essay "There are still men left," he had not dealt forthrightly with his Marxist experiences. He had not made the one-to-one
correlation between the authoritarianism of the fascist South and that
of the Communist Party. But was it communism itself, the ideology,
the ethical and political theory, that was authoritarian, or was it, instead, the men whom he had encountered? And women, too. There was
his memorable experience with Anna Zeltin (Anna Louise Strong).
"Dowager Empress" of the Party, a power in her own right, she was
Wright's superior and secretary to party boss Earl Browder. He arranged to meet her through party leaders, to seek her help. He wrote
later, "I told you of my difficulties with the American Communist
Party; I complained about the Party's lack of correct policy toward the
Negroes. . . . I asked your help against the Fords, the Davises, the
Berrys, the Browders, and the Winstons. . . ."22 In a desperate attempt
to retain his faith in Marxism, he sought her assurance that Davis' and
Ford's words were not paramount, that he did not have to confront the
party black leadership alone, that he could appeal to a higher tribunal.
Anna Strong was that higher tribunal. She could intercede with higher-
ups in the Party on his behalf. Had Ms. Strong intervened, he felt, the

shameful episode with the Office of War Information might never have occurred. She was silent. Abashed, he appealed frantically; he argued, he implored. "That's your affair," she finally said. "It does not concern me."[23]

He had smarted under the rebuff. But he had learned, too, filed valuable data in his mind for future reference. The ethics of communism were as grounded in authoritarianism as those of Jim Crow. Appeals to arbitrary decisions were useless. Codes of conduct were already prescribed, codified. They were carried out by insensitive men and women, enforced by party discipline, and handed down without consultation with those who were most affected by them, as were the rules and ethics formulated by the aristocracies of the South. An FBI informant told the Bureau on August 26, 1943, that "Wright and his wife are certain that the Party will uphold its promises and the future of the Negro is most promising. . . . They feel that in the main Communism offers at least hope." The informer did not mention that Wright's praise was for the spirit, the ideal, of Marxism, not the men who propagandized the ideal.

"When this book, *Black Boy*, is published," he wrote, "there'll be plenty of sticks in it for everybody, from Communists to fascists, to beat me over the head."

He was about to perform a gratuitous act, as much out of a sense of vengeance and recrimination as out of the compelling need to set down the experiences of his past. The harassment by the Communist leaders had ceased. They were unwilling at this time to engage in a public dispute with a man of Wright's reputation. Neither were they in any position to do so. All the leaders, including the blacks, were under intense surveillance by the Federal Bureau of Investigation, and as defections occurred daily, party enrollments reached a record low. For Wright, however, the ferocity of his counterattack would indicate the despair and anguish that the Party had caused him. The wounds ran deep; his disillusionment was severe. The steady axis upon which his world had once turned had been broken, twisted into unintelligible shapes. And the architect of his mental anguish was the Communist Party. *Black Boy* would be a way of evening up old scores. Around the middle of April, 1943, having returned from his lecture at Fisk, he set to work on the book that would make public his break with the Communist Party.

CHAPTER ELEVEN

On May 28, 1943, the SAC of the New York Field Office put his stamp of approval on document 100-41674. This was no reference report. From January 17 to April 7—the period of investigation—the Bureau had employed expert techniques in researching the life of subject Richard Wright. The character of his case was set out: "Custodial Detention-C Sedition." The only question of interest was whether or not sufficient evidence existed to establish his guilt and warrant his arrest. The agent responsible for the report had done an expert job. The errors in the "Reference report" of February 9 were corrected. There were ten copies of the agent's handiwork. Five would go to bureau headquarters, three would remain in New York. "G-2" and "ONI" would receive one each. Under "synopsis of facts," the agent was meticulous, relying upon informers and writings concerning the subject: "Richard Wright, popular Negro writer and former reporter on *Daily Worker*, according to an article . . . by Ralph Warner is a Communist. Other articles in the Worker indicate Wright's Communistic tendencies. He himself in so many words admits his affiliation. Wright formerly lived with a known Communist as man and wife and has been known to associate with members. However, he has not been seen at regular Communist meetings. Selective Service classification 3-A."[1]

As to the question of Wright's guilt or innocence concerning the charge of sedition, after careful scrutiny the agent concluded in the negative. "With reference to the reference report where certain sections of Wright's novel 'Twelve Million Black Voices' were set out as possibly falling within the violation of the sedition statute, a brief review of this book does not indicate that any other portion of the novel is of a seditious nature." What a review of his writings did demonstrate was that "he is at least a fellow traveler if not a member of the Communist

Party," and the agent detailed the "subject's" party activities from 1941 to 1942. Selective Service was contacted, and records of Wright's transactions there were revealed. An informer who presumably had voluntarily come forward was given official status: Confidential Informant [deletion] mentioned in the report of Special Agent [deletion] dated May 28, 1943 . . . is a [deletion] and is being made an informant in view of the fact that the Bureau has expressed a desire not to have them mentioned in reports." Still, there was no evidence that indicated sedition, and the SAC forwarded the report to Washington with the notation that "No further investigation is being conducted and this case is closed."[2]

The phrase "No further investigation" referred specifically and only to the sedition charge. Prospects of imprisoning Wright were quashed. But the prospects of proving that he was a dangerous Communist were very good. On August 29, an informer wrote the Bureau concerning a dinner engagement with Wright. During the course of the evening, the author mentioned a collection of "Russian books" that had been given to him by a friend. When the informer expressed interest in the collection, Wright offered to "let me keep them." "I received them today," the informant wrote the agency, "and certainly as a propaganda agency for Russia they are tremendous. . . . They are illustrated in colored photography and pungent in their message. . . ." Speaking of Wright's hospitality, the informer averred, "I was profuse in my thanks and said I hoped we would meet again. He was most complimentary about my 'intelligent insight into the Negro Problem' and would like to talk further with me. At the moment he is busy with another book about which he did not go into detail. Is all."[3]

The descriptions of the "Russian books" and the informer's intentions concerning them were relayed to bureau headquarters on September 14, 1943, by which time Wright was considered a "key figure," in the New York Office: "As the informant advises, the pamphlets, the Russian books written in English by various authorities, are extremely well executed and of a much higher quality than those put out by the Communist Party, U.S.A. The informant is attempting to secure the set of pamphlets from Richard Wright for her permanent possession and if she succeeds in so doing, they will be turned over to this office."[4] In the eventuality of a Communist takeover of the government, another informer turned dinner guest quoted Wright as stating that the Party would give blacks "the entire South or as much of it as were needed. . . . Blacks would then set up a State and determine for themselves, governmental, economic, and social problems." The informant also noted for the Bureau that Wright's wife "was said to be a rather attractive white woman." At bureau headquarters in Washington, agents contacted their informers in the Party hierarchy itself. "Washington, D.C., Communist Party functionary," stated an agent in a memorandum forwarded to the New York Office on June 9, 1944, "stated in private conversation that Richard Wright was a member of the Communist Party and one of the Party's staunchest members." Another functionary reported the repeated attempts of a local secretary of the Party to enlist Wright as a speaker in November of 1941. Reviewing its own files, the Washington Bureau discovered "that numerous references to this Richard Wright have been made in the *Daily Worker* over the course of years, and that information with regard to him has also been developed by the Special Committee on Un-American Activities, House of Representatives, Honorable Martin Dies, Chairman." There appeared to be enough evidence, the Washington Field Office concluded, to make the novelist a threat to the internal security of the United States. Headquarters informed the New York Field Office: "In view of the fact that Richard Wright is reported to reside in New York City and inasmuch as there is no further investigation to be conducted with regard to him in Washington, D.C., the New York City office is being designated office of origin herein and this case is being considered referred upon completion to that office."[5] The New York Field Office was now in business. Being designated OO (Office of Origin) meant that any communication concerning Richard Wright produced anywhere in the agency network would be forwarded to New York. The go-ahead had been given to launch an even more extensive investigation. For the New York agents, it was a matter of routine. Of all the field offices, their record of keeping tabs on the members of the Communist Party was perhaps the best in the country. Not only were the major Communists located in the area, but most of the "front groups" were also there. The CPUSA (Communist Party of the United States of America) had been designated by the Attorney General as a subversive organization. All of its members were considered threats to the internal security of the United States as defined in the Smith Act, of 1940. Ironically, the Act named for Congressman Howard W. Smith of Virginia was "Modeled after the New York Criminal Anarchy Act of 1902; it made it a crime for anyone to knowingly or willfully advocate, abet, advise or teach the duty, necessity, desirability or propriety of overthrowing or destroying any government in the United States by force or violence. . . ."[6] At the start of the Second World War, the Bureau was ordered by Roosevelt to vigorously investigate "political organizations and affiliations."

And how successful was the Bureau, given the weight of the Smith Act and the presidential mandate? "Into and through the War Years," Ungar quotes Don Whitehead, "the F.B.I. traced the twists and turns of the Communist Party and the fronts which changed their names as casually as a man changes a suit of clothes. . . ."[7] Riddled with informers, the Party "was a pushover for the F.B.I." And the New York Office was far and away the most successful. Agents from this office were present at a "secret meeting" held by the Party's top leaders in February 1944 "during which debate raged over whether to follow a policy of confrontation or collaboration with the established American political parties."[8] In addition to having their telephones tapped, known and suspected Communists had embarrassing information about their private lives leaked to the press. "But why Richard Wright?" asked a friend of Wright's in 1978. The obvious reason, which any agent in the New York Field Office would have given, was that he was a Communist. Anti-Communist sentiment among American citizens was rife even before the war; the Dies Committee, centering upon investigations of alleged Communists in the WPA and other New Deal agencies, exacerbated the sentiment. The Party itself, by its continual vacillations and shifts in policy, added to the American conception of Marxism as ruthless, unscrupulous, and cynical. The Hitler-Stalin Pact did nothing to assuage American feelings. Thus the Bureau, reflecting the director's own particular bias toward "subversives," investigated Communists with more zeal than it did members of right-wing organizations. "The philosophical Communist," Director Hoover declared in 1948, "might just as well be working as an agent of a foreign power because he is aiding its cause."[9] In addition to being a Communist, however, Wright was black as well. He thus symbolized what David Caute called "the convergence of two threats to the American Celebration: *le rouge et le noir*." "For many middle-of-the road white Americans, the issue of blood, of color, stood forth as a vital component of national identity; black tissue in the organism subverted the Celebration."[10] More than one agent involved with the case of Richard Wright believed that "he apparently overlooks the fact that his own rise to success refutes many of his own statements regarding the impossibility of the Negro's improving his personal position." Not only was he black and a Communist, he was also an ingrate. He was a famous writer who had succeeded as a result of the American system. His reported earnings for 1943 and 1944 were higher than the salaries of any of the agents investigating him. He had international acclaim, hobnobbed with the near-great and great of the society. He also had an "attractive white wife." With perhaps an overabundance of zeal and enthusiasm, the SAC, New York, approved the report of his agent, dated July 8, 1944, "Details" of which read: "Although it is noted that referenced report of [deletion] (referring to the report of May 28, 1943) was a Closing Report, in view of the fact that Subject is considered a key figure in

Communist activities in the New York Field Division this case was reopened and the activities of Subject have been followed."[11]

While agents in Washington and New York were gathering evidence to prove that he was a major Communist figure, Wright was making progress with his autobiography, which, among other things, would formalize his break with the Party. ". . . the real hard terror of writing like this," he wrote later, indicating that he was discovering new things about himself, "came when I found that writing of one's life was vastly different from speaking of it, for now I was rendering a close and emotionally connected account of my experiences."[12] He was his own archetype, using the past as a measuring rod of how far he had come from suffering, how high he had leaped over pain and anguish. "Richard Wright," said Baldwin, "was not Bigger Thomas; but he was Black Boy." But he was the black boy before and after, the confused child of Mississippi, Arkansas, and Tennessee, the witness to personal and manmade catastrophe. But he was also the mature man, the successful writer. The black man had left the black boy behind. Looking back, he could discover few black boys of courage, few, like himself, goaded to rebellion, few who were willing to resist to the bitter end. He was a singular child of his age, believing that few were as angered by injustice as himself, alone unable to compromise principle, alone unwilling to allow others to dictate the terms of his living and dying. As he continued to correct and correct his manuscript, feeling his way dangerously through the early years of his life, what had been designed in his mind at Fisk as a book that would demonstrate his oneness with blacks, that would add weight to his oft-repeated statement "I realize that I'm a very average Negro . . . ," became instead a book that portrayed him as singularly extraordinary.

But the problems concerning him were not those that plagued "average Negroes." The FBI, he knew, had questioned his neighbors at Seven Middagh Street. Undoubtedly there were informers, invisible men and women, whom he could not see, touch, ward off. He was still classified 3-A. Theoretically, he could still be inducted into the Army, which would mean leaving his wife and daughter. During these tumultuous months of recording his past, Julia had been a great comfort. She was growing; soon she would begin to explore, feel, and react to her environment. And then there was the Party. . . . There was no chance that they could do to him what they had done to Poindexter. He was beyond that. But the Party would have to respond to him, deal with him. He needed courage to deal with all of this, and he discovered it in his past.

On December 17, 1943, he forwarded the completed version of "American Hunger," the working title for *Black Boy*, to his agent, Paul

Reynolds. The book covered his life from his earliest remembrances up to his departure from Chicago in 1937. "I don't think that there is much that I will ever be able to do on this script," he wrote in an accompanying letter; ". . . on the whole, the thing will have to stand as it is, for better or worse."[13] Ed Aswell, his editor at Harper & Row, was enthusiastic about the book and wanted to publish it by the end of 1944. Wright rejected Aswell's suggestion that it be subtitled "The Biography of a Courageous Negro" and later decided that ". . . *Black Boy* seems to me to be not only a title, but also a kind of heading of the whole general theme." But Aswell also suggested that the book be published in two parts, one volume to cover Wright's experiences in the South, the other those in the North. Coherence could be achieved, Aswell believed, by dividing the book in this way. The editor suggested that Volume Two end with Wright's years in New York, and Wright accepted Aswell's suggestions without question; emotionally he could not now deal with his New York experiences. But, more important, he had over the years built up a profound and lasting respect for this southern white man of courteous, gentle manners and intellectual depth. This was not so on the first day he had sat in the editor's office. He was invited to meet Aswell, he later recalled, after the editor noticed his article "The Ethics of Living Jim Crow." It seemed to Wright that black Southerner faced white Southerner; traditional enemy before traditional enemy. Wright sat tense, waiting to hear his comments about southern life attacked. The editor, however, smiled, looked him in the eyes, told him that no one had written so truthfully about the South before.

The praise coming from this "traditional enemy" stunned him. A southern white man was praising something that he had written, something unflattering about the South, as if there was something that he had done wrong. But this was no trick, no condescension. Aswell respected him as a writer, as a man. His own southern experiences corroborated the writer's. He wanted to be his editor and to publish him at Harper & Row. The bond of trust was formed on that day of suspicion and surprise. Aswell, who was one of the most respected editors in the business, had offered him a contract for *Uncle Tom's Children* and in turn had secured one of the most promising young authors in America.[14]

The book was accepted by the Book-of-the-Month Club, and this meant that publication would have to be postponed until 1945.[15] In the meantime, he set about trying to find a magazine to publish the last third of the book.

Earlier, he had written to Reynolds somewhat apologetically concerning his difficulty with completing a new novel, "The truth is that I've had trouble getting my writing to jell right. And of course, that is something that a writer has to fight out with himself and settle and solve."[16] He tried to solve it by going back to the novel he had interrupted to write his autobiography. The book, tentatively entitled *Black Hope*, evolved around some black "servants" who lived in a house considered the showplace of "a neighborhood in Brooklyn Heights." Only the servants—maids and chauffeurs—were ever seen. The black servant would arise each morning, "get into a shiny car and drive off—alone." Eventually the mystery was discovered. The house belonged to blacks who were the sole occupants; out of fear of harassment by neighbors who would not want blacks living among them, the owners, a black family, "pretended to be servants" in their own home.[17] By the time he returned to the manuscript, he had "given up the original idea, but used the same material to elaborate the same theme. . . ."[18]

Black Hope would also be relegated to the list of unfinished manuscripts. His personal life was again intruding upon his attempts to write fiction. On January 31, he appeared again at the Draft Board, in a state of ambivalence. The Army, he believed, would reject him because of his Communist affiliation. On the other hand, they might accept him in spite of it. And the things that caused him the most anxiety were those about which he knew nothing. They accounted for his sense of "dread," which was so much a part of him that it also pervaded the personality structure of each of his characters. On January 31, he received notice of reclassification: Rejection; the reason, "psychoneurosis, severe psychiatric rejection; [he was] referred to Local Board for further psychiatric and social investigation [deletion]." The sessions with the local board confirmed the original findings and added an explanation for what the government defined as his mental state: "It appeared," an agent later recorded, "from subject's contacts with his local board that his interest in the problem of the Negro has become almost an obsession. . . ."[19] He was exempted from military service. . . .

His difficulty in coming to grips with fiction did not limit his creativity in other areas. He was interested in films, and as early as January 1942, he tried to secure a job making films with The National Film Board of Canada. His ambition was to make a film on the underground railroad. The venture was unsuccessful, but his interest continued. In 1944, he wrote a script, "Melody Limited," based upon the adventures of the Fisk Jubilee Singers, a group of freed slaves who, during Reconstruction, "tour America and Europe to earn money to save and expand their school. . . ." "The aim of the story," he wrote in the opening paragraph, "is to depict the romantic and adventurous manner in which the first Negro educational institutions were built and the role that religion and Negro folk songs played in their building."[20]

He intended it to show the contributions to Negro education by both southern and northern whites. Blacks would also be portrayed, for the first time, as a race of men and women who struggled against great odds to cement understanding between the races. "Melody Limited" was rejected by Columbia Films and The National Film Board of Canada. *The Atlantic Monthly,* however, accepted "I Tried to Be a Communist" for publication, scheduling the article for two installments, in August and September of 1944. And though his break with the Party was now irrevocable, he attended a party held at the Commodore Hotel in June in honor of Theodore Dreiser. Dreiser, like Wright, was a former vice-president of the American Peace Mobilization Committee, a left-wing group established by the Party to keep America out of the war. Dorothy Dudley, Hubert Davies, Isidore Schneider, Edwin Seaver, and George Seldes were guests, and Wright moved among them, engaging in light banter. He took no part in the discussion between Robert Elias and Dreiser, however, concerning the recent shift by the Communist Party. In May of 1944, the Party had transformed itself into a new structure: "The Communist Political Association," and though few were aware of it at the time, the shift would prove devastating to the Party in the coming years. Dreiser, however, welcomed the shift, noting that "it was high time that the Communists worked along American lines as he had urged them to do in the thirties."[21] Wright, on the other hand, realized that little real change had taken place. Communist Political Association and Communist Party USA meant the same thing. The change in name did not mean a change in personnel. The same antiquated men and ideas would dominate the new organization. Nevertheless, the Party's maneuverings were no longer concerns of his, and, his desk fairly clear of work, he began planning a vacation to Canada with his wife in August. Before embarking upon his trip, however, he decided to meet with a "representative from The New York Herald Tribune" in order to set the stage for the dramatic revelations in *The Atlantic Monthly* in August and September.

The FBI, however, was readying a drama of its own concerning his defection from the Party. From May 24 to July 3, 1944, the New York Field Office added evidence to substantiate its case that Wright was a dangerous Communist. The report, approved by Special Agent Conroy on July 8, was conclusive. There were no further grounds for speculation. The "synopsis of facts" was detailed, explicit: "Subject presently resides 89 Lefferts Place, Brooklyn, N.Y. Registered with SS LDB #178; classified 4F, 1/31/44. Subject's agent is Paul R. Reynolds. . . . Subject was sponsor of Councilman Benjamin J. Davis, Jr., C.P. candidate for NYC Council. [Deletion] on subject reflects publicity contacts and other correspondence indicating possible Communist connections as well as fact that Subject receives publications such as 'New Masses,' 'In Fact' and publications from Moscow."[22] The reports of informers were accepted as fact, their testimony used to substantiate the synopsis. Agents also had been extremely busy: the questioning of Wright's neighbors continued. Selective Service records were examined and analyzed and commented upon. The agents discovered that Reynolds was his agent, that, in September of 1943, questions concerning his income had arisen. ". . . Subject had reported that from August of 1942 to August of 1943, he had earned about 6,000. However, on September 10, 1943, he revised his statement and stated that after consulting his Agent, his earnings had been found to be 1907.12."

Based upon research of publications and "according to information from informants," Wright, the New York Office discovered, was "continuing his activities as a writer." He wrote skits and stories in addition to his "better known books," wrote the agent, most of which "concern the Negro." The subject received a great deal of publicity and the report cited as one example "the rather lengthy review of his life appearing in the volume, 'Current Biography. . . .'" The agent summarized the biographical sketch: ". . . beginning with Wright's birth, September 1908, on a plantation 25 miles from Natchez, Mississippi. . . ." The summary abruptly ends one page later, concluding with his return from Mexico in 1940. Three pages of deletions occur in the report at this point. The concluding pages contain notation of "Undeveloped Leads," the avowal "Will follow and report activities of the Subject," and the citing of yet another informer: "In the report of Special Agent [deletion] dated July 8, 1944 at New York, N.Y. The confidential informant is as follows: [deletion]. . . . A temporary symbol is used to further conceal the identity of this informant [deletion]." What, then, was the nature of the deleted material? In the nine-page report, none of the information seemed conclusive enough to warrant the extreme action that the Bureau was about to take. With the exception of the information concerning the Russian publications, Wright's interest in black problems, and his sponsorship of Davis' campaign, all supplied presumably by a new cadre of informers, the updating of information concerning his altercations with the draft board and the question of his status regarding his earnings, nothing is contained in the released file that was not available on May 28, 1943. Yet on June 28, 1944, twenty-five days after the conclusion of the period in which the report was made, the SAC, New York Field Office, forwarded a one-page request to "Director, F.B.I. pertaining to Richard Wright, Internal Security-C. . . ." "It is recommended that a security Index Card be prepared relative to the individual named below. . . ." Under headings marked Native Born and Communist, an X was marked in both places for subject Richard Wright.

The Security Index, "which at its peak had about 15,000 names," was one of the Bureau's more formidable weapons. It was a special list of potential subversives, including "wartime saboteurs" and "persons who might be a threat to the President." Each file card listed background information on the subject, his nationality, file numbers, and organizational affiliation. In addition to the Security Index, the Bureau kept a Reserve Index; included on this list were those who were considered less dangerous and who, during times of emergency, would "be intensively investigated . . . but not detained."[23]

Wright, concluded the SAC, was among the more dangerous. No Reserve Index card. He wanted the power to make an arrest without due process. For this, the Security Index card was necessary. "Once a person was listed in the Security Index, the Bureau would prepare a standby warrant for his or her arrest, to be executed in time of emergency." Headquarters usually worked fast on requests like this. The authorization should be forthcoming by the middle of July, no later than the end of August.

Montreal was supposed to be beautiful in August. The sprawling parks were a symphony of colors, trees and flowers baptized in crimson, gold, and brown. Wright sat contemplative, reflective. A few more days and it would be August; and in a week, maybe two, he would be in Canada. *The Atlantic Monthly* articles would appear while he was away; he hoped he would not be around when the bomb exploded.

He told the reporter that he would not go into specifics. The articles would speak for themselves, more or less. But it was true that he had broken with the Party, that his membership had begun in 1932, and that from May of 1937 until August of the same year, he had been "on the outs with the Party," the final break with which would occur in 1940. During his Chicago days, he had difficulty presenting his own ideas. He discovered that many Communists were "narrow-minded, bigoted, intolerant and frightened of new ideas which don't fit their own."[24] In relation to the Negro problem, there had been a "lamentable regression" over the years. "Publicly," he said, "Communists will deny that there is any substantial change in their militancy, but privately they offer any handy excuse. The militancy of the Negro Question has passed into the hands of Right Wing Negroes. That was not true eight years ago. Most of the battles then were led by Communists.

"I had my way of expressing my conception of Negro experience in writing," he continued; "I thought it would be of value to them. They had their ideas of how I should react as a Communist. There was an irreconcilable gap between our attitudes.

"I do not regard the Communists today as effective instruments for social change." He paused again as the reporter wrote down his last words, which were out now, and beyond recall. His break was now official. In the last speech before his death, he would say that he had taken the Communists as they presented themselves. Later, he had had conflicts with them as severe as those he had had with "the Negro subsidized leaders or . . . the white philanthropic institutions. . . ." Going public was a declaration of war. But the responsibility for that war was theirs. The wounds they had inflicted upon him, the scars that even now would never heal, were far more severe than anything that he might say in retaliation. They had destroyed that most important part of any human being: his dreams. "The Communists," he concluded the interview, "have a terrible lot to learn about people. . . . They are the victims of the very society they seek to change. This too often finds expression in intolerance and narrowness." On July 28, 1944, the New York *Herald Tribune* devoted a "lengthy article" to Richard Wright under the headline "Negro Author Criticizes Reds as Intolerant." On the same day, the New York *Journal-American* headlined its own story "Reds All Wrong, Wright Quits 'Em." The *Journal-American* avowed that Wright until recently "was one of the high priests of the Communist Party." He had defended "Red ideology" as the only possible philosophy for blacks. Now, said the article, he "is hurling epithets at his former Communist Comrades."

At 2:10 P.M. on the same day, the ring of the telephone crushed the silence in the office of Ben Davis. It was Martin Y——. Before turning to Wright, the two men discussed "Union and Party matters." Eventually, the subject of the "Tribune article" was brought up. ". . . we must get the article," Martin advised, "and we must, so to speak, open up a polemic with the guy . . . you know, on its merits. I don't know what's troubling him. . . ."[25] He had not known that Wright would go so far as to make a public declaration. But, having read only the *Tribune* interview, he was as much in the dark about details as was Davis. The viciousness of Wright's attack was due, he thought, to the Party's support of Roosevelt. "I think that's the underlying reason about this charge against us—not being radical."

Davis was uncertain even as to whether or not the Party should respond. But those damned reporters would be calling. "What," he asked the other man, "is your opinion on that—as to what should be said, if anything?" "I think," Martin advised, "we should say that we didn't see the story." It was true. Neither knew all of the facts. "I don't think we should, so to speak, attack him bluntly, off-hand . . . ," he offered.

The councilman still had reservations. After seeing the story, then what? Were the Party to answer his charges, would this not add fuel to the fire? That, Martin told him, would depend upon the content of the article. "In the Tribune today," he added, "it's very nasty." The content would dictate the strategy of counterattack. If his attack was based on the Party's policy toward Roosevelt, "which by the way we should imply even if he doesn't say so, because what could his charges be if we are not radical," he told Davis. But if he accused "us of not fighting for the Negro's interests inasmuch as our position is in relation to Roosevelt, that the Negro should support Roosevelt and everything connected with it . . . it's on this premise that we can polemicize with him."

Davis wanted to avoid a direct confrontation. ". . . well I tell you how I regard him, and that's without seeing the article. I regard him as just another casualty of the movement of the people for freedom today. . . . I regard him as a casualty of the struggle for Negro rights. That's the only way I see it, because I think that we might have a statement but to enter into a polemic with this guy is simply going to prolong that period during which they are going to try and exploit everything he can say about the Communists. . . . But anyway—we'll read it first."26 The other man agreed. They would have to read the article soon, and have "an exchange of opinion" with other leaders. "Yeah," Davis agreed, "maybe we'll get some of our people together on it." He said good-by, and hung up the phone.

At 4:05 P.M., Alexander Trachtenberg, head of International Publishers, picked up the telephone. The call was from M—— at the offices of New Masses. There was a desperate, urgent tone in her voice. She told him that she was "tracking down this Richard Wright stuff for Sam to do a piece on it next week . . . ,"27 mistakenly thinking that Trachtenberg had published the article "How Bigger Was Born." M—— explained her urgency in tracking down the article: ". . . he denounces the Party and etc. He has two pieces coming out in the Atlantic Monthly." Trachtenberg sprang to attention. So that was the cause of the urgency. And that was the reason, he surmised, that the Book-of-the-Month Club "had chosen his new book."

"He has two pieces coming out—'I Tried to Be a Communist,'" the caller to the FBI went on. She quoted from the Tribune article, used Wright's words: "intolerance, narrowness, bigoted, intolerant of new ideas. . . . And so we're going to do a piece on this man for next week," she told Trachtenberg, "and that's why I was trying— I just talked to Sam, and he's up in the country and I'm going up there tomorrow, and I was trying to gather this stuff together for him. . . ."

What he had published, Trachtenberg recalled, was "Bright and

Morning Star." There was a preface to that and something about funds from the sales going into the "Browder Defense Fund." The caller thought that would be useful. She wanted all the ammunition she could get. This was a major campaign. It was a small-scale war. She asked the publisher to send the material by first-class mail, special delivery. She needed it right away. She was catching the train first thing in the morning. By next weekend there would be a carefully written, detailed statement ready for the media.

On the same date, time indeterminate, a three-page memorandum marked urgent was sent via teletype from the New York Field Office of the FBI to Headquarters, in Washington, indicating that Wright, in an article "in today's New York *Herald Tribune*," had criticized the Communist Party. He discussed his past affiliations from 1932 to 1940 and the difficulties he encountered trying to "present his own ideas to the Party." The "remarks were prompted by questions growing out of an article" scheduled for release in *The Atlantic Monthly* for August and September. The memo is sprinkled with quotations from the *Tribune* interview, including the writer's derogatory remarks about the Party, his assessment of its value to the struggle of "the American Negro," the narrow-mindedness and bigotry of party leaders. The break appeared substantial, real. The tone of the interview was that of a disillusioned, bitter man. But the Special Agent in Charge had not, however, seen the original article. His judgment, like that of the Communists, was formed on the basis of the newspaper interview. But what if the article substantiated the interview? What if the writer was as bitter as suspected? The Security Index card was still pending. There had been no answer from Washington concerning that. Perhaps now it may not be necessary. If Wright was no longer a Communist, perhaps he might become an informer. "At the present time," the SAC told Headquarters, "the NY Office has under consideration the advisability of interviewing Mr. Wright."[28]

Headquarters was receptive to this idea, though it advised the field office to proceed with caution. On August 4, a memorandum was forwarded to New York giving tacit approval to the sentiments expressed "concerning the reported disaffiliation on the part of the subject with the Communist Political Association." Washington advised the New York Office to attempt to obtain "specific information concerning exploitation of the Negro race by the Communist Political Association." If such an interview took place, the agents should make a previous study of the writer's articles and particularly pertinent comments "regarding the Communists." But, warned Headquarters, the interview must "be most discreet." This was extremely necessary in view of the fact that Wright "lamented" the Party's "regression" on the Negro question. "From a review of the teletype you submitted in this regard," the memorandum concluded, "it would seem that Wright does not think the Communist Political Association revolutionary enough at the present time with respect to the advancement of the Negro. This should be considered seriously prior to any action on your part."[29]

CHAPTER TWELVE

The first installment of "I Tried to Be a Communist" appeared in *The Atlantic Monthly* at the beginning of August. Wright was in Canada on his first vacation trip since 1940, which would be both a vacation and, he admitted to a friend, a search for "a place to live."[1] Montreal, Ottawa, and the Gatineau country of Quebec were on the itinerary. Was the search for a home away from the United States caused by a premonition of the furor that awaited him on his return? In times of extreme crisis, facing what he considered unbearable pressure, he became a wanderer. The serene ambiance of Canada, snow-capped mountains, lush fields of dewy grass, "peaceful area[s] where the animals came to eat on the threshold of his house and where it was agreeable to do nothing,"[2] must have seemed particularly inviting. The chaos and the turmoil were miles away! But he found no place he'd consider settling in.

Meanwhile, readers as varied as FBI agents and Communist leaders found in *The Atlantic Monthly* a critique not so much of communism as of Communists. He was not opposed to their objectives, but to their means, to their cynicism, and most of all to their authoritarianism. When he wrote, "I will be for them, even if they are not for me," he was pledging his continuing faith not to men but to an ideal. In clinging to this elementary faith, he was a special kind of defector. He did not castigate the Soviet Union. Nor did he, as others were soon to do in the "subversive trials" of the late forties and fifties, denounce the concept as an evil plot against God and man. Against the Communists, though, he enumerated the following crimes: the abrupt termination of the John Reed Clubs, eliminating opportunities for a number of young, untested writers; the animosity directed toward him by his Chicago cell; the bigotry of comrades who could not secure him living accommodations; the forced interruptions of his writing to do organization work for the Party; the successful attempt to mobilize black actors against him on the WPA Federal Theatre Project, which resulted in his transfer; the spectacle of the trial of Poindexter; his forceful, physical ejection from the Communist ranks during a May Day parade.

Wright's chronology of events is confusing. The articles, like the book *American Hunger*, the final third of the autobiography from which "I Tried to Be a Communist" was taken, published in 1977, seem to coalesce episodes from his Chicago and New York experiences. He places the confrontation with Anna Zeltin [Anna Louise Strong] during the Chicago period, but, later, he reveals in an open letter to the one-time Communist Zarina that the altercation between them took place in New York. His personal animosity toward the leaders notwithstanding, he took great pains to hide their identities behind pseudonyms. Descriptions of Ed Green, Buddy Nealson, and Ross, among others, correspond to descriptions of John P. Davis, Harry Haywood, and David Poindexter, respectively. The Communists from his New York period seem absent from these sketches. Benjamin Davis, Max Yergan, William Patterson, Alexander Trachtenberg, and James Ford are nowhere to be found among the list of characters.

On August 25, the New York *Age*, a black tabloid, said about *The Atlantic Monthly* articles that "it would be interesting to note the answer of the Communists to this harsh criticism by so prominent a former member." By August 28, Danton Walker noted in the New York *Daily News* that "Richard Wright, author of 'Native Son,' has started an uproar." The Party was on the defensive, and Davis' reluctance to "polemicize" with Wright must have been overruled. The Party entered the fray, firing off some of its biggest guns.

Davis led the attack. Having once criticized *Native Son*, the skilled Marxist rhetorician began his article "A Few Words on Richard Wright and New Ideas," for the *Daily Worker*, by praising the writer and citing *Native Son* as evidence of his promise. Wright's "outlook," perceptions, vision, those intangibles that helped to produce his masterpiece, resulted from his membership in the Party. Now, because he was personally peeved and perhaps in "conspiracy" with the Party's enemies, the writer resorted to "public and wholly unjustifiable attacks" upon those responsible for his success. Not only this, but in an attempt to impress the "superleftists," Wright fabricated his story. Davis argued that if Wright left the Party in 1940, as he claimed, why did he wait until 1944 to make his departure public? The writer was an ingrate, a renegade, who had joined the ranks of such "Red baiters" as Norman Thomas. The real reason for his defection was clear. Roosevelt faced a difficult reelection campaign, and the fate of black Americans hung upon his reelection. Thus, "I Tried to Be a Communist" appeared to be a fabricated political document designed to aid those who condemned the President as "soft on Communism." In aligning Wright with those who opposed Roosevelt—a popular President with black Americans—Davis depicted his adversary as a traitor not only to the Party but to the cause of civil rights.

As befitting his position as vice-president of the Communist Political Association, Davis had taken the high road. But party functionary and lower-echelon Communist Robert Minor traveled the gutter in his attack in the *Daily Worker*. Not only did he accuse the writer of opportunism, but naïveté as well: "He sat in meetings for years," wrote Minor, "and did not discover that the only thing required is that you be loyal to the people's cause."[3] It was the people's cause that Wright was betraying, not the Party's. In doing so, he tried to "accentuate racial divisions" by obvious "anti-semitism," by repeated references in his article to "'a Jewish chap,'" "'a Jewish boy,'" "'his Jewish wife.'" Minor concluded that the movement could do without such individuals and most assuredly the movement could do without Richard Wright.[4]

Agents of the FBI monitored the controversy with cool detachment. The New York Field Office forwarded a blow-by-blow account and analysis to Washington Headquarters in a report made on September 5. The writer was still designated a "key figure," and the character of his case remained "Internal Security-C." Approval for the Security Index card had not yet been granted, but the writer, nevertheless, had been kept under close scrutiny. New informants had been uncovered. The field office had clarified his status as an ex-Communist. *The Atlantic Monthly* articles were carefully read and analyzed. Excerpts were quoted liberally, and a Xeroxed copy of Part Two was included for the benefit of Washington. In the customary "synopsis of facts," Agent [name deleted] observed: ". . . Final results of 30 day [deletion] set forth reflecting general correspondence of Subject. Subject author of two articles appearing in *The Atlantic Monthly* for August and September. . . . Theme of articles seems to conclude with thought that subject broke with Party because his friends in the Party, including those of his own race, were unable to recognize him as their friend. Articles do not appear to attack Communist Party as a revolutionary club, but because of failure of individuals in Party to properly recognize and deal with problems in society. Articles received wide-spread newspaper publication. Reports of informants and publicity indicate prominent Party members concerned over Wright's articles."

The report dealt with the genesis of the articles, beginning with Wright's interview in the New York *Herald Tribune*. The *Journal-American* column is also reported, along with commentary published in the Pittsburgh *Courier*. Rebuttals by Davis and Minor are summarized. The recordings of the conversations between Davis and Martin and between Trachtenberg and the woman M——, made on July 28, are printed in their entirety. "I Tried to Be a Communist" is lengthily reviewed and commented upon. Quotations concerning the writer's participation in the dissolution of the John Reed Clubs, his problems with his local unit, and his assessment of the Ross trial drew special attention. They quoted from Wright's discussion that the Communists had been blinded, their lives "truncated and impoverished by the oppression they had suffered" at the hands of the Americans. Their consciousness had been so corrupted by "American life" that they counted him among their enemies. The agent noted that this "is believed significant in indicating that Wright disapproves whole heartedly of the American way of life and living even though he has publicly at this time announced a breach with the Communist Party organization."[5]

The report concluded: "In view of the fact that the publicity and the information furnished by informants indicated Wright's break with the Communist Party was an actual fact, it was felt that a discreet and careful interview with Wright might be productive." This would have to wait, the agent wrote, until the writer returned from his vacation, around "September 15, 1944."[6]

On his return from Canada, in the middle of September, Wright stayed relatively clear of the controversy he had initiated. Canada had been refreshing. He had brought back impressions that would last, that would eventually find their way into various essays. He was most impressed with the people of French Quebec, a people "at one with their culture." Their personalities were formed by this kinship between themselves and their natural heritage. They were a serene people, "even tempered; no one strove too hard for a personal or an individualistic vision of life. No one sought a separate or unique identity . . . the individual and his group are one." How different this was from America! Yet he realized that the people of Quebec were "romantics"; the peaceful, serene life belonged to the age of feudalism. Such melancholy musings probably caused him to focus more attention upon the chaos in his own life. He had not completely examined the words he had written in "I Tried to Be a Communist": ". . . I knew in my heart that I would never be able to write that way again, would never be able to feel with that simple sharpness about life, would never again express such passionate hope, would never again make so total a commitment of faith."[7] The doubts concerning his talent were reflected often in his journal during 1945. At the beginning of the new year, he secretly charged himself with the necessity of creating a "new language" to depict his vision of the world, to emphasize what he and he alone felt.

"Black Hope" was therefore laid aside for a new project, "The Jackal." His work with juvenile delinquents led him to conceive of a story in which a youth gang kidnaps a woman. After the crime, the boys become impressed with the enormity of their act. They are caught in a nerve-wracking dilemma, the options of which are equally dreadful: to let the woman go or to keep her. Both would result in eventual imprisonment. "In this way," writes Fabre, "Wright planned to study the pathological behavior resulting from fear and anger."[8] "The Jackal," too, would join the list of uncompleted manuscripts. He was able, however, to complete an exchange of letters with Antonio Frasconi. Short, some six pages in length, Wright's letter is among the more important works of his career. Whatever his difficulties with fiction, the letter to the Uruguayan painter and woodcutter shows the mature writer at his rational best, using prose as a successful vehicle for responding at last to his critics. Frasconi, a progressive, long-time sympathizer with the Negro, was determined to confront, in a book of woodcuts, the black situation as it existed, in order to point up the extremes of American racism as reflected in the riots of 1943; even though it was widely felt that now "more than ever it is necessary to maintain the unity forced by the anti-fascist war."

Wright's published reply to Frasconi offered advice that was logical and well thought out. Beside the rash, shrill, often vitriolic utterances by such Marxists as Davis and Minor, Wright seems almost restrained by contrast. He begins by stating sympathy with the Uruguayan's dilemma, and moves immediately to raise the issue to the level of morality. The Party was accusing him of immorality, of being hypocritical. But, he asked, "Are we not confronted here with the attitude of 'moral slackers,' 'moral dodgers,' who wanting to conquer the fascist enemy do not want to rid their lives of the fascist like practices of which they have grown so profitably fond?" Are not the true immoralists those who in times of political expediency refuse to speak out against a segregated United States Army, a segregated Red Cross, a segregated American way of life—were these not the true immoralists? The greatest crime of all was to keep silent, not to seize the opportunistic moment and to condemn the condemned still further. Paint, draw, engrave, he admonished Frasconi, ". . . let all facts that impinge upon your sensibilities be your subject matter, and let your heart strike the hour as to when you should give what you have to others."[9]

The morally committed writer, he was saying to the artist, and to his former comrades now hostile adversaries, must not, cannot listen to the chiming of a clock wound and set by others. He must instead move according to his own inner clock. Boldly, he positioned himself to the left of the Party, proposing that the freedom of the artist is outside of authoritarian order and law. But he was implying also that it was he, not the men of the Party, who believed in the moral intentions of humankind. He may have been able to crystallize the themes of man's alienation and status as an outsider in his exchange with the Uruguayan artist because earlier he had written of such ideas in "The Man Who Lived Underground." Written in 1941, the story centers upon Fred Daniels, inhabitant of a surrealistic world whose perimeters are bounded by guilt and fear. Picked up by the police, accused of murder, beaten and tortured, he manages to escape from custody and disappears down a manhole. It is metaphorically an escape into his unconscious, and from the vantage point below ground he gains perspective upon two worlds. The underground, like the psyche, is a place of irrationality and chaos; structure and order are missing here, occurrences are frequent, sudden. The world above ground, however, was authoritarian, proscriptive, imposing its own patterns, warring against irrationality, against impulse, against spontaneity. For Daniels, though confusing and exacting, the world below ground is more attractive. Here in this subterranean passage of his unconscious, there were no absolutes and no codes based upon original sin. There was guilt, to be sure, but it was a universal guilt imposed, irrespective of race or color, upon all. "Yes, if the world as man has made it was right, then anything else was right, any act a man took to satisfy himself, murder, theft, torture."

While the themes of the exchange with Frasconi, therefore, were of courage and determination, those of his journal entry for January 20–21, 1945, in which he reminisced, were much like those about the future work, of "The Man Who Lived Underground," despondent, despairing, pessimistic: "When the war is over and if I'm lucky I want to leave the hatreds of race and the pressures of the United States behind and go and live in a foreign land where the currency is cheap and give myself up to this great work. . . . The book will really be an expression of my own spiritual hunger. I had once thought that Communism was an instrument for that, but now I don't know. They beat you down too much with dictatorial methods of work and feeling and thought. . . . Oh, God, how lonely I am with this burden of consciousness."[10]

He was more concerned at the moment, however, about *Black Boy*, scheduled to be released in March, than about a future work. He knew that he would be attacked, that his critics could not understand the motives that had prompted him to write such a book. Nevertheless, he had written a book true for the most part to his own experiences and, he believed, to the experiences of black boys everywhere. He was especially concerned with expected attacks from black critics, perhaps understanding quite well that they would view many of his comments as stemming from self-hatred. And though, in his journal, he had admitted to feeling a sense of self-hatred, he would deny that such feelings influenced his book.

He would rather believe that blacks remained imprisoned in emotional ghettoes and were not free enough to face their experience in all of its nakedness. Few were capable of seeing themselves, as he did, in the quote from Vachel Lindsay's poem *The Leaden Eyed* "Not that they starve, but starve so dreamlessly / Not that they sow, but that they seldom reap, / Not that they serve, but have no gods to serve, / Not that they die, but that they die like sheep."[11] From the perspective of his own ordeal and his Marxist training, he saw black people as people in constant torment and agony, and few black critics were willing to accept this view of black life. True to his expectations, therefore, they attacked the book, and even his old friend Ralph Ellison, explaining his reasons for writing a somewhat critical review, stated: "It was an attempt to get Dick to see certain things. . . . In *Black Boy* he cut his ties with Negroes."[12] The long-held doubts, confusions, and ambivalences about blacks, partly covered by the blanket of Communist ideology, were revealed in the autobiography in stark, open nakedness.

Few of his critics grasped this point more quickly, nor, perhaps, with more relish, than Benjamin Davis. Almost one year before, the Party had been thrown on the defensive as a result of Wright's assault in *The Atlantic Monthly*. For the astute, crafty Communist, things had looked bleak indeed. A politically knowledgeable adversary in Wright's situation would have bombarded the press with statement after statement, kept up the attack, forced the Communists into divisive political battle. But Wright had done none of this. He had dropped his bomb and more or less retreated from the battlefield. The Party had had time to regroup, counterattack; now, on the offensive, Davis immediately reviewed *Black Boy* upon its appearance, calling it "a furious and terrifying story of the impact of the Jim Crow system upon human beings in the deep South."

As was expected, Davis opened with praise for the intention and the theme of the work. Yet, here and there, thrust and counterthrust were directed at the author—at the book's exaggerations and at its "intensely subjective tone." "*Black Boy* says some wholly unacceptable things about the Negro's capacity for genuine emotion," wrote Davis. The fault is that of the writer, whose own ego is too intensely involved. He is limited by his subjectivity and thus unable to view black people outside the boundaries of his own emotional needs. "Some circles" have elevated this man to a position of spokesman for blacks, and yet his thinking and perceptions are fuzzy, confusing. In the interests of those he presumes to speak for, he has the obligation to overcome "this limitation of subjectivity imposed upon him in order that he may see clearly, and participate with the forces which would destroy the myth of white supremacy. . . ." The writer, concludes Davis, "wields a brilliant and stormy pen . . ."; few are his equals. Yet there are brilliant writers on both sides of the racial struggle, and the reflective artist and the artist who points out the inequities must be one and the same. Inequities exist in the real world, outside one's own subjectivity; black life has negative as well as positive aspects, and Wright is unable to see the positive because he is alienated from the people, particularly from progressive forces seeking to improve their lot. While not responsible for the conditions of black boys, he is, Davis contended, "responsible for his own . . . act of withdrawal from the forces" paramount in the fight for a better world. "He can blame himself."[13]

Davis' charge of subjective parochialism and narrow-mindedness was echoed by black and white critics alike. Speaking for the liberal community, Orville Prescott, in the New York *Times*, took notice that the book was obviously "not the work of an objective artist or an open mind." For Prescott, "It could not have been. The neurosis, the overemphasis, the lack of balance, and the emotion recollected in turmoil are the bitter fruit of an old injustice."

Prescott also voiced the objections of such intellectually astute black leaders as Du Bois, noting that "Part of the raw shock of 'Black Boy' is caused by Mr. Wright's excessive determination to omit nothing, to emphasize mere filth." As for the writer's isolation from blacks and whites, Prescott wrote that "other Negroes resented their lot but did not feel at all so acutely as he did." However, he concluded, the book was "powerful, moving and horrifying."[14]

Condemnation of the book was strident and intense. Speaking for a score of right-wing reviewers, Senator Bilbo, of Mississippi, took to the floor of the United States Senate on June 7 to call *Black Boy* ". . . the dirtiest, filthiest, lousiest, most obscene piece of writing that I have ever seen in print . . . it is so filthy and dirty." But, he concluded, "it comes from a Negro, and you cannot expect any better from a person of his type."[15] No less rabid, excessive, and abusive were the avalanche of letters that arrived at the FBI. One such letter maintained: "Richard Wright the Negro who wrote black boy and Native Son books are doin no good and a lot of harm they are causing disunity and spreading race hatred and if you people dont want America tores up same as Germanny you had better put a stop to such people as . . . that poor crazy old Richard Wright." Other letters referred to him as "a black nazi," "one of the biggest spreaders of race hatred," and asked that his books be banned. "I am an American Negro," wrote another angry correspondent, "and proud of it because we colored people in America have

come a long way in the last seventy years. . . . We colored people
dont mind the truth but we do hate lies or anything that disturb our
peace of mind." Another writer questioned the authenticity of author-
ship: "Granting that the Negro called Richard Wright actually wrote
the book, it is my opinion that all the publicity given to the book is
being financed by some person or organization—for propaganda pur-
poses. . . ." The letters were titillating, somewhat amusing. Some were
simply embarrassing. But they offered little help to the Bureau in its
own dilemma concerning subject Richard Wright. In the report concluded on September 5, 1944, the New York Office had made known its
intentions concerning the subject and his recent defection from the
Party: "Will, after careful consideration, discreetly interview subject
Wright concerning his association with the Communist Party." On
February 26, 1945, however, the office had second thoughts about its initial objectives. "After very careful consideration it is felt inadvisable to
interview Wright particularly as the basis of his break with the Communist Party, as appears from his recent articles . . . is the Communist
Party's failure to be sufficiently radical and militant with respect to the
advancement of the Negro. These articles also indicate a complete disapproval by Wright of the American way of life." The decision was
also prompted by the report of Wright's local draft board, which
deemed him mentally unstable, suffering from severe psychoneurosis,
his "interest in the problem of the Negro . . . almost an obsession."
    The Bureau was no longer dealing with a Communist; it was now
dealing with a crazy man, and a change of status was necessary. "In
view of the subject's public break with the Communist Party," the
memorandum declared that Wright would no longer be considered "a
key figure by the New York Field Division." However, "due to his militant attitude toward the Negro problem," the office insisted on maintaining "A security index Card on him. . . ." "This investigation," concluded the memorandum, "is being placed in a closed status by the
New York Field Division. In the event further investigation becomes
necessary, it will be reported under a Security Matter C character." On
April 17, the New York Field Office forwarded another memorandum
to Headquarters, correcting an important mistake on the memo of February 26. Permission for "Security Index Card had never been granted
by Washington." Therefore, "no security index card is being maintained in the New York Office on the subject unless contrary advice is
received from the Bureau," concluded the memo, in which several paragraphs of material are deleted.
    "Contrary advice" was swiftly forwarded from Washington. The fact
that Wright was no longer a member of the Communist Party did not
lessen his danger as a subversive, and he was reclassified. "In view of the

militant attitude of the subject toward the Negro problem, . . ." Headquarters advised, "it is believed that you should submit a recommendation for the preparation of a Security Index Card in this
case. . . . You may consider this letter as the Bureau's approval of such
a recommendation and you should place a Security Index Card in your
files at this time."[16] On May 18, 1945, a revised index card, "a white 5″
× 8″ card," was prepared and filed in the confidential Security Index
Card File in the Office. "It is advised," the SAC informed Washington,
"that the original security Index Card maintained at the Seat of Government [Washington Headquarters] be revised in agreement with the
caption above set out." Under the caption "Communist," the X had
been obliterated from Wright's revised card. With the power and authority to arrest him without warrant, the Bureau was content to rest its
case against Richard Wright for the time being.

It had stepped up its attack on the Party itself, however, and some of
the members were apprehensive about Wright. "The only thing that really concerned us," a Marxist leader remarked, "was if he would talk to
the F.B.I. Frankly, he was a strange man, and we just didn't know."
Wright had no idea of informing on his old comrades, nor was he anxious to continue the warfare—or any relations—between them. As far as
he was concerned, his adventures with communism were over. In January, he wrote in his journal that communism failed to give people the
tools that were fundamental to thinking; reality was not what one interpreted for oneself, it was "what Earl Browder says it is. . . ."[17] He
was free now to think for himself, to interpret reality in his own way.

For some time, Wright and Ellen had had ideas of living in the intellectually, artistically stimulating area of Greenwich Village, the most
liberal section of New York City. Julia, now almost three years old and
growing more inquisitive and curious every day, would be somewhat
safe from the more overt forms of racism in such an environment. His
rupture with the Party concluded, fearing the eventual attacks by blacks
about *Black Boy*, the always attentive Wright became even more so regarding his family. "Ellen," wrote Fabre, "had become the essential element of his stability, and he left more and more of the practical responsibility for their life to her."[18]

Among the practical responsibilities was buying a house, and he had
wanted this to be a joint undertaking. A house was soon found for the
couple on Charles Street, in the heart of the Village, but the vaunted
liberalism of the Village did not apply to blacks, who were unable either to rent or buy houses there. As a result, the Wrights were forced to
engage in subterfuge: on the advice of their lawyer, the couple was established as "The Richelieu Realty Co." "President and sole owner of
the corporation is Ellen Wright, wife of the author, Richard Wright,

who has acted as agent for the real estate firm."[19] When the neighbors discovered who the real owners of the house were, they attempted to prevent the family from moving in: one such attempt involved an offer to buy the house at almost double its cost. The Communists, upon discovering the identity of the owners of the new house, and unable to resist a swipe at Wright, also reacted. One, Franklin Folsom, threatened a rent strike. Others, either sympathizers or party members, took the Wrights to court. A similar attempt to purchase a farm in liberal New England ended in failure. The owner of the property, who had at first accepted the Wrights' deposits, suddenly discovered complicated legal difficulties involved in the sale. Wright withdrew from the transaction only to discover later that the farm was still on the market.[20]

He was no stranger to such rebuffs. As a black boy, he had suffered them daily. But, no longer the black boy, he was a world-renowned author. *Black Boy*, controversial though it was, was an immediate best seller. In five months, over a half million copies were sold. Translation rights were sought by publishing capitals throughout the world. Radio programs and talk shows were devoted to discussions and debates concerning the book; national magazines vied with each other for background material on the author's early life, and reprints were demanded by editors of magazines, large and small. Praise came from famous writers. "It needed to be said," wrote William Faulkner, "and you said it well." ". . . just finished reading *Black Boy* and wanted to let you know immediately how deeply it impressed me," wrote Henry Miller. ". . . now when one Negro can write as Richard Wright does, writing as a Negro about Negroes, writes not as a Negro but as a man," wrote Gertrude Stein, ". . . the relation between the white and the Negro is no longer a difference of races but a minority question and ends not in ownership but in persecution." Meanwhile the world-renowned black writer was undergoing the same kind of oppression as the black boys in the many ghettoes of America.

But the repercussions to Wright were much more severe now. The black boy of before had had a world before him to be conquered. For the writer, the victories had been won, status achieved, success assured. And yet the fundamental recognition of humanity had not come. "What have I got out of living in America?" he had asked in the last pages of *Black Boy*, and answered despairingly, ". . . all that I possessed were words and a dim knowledge that my country had shown me no examples of how to live a human life. All my life I had been full of a hunger for a new way to live." "Can a Negro ever live like a man in America?" he angrily asked in his journal.

It was one of many angry questions asked in a journal that he took great pains to hide lest even his wife become privy to its secrets. The

January 1945 recordings are replete with pessimism, concerns about his writings, even about the purpose of writing. As a beginning writer, he had wanted to influence the people for whom he wrote; the truth, however, was that only those whose consciousness had already been raised were affected. And more and more, his recordings became bitter, almost hostile, regarding the lack of militancy and honesty of his black colleagues. None had the courage, like him, to admit the all-pervasive fear of their American experience, and none were sufficiently militant to want to do something about it. Freedom, he had told Nehru's sister, Madam Vijaya Lakshmi Pandit, would come for the Indian people only when enough Englishmen were "butchered" to force an end to their tyranny. Oppressors never surrendered power out of moral piety.[21] He did not advocate violent resistance to American oppression, but he demanded a militancy commensurate with what he believed his own to be.

In fact, blacks in America were more colonized than blacks anywhere else in the world; they were stripped of their own culture and denied access to that of the larger society. "Stunted, stripped, and held captive within this nation," they were prevented from growing into political, intellectual, and economic manhood. The idea of blacks as wards of society was so deeply ingrained that few white men could remember the day when such perceptions did not prevail.

In *Twelve Million Black Voices*, Wright had noted his ambivalence about white America's motivations; oppression of blacks, he had argued, resulted from economic and class and racial conflicts. Now, three years later, he offered a more charitable, historical rationale. In June, vacationing in Quebec once again, he wrote the Introduction to *Black Metropolis*, a book by his friends St. Clair Drake and Horace Cayton. The black situation could be viewed in moral and racial terms, less in terms of economics and class. The nation had grown, developing "supreme confidence in the natural dignity of man," and believing that "reason and freedom could lead to . . . paradise on earth." Having reached this plateau, however, Americans made their first mistake: enslaving others to serve to help build an empire based on the belief "that all men were naturally free. . . ." Unfortunately Americans, who possessed "in their hearts those impulses that made dignity and nobility a given human right . . . could not play the role of master with a singleness of heart."[22]

In order to hold onto his newly achieved civilization, rather than for economic or class reasons, Western man was forced to retain blacks in perpetual childhood and to assuage his guilt feelings by inventing rationales for doing so. The rationales were becoming more difficult to sustain in the industrial age. Such new concerns pushed men and women away from the land into the cities, mandated new modes of living, offered new opportunities for spiritual and intellectual development. During his years as an inspired Marxist, he had believed that solutions to the problems of blacks would come about as a combined effort by black and white progressives. Now, split from the Party and increasingly alienated from blacks, he viewed salvation as the work of white people, because it is due to conditions imposed upon them by white America that blacks have not progressed. Blacks move through America frightened, fearful, he writes to Gertrude Stein on May 27, 1945. They feel unwanted, they "look like children who want their mothers to love them but know that their mothers never will."[23] In comparison to blacks in other lands, those in America are the least healthy, the most damaged in terms of personality and emotion. The fact that they "belong nowhere" is visible in their "behavior."

In part, his negative appraisal of blacks may be attributed to his own helplessness and inability to deal with such overt racist situations as those involving the Charles Street house and his failure to purchase a farm. In the unpublished essay "I Choose Exile," written in 1950, he recalls riding back to New York after the episode in New England, and the anger he felt at the time. He would leave America, he promised himself, leave the land of his birth, "Defeat the culture that shaped me. . . ."[24] But he had not yet decided to exile himself from America, and to live here and to combat racism he needed allies. The Introduction to *Black Metropolis* moved him close to liberal progressive whites even as it distanced him from the more intellectual blacks, as few blacks were willing to assert that every facet of black life was dominated by white censors or that black survival was impossible without the leadership of whites.

In October of 1945, he wrote to Gertrude Stein that in the event she came to the city and lectured, she should "say some hard and sharp things to Negroes too." They should be made ashamed of "their fear and timidity."[25] He himself now "took time out from writing . . . about" the Negro problem and talked to audiences of whites and encouraged others to do the same: ". . . preach and yell and educate and talk to them. . . . I make speeches about the problem, confining myself almost always to white people, that is, white audiences. . . ."[26] His attacks on moderate Negroes during his Communist days were, for the most part, orchestrated by the Party; now, however, they assumed a form peculiarly his and were almost hysterical in intensity. In the Introduction to *No Day of Triumph*, by Saunders Redding, he argued the need for a more viable leadership, applauding Redding for being "the first middle class Negro to break with the ideology of 'the talented tenth.'" In April of 1945, he came close to accusing his old friend

Elmer Carter, former executive director of the Urban League, of being unwilling to accept the cold facts of black life. Even the tacit alliance that he had once thought possible with progressive blacks was shattered. More and more he sought to cement his relationship with progressive whites.

CHAPTER THIRTEEN

He returned from his second trip to Canada, at the end of the summer, refreshed. Complications had arisen regarding purchase of their Charles Street home, so the family moved into a Village apartment at 82 Washington Place. Wright then began an extensive lecture tour, under the stewardship of Harold Peat, "to enlighten his fellow citizens on the "so called Negro problem." His itinerary was extensive. In Connecticut, he talked to a convention of schoolteachers about Afro-American literature. In Washington, at Howard University, he followed Mrs. Eleanor Roosevelt to the rostrum to speak on "the unfinished task of democracy." "The Negro Contribution to American Civilization" was the lecture given in Camden, New Jersey, and "The Role of the Negro in the Arts and Sciences," was given in Des Moines, Iowa.[1] In January, he joined other literary notables, black and white, in attending the funeral of the black poet Countee Cullen. And as always, he found time to aid other writers, black and white.

One such writer was Chester Himes. By the time he met Richard Wright, in 1945, Himes was already a published writer, his career dating back to 1934. He was born in Jefferson City, Missouri, in 1909 of middle-class parentage and attended Ohio State University. All hopes of completing college disappeared when he was sentenced to the Ohio State Penitentiary for robbery. "I grew to manhood in the Ohio State Penitentiary," he wrote in 1972. "I was nineteen years old when I went in and twenty-six years old when I came out. I became a man, dependent on no one but myself." He also became a writer, contributing short stories, mostly about prison life, to *Abbots Monthly Magazine* and *Esquire*. When Doubleday published his first novel, *If He Hollers Let Him Go*, Wright reviewed it for *P.M. Magazine* along with Arthur Miller's *Focus*. The review was mostly favorable, and a long-lasting friendship developed between the two writers. "From the time I had met him after the publication of *If He Hollers Let Him Go*," Himes wrote, "until his death, Dick and I had a somewhat secret understanding that I wouldn't ask him for any favor he did not want to do, and he wouldn't do it."[2] What Wright did do was offer his fellow writer financial aid and encouragement throughout those years.

James Baldwin, on the other hand, was an unpublished writer when he met the internationally known novelist, in 1945. "I introduced him to Wright," said Henrietta Weigel, "but they were cool to each other. I was disappointed, childishly believing that Wright, having experienced the difficulties of being a black writer in the U.S.A., would at once take Baldwin 'under his wing.'" Whatever Ms. Weigel's account of the first meeting between the two writers, Baldwin remembers that, at the age of twenty ("broke, naturally, shabby, hungry and scared"), having completed part of a novel, "In My Father's House," a mutual friend "arranged a meeting between him and Richard Wright."[3] The Wrights were still living in Brooklyn. Wright, casually dressed, affable, gracious, welcomed the intense young writer. Baldwin was impressed, overawed, frightened. He had never met a writer of Wright's stature before. In the Harlem in which he was born in 1924, knowing writers or having ambitions to become one were not fashionable.

The bourbon offered by his host and readily accepted did little to put him at ease. Awkwardly, he talked about his novel, rambling, hesitantly. ". . . Wright was understanding as well as receptive."[4]

While a structure such as the John Reed Clubs was no longer available, he would do what he could for young writers who sought him out. Wright agreed to read part of Baldwin's unfinished novel. With some trepidation still, Baldwin mailed him the first "section." Wright read it, was impressed, and helped the younger writer to secure a Eugene F. Saxton Memorial Trust Award. Recalling his first meeting with Wright, years later, Baldwin admitted, ". . . I was scared shitless of *him*."

But his well-deserved reputation and acclaim frightened few others. He cashed in on both in aiding his friend Dr. Wertham to help found the Lafargue Clinic, "where starting April 8, 1946, delinquents and the sick could come and confide their problems to a devoted staff for 25¢. . . ."[5] This first mental clinic for Harlem blacks was given added exposure and, no doubt financial assistance, by Wright's article "Psychiatry Comes to Harlem." His differences with the moderate Negro leaders notwithstanding, he accepted invitations to lecture for civil-rights groups and maintained his friendship with members of the Urban League and the NAACP. Nevertheless, his more solid relationships were maintained with whites of the liberal caliber of Dorothy Norman and Wertham. And despite his numerous, seemingly never-ending round of activities, he still, as John Hammond told Michel Fabre, "felt very much like an outcast those days since the Communists had organized a powerful vendetta against him."[6] More and more, he thought of exile, of moving outside the racial pressures and confusions of America. He had confided these thoughts to his journal of January 28, 1945, in commenting upon his reading of Gertrude Stein's *Narrations*. The writer's dialogue, he reflected, brought back memories of the speech of his grandmother, and he wondered how "one could live and write like that," concluding that one could do so only "in Paris or in some out of the way spot where one could claim one's own soul." He could not do that in America. "All the more reason," he added, "why I dream of leaving my native land to escape the superficial things I think I know. That's why I left the south, and now I want to leave the country and some day I will, . . . by God."[7]

As 1945 drew to a close, Wright's sense of urgency and restlessness concerning the American racial situation increased. His new neighbors in Greenwich Village were no more hospitable than his old neighbors had been in Brooklyn. Wryly he commented to more than one friend that though he was accepted as a writer in the Village, "he could not get a hair cut there." He and his wife were subject to constant insults from shopkeepers and storeowners, and few restaurants in the area received black customers with "civility." "To be in Washington Park during the forties," remarked a black poet, "was to take your life in your hands. To be with a white woman was to commit suicide." "Ellen and I," Wright confided to his journal, "never think of the disparity of race." It became apparent only when someone forced it to their consciousness. But race was only one of the burning issues facing postwar America. Equally as important was the coming "cold war," which erupted almost immediately after conclusion of the "hot war" in 1945. By the time the Japanese signed the formal surrender, on September 2, the always precarious relationship between the Soviet Union and the United States had begun to disintegrate. Many Soviet cities lay in ruins; the Russians were badly in need of minerals and foodstuffs. To forestall large-scale revolt and to maintain itself in power, the Stalin regime became even more oppressive, and the Soviet Army, which had entered many Eastern European countries as liberators, remained as conquerors. The supplies obtained from these countries made it possible for the Russians to spurn the Marshall Plan, designed to force dependence upon America, and enabled them to challenge American hegemony in Asia and Western Europe.

If Russia was a stricken giant in the first months after the war, America seemed to many a colossus. American cities were untouched by war, the people were prosperous.

However, each stood as a barrier to the territorial ambitions of the other. Unwilling to initiate a hot war, the Americans became fully involved in a cold one not just against the Soviet nation but the Soviet ideology as well. The Russian Communists were, for the most part, immune, but the Communists at home were extremely vulnerable: The Communists, announced Truman's Attorney General, Tom Clark, in June of 1946, are engaged in a "conspiracy to divide our people, to discredit our institutions, and to bring about disrespect for our government."[8] As feelings against Russia increased in the United States, American Communists came to be regarded with increasing hostility by the American people.

The Congress responded to this increasing hostility. In January of 1945, new life had been breathed into the House Un-American Activities Committee (HUAC) under the chairmanship of John S. Wood, of Georgia, and the powerful influence of the man who had helped resuscitate it, John E. Rankin, of Mississippi. Rankin, who had joined fellow Mississippian Bilbo in an attack on *Black Boy* on the floor of the Senate, asserted that the Fair Employment Practices Commission was "the beginnings of a Communist dictatorship the like of which America never dreamed of." He declared on another occasion that "Communism . . . had hounded and persecuted the Savior during his earthly ministry, inspired his crucifixion, derided him in his dying agony, then gambled for his garments at the foot of the cross."[9] With the backing of Rankin, Congress authorized HUAC "to investigate: (1) the extent, character and objects of un-American propaganda activities in the United States, (2) the diffusion within the United States of subversive and un-American propaganda that is instigated from foreign countries or of a domestic origin and attacks the principle of the form of government as guaranteed by our constitution, and (3) all other questions in relation thereto that would aid Congress in any remedial legislation."[10] One of the first witnesses summoned before the Committee was Wright's old antagonist Benjamin Davis, Jr.; HUAC, however, was not the only adversary that Davis and his comrades had to confront after the war.

The Communist Political Association came under fire from none other than one of its own. In April 1945, French party theoretician and second-ranking Communist of the French Communist Party René Duclos published a letter entitled "On the Dissolution of the Communist Party of the United States." The charges he made against the American Communists are the same as those made two years earlier by Wright in "I Tried to Be a Communist." Under the leadership of Browder, charged Duclos, "the Party . . . relinquished its function as the only independent spokesman of the American working class; . . .

abandoned the Marxist theory of class conflict, substituting the mild reformism of the social democrats . . . [it] played into the hands of the bourgeoisie and the monopoly business interests."[11] On June 2, Davis and his fellow members of the National Board met to plead guilty to the charges leveled by Duclos, and inadvertently to those made by Wright: ". . . These errors were facilitated by non-labor bourgeois influences which unconsciously affected some of our policies as we participated and functioned ever more actively in the broad camp of National unity. . . ."[12] James Ford, who had vociferously deplored the criticism and militance of Wright, offered his personal confession: "I share fully in the responsibility for the opportunistic line which had led our organization into the swamp of revisionism. . . . What are the sources of my error? I had a fear of factionalism. . . . And I know what disastrous consequences factionalism would cause in all or any phase of work of the Communist movement, especially Negro work."[13] It was Edna Lewis, however, from Wright's old Communist cell in Harlem, who sought consideration for the entire black leadership: "Negro Communists have a special responsibility to the Negro people. Our knowledge of their suffering should have kept us on guard against accepting a program of compromise to last for many generations as proposed by Earl Browder."[14] One month later, in response to the Duclos attack, the Party transformed itself once again into the Communist Party of the United States.

Wright had little time and less inclination to gloat over his unexpected and unintended vindication by Duclos and indirectly by the Politburo itself. Personally, he was feeling the effects of the cold war. In 1946, signs reading "Negroes Vote at Your Own Risk" began appearing throughout the South; murders of blacks in and out of uniform took place while black veterans were beaten and other blacks intimidated. The racial situation became so acute that in 1947 the NAACP addressed an appeal to the United Nations: "An appeal to the world, a statement on the denial of Human Rights to minorities in the case of citizens of Negro descent in the United States and an appeal to the United Nations for redress." The appeal fell on deaf ears, both in the world organization and among progressives in America.

The progressives, Wright's new allies and singular hope for salvation for blacks, were in disarray. As the governmental investigative machinery began to move, as HUAC prepared for war on Communists both real and imagined, the liberal left began to express an anticommunism of its own, one, according to Arthur Schlesinger, Jr., "graduated in mode and substance according to the threat. . . ." "We cannot take chances with the ringleaders of a conspiracy," wrote Max Ascoli, editor of *The Reporter,* as the court upheld the conviction of Communist leaders tried under the Smith Act, "that if successful, would pervert and destroy our institutions." And Wright's champion and judicious critic Granville Hicks, an ex-Communist, insisted that all Communists were agents, or potential agents, of the Soviet Government. Robert L. Heilbroner, in an attempt to explain the liberal retreat, wrote: "It is, I think, the fear of losing our place in the sun, of finding ourselves at bay, that motivated a great deal of anti-communism . . . !" As the *Hiss* and *Rosenberg* cases exploded into tragedy, and as HUAC launched its vendetta against the Hollywood film industry, progressives, for the most part, shrouded themselves in silence, or worse, capitulated to or joined the right-wing assault on freedom and liberty. Deeply pained and becoming increasingly more disillusioned, Wright averred: "There's no hope for this country. It is sliding into fascism."

The feelings of estrangement, of being a man alone, intensified, and he withdrew further into his family. He writes in his journal about the youthful beauty of his wife and of the growing curiosity and inquisitiveness of his young child with warmth and affection, noting that she delighted in coming to watch him work, and promising to buy her a typewriter when she became older. He worried about leaving them alone in the Village when he was away on a lecture or business trip. More and more, he came to realize the irony of his situation. Almost weekly he stood before audiences, predominantly white, and argued the case for equal treatment of blacks, sometimes being reassured by the sympathy and understanding of his audience; then he returned home to a neighborhood in which he could not adequately protect his family, could not shield them from abuse or invective. And it was not only the misguided poor whites of the Village, who cared little about the black situation; no, the pseudo liberals were as unconcerned, as unfeeling; and the progressives in their retreat from the cause of human rights must have reminded him of former allies, the Communists.

Few seemed to share his sense of urgency or desperation over the changing American scene; apologies for inaction came from all quarters. As the southern racists in Congress began to equate the civil-rights drive with communism, the progressives answered by swearing their anticommunism. Blacks were not only totally alone now; they were helpless. The inevitable outcome would be more riots—more Detroits, and New Yorks; there would be more patients for the Lafargue Clinic, more black children in institutions like Wiltwyck. But how much of Wright's understanding of the American scene was based upon his own angst, his own despair? Was not the trauma that America was undergoing natural in the aftermath of war? He may have been too effusive in seeing the rise of American fascism parallel the rise of German fascism. Or perhaps the books he read had shaped his perceptions. He did not understand the existentialist writers—Kierkegaard, Heidegger, Nietzsche, Unamuno—but, in postwar America, he divined the environment that produced the alienated, the estranged, the outsider. And yet he had no real measuring rod by which to gauge his society. He had gone to Mexico and Canada and had been favorably impressed. But he had not traveled across the Atlantic, had not seen the cultures and people, the cities, of continental Europe. Such an opportunity would offer some means of comparison, some way of testing his own assertions about himself and his country as well.

The opportunity that he longed for came suddenly, unexpectedly. The shrill blast of the telephone on that crisp, windy December morning of 1945 had angered him. His work was being disrupted; his wife and child, still asleep, would be awakened. His own passion for calling his friends in the early morning forgotten, he strode, visibly annoyed, to pick up the receiver. The static was deep and the voice of the foreign government official at the other end barely audible. Anger turned to surprise. Wright was asked to visit France as a guest of the government. Out of euphoria, exuberance, and surprise, he exclaimed, "It is not possible." The static became deafening, jamming the reply on the other end. No doubt, he was oblivious to whatever remained of the conversation. He wanted to rush and tell his wife the good news. France was the one country that he most wanted to visit. The opportunity for reflection was now his. He needed a passport; he had to check with friends about the weather, the people, what to expect in Paris. He wanted to be able to say a few French words; he had to find something to do with the cat, Knobby, such a favorite of Julia's. The work he had begun on his new novel could wait; the other things were paramount. He would have to begin preparations immediately.

The French caller took Wright's cry of surprise, "It is not possible," literally, and concluded that the writer would not accept the invitation. Wright, however, had immediately begun making preparations to accept the invitation; while he waited for an official welcome, he attempted to get his government to issue him a passport. Receiving a passport, as he described it in "I Choose Exile," was an excruciating task. He supposedly applied in January of 1946 and was rebuffed.

Once the French officials discovered the error, they issued him an official invitation; he appealed to such influential friends as Dorothy Norman, Gertrude Stein and the French cultural attaché, Claude Lévi-Strauss, to secure a passport. These efforts on his behalf seemed to avail nothing; on April 29, he went to Washington and appealed in person to the government; he enlisted the aid of other friends and finally contacted "Fascists, friends of Evelyn Walsh McLean. . . . [He] received his passport one hour later. No questions were asked."[15] The State Department's records concerning the affair stated simply that Wright was "to represent the publication, 'Twice A Year,' to the French public, writing articles about French literary developments, reestablishing contacts for the distribution of the periodical, and seeking manuscripts for reproduction in America," and that his wife would accompany him.[16] On April 29, 1946, his passport was issued to him and was validated for travel to France only. It was possible that the strange, melancholy attitude that Baldwin noticed in the writer a few days before he was to embark had to do with the mystery surrounding his passport. He talked a lot, Baldwin recalled, concerning a friend who, in trouble with the immigration officials, had been deported. He was not being deported, but his government was overly suspicious of his reasons for visiting another country, and the immigration statutes already in force would have allowed them legally to detain him.[17] Instead they allowed him to leave, with the intent of closely monitoring his movements. "Will verify subject's residence and ascertain his activities upon his return to the United States from France, presumably in September, 1946." Reads a memorandum, "If possible, secure the subject's reason for his trip to France."

Governmental surveillance notwithstanding, ". . . one hour after setting foot on French soil," he wrote in 1950, racial tension and feeling disappeared.[18] Certainly the somber mood noticed by well-wishers who attended a farewell party on the S.S. *Brazil* on the day of departure had disappeared by the time the ship reached Le Havre, France, on May 8.

The Wrights were ushered through customs by attentive, unusually polite officials and directed to a boat train to the Gare St. Lazare and Paris. Giant ships, lying like overturned dinosaurs, half in and half out of the water, were reminders of the recent catastrophe at Le Havre. But the French countryside through which the train sped was different. Wide-open fields and spaces reminded him of the South. For the moment, concerns about the American situation seemed to have disappeared.

As they pulled into St. Lazare Station, the family was besieged by a crowd of critics, reporters, dignitaries, politicians, friends, and the curious. Wright was given a reception accorded heads of state, and France turned out her most important cultural ambassadors to meet him. The American Government, through the embassy, had dispatched a sleek limousine for the occasion. He was jubilant. Nowhere in America could he have received such a reception, not only because he was black but because Americans had little respect for writers. And somehow this was most important. He was a black writer to be sure, and he never pretended to be otherwise. But the French were looking beyond the color of his skin; they were seeing a human being, a writer. "His visit to

France," wrote an interviewer who talked to him after his return from Paris, "had been a unique experience in freedom; there he was not a Negro but a human being, accepted and even welcomed."[19] It was a triumphal moment, even one of vindication. He had survived the ruptures with the Party, the hassles with the government. He answered the questions of reporters before being whisked away at the head of an entourage that included such literary notables as Maurice Nadeau and Claude-Edmonde Magny—the black boy from Mississippi making his entry into Paris proper. Down the Champs Élysées, past wide boulevards and tree-lined streets, the breathlessly red, white, and pink flowers of the Tuileries; past the stately architecture of centuries-old buildings; the ominous gargoyles, pale gray in the spring coolness, atop Notre Dame; past the Louvre and the bronze colored figurines of men and women adorning the buildings, the grounds of what a German general described as the most beautiful city in the world. The entourage paused long enough for a lunch at Gertrude Stein's residence, and the family was off again, this time to the Hotel Trianon-Paris, on the Left Bank, to encounter more reporters, French officials, guests of the hotel, and clerks, bellhops and concierges.

In his interviews with reporters, he was polite, comfortable, relaxed. When asked if his own success and that of blacks like Marian Anderson and Paul Robeson did not produce better relationships between blacks and whites, he answered that no matter the measure of success, no black American overcame "the difficulties and disabilities of being a Negro." The lives of us all, he continued, "flow through banks and channels built for them by white Americans."[20] That was what he felt, what he believed. He was informing, not attacking. Finally, left alone to settle his family into the hotel suite, he reflected on the past days and hours. Do not, an American official had pleaded with him, let the Europeans "use you as a brick to hurl through our window." The official was afraid of what Wright might say about America. Far more important to him, however, were the personal experiences he would remember having had in France. Among other things, he would remember his ease in finding an apartment without race considered a factor; and the woman in the French countryside who invited him in to meet her son-in-law, a black man married to her French daughter.

And he would remember, much more fondly, his first long visit with Gertrude Stein. His fascination with the American writer in exile began during the early days of his career. Hers were among the books that he had read and reread; he had been caught by her use of language, her masterful manipulation of words. In 1945, he reviewed her book *Wars I Have Seen* for *P.M. Magazine* and suggested that future generations would benefit from reading the book. Carl Van Vechten called Miss

Stein's attention to the review, and after reading *Black Boy*, she wrote
him a complimentary letter.[21] Though they had not met, an enduring
friendship ensued in letters. With Stein still active, though suffering
from cancer, the two promenaded through the beautiful Luxembourg
Gardens, in and out of the narrow walkways off St. Michel and St. Germain des Prés. He would have one more visit with her before she entered the "American Hospital on July 19."[22] It was on this visit that she
advised him to go to Spain, advice he was to take years later.

He also met Simone de Beauvoir, the black French writer René Martin, Jean Paul Sartre, André Gide, André Malraux, Roger Maran du
Gard, and Maurice Merleau-Ponty. And, everywhere, he signed auto-
graphs, acted the gracious guest. By the end of the summer, much of
this social life behind him, he moved into an apartment on Boulevard
St. Michel. He did little work on his new novel, though he found time
to write the short story "The Man Who Killed a Shadow" and to review Gertrude Stein's *Brewsie and Willie*. And he reflected upon the
absence of tension, of racial feeling, almost everywhere. ". . . There is
such an absence of race hate," he wrote his editor on May 15, "that it
seems a little unreal."[23] At home, however, the FBI was taking another
look at his case. "Reference is made to the report of [deletion] New
York, June 18, 1946," states a memo forwarded to Washington on that
day, "wherein it was set forth that the subject is presently in France
where he intends to remain until September, 1946. In view of this fact,
instant case is being reopened 'pending inactive status' in order that the
subject's residence and activities may be checked upon his return to the
United States." On June 18, 1946, SAC Conroy, of the New York Field
Office, initialed a report compiled over the period of June 5 through the
fourteenth. The Bureau file (the file maintained at Washington) is
cited for reference, along with several letters, dated: 2/26/45, 4/17/45,
5/7/45, and 3/12/46. The 1945 letters refer to the matter of the Security Index card; but, in the letter of February 26, the SAC informed
Washington of his intention to question Wright concerning his "association with the Communist Party." The April letter pointed out that
Wright was no longer being carried as a "key figure" in the New York
Field Office, and in a letter of reply (May 7), Washington informed
the New York Office that Wright's "militant attitude towards the
Negro problem" mandated maintenance of a Security Index card. The
March 12, 1946, letter is missing from the files, and so, too, are what is
designated "Bureau letters to SACs, 1946 Series," of that date. Wright's
desperate attempt to obtain his passport had gained urgency during the
months of March and April. Did the deleted letter refer to these transactions?

The June 18 document details the Bureau's interest in Wright's trip

to Paris. "Subject . . . [left] U.S. for France, May 1946, with return set
for Sept. 1946. Reason for trip unknown." Under "Details," the Bureau
noted that the Selective Service records contained notice of Wright's
change of address from Brooklyn to Manhattan and ". . . a letter dated
April 14, 1946, wherein Wright advised he planned to leave the United
States on May 1, 1946, for a period of three months in France. The
reason for this trip was not given in his letter." In a long deletion,
which appears to refer to information given by an agent or an informer,
the Bureau learned that Wright was "writing a novel," though the completion date was unknown, and that he had left for France. There was
also a notation concerning his lack of ardent critical attack upon the
Party. The case was designated "pending," and the agent vowed to verify Wright's residence and monitor his activities upon his return to the
United States and to find out the reasons for his trip to France.[24] On
September 5, 1946, the following communiqué was issued to SAC, New
York, from Washington: "Your office is instructed to follow the activities of the instant subject in the Communist field closely upon his return from France. Continuing investigation, every effort should be
made to obtain admissible evidence tending to prove the subject's
membership in, or affiliation with, the Communist Party. In the event
you are unable to develop such evidence, further consideration should
be given the advisability of cancelling the Security Index Card on this
individual."

Four months of investigation produced no evidence of Communist
involvement. On February 19, 1947, SAC, New York Field Office, referred to the Washington letter of September 5 and its own report of
June 18. It was noted that Wright had given "An Interview with Richard Wright" that appeared in *The New Leader* of February 1, 1947,
"an anti-Communist publication of the Social Democrats," and that
the article was a translation from an interview given by Wright in Switzerland, "in *Die Weltwoche.*" In Zurich, noted the report, Wright "expressed his resentment of racial discrimination in the United States."
But informants had been able to supply no information of present
Communist involvement. Agents also were unsuccessful in discovering
any link between Wright and the Communists "since he severed connections with the Communist Party." Therefore, in light of this fact
and the additional one that Wright "may not return to the United
States for some time," the SAC advised Washington that the case was
being closed unless Headquarters directed otherwise. Yet, in reference
to Headquarters' advice concerning cancellation of the Security Index
card made in the communication of September 5, the New York Field
Office averred: "In view of the subject's past activities, it is believed
that the security Index Card in this case should not be cancelled."

Throughout the years, Wright was to be queried by one government agency or another concerning his knowledge of such alleged Communist-front organizations as the Abraham Lincoln Brigade, The National Council for American-Soviet Friendship, and the Marxist-oriented Young Communist League. In 1946, the government stepped up its campaign against black singer Paul Robeson, summoning him before HUAC for the first of many inquisitions that would eventually strip him of his passport and his means of making a living. During 1946 and 1947, the FBI began "pulling out all stops," compiling the massive dossier of material to be used in the case "against eleven members of the National Board of the Communist Party in 1948." In 1946 and 1947, the FBI compiled "a 1,350 page brief supplemented by 546 exhibits, together with two supplemental briefs and a further 300 exhibits. . . ." Among the defendants in the Foley Square trial were Benjamin Davis, Jr., and Henry Winston.[25]

The efforts of the Bureau were aided by informers, agents who had infiltrated the Party, and anti-Communists turned government informers. Wright was familiar with many of the organizations and individuals destined for the Bureau's dragnet. He had been close to the higher echelons of the Party. He had had a working relationship with Davis and Winston, had shared platforms with Paul Robeson. On learning of his initial break with the Party, the New York Field Office requested permission to "interview him" concerning his knowledge of the Marxist apparatus. And it was hoped Wright would help. Now that his writings and interviews demonstrated a definite anti-Communist stance, the Bureau wanted Wright as an informer. But, given his reputation, the Bureau perhaps had to offer as compensation the removal of its own carefully documented case against Wright himself, as called for in the Washington document of June 18. And was further compensation to be offered by removing the Security Index card, called for by Headquarters in the same document? Or was the government clearing its dockets of one-time Communists in order to focus its attacks on the actual ones? Whatever their reason, in the summer of 1947 the New York Field Office cancelled its Security Index card on Richard Wright. The memo forwarded to Washington from New York on January 19, 1948, reads: "A review of instant file reflects that since subject's severance of his connections with the Communist Party, and his public criticism of its policies during 1944, he has not engaged in any Communist activities; that, in fact, according to information submitted by ND 352 on July 2, 1947, *subject was definitely not in a Marxist frame of mind as indicated by certain critical comments he made concerning conditions within the Party.* [Italics mine.] In view of the foregoing circumstances, Bureau authority is requested at this time for the cancellation of the Security Index Card maintained on Subject by the New York Office." Authorization was granted on February 5, 1948. But could criticism concerning the Party be equated with giving information concerning it and individuals? Was Wright, then, playing a desperate game of his own, trying to outmaneuver his antagonists, gaining much-needed time for his eventual final exile?

Contrary to information fed the FBI, the Wrights remained abroad throughout 1946, returning to America in January of the following year. From France, he visited Switzerland, where he gave a series of interviews and discussed "a German edition of *Black Boy*." In London, he met members of the Coloured Writers Association, "composed of young writers, Hindu, African, British West Indian and Asiatic" and other Third World cultures. He also met and talked extensively with the Trinidad-born African leader George Padmore. "An extraordinary man," often called "the founder and guiding spirit of the African revolution," Padmore emigrated to the United States in the nineteen twenties and attended Howard University. While at the university, he joined the Communist Party, worked with the Party in America, and "ultimately became head of the Negro Department of the Profintern, the Communist Trade Union International, with an office in the Kremlin."[26] In this capacity he kept in contact with "African Nationalist Revolutionaries," throughout the world; helping to "organize activities" in Africa, he also became a trusted and leading adviser to Kwame Nkrumah, of Ghana. In 1935, however, as Communists espoused the United Front thesis, "seeking the alliance of the Democracies against fascism," Padmore broke "decisively with the Comintern." It was not the fascists, but the democracies, Britain and France, that maintained the colonial status of African people.

No doubt, the similarities of his and Padmore's experiences with the Party drew Wright to the Trinidadian. But he was drawn also by the tremendous courage the revolutionary displayed. For Padmore, the issue was clear-cut, the options reduced to one: the Party had become reactionary, willing to sacrifice the freedom and rights of African people; he could not remain in such an organization; thus he came to England to continue his work, directing much of the revolutionary activity of African nationalism from his home in London. Here, for Wright, was a man whose fierce independence equaled his own. Dedicated and strong of will, Padmore was Wright's mirror image.

But there were others like Padmore, and in London and Paris he met them. Peter Abrams, the South African writer, "the second Negro to . . . [graduate] from the University of Johannesburg," who endured situations analogous to those "of the Negro on the plantations in the deepest south," Léopold Senghor, and Aimé Césaire, revolutionary poets and writers; Peter Blackman, from the West Indies, and Mohammed Mahgoub, from the Sudan. All were deeply concerned with racism and oppression, and their energy and vitality suggested to Wright dimensions of the racial problem that he had not theretofore seriously entertained. "The voice of the American Negro," he told the P.M. interviewer on his return, "is no longer a lone voice. You hear echoing voices in the people of Burma, China, South Africa. Three quarters of the world's population is colored. The attitude toward the Negro problem is entering a new phase."

The Wrights returned around the nineteenth of January, 1947. The furor caused by purchase of the Charles Street house had finally abated, and the family settled into the comfort of their new home. He had brought back a storehouse of fond remembrances, and freely praised the Europeans for their humanity and their courage. Yet he did not want to remain abroad, did not want to go into exile. It was enough to know that there were others engaged in the fight against racism and injustice, that the constant retreat of white liberalism in America and the impotence of American blacks were balanced by courageous blacks and whites of Europe, distant allies to be sure, but people whose sense of commitment was as sincere as his own. Why had he returned to New York, feeling the way he did about Europe? He mentally repeated the interviewer's question.

Proudly he looked around the interior of the freshly painted living room. The building, all three stories of it, was his. He had settled his family in one large apartment; the others, he would continue to rent out. Near him, his working desk was clear of things brought from Europe and those accumulated over the years. "Pictures," the P.M. interviewer noted, "were even stacked in the fireplace." But sofa, chairs, table and desk were carefully arranged. It was not difficult to understand why he had come back to America. He was an American. His roots were here; his days of anguish and his days of triumph and success had been born here: "The French," he said, "are in France and the Americans are in America. My work is here. My main job is in this country. . . . I belong here. . . . I was fashioned in this peculiar kind of a hell."[27]

He discovered before long, however, that readjustment to America after eight months of freedom from racial and governmental tension was difficult. He swung back into a vigorous program of activity, serving on the board of the Lafargue Clinic and for a short time on the executive committee of the Authors League. He wrote reviews and continued to give interviews; and he welcomed to the United States such notables as Simone de Beauvoir, often turning his living room into an intellectual, political, and social round table for discussions and debates. "I met at his Charles Street house Simone de Beauvoir (who was a champion, along with Jean Paul Sartre, of existentialism)," Owen Dodson recalled. "This philosophy impressed Dick wholeheartedly. . . ."[28] So, too, did the outspoken Ms. de Beauvoir, whom Wright escorted about the city, taking her to Harlem to meet Adam Clayton Powell, Jr., to dance at the Savoy Ballroom, and to "listen to spirituals in a small church. . . ."

But the stepped-up campaign against subversives, real and imagined, was rushing to a dramatic conclusion. The House Un-American Activities Committee was poised to begin the assault on Hollywood that would lead to the eventual blacklisting of hundreds of writers, directors and actors. ". . . some of the most flagrant Communist propaganda films," averred a HUAC report, were produced by the Hollywood film industry. In September, forty-one witnesses were subpoenaed by the Committee, of whom nineteen were "expected to be 'unfriendly.'" Thirteen of the nineteen were Jews.[29] Prominent among the targets of both HUAC and the FBI were past associates of Wright's: not only Ben Davis, Ford, Winston, and Yergan, but also Robeson and Canada Lee, who had starred in the stage production of *Native Son*. The target year for both HUAC and the Justice Department was 1948, when the fierce campaign to eradicate "the Communist threat" by jailing suspected subversives, known Communists, and sympathizers was to begin. Pressure, upon those with knowledge of "the conspiracy," to testify was intensified. What he had wanted as an American, Wright would later write in explaining the reason for his self-imposed exile, was the right to refuse to spy or inform on those who held differing political views. There is little reason to doubt that the FBI acted on its stated intention to interview Wright. The CIA, Chester Himes told John A. Williams in 1970, was interested in Wright because "they thought that he might have had information concerning the Communist affiliations of people in high places in government. . . ."[30] But, in 1947, it was the FBI that was interested, for the same reason.

How, then, could he satisfy this interest without becoming one of the government's many "black informers"? One way was to repeat his public criticism of the Party, to reiterate his charges that the leaders were egotistical, cruel, self-righteous men and women, or censure them anew for their conduct on the "Negro question," and continue to proclaim his own fierce anticommunism. Such a strategy could only be short-term. In time, the Bureau would demand specifics, would want validation of names, organizations, information more damaging to old comrades. There were two options: give the government the information it demanded or face investigation and probably trial himself. But there was a third option: he could choose exile. ". . . had I not fled my native land," he would later write, "I would have perished in the atmosphere of political hysteria of McCarthyism. . . ."³¹

Pressure to become an informant for the FBI was only one of the factors pushing him toward exile in the spring of 1947. After returning to America from his first visit to Europe, he told William Gardner Smith in 1954, he was affected by the contrast between France and America. The Americans appeared cold, frantic, materialistic. Beside the "haunting, picturesque grey rooftops of the Paris he had left" and "the fantastic formal beauty of the Luxembourg Gardens," New York streets and parks appeared dismal. There was a slow-paced, easy grace about Paris that was missing in New York.³² And as always, there was the daily confrontation with American racism: "Every Negro in America," he told Smith, "carries all through his life the burden of race consciousness like a corpse on his back. I shed that corpse when I stepped off the train in Paris."

Once, in a restaurant near his home, he was served salt in his coffee when he and a white companion sat beside each other. The waitress' manner suggested that that was the way coffee was served there.³³

And physical violence was a real possibility in those first months and years after the war. Gangs of young Italians thundered through the streets of Greenwich Village assaulting blacks; some were pulled from cars and beaten. Those unfortunate enough to be in the company of whites were, on more than one occasion, severely beaten. The rage and anger against blacks exempted neither women nor children, and Wright was concerned about possible injury to his wife and child. Julia was now six years old, a vibrant, energetic child to whom books and typewriters were important, who could not distinguish between blacks and whites, many of whom were visitors, and friends. It was doubtful that she could discern the contours of a world in which skin color was important.

Once, long before, he had maintained something of that same innocence. As a young boy, he had not been able for a long while to discern the fundamental difference between the white color of his grandmother and that of "white" people. He had not known that there was a demarcation line between one human being and another on the basis of pigmentation. He had always wanted to visit France, he said, because he wanted to live for a time in "a nonracist atmosphere." He wanted for Julia permanent escape to such an atmosphere; no black child should have to undergo the searing experiences he had written of in *Black Boy*. After she was refused the use of the ladies' restroom by an employee at Bergdorf Goodman's ("There are no restrooms for *you!*"), he realized how limited the scope of his protection was. "A pain so sharp," Constance Webb wrote, "that it hurt his throat burgeoned; it made his skin

feel as if every pore was overloaded with grief or rage. There was hate
alternating with pain. 'Sometimes I look at my sweet child and I wonder just how much does she know—I feel certain that she knows already
much more than she knows she knows. Yes, my baby is getting quite
old enough to understand it all.' "[34]

More and more, images of Paris, racism-free, beautiful, and serene,
tugged at his memory, beckoned. Twice before, he had left situations
and regions where his own security was threatened; now that of his family was threatened also, and he was becoming aware of the fact that he
would pull up anchor again. When you're born in the South, James
Baldwin related, you can always leave to go North; but when you're
born in New York, there is no place to go but out—of the country.
Wright had not been born in New York, but beyond the liberal pretense and such reactionary reality he had found in that city, there was
only the outside. In "I Choose Exile," he speaks of his decision in cata-
clysmic, almost cathartic, terms. He was through, done with struggling with American racism; he would leave for Europe. He would, in
so doing, have defeated the culture "that shaped" him. But he would
also have thrown up a protective curtain around Julia. Around the beginning of April, he confided his intentions to his wife.

He did not know how long this sojourn would last, but he planned
for a stay of some length. He arranged monthly payments to his
mother, from his account maintained by Reynolds. He purchased a new
car and learned to drive. He put his new home up for sale and left his
business affairs in the hands of his capable lawyer. He arranged for temporary lodging in France with a friend, Odette Lieutier, until he could
find an apartment for his family. On July 30, 1947, after a party in his
stateroom, he stood solemnly, watching intently together with his wife
and daughter, as the S.S. *United States* moved out into the Hudson
River.

The day was hot, humid, the air heavy with moisture; the dark,
crusted layers of the New Jersey Palisades were barely visible in the af-
ternoon haze. Silhouetted against the reddened sky, they appeared from
the ship deck like brooding specters. The skyscrapers of New York were
near, but they, too, seemed surrealistically etched against the hazy sky.
The reconverted troop carrier moved past other ships, some turning
their engines in preparation for their own voyages, past the Statue of
Liberty, where Wright blanched, reflected, past Ellis Island and the
antiquated buildings that once served as the first way station for exiles
from many lands. He reflected for a while on his going-away party, and
was a little ashamed of his attitude. His friends had been there:
"Ralph, Marie, Willard, Nello, Taska," along with others, but he had
been bored, had wanted the ceremony to end, had wanted to be on his

way. He was, he later confided to his journal, leaving the land of his birth, everything, and there was now no place that was home to him; he had no place to go back to.[35]

He thought of his belongings down in the hold of the ship: Knobby the cat, his Oldsmobile, trunks laden with books, clothing, pictures, pieces of furniture; he thought also of freedom, what his new novel was about. The sometimes violent heaving of the ship made him slightly uncomfortable, and this was exacerbated by the changes induced by his presence in others aboard ship. "I was returning to Europe for the first time since 1939," writes the French novelist Caroline Caro-Delvaille. ". . . Richard Wright, his wife and daughter were aboard, subjected to all the persecutions and ostracism that could spring up in the minds of the steward and officers on board, not to mention many of the American passengers."[36]

"When I come to sit down," he related to the novelist, "the people around me ostentatiously get up; with a visible disgust they make way for my wife, because she is white and has disgraced herself by marrying me."

What, then, was he seeking in crossing the Atlantic? he asked himself in his journal. Was it possible that he was seeking love, brotherhood, a chance to make others understand the man in him as he understood the man in them? Physically alienated from his homeland, the American in him wanted to reach out to them, to grope for common ground. Yet he could not. "They were passing me by," he related, "pretending not to see me. I was rejected." The words confided to his journal of July 31, therefore, were of resignation and of anger. The American passengers, he wrote, were unsophisticated, "internationally wet behind the ears." "Beside the people of the Continent," he wrote in a later entry, "they appeared like country apes. We are so young, so raw a people, so crude, so lacking in human feeling and sensitivity."[37]

As the long voyage continued, he was able to establish communication with some of the passengers, mostly foreigners like Ms. Caro-Delvaille and an Irishman, he wryly noted, who loved America more than he ever could. The Irishman had found paradise in America, had been treated better than blacks would ever be treated. Perhaps he, a foreigner in another country, would fare likewise. On the other side of the Atlantic were people of differing nationalities, and among them international brotherhood might be established. All that could have been on American shores might be realized on the Continent. It was small comfort, but comfort nevertheless.

On August 5, the ship docked at Southampton, England. Wright was recognized by the ship's steward and taken to meet the crew, who obviously sensed in the author of Black Boy a sympathetic listener.

They told him of their anger and outrage concerning their working conditions, told him of the inequities they suffered. He felt something of their outrage, but he confided to his journal that they should have done something about their condition. Undoubtedly he reflected upon the fact that he had moved to do something about his own. After disembarking, he and the family drove up to Folkestone in the large, cumbersome Oldsmobile, for the final journey into France.

Later that night, in his hotel room at Dover, overlooking the English Channel, he peered down through the haze settling slowly. On the other side lay Boulogne, a quiet, sleepy village from which he would motor into Paris. He was truly now a man alone, a man understood by no one, isolated with his own thoughts. What he wanted most of all was to live freely, and few people could understand that. But he knew it was the intensity of this desire, this obsession even, that had driven him from Memphis to Chicago, from Chicago to New York, from New York to Paris. And after Paris? He did not know. It was sufficient that Paris had once before offered him a sense of freedom, introduced him for the first time to whole days when he did not feel "like a Negro." It was, after all, in Paris, some weeks later, that he could confide to his journal that he was enamored of life and had no free time "to act free." Now he was anxious but also excited. On the next morning, the Wrights crossed the Straits of Dover. He retrieved his car and baggage, cleared customs, and set out toward Paris. The final odyssey had begun.

CHAPTER FOURTEEN

The August sun had set by the time the Wrights arrived at 9 rue de Lille, the home of Madame Odette Lieutier, their landlady from the previous visit. Again he was impressed by the magnificent beauty of the city. "I could tell a difference immediately between France and America," he confided to William Gardner Smith. "I could feel the difference in the air."[1] Civilization, he noted later, was the one French quality that the Americans did not possess.

The two-room apartment, overlooking a garden, assigned the Wrights by their host, would serve as temporary accommodations. Julia would share a room with the maid, Alice. There was the problem of working space, and he rented a hotel room across from Madame Lieutier's to serve as a small office. He was anxious to begin work again. Progress on his new novel had been slow. Once he was settled in his new home, he could accelerate his efforts. But he was an internationally known writer, and the guests who streamed constantly to welcome him back to Europe were many. Among the guests and callers were George and Dorothy Padmore, from London. Carson McCullers and her husband, Reeves, were among them. The fears Wright had had for Carson back when they shared the house at Seven Middagh Street were close to being realized. Frail health and constant drinking had left her almost an invalid who could have reminded Wright of his mother. He was filled with pity for the white writer, tried to comfort her, to pay her some of the attention that she desperately needed—attention not given by her husband, Reeves.

Such friends as Peter and Dorothy Abrams visited from England, and he delighted in showing them the magnificence of his new home in exile, introducing them to restaurants now becoming his favorites—Deux Magots and the Café Tournon. And whether in the company of guests or alone, on the streets of Paris passersby stopped him, greeted him. He would respond graciously; he was Monsieur Richard Wright, whose picture they had seen in the paper. He was such a celebrity, Himes quotes his own translator, "that if he had called a press conference at the foot of the stairs leading up to the *Sacré Coeur* and said, 'Gentlemen, I want you to run up these stairs,' they would have done so."

It was not long, however, before the romantic aspects of Parisian life succumbed to reality. Angrily he summed up his negative reactions to Paris and the Parisians in his journal. They were, on the whole, an impractical people. For two hours and more in the middle of the day, they closed their stores. They were abominable cheats. The women walked around half naked. Service people were often derelict in their duties; when the iceman did not respond readily to a request for ice, he was forced to purchase some himself. Somewhere, he mused in his anger, there had to be a "blending of the tolerant way of life of the French and the love of comfort of the Americans."[2] And there should be some way of assuring a man water enough for a hot bath after a long day's activities.

The truth is that he had returned to a Paris in the chaos and turmoil of a general strike, and he was piqued. Subway service was terminated; gas and water were cut off for interminable lengths of time; the streets overflowed with garbage and debris, and rats multiplied. The police and the workers regarded each other as the enemy, and clashes erupted between the two spontaneously and often.[3] The chaos of Paris triggered remembrances of his past in America. On his thirty-ninth birthday, a sense of despondency crept into his journal as he reflected on his past years and concluded that he had not accomplished very much. And a visit to a night club brought back despondent remembrances of the pains of yesterday. He had hated the place, he noted on September 22, because it reminded him of those desperate days of hunger, fear, and loneliness in Chicago. He could not, he recorded somewhat wistfully, tell his friends of his feelings. He confided his lack of "nourishing experiences" to his journal.

His depression was short-lived, however, and soon he settled down to the life of a famous Parisian intellectual. His itinerary was full: public appearances, book signings and lectures, interviews with foreign and American journals. A new apartment had to be secured: not only were Madame Lieutier's two rooms small, but he suspected that she was using drugs, and worried about the bad influence on Julia. After a careful search, the family located a six-room apartment on the Avenue de Neuilly. Amid the chores of settling in, he found time to sit on park benches to read books, including Camus's *The Stranger*. His critical comment on Camus's novel, recorded in his journal, was that it lacked "passion." But he was impressed by the writer's use of fiction "to express a philosophical point of view." He found time also for long discussions with Sartre and De Beauvoir.

Sartre, Wright felt, was the only Frenchman who translated that country's experience during the Nazi occupation into universal terms. His ideas led him into "areas" where one discovered what was "good." The discussions with De Beauvoir and Sartre often lasted late into the night and centered almost always upon the concept of freedom and the burden it imposed on the individual. It was an existential concept that haunted the black American writer, as various notations in his journal show. It was also one of the central theses of his new novel, which he was still having great difficulty in bringing himself to work on with any consistency. He was more consistent in his efforts on behalf of *Présence Africaine*, the magazine launched by Alioune Diop to explore and define "the African personality" and its universal implications. Wright was among the sponsors of the magazine, who also included Sartre and André Gide, Léopold Senghor, and Aimé Césaire. He served on the board of the magazine and was instrumental in having the works of such black Americans as Gwendolyn Brooks, Horace Cayton, Frank Marshall Davis, and C. L. R. James published. In the pages of *Présence Africaine*, "the Négritude Movement" was given full exposure, and in time the magazine and many of its African supporters and contributors became targets of investigation by the French security police and the CIA. Wright's declaration in his journal of September 16 that he had to see the continent of Africa in order to write "the only book about Africa that will be written in my time"[4] may have been inspired by his close association with Africans in London and Paris. His declaration of intent concerning Africa, noted in his journal, appears among many notations concerning freedom—the importance of it, the necessity of it. The relatively serene and peaceful environment of France led him to view the concept as being more meaningful than it was in the racially restricted environment of his homeland. Back in America, however, the concept was being put to the test as never before in the nation's history, and the speculations concerning it centered primarily upon whether or not it could survive the onslaught against it.

On October 20, 1947, J. Parnell Thomas (Republican, New Jersey), the new chairman of HUAC, summoned the packed hearing room to attention. Rankin, the leading Democrat on the Committee, had proposed these investigations himself, speaking contemptuously of "the loathsome, filthy, insinuating, un-American undercurrents . . . running through various pictures." He had proposed levying a ten-thousand-dollar fine and a ten-year jail term on teachers who aided, abetted, or sympathized with "Communist ideology."[5] The prospect of viewing such well-known Hollywood personalities as Gary Cooper and Robert Taylor caused a black-market run on seating. Inside, facing Rankin, Thomas, and the other members of the Committee, the "Hollywood Ten," as they would later be named, including Ring Lardner, Jr., John Howard Lawson, and Dalton Trumbo, along with witnesses and attorneys, sat illuminated by klieg-like lights. With the banging of the gavel by Thomas, the Hollywood version of "the night of the long knives" began. Before the ordeal ended, in the nineteen fifties, from California to New York a chorus of names were uttered in varying degrees of harmony, orchestrated by the members of HUAC. Hollywood's biggest names bowed, trembled, pleaded, and informed on others, in an attempt to satiate the Committee with information concerning the Communist conspiracy. Such matinee idols as Larry Parks, Humphrey Bogart, and Edward G. Robinson underwent confessional catharsis before HUAC. Writers such as Budd Schulberg and Bertolt Brecht repudiated the "errors" of their ways. Elia Kazan appeared and named Clifford Odets as a subversive; Odets, when given his opportunity to appear, named Kazan. The black actor William Marshall's career was ruined as information by informers eventually caused him to join hundreds of others on the Hollywood blacklist. Actor Canada Lee was dropped "by his television sponsor the American Tobacco Company." In desperation, unable to earn a livelihood, in an attempt to regain the good graces of the film industry, "he delivered an attack upon Paul Robeson." There were heroes also, who refused to take part in the orgy of defamation and slander. Despite economic and professional sanctions, Robeson steadfastly refused to cooperate with HUAC. Dalton Trumbo, John Howard Lawson, and Ring Lardner, Jr., stared down their inquisitors. Adam Clayton Powell was one of only two in the House of Representatives who voted against funding for HUAC. Pete Seeger refused to sing before the Committee, and Arthur Miller pointedly refused to answer questions about other individuals. He was among the few who did so. Hundreds of writers, directors, producers, and actors were blacklisted. HUAC had demonstrated its tenacity regarding the "Communist conspiracy." The bureaucrats of the Department of Justice could do no less.

On July 28, 1948, a federal grand jury indicted eleven members of the National Board of the Communist Party, among them Wright's old friends and antagonists Henry Winston and Benjamin Davis. They were charged with conspiring to "organize" the Communist Party of the United States, a group that advocated overthrow of the government by force and violence, and with teaching this doctrine themselves. The Justice Department wanted this conviction badly, in order to turn the Smith Act of 1940 into a potent weapon against the Communist Party.

None of the National Board members was on trial for committing acts of violence, but for simply "conspiring" to do so, and a "favorable" verdict against them would give the Department unlimited power to move against other suspected and former Communists. Overnight the Smith Act in fact became a weapon of legal terror, as men and women accused of holding opinions contrary to the government were brought to trial across the nation.

Day after day, during the nine months of one of the longest trials in American history, men with whom the exiled writer had had a working relationship confronted the super-patriotic delegation of the prosecution, the legal representatives of the United States Government. To their surprise, they also confronted old party members turned professional informers, some of whom had been in the employ of the government all along, and a massive array of sworn documentary testimony from ex-members who volunteered to give or were coerced into giving information to the FBI. They also faced the irony of circumstances: At the outset of the trial, the defendants contested the exclusion of blacks and other minorities from the jury. The intent was to throw the prosecution on the defensive with the charge that the government was racist and adhered to policies of racial exclusion and oppression.

It proved to be a tactical error. The government in fact practiced racial policies of almost unlimited inclusion: among its major witnesses were black agents and informers. The agents, recruited by the Party because they were black, were sent off to Moscow for political education, and quickly started on the path to leadership. The informers, noted David Caute, "comprised a sad crew of Uncle Toms. . . ." One such informer, William O. Newell, made his debut at the Foley Square trials. He was so successful that later he offered his expertise upon the menace of the Communist conspiracy in Smith Act trials across the country. William G. Cummings, an ex-Communist turned informer, shocked his former leaders by his appearance in the courtroom at Foley Square. Over a period of eight years, he was to earn over eleven thousand dollars for information given to the FBI and offered in court trials involving Communists and Communist organizations. The black agents and informers took their places side by side with the white ones; their mannerisms and actions contrasted sharply with those of the two black Communist leaders. During the course of the trial, Winston became so agitated that his bail was revoked and he was remanded to jail. He suffered a heart attack, but Judge Medina refused to allow Winston's personal physician to tend him. Davis, the calm, rational party statesman, induced obvious discomfort in both his white and black accusers.

He had survived the party purge after the Duclos attack, and he was highly regarded by his Harlem constituency as well as by members of

the Communist International. Only two months prior to the beginning
of his trial, he had proved his value as a leader. In August of 1949, Paul
Robeson was to give a benefit performance in Peekskill, New York,
where anti-Communist fervor ran rampant and threats of physical violence to the purported gathering of "Blacks and Jews" came from all
quarters. Even the government of New York supported the attempt to
prevent Robeson from performing. On the first scheduled date of the
concert, the audience and performers were violently assaulted by
members of the American Legion. Davis, unperturbed, demanded that
the concert be held one week later. He summoned over three thousand
"friendly security guards (fur workers, longshoremen, seamen)" to be
prepared to trade violent blow for violent blow.[6]

Now, standing before his accusers, this was one of his finest hours.
The outcome, he knew, was not in doubt. Red hysteria would doom
them all. What was important was that he maintain his sense of historical perspective. History would reveal that it was not the Communist
Party that was on trial but the American Constitution. "We are
confident," he told the court on his day of sentencing, "that the American people are going to realize what is happening here and that they
will realize that their liberties, their peace, and their democracy are im-
periled. We have all the confidence in them because the future belongs
to the people of America, Negro and White." Davis was sentenced to
five years in federal prison.

Far from the dock in Foley Square, in Paris, Wright was less concerned about the fate of his one-time comrades than he was about the
global implications of America's turn to the right. "From the vantage
point of the grim realism of Europe," he had written Dorothy Norman
in March of 1948, "events in America take on fantastic shapes . . .
compared to the hard necessity of European reactions, American reaction seems irresponsible. To be anti-Fascist or anti-Communist in
France is a totally different thing from being anti-Communist or anti-
Fascist in America. . . . The questioning . . . of the Hollywood actors
by the Un-American Activities Committee is quite incomprehensible
here, and people keep asking: 'How many Communists have you in
America?' And when you answer: 'Not more than a hundred thousand,'
they don't know what to say. Frenchmen are used to dealing with Communists by the millions, not by the thousands."[7]

The paranoia leading Americans to assault the Bill of Rights and to
fear communism was historical. Both could be traced back, he was to
imply later in another context, to the "barbaric treatment of the
Negro." Such treatment was not as terrible, though, as what racism led
America to: "destructive warfare . . . against the concept of the free
person, against freedom of conscience, against the rights of man, and

against herself."[8] During the winter of 1948, he visited Italy, England, and Belgium. Their people, he found, sought some unifying force around which to structure their lives and their countries. In Italy, he found "an odd and vibrant spirit."

He discovered that concern about the United States dominated European thinking and that American influence was pervasive. American currency was the most stable and most sought after. American movies and novels proliferated, along with Wheaties and Fords. European economic and military needs, partially satisfied through American aid programs and military pacts, gave America great power in European affairs. In England, too, like the rest of Europe, the aftermath of the war and the great floods of 1947 had brought American hegemony and economic and political chaos. Even France no longer appeared to be the stable nation he had found on his first visit. "I've seen some strange things here in Paris since last August": the disruption of the French currency, which made the black market the dominant economic institution; corruption, high prices, demonstrations, lack of material goods and comforts. The lack of ideological direction, so pronounced in the rest of Western Europe, was even more evident in France. The country had become a testing ground between left and right, and the Gaullists and their leader, General Charles de Gaulle, waited in the background. This once great bastion of freedom seemed free no longer. Again the safety of his wife and daughter was foremost in his thoughts: he kept three tickets at the ready; complete chaos and a decisive victory by either left or right would propel him out of the country.

"Yet," he wrote, "something happens when life sinks to such a low pitch of being. In extreme situations like this men have leaped out and greeted themselves and the world anew." But the spiritual impetus for this creation would not come from America, where daily the rights of man were being trampled by HUAC. Nor from the Soviet Union, where the concept of freedom was almost nonexistent. And certainly not from tired Western Europe, confronted with the task of maintaining its own identity in the cold war between America and Russia. In various ways, both right and left, East and West, defined man as a kind of animal to be satiated by material comforts, in a world in which full stomachs and freedom would be synonymous. It would lead inevitably to "a total extinction of the very concept of what it has meant to be a human being for 200 years."

However, the Third World force, poised between East and West, seemed perhaps man's last hope for retaining workable concepts of freedom and man. It had not succumbed to the evils inherent in industrialization and technological advancement and had time, therefore, to create the new man of the modern world, one who would utilize technology and industrialization as a means of enhancing the validity and importance of man. As he had once believed blacks to be the spiritual saviors of America, now he envisioned the Third World as the spiritual saviors of humankind. It was the barrier between both left and right, between American and Soviet hegemony. In an interview published under the auspices of Michel Gordy (himself an object of investigation by the FBI) in the *Lettres Françaises* of January 10, 1947, Wright had made clear his position as a "committed intellectual" aligned with neither East nor West but fervently committed to creation of "a third force." Wright's new position, philosophical though it was, did not escape the notice of the United States Government. "It should be noted," a dispatch to Washington read, "that whereas Richard Wright continues to maintain an anti-Stalinist position since his expulsion from the CPUSA, he has wittingly or not been serving Communist propaganda ends by frequent contributions to neutral publications such as *L'Observateur* and particularly by his insistence on portraying abroad only the seamy side of the race question in the United States. While flirting with Titoism and Sartroism, he has maintained a position, so far as the East-West conflict is concerned tantamount to 'a plague on both your houses.'"[9]

Despite his trepidation about the French political scene, his philosophical position now arrived at, feeling more comfortable in his role as an important Paris intellectual, he settled down to his life as an expatriate. The family moved again, this time into the heart of the Latin Quarter, into a spacious apartment overlooking the Luxembourg Gardens. To his new apartment, noted Ollie Harrington, "came the great, the not so great, and those who would never be great. All were welcome." Jean Paul Sartre, Simone de Beauvoir, Arna Bontemps, Gunnar Myrdal, and E. Franklin Frazier, Frank Yerby, Ralph Ellison, James Ivy, and Saunders Redding were among those who came. They discussed America and Europe, Africa and the Third World, bantered about people and events. "Wright," said one guest, "was a great raconteur. In that high squeaky voice, he brought down the house with the punch line of every joke—some of them were, what would you say, kind of rees-cuee?" His prize, however, was young Julia. Bright, precocious, she held her own and better with French students at the Lyceum. She was beginning to speak French as if it were her first, not second, language. "That child Julia," he confided with obvious pride to Ollie Harrington at one point, "she worries me. She won't do anything but study."

But there were personality quirks also, revealed now, in this atmosphere of relative peace and calm. "I remember the first time I met Wright," recalled another black American, soon to become one of the

writer's best friends; "it was like something out of Mississippi. I was
hungry as hell. But Dick and his family went into the dining room to
eat—he left me, still hungry as hell." He had this crazy habit, Chester
Himes remarked, of calling his friends in the early hours of the morning.
He had the habit also, Himes later recorded, of poking his nose into everything out of the ordinary, everything strange. When James Baldwin
arrived in Paris in 1948 to commence his own exile, he ran into Wright,
who was sitting in the Deux Magots, one of his favorite restaurants,
with the editors of Zéro magazine. "Hey boy," Baldwin recalled the
greeting, noting that Wright appeared "more surprised and pleased and
conspiratorial than ever, and younger and happier." He was calm, courteous and he introduced the younger writer around. He did not, however, perhaps as Baldwin wished, adopt the younger man, fatherlike, as
a protégé, and guide him through the pitfalls of this new and frightening environment.

But Baldwin was only one of the growing black expatriate community in Paris that had made Wright their leader. They were writers, artists, students, ex-GI's, composers, musicians, and representatives of various governmental agencies such as UNESCO and the United States
Information Service. And there were those, a growing number, who
served as agents or informers for the CIA, the FBI, and the American
Embassy. The Café Tournon, situated atop a hill, directly in front of
the Luxembourg Gardens, near Wright's new apartment, was the place
of rendezvous. Here blacks met to fraternize and debate racial problems,
to drink scotch, and to become involved in the heart of the bohemian
life of the Left Bank. The cafe was far from the colonial-style mansion
on the Champs Élysées that housed the American Embassy and was
the focal point for another community of Americans, predominantly
white. But, for whites and blacks alike, Wright was the most celebrated
of the Left Bank Americans.

Perhaps too austere and imposing, he was not, however, the favorite
of the Paris black community. This position was occupied by his old
friend Ollie Harrington, a one-time war correspondent and cartoonist.
"Ollie," related Chester Himes, "was the center of the American community on the Left Bank in Paris, white and black . . . he was a fabu-
lous raconteur. . . . He used to keep people spellbound for hours. So
they collected there [at the Tournon] because of Ollie."[10] When Harrington arrived at the American colony, Wright gained his most faithful and lasting friend, despite the fact that they were somewhat separated by ideology. Wright's flirtation with the Communist Party was
behind him, while Harrington's would grow to full romance over the
years. Still, the handsome, freewheeling Harrington and the somewhat
correct, puritanical Wright shared ideas about racism and American so-

ciety. They also shared an antagonist, in the person of Agnes Schneider, American consul in Paris. A cold warrior, ever watchful for subversives or Communist sympathizers, and considered extremely racist by members of the black colony, she had almost absolute power over Americans in Paris. At her behest, passports could be confiscated; and sometimes the owner would be shipped back to America. Or she could render the holder passportless, as was the fate she rendered to Harrington, confiscating it and holding it for a number of years. Backed up by the legal attaché of the American Embassy (the FBI agent in charge in foreign countries), her information on Americans, on their former as well as present political and social activities, was complete.

Even now, Wright's activities were being carefully monitored by U. S. Government agents: "On November 30, 1948," bureau files noted, "an informant of unknown reliability who was visiting in Paris, France, advised that he was approached by Richard Wright, whom he described as a 'well-known Communist writer,' who had requested him to jointly cooperate in writing a book showing the methods used by the Communists to ensnare the Negroes into the Communist movement." The partially eradicated name following the notation was Max Yergan. An old friend and fellow Marxist, Yergan had broken with the Party shortly after Wright. If Yergan was not then in the employ of the FBI, he may have been trying to avoid possible recriminations for his Communist past by informing on others. Whatever his new role, there was little to report to the investigative agencies of a subversive nature concerning Wright during his first year in exile. His flirtation with what the FBI called "Sartroism," referring probably to Wright's collaboration with Sartre in an attempt to make the non-Communist Rassemblement Démocratique Révolutionnaire "into a powerful movement" had already been noted. The group, however, was, from the outset, strongly anti-Marxist, and when it moved from this position, Wright broke with it.

There was little of a political nature in his lectures on the relationship between Europe and America given at the American Church; nor in his lecture to the Club Maintenant on Afro-American literature.[11] He attended parties and receptions, and openly spoke about racial conditions in America on such occasions as receiving the French Critics Award for the newly published translation of Black Boy and affairs given in his honor by the publisher Gallimard or Les Temps Modernes. But his attacks on American racial conditions were balanced by his attacks on the Communists. In November of 1948, he agreed to allow publication of "I Tried to Be a Communist" in an anthology, The God That Failed. In 1949, he spoke out against Robeson's assertion that blacks would not defend American interests in a war with the Soviet

Union, and on April 4, 1949, he unleashed an attack on the Communist Party of the United States in an open letter to the Paris Edition of the New York *Herald Tribune,* and on Anna Strong, his one-time Communist superior, who had fallen on bad times. She had emigrated to the Soviet Union presumably to escape the investigative agencies in America. Soon she fell into disfavor with Soviet authorities, was arrested, charged with spying, and ordered expelled, only to return to America to face inquisition and possible imprisonment by the Justice Department or one of the congressional investigative committees. In a desperate attempt to avoid both, she published a series of six letters to the European edition of the *Herald Tribune,* in which she tried to downplay her position in the Communist hierarchy.

Reading Strong's apologia, Wright was jolted back ten years, when he had sought her help in his own battle with "petty Communist officials." They had talked, he recalled, as one comrade to another, and he had told her of his own difficulties with "the American Communist Party, but his appeal was summarily rejected" and he was "abruptly and brutally" dismissed. Having never forgotten the incident, he now seized the platform offered by the *Herald Tribune* to strike out at her and the American Communist Party: "Comrade Strong," he wrote, "for thirty years you defended, created, rationalized, perfected, and justified the very cruelties which you now lament. . . . You too have listened to comrades in the Communist Party voice appeals and complaints similar to yours and you turned your head away. . . ."[12]

It is a bitter denunciation, motivated no doubt in part by an attempt to settle old scores. But the public attack had come at a most inopportune moment for the Communist Party in America. At the very hour of publication, two of the Communists Wright named, Davis and Winston, were on trial at Foley Square. The Justice Department, through its prosecutor, John F. X. McGohey, had specified the charges against the defendants and established the criteria for other such trials. Among the charges enumerated were the following: indoctrination of members and gaining recruits by exaggerating minority grievances; encouraging admiration and support for "the bolshevick revolution by attacking capitalism, portraying the armed forces as tools of Wall Street imperialism," and arguing that warfare between America and the Soviet Union would be "imperialistic and unjust and a cause for civil war."[13] Wright does not directly accuse his old comrades of these specifics, but, indirectly, his letter suggests that the Communist Party of the United States was guilty of many of them.

What, then, was the reason for his untimely attack? Did he simply feel a moral necessity to speak out? Was it his way of attempting to silence the attacks made upon him by the French Communist Party? If so, why the onslaught against the CPUSA, which, given its own burgeoning troubles, was in no position to orchestrate attacks upon him either at home or abroad? Or, more to the point, was he attempting to convince the American Government that his own anticommunism was as fervent as ever? "Comrade Strong," he wrote, "you are in a position to help cleanse the soiled political instrument which the oppressed want to use in their struggle for a better life. You are free. You can make any choice you like. You can step out of that morass of psychological slavery in which you floundered when you wrote your articles and you can renounce that devious political game in whose names people become so lost that they cannot tell the truth even when they try. . . . You can still confess openly, honestly, completely and with a deep sense of responsibility toward the oppressed of this earth and their future. . . ."[14] Were these simply the words of a morally committed and concerned man? Or were they words designed to point out the true position of the anti-Communist—his, in contrast to that of others? If the latter, the venture was doomed to failure. His own assertions and anti-Communist activities to the contrary notwithstanding, the United States Government was not altogether assured that Wright was not, at the very least, "a philosophical Communist."

The attack on Anna Strong occurred four months before he visited the United States for the first time since his exile. The reason for his trip concerned the filming of *Native Son*. In the summer of 1948, he was approached by the producer Pierre Chenal and his partner, James Prades, of Uruguay, who expressed interest in making the novel into a movie. Wright agreed to join in the partnership and to play the role of Bigger Thomas. On his own initiative, Chenal bought the rights to the stage adaptation and wrote the script himself, changing some of the scenes from the stage version and adding others. And when "political pressures" prevented the filming of certain scenes in Italy and France, Chenal boarded the *Queen Mary* on August 20, en route to New York. The working plan was to film certain portions of the movie in Chicago in September and the remainder in Argentina in October. After a brief stay in New York, Wright went to Chicago. He had written his agent to maintain secrecy concerning the project, and the facts were not revealed by Reynolds until Wright and the company, Sono Films, were already in Buenos Aires.[15]

He was a changed man, this prodigal come back to his first home away from the South. He had not been in Chicago in close to four years. The family with which he had begun his trek had now, like himself, departed. They were back in Mississippi, and the home he had purchased for Ella now sheltered another family. Although some old friends were still there, it was now a strange city, dirty and even more overcrowded, with a lack of trees and vegetation that affronted his sensibilities now after almost two years in Paris. And the overt racism and corrupt officials turned his stomach. He had taken precautions for securing a room at the prestigious Palmer House, having wired ahead to Louis Wirth, a white man, asking him to make reservations in his behalf. But when Wright tried to reserve rooms there for Prades, due to arrive for work on the film, he was informed by the white clerk that no rooms were available. Sizing up the situation, Wright asked a black waiter about the clerk's assertion. The waiter validated his own suspicions: the hotel was half empty. He called a white friend, who came down and explained the situation to the management: moments later, a reservation was issued in the name of James Prades. The overt corruption that he encountered on this trip annoyed him, though he was no stranger to Chicago corruption. Years before, he had observed the practice at work when he worked for the Republican and Democratic candidates. But the corruption now was more blatant, seemingly more widespread. When the crew filmed scenes in white neighborhoods, the police gathered as if at a barbecue to accept the ten-dollar bills the producer handed out to ensure that the filming would proceed uninterrupted. The police took their graft in the full light of day and public exposure. Sometimes they even lingered to watch the film being shot; at other times, they protected the crew from other policemen and enraged whites.

He offered his final appraisal of the city in "The Shame of Chicago." "Powerfully and impressively ugly . . . ," it was a city where the paraphernalia of affluence, "packards, oldsmobiles, chevrolets, all gleaming and new" stood in glaring contrast to the squalor and the slums. The once deserted tenements in which, in the novel, he had Bigger hide while trying to elude the police, were deserted no longer. They had not been renovated, either. Men, women, and children had been forced to find homes in those condemned buildings, as a result of overcrowding during the war. Now families much like his own on their first arrival in Chicago shared squalid quarters with rats and other vermin. Still, as before, those houses were populated by blacks, while the whites retreated farther and farther away from the South Side. They reminded him of two armies each nervously circling the other; the whites motivated by centuries-old hatred and hostility, the blacks by fear and rage. The whites were willing to go to the bitter end to maintain their privileges: their white neighborhoods, schools, separate way of life. Blacks struck out through violence, crime, and riots. The movement of these two armies was toward a Wagnerian "twilight of the gods" ending in the world-horrifying spectacle of the Cicero riots. The situation of blacks, he concluded, the filming done and the crew heading toward Argentina, remained as hopeless as before.

The entire production company of Sono Films gathered in Buenos Aires; along with Wright, the cast included Gloria Madison, who played Bessie; Joan Wallace, who played Mary Dalton; and Nicholas Joy as Mr. Dalton. Jan Erlone was played by Gene Michael, Mrs. Dalton by Ruth Roberts, the attorney Boris Max by Don Dean, and Bigger's sister, Vera, by a Brazilian, Lydia Alvas. Wright was particularly grateful to Ms. Wallace, who took the unpopular role opposite a black male character and whose career suffered, later, as a result. *Publishers Weekly* announced on October 1, quoting Reynolds, that "A four month schedule" had been set "for the studio work in the Argentine." However, dissension and intrigue among the principals, added to technical difficulties, more than doubled that time. Wright discovered too that he had been misled about costs and shooting time, even about his original contract, which had guaranteed him 17 percent of the profits plus expenses but which was changed in the Spanish translation. Later it was stolen from his room. He told Attilio Mentasti, who had earlier become a partner in the production along with Chenal and Prades, of his suspicions over the legal maneuvers of the other partners. Together he and Mentasti drew up another contract, which granted Wright one fifth of the profits. The film was completed in June of 1950, and the total operation was finished in October. On November 4, *Native Son*, starring Richard Wright as Bigger Thomas, premiered aboard a Pan-American airliner en route to Nice.

Much of the film was left on the cutting-room floor in Argentina. What remained for the viewing public was a film that followed the novel only in terms of theme and message.[16] Sensationalistic episodes were added, probably with an American audience in mind. Running commentary upon the action of the film disrupted overall continuity. Bigger Thomas was described as a young man of ambition, unable to realize his potential because he was black. "When you are black," ran the commentary from the script, "it is better to keep your dreams locked in your heart." Bigger was changed from the fearful ghetto youth of *Native Son* into a young tough seeking vengeance upon the white world. Brandishing a gun at one point, Bigger wears it as though it were his badge of equality. Bessie, the frightened, timid automaton of the novel, is depicted in the film as an ambitious singer, passionately, jealously involved with Bigger. But Mary Dalton undergoes the most sensationalistic transformation. In the novel, she appears flighty, overbearing, but innocent, while, in the film, she becomes a sexual object for Bigger. He first encounters her in a "flimsy negligee" and she places her arms around his shoulders and makes flattering remarks. On the night of the murder, Bigger is shown crushing her in a brutal, passionate embrace. It is the dream sequence alone, which Wright introduced into the play, however, that lends creativity and novelty to the film. But how much of the script was changed or simply left on the cutting-room floor would be difficult to determine. Wright attributed the financial failure of the film to the cuts, particularly to those demanded by the censors in New York, which he strongly protested. Even the FBI was told of his discontent with the venture. An informant reported to Army Intelligence "that Wright had made a picture in South America early this year and since has lost a lot of money promoting a dance group. Wright had asked [name deleted] to write some music for a new show which Wright wanted to do in order to recoup his fortune."[17]

The film completed, he visited Haiti for the first time, intent upon taking notes on the black country for possible publication of "a travel journal."[18] He visited Rio, and along with Eric Williams, "vice-president of the research committee for the Caribbean Commission," heard his first tin can band at the Port of Spain City Club. His reactions to this experience were almost childlike. "I've never seen or got such a treat." When the band played, he sprang to his feet, convinced that the sounds that he heard came from "a steel band." When he discovered that the music was made "on the steel heads of gasoline drums," he divined this as one more instance of black genius and creativity.[19] He met and talked with Haitian intellectuals and writers and was intrigued by the voodoo cults and the revolutionary history of this former French colony which had given birth to the rebel Toussaint L'Ouverture.

Still, he was impatient to get back to Paris to spend time with the newest addition to his family, daughter Rachel, who had been born on January 19, 1949, at the American Hospital in Paris. The treatment accorded Ellen Wright during the birth of her second child was more gracious than what she experienced during the birth of Julia in a Brooklyn hospital seven years before. Whatever the American staff felt about interracial marriages, prudence demanded that their remarks and attitudes be uttered, if at all, in private. Wright was now the father and protector of *two* young girls. Julia's health and vitality had more than convinced him that he was right to raise his child away from American racism. The safety and well-being of his family demanded that he remain abroad. Still, as he told an interviewer before sailing back to France on August 19, though he may complain about America, he was still an American citizen. "The only thing that Paris has," he remarked, "that the United States does not seem to have is humanity."[20]

The presence or absence of American humanity, however, was not the pressing question for civil libertarians and the left in 1950. Of much more immediate concern was the continual massing of power by the investigatory agencies of the federal government. In February of 1950, Senator Joseph McCarthy, of Wisconsin, mounted a platform in Wheeling, West Virginia, brandishing a sheaf of papers that he claimed contained the names "of 205 Communists employed by the State Department."[21] In the same year, President Harry S Truman charged, at Cornell, that sit-in demonstrations in the South by black and white students were inspired by the Communists. In August of 1950, the State Department revoked the passports of several Americans desiring travel abroad, including that of Paul Robeson. And in that same year, the liberal democrats of the United States Senate were overwhelmed in their attempt to defeat the Internal Security Act of 1950. Among the more ominous features of the Act was the emergency detention clause, which enabled the government, during times of "national emergency," to imprison without benefit of trial any American citizen who had held membership in the Communist Party since 1949. Camps were to be provided during such times of emergency. The clause amounted to a virtual cancellation of the constitutional right against unlawful search and seizure. The burden of proof was on the defendant, as the words of informants or unscrupulous agents could seal the fate of a suspected Communist, under the clause. For many Americans like Wright, past association with the Party added an extra burden.

The power of the Attorney General to officially list subversive or radical organizations for possible action by the federal government had received added powers in 1947 when Truman issued Executive Order 9835. The order "launched the Federal Loyalty Program," and the Internal Security Division of the Justice Department was able to add more organizations to the list. The creation of the Subversive Activities Control Board, by the McCarran Act, gave the Attorney General the power to act more decisively against suspect organizations. On a petition from the Attorney General and after hearings, an organization could be ordered "to register under the act as 'Communist-action, Communist-front,' or subversive."[22] Those groups so ordered would have to file lists naming their officers, "maintain supervised records, and to label their mail." On November 22, the Attorney General "petitioned" the Board to order the Communist Party to register under the Act. Had it registered as a Communist-action group, the Party would have been forced to list its members, in addition to its officers; members would be barred from elective office or work on defense contracts awarded to private industry. The literature and radio broadcasts by such organizations would have to bear the stamp: "Dissemination by _____, a Communist organization . . . "Section 6 made it illegal for members of registered organizations to apply for a new passport or for renewal of an old one. The McCarran Act, vetoed by President

Truman, became law when the Congress overrode the presidential veto.

The Act was a potent weapon in the arsenal of congressional and governmental agencies charged with tracking down subversives. Secretary of State Dean Acheson acknowledged in 1952 what by then was common knowledge: Passports would be withheld from those whom the government "had reason to believe" were members of the Communist Party and whose "conduct abroad is likely to be contrary to the best interests of the United States," or from those who, while abroad, might "engage in activities which will advance the Communist movement. . . ."[23] Reportedly, "three thousand Americans" were barred from traveling abroad; in other cases, "evidence" of the willingness of "ex-Communists to cooperate with governmental officials" had to be shown before issuing passports.

Revocation of passports from those already abroad often forced Americans to return. Dr. Walter G. Berman was already in Denmark delivering a lecture in 1953 when his passport and that of his wife were suddenly revoked. He was accused of attending "a Communist meeting." William Patterson, in Paris to present a petition on genocide before the United Nations, was warned in time to enable him to change hotels and escape authorities coming to revoke his passport. The government was therefore armored against the suspected subversive at home and abroad. Proof that one was a Communist or, in Acheson's words, engaged in conduct abroad that "is likely to be contrary to the best interests of the United States" could bring the recalcitrant back to America to face the wrath of any of a number of congressional or other governmental agencies. For a long time, foreign intelligence had been in the hands of the FBI, through the legal attachés of the American embassies and the Office of Strategic Services. In 1946, the Central Intelligence Group was authorized by the President. When the National Security Act was passed, in 1947, the Central Intelligence Group was re-created as the Central Intelligence Agency.[24] The agency is charged primarily with collecting information abroad that might affect the security of the United States. Outside of this mandate, the Agency has been involved in such clandestine operations as attempts to subvert foreign governments and investigation of Americans at home and abroad, and has been financially and politically involved in such organizations as the Committee for Cultural Freedom. By the time Wright arrived back in Paris, in August of 1950, the CIA was deeply involved in the black expatriate community.

CHAPTER FIFTEEN

Wright had returned to Paris somewhat disappointed over the probability of failure of his film. He had lost much of his own money on the venture. According to an FBI informant, he had incurred the wrath of some of the black expatriate community because he had promised them roles in the picture and had not followed through. He was glad to be done with the venture, eager to move on to other work. The nine months spent on actual shooting of the film had left him little time to work on anything else. His novel, which he had informed his editor he was reworking, was nowhere near completion. The only major piece of published work bearing his byline was the anthologized essay "I Tried to Be a Communist," included in *The God That Failed*, published in 1949. Edited by Richard Crossman, the book was suggested by the ex-Communist Arthur Koestler, who, along with Wright, André Gide, Ignazio Silone, Louis Fischer, and Stephen Spender, was among the contributors.

After viewing the contents of the book, one F. J. Bauman forwarded a memorandum to a Mr. A. H. Belmont, that ended up in the offices of SAC Tolson of the New York Field Office. "The purpose of this memorandum," wrote Bauman, "is to submit for your consideration certain pertinent ideas which may be of some interest and value to the security work being conducted."[1] "The former Communist Intellectuals" wrote Bauman, described their affiliation with communism, and the book had been favorably received in the United States. "Writers today," he noted, "seem to rush to praise lavishly any Communist who has left the movement. There seems to be a tendency to make heroes and prophets and seers out of ex-Communists." This lavish praise is heaped upon them without much consideration as "to the present convictions held by these ex-Communists."[2] Much of the memo concerns the article by

Wright. A Xeroxed copy of the article is included in the memo. Approximately three paragraphs pertaining to him are deleted. There is a brief biographical sketch. A bureau notation cites the period of Wright's membership in the Party as extending from 1932 to 1940. The sections dealing with the writer fall under three general headings: "Reasons Why Richard Wright Accepted Communism," "Reasons Why Richard Wright Rejected Communism," and "Richard Wright's Present Convictions." The latter brought forth questions and speculations from the author of the memo. He found it odd that even though Wright acknowledged suffering at the hands of the Party, he still vowed "I'll be for them, even though they are not for me." Whatever the ex-Communist believes in now is not clear. He "complains" that never again will he be able to to make a commitment of faith so total as that he accorded the Party. "He surrounds his present state of mind with vague, dramatic and almost meaningless words." In his own "Observations," Bauman concluded, it appeared that though Wright and the others were ex-Communists, "they have not accepted the principles of democracy known and enjoyed in the United States. On the contrary, they seem to entertain still a certain degree of sympathy and affection for what they consider to be the ideal form of Communism." Clearly, one agency of the United States Government did not look upon the restatement of Wright's old disaffection with the Party, as forwarded in the Crossman anthology, as proof positive of his break with communism. A formal Communist, in the sense of being a card-carrying member, he may not be. But his ideas could well lead to suspicion that he was "a philosophical Communist," and the Internal Security Act of 1950 enabled the government to deal with philosophical Communists as well as actual ones.

Wright had hoped, however, that a restatement of his attitudes would end all doubt as to his status as a Communist. He was a supporter of neither East nor West, nestled in neither the camp of the right nor that of the left. His own deep concern and commitment was toward the Third World. He was opposed to racism and discrimination, to injustice and oppression, and he saw these characteristics in both East and West. Even in France, racism had begun to breed and grow, multiplying like disease germs, and after a brief vacation in Switzerland, he returned to Paris to lend his tremendous influence and energies to exterminating the germs.

Even before leaving for Argentina to work on the film, Wright and other aware black Americans had become alarmed over the growing incidence of racism in Paris. A small group, initially composed of Wright, Ligon Buford, ex-director of the World Refugee Office, and journalists William Rutherford and Ollie Stewart, discussed the topic, sometimes at Chez Inez, where the management—Inez Cavanaugh, Al "Fats" Edwards, and Al Simmons—joined in, and at other times at the homes of other concerned Americans, such as Jay Clifford, a retired American customs official. The expatriate Americans foresaw a crisis in the expansion of American influence, politically through the Marshall Plan and the Atlantic Pact, and militarily through SHAPE. More and more Americans were joining the community, centered around the American Embassy, working for either governmental agencies or the multiplying number of American corporations. The low French foreign-exchange rate drew thousands of American tourists to Paris each year, and the Korean War increased the number of American military personnel, designed to bolster the European alliance. Most of the newcomers were white, and they brought their American brand of racism with them.

The black community, which had enjoyed a relative degree of freedom from racial restraint, felt threatened. American racism was infectious. None of the "American commercial firms in France employed blacks," Wright told a conference held under the auspices of *L'Observateur* in 1951, and proceeded to name the following: "The Guaranty Trust Company of New York; J. P. Morgan and Company; The American Express Company; The Chase National Bank; Kodak; Standard Oil; Shell Oil; United States Steel. . . ." In addition, no black had ever been employed by the American Hospital during its twenty-five-year existence. White American tourists forced French hotels to enact racially restrictive practices, and clashes between black civilians and white military personnel were on the increase. "The white folks," said a member of the group, "were damn' hot about all them black brothers running around with them pretty French girls." Agnes Schneider, Chester Himes later wrote, "became so disturbed by the rumors of interracial sex taking place . . . she began confiscation of whatever soul brother's passport she could lay her hands on."[3] In defense of their liberties, therefore, Wright told the *L'Observateur* conference, "and as a gesture of friendship and solidary toward their French neighbors," the black Americans organized a group, ". . . the Franco-American Fellowship, whose aim is to raise again the concept of freedom, generosity, the dignity and sanctity of the individual."[4]

The Franco-American Fellowship held a "pilot meeting" on October 5, 1950, "quite late, as I remember," Baldwin later recalled, "one evening in a private room over a bistro. It was in some extremely inconvenient part of town, and we all arrived, separately by twos. . . . (There was some vague notion . . . of defeating the ever present agents of the C.I.A.)" Wright explained the group's objectives, and told the black expatriates that he had enlisted the aid of such French personages as Sartre and De Beauvoir, and that the American Embassy was disturbed over the formation of the group. Noting the large number of artists among the expatriate community, he avowed that the Fellowship would be cultural as well as political. The inaugural meeting was held in December and addressed by Sartre and Louis Fischer, the American author. By early 1951, the group had over sixty members. In February the group investigated the charges by a black nurse, Margaret McCleveland, that she had been denied a job due to racial discrimination at the American Hospital. In the same month, the group protested the plight of "The Martinsville Seven," condemned to the electric chair by the Virginia courts on the charge of rape; the impending execution of Willie McGee, convicted of rape in Mississippi; "and sent messages of support to other organizations concerned with racism and anti-semitism." The group sponsored social and cultural functions as well and held lectures and conferences at which various topics were debated. "Among the topics discussed," an informant told the FBI, was "The Danger of Wall Street Capitalism," and the most persistent theme echoed in group discussions centered upon things "wrong with the United States." In April, the CIA monitored the conference held at the Club de L'Observateur, in which Wright occupied the speakers' rostrum with the Marxist Daniel Guérin, who had been denied an American visa and who had been supported by the Fellowship.

The CIA agent was more impressed by the attendance, about seventy people, and audience at this meeting than those he had previously attended. The audience was "primarily French, but there were also Americans, including Negroes," and seemed to "be a good deal more intelligent and interesting," noted the agent, "than at the last meeting I attended."[5] It was observed that, though the conference was supposed to deal with literature in the United States, "more emphasis was placed on the Negro problem in the United States and France." Guérin and Wright seemed to be angry men, "angry at the American system and at white Americans abroad." Wright went out of his way to draw "a dismal picture of life in America and made a few questionable generalities." Among the few questions asked concerning Negro literature, the one about *Native Son* led to a long discussion about the Negro soul. Guérin's questions to Wright on the relationship between blacks and the Communist Party were raised in a manner that would put the Communist Party in "the best light." The agent was bored by the question-and-answer session. Many of the questioners dealt with examples of racial prejudice in America. Another brought up the problem of the French attitude toward the Arabs; another questioner drew the response from Wright that "until now, the American black had not sought solidarity with his African brother."[6] The agent found the colloquy between Wright and Guérin to be the most interesting part of the evening. Prompted by Guérin, Wright explained "the background of the Franco American Fellowship" and offered commentary upon the problems of blacks in America and upon his relationships with white Americans and the French. The concealed recorder was taking down every word. Fortunately, when Wright spoke, the audience became almost totally silent. His high, squeaky voice registered well, his words came through the transmission, loud and strong. The agent was satisfied that he would have little difficulty in transcribing, word for word, the proceedings, and that the copies forwarded to the State Department, the FBI, Military Intelligence, and the Agency, would be clean and accurate.

Adopting an attitude of interest but subdued detachment, the agent heard Wright tell the audience that blacks had sought France out as "a land of refuge." Until the Americans began to export racism, it had remained such. Now blacks were concerned about their future relationship to France, worried about the changing French attitude in light of its need of American aid. This attitude was being influenced by the white members of "the American colony." They were more violently race-conscious here than in America. Among the white members of "the American colony and the American Government Agencies," there was no trace "of liberalism" to be found. ". . . the Americans who come to France damn French culture and practice their own brand of racism." The Franco-American Fellowship, Wright intoned, was organized to offset American racism and to "keep the spirit of confidence between the French and the American people."[7] Later the agent would include in his report the entire essay "American Negroes and France," written by Wright to outline the aims of the Fellowship and published in L'Observateur.

But, for now, Wright was saying other things. Truman's directive officially abolishing segregation in the armed forces was issued as a result of American concern over the cold war. Despite the directive and a small measure of progress, segregation continued to exist in the Army and the Air Corps. He responded to Guérin's question concerning his experiences in the Party by saying that "he joined the Party because he was—and is—a revolutionary and, like all revolutionaries, sought a political instrument." The Party was a "militant organization" at that time and concerned itself with problems facing blacks. Later, the Party shifted to the right. When blacks, presumably like himself, "brought their grievances to their main leaders, the Communists paid no attention to them." The Party admitted its own mistakes after the war, but the damage was already done: it had lost the support of the black population. Were there, Guérin asked, "beneficial things the Communist Party did for the Negro prior to the war?" Later the agent summarized the answer for his superiors: "Mr. Wright contended that the Communist Party had the choice to champion civil rights themselves if they had wanted to. He pointed out that prior to the war, the Communist Party had helped the Negro in such fields as labor and law (the Scottsboro case). He concluded by saying that there was, as there is today, a need for a revolutionary party in the United States. He said that the world had heard of the cases of Coplon, Hiss, Pennington, and the eleven [Foley Square] Communists. There was no instance, he said, where a Communist stood up and said, 'yes, I am a Communist and I have done what I have done because your system is wrong.'"

On November 27, 1951, seven months later, the American Embassy "furnished information to the Department of State . . . indicating that the subject Wright was willing to go to any length to attract attention to the problem of racial discrimination in general and to its manifestations in the United States in particular. It was further stated that the subject has been using as an instrument for his publicity, a group to which he has given the name of 'Franco-American Fellowship.'"

Whatever immunity Wright may have enjoyed since cancellation of the Security Index card maintained upon him by the FBI in 1948, and as a result of his formidable international reputation, had ended. His leadership of the Franco-American Fellowship angered agents of the military, the FBI, the CIA, and the State Department. The Fellowship itself was a major embarrassment to the American Government. The Soviet Union continued to score propaganda points against America, based upon U.S. racist practices. The country was engaged in a war in Korea, pitting a white nation against one whose people are brown-skinned. When the Chinese entered the war on behalf of the Koreans, many of their propaganda leaflets reminded black Americans of their kinship with the nonwhite peoples of Asia. Truman's directive ending racial discrimination in the armed services provoked violent clashes between black and white GI's in Europe. In America, the NAACP made plans to bring the issue of black racial oppression before the United Nations, and the American Communist Party, in a feeble offensive, drew up a petition of genocide leveled at America for its treatment of blacks and dispatched Patterson to Paris to present it before a special session of the world body. Racism, the government realized, was America's Achilles' heel, and it wanted to protect itself as well as possible.

Theretofore, the case of Richard Wright had been a trying one. He had a coterie of international supporters and friends; numbered among them were such influential people as Gunnar Myrdal, Aimé Césaire, Sartre, and members of the French Government and press. He had criticized American and Soviet policy in even-handed fashion, and though he had spoken out against racism and prejudice often enough, prior to the formation of the Fellowship he had initiated no action. Now his powerful voice was being heard from one end of Europe to the other. In December of 1951 alone, bureau files show him participating in two notable events, one that called attention to America's racial problem and the other leftist in orientation. On the twelfth, Wright participated with members of the International League Against Racial Discrimination and Anti-Semitism, along with Katherine Dunham and Alioune Diop, in an affair that gave Ralph Bunche "some 90,000 francs . . . for the widow and the children of . . . [Willie McGee]." McGee, having exhausted his appeals, was executed in May despite worldwide protest. The men who killed McGee, Wright wrote in an article published in France under the title "Behind the McGee Case," stood condemned by world opinion, and the damage done to the American image was severe enough to force "several high American officials" to consider "the folly of racial prejudice."[8] On December 16, 1951, Wright was photographed with Jean-Louis Barrault and Madeleine Renaud, at the Center for International Relations, at a party given to "initiate the New Story International Contest for Young Writers." Wright's name appeared on the invitation, along with those of Sartre, Stuart Gilbert, and Harold Kaplan; and along with William Saroyan, Tennessee Williams, Gilbert, and Sartre, Wright was named to the board of directors. And as the government informants noted, he continued his work with the Franco-American Fellowship. However, now that the government was armed with the provisions of the Internal Security Act of 1950, Wright was in a position analogous to that of Anna Louise Strong before. The government could legally confiscate his passport, order him back to America, where he would undergo the ordeal now faced by his old associates Langston Hughes and Paul Robeson. All that was needed was evidence that Wright's conduct abroad was detrimental to the interests of the United States, and substantiation of Communist ties despite his protestations to the contrary. The government not only had Wright's own words to buttress any case it desired to make; it had the painstaking work of agents and the testimony of a number of informants.

On December 16, 1951, an informant reported that "The Franco-American Fellowship Group was organized almost entirely by Richard Wright . . . and was supposed to be a sponsorship for young writers, artists, and poets, who were students in France. . . ." Several of the students made statements to the effect that the group was leftist in the nature of its discussions and that the persons who defended the French and American concept of democracy were not given the same hearings as the "Existentialists" and "left" partisans. The main opposition to the group, the informer related, came from James Baldwin, who "attacks the hatred themes of Wright's writings and the attempt of the Franco-American Fellowship Group to perpetuate 'Uncle Tom literature methods' when the day has come for a more 'realistic' and 'analytical' approach to the Negro problem."[9] The lengthy document reported that members associated with the Fellowship had been observed passing "out Communist literature at the American Express Company and had been giving this literature to Military Personnel." The group was identified as "the Communist Group of artists and writers that Richard Wright has organized in Paris."

On the eighteenth of December, the informant issued another statement: "Richard Wright is active in the Communist Party in France and has been engaged in spreading the Communist Doctrine through the Franco-American Fellowship Group. *Mrs. Richard Wright* is the active *Communist member* [recorder's italics] of the family and has made a point of insulting Negro personnel who hold views other than Communist. Source has known Wright since his first appearance in Paris. . . . Source stated that Mrs. Wright seems to be the power and [deletion] in the entire group. . . . Source stated that Wright had boasted that he had 'the State Department in my pocket—they call me in for conferences, the fools.' " The information was analyzed, amended, edited, and made part of the Bureau's overall file. It was also handed over to the "Legal Section, Passport Office, Department of State," and made part of the "passport file of Richard Wright."[10]

Though the recording agent acknowledged in his report that the "source" who had supplied the information regarding Baldwin's antagonism to the Fellowship in general and to Wright in particular, seemed to "be anti-semitic" and to have a "mental quirk," no effort was made to correct or substantiate the information when disseminated to other agencies. Over the years, as Baldwin's reputation grew, the government considered it important to have Baldwin's purported opposition to Wright on file. The informant, a black musician from Philadelphia, was evidently acquainted with both Baldwin and Wright. Like practically everyone else in the black American colony, he knew about the dispute between the two writers occasioned by publication of Baldwin's essay "Everybody's Protest Novel," in *Zéro* magazine, in 1949.

The essay was a critique of the value of protest literature in general. Wright was mentioned only in the concluding section, where Baldwin, as he had earlier done with *Uncle Tom's Cabin*, points out the limitations of *Native Son* as a moral vehicle. Even before he had read the essay in print, Baldwin wrote, he encountered Wright in a cafe, the Brasserie Lipp: "Richard accused me of having betrayed him, and not only him but all American Negroes by attacking the idea of protest literature."[11] The younger writer was on the defensive. What he had wanted from the older, established writer was approval. How much was the inclusion of *Native Son* in the body of the essay, almost as an afterthought, an attempt to force recognition? He had come to Paris, lonely, angry, and broke. He had encountered Wright on his first day in this new country, and the greeting had been as formal and businesslike as on that first meeting day in the apartment in Greenwich Village. The two sometimes drank together, debated together, fought each other; but the kind of paternal attention Baldwin needed and wanted from the older man was not forthcoming. ". . . I wanted Richard to see me, not as the youth I had been when he met me," wrote Baldwin, "but as a man." But he wanted the writer to also accept him as an equal, to accept his right "to disagree with him."[12]

Acceptance on all counts was difficult for Wright. A self-righteousness bordering almost upon arrogance caused him often, far too often, to become incensed at adverse criticism. "Don't you know," Michel Fabre explained the reason for Wright's rupture of his friendship with Margaret Walker to her, "that those people in New York told him some awful things they said you had said about him. And it turned him livid with rage. And he believed you were ganging up on him." "Richard thought," Baldwin noted, "that I was trying to destroy his novel and his reputation. . . ." But to destroy either was beyond Baldwin's ability or ambition. He had, as he confessed, used Wright's work as a stepping-stone to his own. But this was the stuff of literary quarrel, and the two men fought the battle "of the relevance or irrelevance of protest literature" throughout the years of their exile. Why, then, did the government insist upon projecting this literary quarrel into the political arena, to posit Baldwin, who had worked with the Franco-American Fellowship, as being opposed to Wright and the group?

Despite his attitudes toward blacks and America and the white liberal anti-Communist Left, Wright's reputation was still secure. It was the only currency he had against the government in the event that he was summarily forced back to America. Unlike Du Bois and Robeson, and his old comrades who had fought the battle of Foley Square, he did not have the party apparatus to support him. Black Americans, in the main, he believed, were still basically impotent and would be unable to come to his aid in the event of danger. The liberal Left was weaker still, trying to recover from the vicious campaigns waged against the Left. All that Wright had in his own defense was his tremendous reputation. He was still the most famous black writer of African descent. Hundreds of thousands of copies of his books had been published in all languages. A campaign against him would have to begin by weakening his appeal. The article he had written for *Ebony* magazine was delayed in publication until December 7, 1951, and then only with a fierce editorial by the publishers, John Johnson and Ben Burns. "I Choose Exile" was rejected by both *Ebony* and *The Atlantic Monthly*. "While Wright sits out the threat of totalitarianism," wrote a reviewer in *Time* magazine in 1953, following publication of *The Outsider*, "an abler U.S. Negro novelist sees the problem of his race differently. Says Ralph (Invisible Man) Ellison: 'After all, my people have been here for a long time. It is a big wonderful country, and you can't just turn away from it because some people decide it isn't your country." And Wright came under attack also in an essay published in an American Cultural Services publication, *Perspective U.S.A.*, under the title "A No to Nothing," authored by Richard Gibson, believed by members of the black American colony to be an undercover CIA agent. "Gibson," remarked a well-known black writer, "was in the service of the government. I was associated with the Fair Play for Cuba Committee, Gibson joined the Committee after leaving Paris and I found out that things said during meetings to Gibson only were later thrown at me by the F.B.I."

The government's preoccupation with the Franco-American Fellowship was not matched by that of its founder. With the organization successfully launched, Wright retired from the presidency, having devoted time, energy, and some of his own money to the organization. By the end of 1951, the organization itself had virtually ceased to exist. "It seemed, indeed," wrote Baldwin, "that Richard felt that, with the establishment of this club, he had paid his dues to American Negroes abroad. . . ."[13] What he had done, however, was to gain needed time from work on his new novel. His travels through Europe, his work on the film version of *Native Son*, and his activities concerning the Franco-American Fellowship had enabled him to distance himself emotionally from the Party and to be better able to assimilate his Marxist experience for presentation in fiction. "The break from the United States," he told William Gardner Smith, "was more than a geographical change. It was a break with my former attitudes as a Negro and a Communist—an attempt to think over and re-define my attitudes and my thinking. I was trying to grapple with the big problem—the problem and meaning of Western Civilization as a whole, and the relation of Negroes and other minority groups to it."[14]

By the beginning of 1952, he felt capable of dealing with "the big problem" in fiction. The novel that had taken so long to complete was bundled up and taken, along with his typewriter, to London. He arrived in England on February 16, and five days later renewed his passport, giving his address as 28 Glenluce, London, and his occupation as that of writer. Between intermittent discussions with George Padmore and his wife, he worked diligently in the one-room flat and completed the novel in May of 1952. Almost one year later, on March 16, *The Out-*

sider was published by Harper & Row, and on April 12, Wright received his author's copies from Chester Himes, who brought them to Paris at the beginning of his own exile.

Partly autobiographical, *The Outsider* was as much his own spiritual odyssey as it was that of his hero, Cross Damon. His experiences in America, his disaffection with communism, his view of a Europe in turmoil based upon his travels during his first year in exile, the long nights spent with Sartre and De Beauvoir debating the meaning of freedom, the silent questioning in his journal of the meaning and nature of man, and his often deeply felt periods of alienation combine to present a picture of a solitary individual intent upon re-creating the idea of man in the modern world. The major causes of the present chaos, Wright told Smith, was "the Industrial Revolution, and the dislocations caused by it. . . ." The old isms, communism, fascism, Nazism, were modern man's "experimental attempts" to discover new methods of organization for life in an industrial universe. These isms had failed. The job still needed to be done: "The first item on the agenda of modern man is the organization of modern life. Societies must guarantee to men that man can remain human, despite the factory system."[15]

To do this, however, man must be born again. The old burdens of responsibility and obligation must be cast aside. At the beginning of the novel, Damon is writhing under tremendous burdens. He is black, and because of this, relegated to the ghetto of Chicago's South Side. He is married to a woman whom he no longer loves. He is emotionally tied to a mother whom he both loves and hates. And he has a young mistress who, in trying to blackmail him into marriage, threatens the secure job that he holds in the Chicago Post Office. Like the author himself during those first years away from the South, Damon is mired down by family responsibilities, by an emotional mother who saddles him with feelings of guilt and dread, and by a job that promises little. Just as writing was the mechanism by which the author prevented himself from being overwhelmed by his own despair, reading and study accomplished this for Damon. He attended night classes at the University of Chicago, and he read widely in the works of Heidegger, Nietzsche, and Husserl. And as numerous works read by Wright in his dimly lit room in Chicago, years back, had given a message to him, so, too, do these existential authors speak out to Damon: "It's up to us to make ourselves something," Damon argues; "a man creates himself."

But what mechanism would enable Damon to do this? Wright had had an instrument; the Party was a vehicle that enabled him to re-create himself. It had been his ticket out of the black belt; his and numerous other blacks'. Now, feeling the full effects again of his dissatisfaction with the Party, he had to create another vehicle for his protagonist. Unlike himself, Damon would be given the opportunity to begin his entire life from the very beginning. Homeward bound one day, he is involved in a train crash. He survives, but his overcoat and identification papers are left behind. Later, the authorities use these to identify another victim, a man burned beyond recognition. Damon is pronounced dead and is free to begin the search for himself.

He journeys to New York, assumes a new name, becomes involved with the Communist Party and a hunchbacked district attorney, Eli Houston. Through his relationships with the Party, he becomes a tenant in an apartment owned by Gil Blount, a party leader, and his wife, Eva. The Party has initiated a campaign to force the "fascist owner" of the building, Herndon, to rent apartments to blacks, and Damon is expected to serve as the focal point of confrontation leading to court action. But when the landlord discovers that Blount has allowed a black to rent a room in the building, the Communist plan to provoke a court case goes awry. Blount and Herndon engage in a bloody fight. Damon, who retreated from the scene after the initial altercation, returns to find both men weakened. Impulsively, he murders them both, justifying his actions only by the rationale that he had hated them, that both represented the same form of tyranny and fascism, that the ideals of both were to lead man back into the dark ages of conformity and tyranny, of oppression and slavery, in the name of progress. After the murders, however, he realizes an all too close affinity between them and himself: "Oh, Christ, their disease had reached out and claimed him too. He had been subverted by the contagion of the lawless; he had been defeated by that which he had sought to destroy."[16]

The murders bring him into contact once again with Houston, whom he had first met on the trip to New York. In the district attorney, Damon finds a man much like himself, an outsider, an intellectual, a man also burdened with the idea of freedom: "A lawless man," Houston tells him, "has to rein himself in. A man of lawless impulses living in a society which seeks to restrain instincts for the common good must be in a kind of subjective prison."[17] The conflict between nihilism and freedom was one that preoccupied the writer as much as it did his characters. How much of the criminality, the lawless impulses, that he harbored in his own unconscious, resulted from the religious mores of his family, the rigid authoritarianism of the Party, the status now incumbent upon him as a famous man? Was he not imprisoned by all this, and how often had he sought to break the bars of that prison and for how long? On that day when he had tortured the kitten to death in the flat in Memphis where his father lay asleep, was it simply a means of antagonizing his father? Or was it a vehicle for giving release to the violence contained within him? Was his interest in the murderer Clinton

Brewer propelled by humanitarian motives alone, or was it a way of identifying with his own deeply buried violent feelings and emotions? All of his life, he had had to keep a tight rein over his emotions; it was important that no one know what he really felt deep inside. And this was the bane of most men. Most feared their own destructive, nihilistic tendencies. Most feared the test that would warrant their going to "the bitter end."

But there were men like himself, and his character Houston, who realized that they were "lawless" men. They were in touch with feelings and emotions, could resist the attempt to give their passions free rein. The cell of their prison was ventilated by their concern for the common good, their own selfish instincts moderated by compassion and humanity. These attributes distinguished them from the Damons, the fascists, and the Communists, and in turn, from twentieth-century man. They were the outsiders, men in a void, somewhere between a dying world and one waiting to be born anew. They were not the new man, but they were his forerunners, realizing the great truth that freedom is relative, not absolute, that it is not divine, that it recognizes the necessity for limits.

His protagonist Damon, therefore, was a warning to man, not an example. After another murder and the suicide of Eva, whom he has taken as his mistress after Gil's death, he is executed by agents of the Communist Party. In the agony of dying, he realizes the final truth: "Alone a man is nothing. . . . Man is a promise that he must never break. . . . I wish I had some way to give the meaning of my life to others. . . . To make a bridge from man to man. . . ."

Richard Wright, Margaret Walker observed, was not nihilistic, but he partook of some of its negativism. "He was completely a secularist and secular existentialism was his final belief. It is best expressed in what I regard as his most autobiographical piece, *The Outsider*. Cross Damon has a lot of Richard Wright in him. . . ."[18] But there is "a lot of Richard Wright" in Eli Houston, also, and this balance makes *The Outsider* a very antiexistential novel indeed. For Wright, who, out of fear and dread, had had to curb his own instinctual longings, to subdue his passions for so long, ofttimes to the point of psychological ill health, it was difficult to accept a philosophy that reduced the individual to feeling and impulse. Rationality had been his own key to salvation, and he had had to struggle to achieve it, first against his family and later against American racism. He had won his struggles, much like those engaged in by modern man moving all too rapidly into a world of industrialization and technology that he did not understand. And he had won it, because he had believed in the power and strength of his own reason and intellect. It was Descartes, then, not the existentialists, who had been correct after all. Man was a rational being.

The book that he had been unable to complete for over four years, he brought to a conclusion in three months. The real work was over. There would be revisions to make, sections to be rewritten. But the book had flowed smoothly, had come, finally, fast and well. "It can't be said," he told Smith, "that I write books; books happen with me. I become deeply involved with certain problems. The way I attack them, and think them through, is by writing books." He had finally thought through a great many problems and attacked them in *The Outsider*. Still, he had no illusions that his American public would understand his book or applaud his efforts. He did not know, he wrote his agent on May 1, if the novel was good or bad, and later, on June 28, he voiced concern about the American scene and its receptivity to a book like *The Outsider*. Americans now existed in a turbulent, hysterical atmosphere, and only the "official view" was desired. His book, he believed, described the world of the present, but he had few hopes of anybody liking or accepting it, "especially Americans."[19]

His pessimism and doubts to the contrary, working so diligently on the book had spurred the once dormant impulse. *The Outsider* had scarcely undergone final revision before, back in Paris once again, he was at work on a new book. When Smith interviewed him for *Ebony* magazine, Wright was able to tell the novelist and fellow expatriate that he had now completed another novel, one that, "like all my future books, I think . . . will take up aspects of the problems broached in *The Outsider*." He managed to generate a great deal of enthusiasm for "my little book," as he called *Savage Holiday*, and for its central character, retired insurance executive Erskine Fowler. Men like Fowler fascinated him. He was a successful man; he shopped at New York's most expensive men's stores; he belonged to first-rate clubs, was well liked, admired, and respected by his peers. He lived in a fashionable section of New York City, and though retired from his company against his wishes, his financial position was secure. For Wright, however, such men lived on two planes of reality. His natural suspiciousness of order and decorum, of those who projected images of supreme confidence in a world where most men could not hide their insecurity, led him to want to reveal another Fowler, one buried deep in the unconscious.

Fowler's other "self" has been locked away all these years, as a result of his inability to face the truth concerning his relationship with his mother. She was a sexually alluring and promiscuous woman, who granted her favors to many men. He had been rejected by her, even as he desired her himself, desired to replace the other men in her affections. He had felt guilty about his incestuous feelings. To punish himself, he had imprisoned his emotions behind a façade, locked the doors upon his feelings and passions. And as the imprisonment of his true nature had been caused ostensibly by a woman, it was only natural that a woman also be the agent of its release. Voluptuous Mable Blake is such a woman. With her young son, Tony, she occupies the apartment next to his. His relations with her had always been proper, polite. According to the gossips, she was a promiscuous woman, but had it not been for Tony's accident, he would probably have learned little more about her.

It was a freak accident, but he worried that no one would believe him. He had often opened his door after a shower, or while casually lounging, nude, to retrieve the morning paper. On this day, he had to move farther into the hall to get it, and the door slammed shut. There was no option other than to climb through his terrace window and back into the apartment. The young boy had been playing on the terrace adjoining Fowler's. The shock of seeing the nude man climbing over the iron railings caused the boy to reel back suddenly and fall to his death. Afraid of what others might make of his story, Fowler remains silent, and Tony's death is called accidental. But, for the second time in his life, Fowler is consumed by overwhelming guilt. But now he could assuage the guilty feelings centered around his mother as well as those occasioned by his participation in Tony's death.

He could marry Mable Blake, guide her away from her errant, promiscuous ways. But the doors to the unconscious creak open wider and wider each time he looks upon Mable's inviting body. He pays court to her, even proposes to her. He wants her to give up other men, but he discovers that she has not. His sudden attentions make her suspicious concerning the supposed accident of her son. Through anonymous telephone calls, she informs him that she knows about the dreadful events of that day. Later, she reveals herself as the caller. By this time, the hidden Fowler has completely emerged from inside the prison. He is buffeted by two equally pressing but conflicting needs; he wanted to reestablish his relationship with his mother, and to possess her sexually, vicariously, through Mable. But he also hates Mable for bringing him to this impasse, for forcing him to move beyond his façade of decorum, to acknowledge his own lust and passionate desires. His sense of outrage is vented upon the woman in a scene bearing close resemblance to an orgiastic religious ritual: "With machine-like motion, Erskine lifted the butcher knife and plunged it into her stomach again and again. Each time the long blade sank into her, her knees doubled up by reflex action. He continued to hack into her midriff and, from the two-inch slits which appeared in the flesh of her abdomen, blood began to run and spurt."[20]

Wright had less hope for the success of *Savage Holiday* than he did for *The Outsider*. Despite his comments to Smith, the book was in the vein of the other only in that again he was concerned with passions and feelings and the dangers caused by repression of one's natural emotions and instincts. His distance from the stresses of America, and his relative racial peace and calm, had freed him to the extent that he could deal with those subconscious forces and urges that had been his as well as Damon's and Fowler's. The oppressiveness of women are central to both books, and the mothers who produce guilt in his protagonists have similar characteristics to those of his own mother. Over the years, he had been able to free himself from many of the moral proscriptions handed down by Ella, but at what cost? Was the price that he paid an overwhelming guilt that enabled him to re-create Fowler's murder of Mable, on the printed page, through the extreme violence and eventual murder meted out to most of his female characters from Mary Dalton to Mable Blake? The question was not central to his own plans for *Savage Holiday*, and he thought first of issuing the novel under a pseudonym. When it was accepted by a paperback house, he was more than pleased. The book would escape the serious scrutiny of major book reviews.

The *Outsider* was reviewed, and extensively so. Granville Hicks and L. D. Reddick were among well-known critics who liked it. On the whole, however, the reception was much as he had suspected it would be. His old friend Saunders Redding was among the leading critics who panned the book. Redding argued that Wright had stepped outside of his milieu; he had been among the existentialists too long and away from the chaos and turbulence of America. The book was therefore a political and literary disaster, and if Wright was to repeat the example of *Native Son*, he must "come back home." *Time* magazine echoed Redding's comments concerning the relationship between *The Outsider* and Wright's exile and suggested that Wright's absence from the country prohibited him from understanding the extent of black progress. It was a curious criterion, Wright knew, upon which to judge the merit of a literary work, so he had no intention of ending his exile. When the suggestion was made that he come to New York for publication of the book, he refused, fearing that he might be summoned before the Un-American Activities Committee and forbidden to leave again.[21] He later told Smith, "I am like many writers before me and during my time, who have felt freer to deal with the subjects they were born with while in exile." Nevertheless, concern about his exile was to become more pressing in the coming years, and few would understand his reluctance to return to America.

CHAPTER SIXTEEN

Chester Himes arrived in Paris on April 11, 1953, having traveled from Le Havre on the final leg of his journey. Wright had reserved a room for his old friend from America, and together with a companion, Yves Malartic, had gone to the Gare St. Lazare, to meet him. In the large crowds and wide area of the station, the friends missed each other. Himes caught a cab and made his way to number 14 rue Monsieur le Prince. But Rachel had been ill, and Wright had left word with the concierge not to admit anyone to the apartment. Himes went to his reserved room and retired for the evening. Wright, in the meantime, had accompanied Malartic to a cafe across from the station to await other trains. At each arrival, the two men posted themselves at the second-class car entrances, and as train after train passed and Himes did not appear, Wright became alarmed. Malartic fed his anxieties. He talked of the terrible things that could happen to the noninitiate in Paris; Wright's imagination took over, and he conjured up visions of his old friend waylaid in some French alley. "As all his friends knew," wrote Himes, "Dick had an excitable temperament and was given to such self-indulgent exaggeration that the buzzing of a blowfly could rage like a typhoon in his imagination."[1]

Wright was for calling the police. Rushing back to his apartment, he informed Ellen of the situation. His wife advised calm. There was simply a mixup. At the very least, the affair could wait until morning. When Himes did not show up during the night, on the way to the police station Wright stopped by to cancel the room, only to discover the missing Himes. "I could see he was alive with curiosity," Himes observed. "He had always been extremely curious about me. He knew of my prison record . . . and he suspected I had lived a life of wild and raging fury." Wright guided his old friend to the Monaco for breakfast, found him a permanent room in the Hotel Scandinavie, across from the Café Tournon, a few blocks from his own apartment, and took him home for lunch. Himes renewed his acquaintance with Ellen, saw Julia, whom he remembered as "a tiny tot" in New York. She had blossomed out now, into an energetic, vibrant teen-ager. She was "the spit and image of her father," he noted. Rachel he saw for the first time. Now almost six years old, frolicsome and playful, she was, Himes observed, like a dark-blond doll. ". . . it was immediately apparent that she was her father's pet." Wright was anxious to get his copies of *The Outsider* and the reams of typing paper that Himes had brought from America for him, and he ushered the writer into his Citroën for a drive to customs. Shortly after commencing his exile, he had disposed of the big, cumbersome Oldsmobile that he had brought from America. The car had been trouble, too large and unwieldy for maneuvering in the French traffic and an ostentatious display of American wealth.

At the customs office, the two men discovered that Himes had left the keys to his trunk in his hotel room. He was not able to open it for inspection. Wright remonstrated with the official, declaring that Himes had brought in no contraband or otherwise prohibited material. The official was unmoved. Wright proposed that the official break into the trunk with a crowbar. Himes looked on in bewilderment. The official explained that he could not do this. Suddenly, Wright's eyes brightened. A mocking smile spread his lips. He noticed packing cases of Kleenex and toilet paper, collected by a chauffeur, presumably for the American Embassy, thinking, perhaps, of the rough French toilet paper. Wright steered the official's eyes to the cartons and announced, "They can't even wipe their ass on French paper."[2] The official laughed, and handed over the trunk. It was dark by the time the two managed to get the heavy trunk to Himes's room, but Wright, after retrieving his ten copies of *The Outsider*, steered Himes back into "the dark narrow streets." They went to the English bookstore, where Wright lectured the young bookstore owner on how the books should be displayed in the store window for quick, proper viewing by passersby. Later, he took his old friend to a night club in the Latin Quarter, La Romance, not far from his apartment, and introduced him to the Frenchwoman who ran the club, a staunch anti-American.

During the following days and weeks, Wright introduced Himes to the cafes of Paris and to friends and acquaintances. He steered him also to the soul-food restaurant opened in Paris to a thriving business by Wright's enterprising friend and fellow exile Leroy Haynes, an ex-GI from the South who, in addition to being a shrewd businessman, was a part-time actor. Wright introduced Himes one by one to members of the black American colony. Though Wright was still grudgingly re-

spected by the black expatriate community, his influence was beginning
to wane. A justifiable suspiciousness had become permanent among
black Americans. Informants and agents of the government moved
clandestinely among the American community. Passports were being
confiscated, people were being asked questions, by agents, relating to
conversations whispered supposedly in private. The government still
maintained surveillance of the activities of Wright. On March 3, 1952,
"Mr. William A. Crawford, Political Section, American Embassy," forwarded a confidential dispatch, to the Paris legat, concerning a debate
that had occurred between Wright and Michel Gordy, a journalist
who had interviewed Wright for several journals, among them *Les
Étoiles*, which were "hardly complimentary to the United States." By
1952, in fact, it was considered the best politics, an informant told Military Intelligence, for those with jobs requiring loyalty clearance "to stay
away from the Wrights. . . ." Envy and jealousy also were contributing
to the beginning erosion of Wright's influence among black Americans,
though it remained as high as ever among the French, despite his break
with Sartre and the existentialists over what he had thought to be
Sartre's movement back toward positions taken by the Communist
Party. For the time being, his relationships with the Africans and the
members of Présence Africaine were secure.

Through Wright, Himes met William Gardner Smith for the first
time. The Philadelphia-born author of *The Last of the Conquerors* had
begun his exile around 1948. He was a young, pleasant-looking, brown-
skinned man, Himes remembered, who spoke rapidly. He was regarded
highly by most members of the black expatriate colony, but, despite his
article on Wright, written for *Ebony*, Himes thought that Wright did
not like Smith. Smith had written another book, which was selected by
a book club in France, while none of Wright's books was so selected.
Smith may have thought himself a little superior because of this, Himes
conjectured, and concluded that Smith was not so much egotistical
as young and naïve. Wright's coolness toward Smith was probably
prompted by Smith's close association with Gibson. Himes was rein-
troduced to Ollie Harrington, and later, when the president of World
Publishing Company, Ben Zevin, and his wife visited Paris, Himes introduced the publisher to Wright.

Later, at La Méditerranée, where Wright took the couple, Himes,
and Ellen to dinner, Zevin was somewhat startled at the attention given
Wright by restaurant owners; ". . . the proprietor had sent all of his
staff—chefs, waiters, doormen, everyone who wore a uniform—out into
the street to form two long rows to Dick's car through which we passed
like royalty,"[3] Himes wrote. Later, back at the Wrights' apartment,
after a visit to a night club, Zevin accused Wright of having deserted

the black struggle. The author chose, the publisher argued, to be "a big frog in a little pond" here in exile while leaving the fight to more dedicated men, like himself. Wright was called upon to defend his exile, and during the heated exchange, he voiced his opinion that what was needed was an all-out assault upon prejudice, not the polite self-satisfying gestures made by the publisher. Himes quickly acted as inter-mediary, and later the two men patched up their differences at a dinner sponsored by the Wrights. The evening became festive, and Wright, Himes noted, became relaxed and somewhat jovial. Later, Himes witnessed a similar change in attitude take place with Wright during a meeting with another well-known American. The two men were passing the time waiting for a cocktail party, to which they were invited that evening, to commence. While sitting in the study of Wright's apart-ment, wrote Himes, Wright answered the ringing of his doorbell and brought back "a surprise visitor": David Schine, "chief consultant" to the Senate Subcommittee on Investigations, chaired by Senator Joseph McCarthy. Schine owed his position, indirectly, to the elections of 1952, which brought Eisenhower and the Republican Party to victory. His own role in the election was minimal, but McCarthy played a major role and was appointed chairman of the Senate Committee on Govern-ment Operations. The senator then appointed himself chairman of the Subcommittee on Investigations and appointed twenty-five-year-old Roy Cohn the Committee's chief counsel. Cohn immediately brought his friend, equally young, wealthy David Schine to the committee as "chief consultant."[4] The names of the two men were linked with that of the Wisconsin senator, whose name would come to symbolize the era of witchhunts, assaults upon civil liberties, and no-holds-barred warfare on "subversives." In the course of a whirlwind assault on the "vital center of the liberal establishment," wrote David Caute, "he [McCarthy] suc-ceeded in melodramatizing the American inquisition across the world."[5] Cohn and Schine were principals in this endeavor, and among their more notable ventures was a tour of United States libraries overseas in an attempt to gauge the extent of subversive material in the libraries' catalogues and on their bookshelves. During this excursion, Schine, unaccompanied by Cohn, had appeared at the Wrights' apartment.

The visit to number 14 rue Monsieur le Prince, however, had nothing to do with libraries or books. "A man named Jarrel" had been ap-pointed to a position with the Department, and McCarthy wanted to rescind the appointment. To this end, Schine was engaged in collecting information about Jarrel. He had heard that Jarrel had been a member of "the John Walter Reed Club" in Chicago, during the period of Wright's membership. Schine wanted validation of this fact from Wright, plus any information he had on Jarrel. Wright told the investi-

gator that he did not know Jarrel. That he had never been a member of
the club, himself, that he "did not know any members."⁶ The chief
consultant was enraged, as Wright's one-time membership in the Chicago John Reed Club was a matter of FBI record. Did he believe that
his position in France offered him some kind of immunity? Schine told
the writer about the Committee's assault on Langston Hughes, how
"he and Cohn pressured . . . Hughes into stating before the committee
that he regretted some of his un-American political activities and writings."⁷ He reiterated his questions concerning Jarrel, but Wright offered
the same answer as before. After Schine left, Wright turned to Himes:
"That stupid son of a bitch thinks he can threaten me; I'll never testify.
I've written everything I have to say about my Communist affiliations."
Was this simply bravado, a recognition of the fact that Schine really
had no official status, that, by being abroad, Wright *was* immune from
congressional committees? But what might his attitude be were such
questions asked by the State Department itself, by its representatives in
the Passport Division? They might have the kind of power that Schine
did not have, and failure to answer them might force Wright back to
America. Having affronted Schine in Paris, he dreaded what might happen were he to face the infuriated investigator in America. He was, perhaps, not altogether unhappy when a phone call from James Baldwin
cut short his conjectures.

Baldwin was broke and wanted the loan of ten dollars. Whatever
Wright's concern about Schine's visit, Baldwin's call reenergized him,
brought to his face "that look of malicious satisfaction which his close
friends had come to know so well." Himes was all too familiar with that
look and the kind of energy it seemed to generate in his friend. Once,
when Himes was forced to move to another room, he discovered that
two lesbians lived in the room directly beneath his new one. On visiting
Himes, Wright had noticed the two girls, and at the first opportunity
rushed to engage them in conversation. "He had a sharp curiosity,"
Himes explained, "about the sexual behavior of odd couples, lesbians,
and prostitutes." Wright engaged the girls in intense conversation, that
look of "malicious satisfaction" apparent in his curiosity and excitement. The girls became embarrassed, retreated to their room, only to
find Wright following as far as the threshold, peering "about inside
their room as though it were a cage at the zoo." Finally, one of the girls
slammed the door in his face. "He was greatly stimulated by these encounters . . . ," Himes observed.⁸

Now he looked forward with relish to another confrontation with
Baldwin. He had helped Baldwin get an "eighteen hundred dollars"
award "and a renewal for nine hundred from Harper & Brothers" to
help him in writing his first novel. Baldwin's way of paying him back,

he told Himes, had been "by attacking him" in published articles. Now
the look came to his eyes again; "Baldwin has the nerve to call me to
borrow five thousand francs [ten dollars]."

The two men found Baldwin waiting at the Deux Magots. Wright
had hardly seated himself before he moved to the attack. He accused
Baldwin of ingratitude; he attacked Baldwin's censure of protest literature, reiterating his argument that all literature was protest. Baldwin
was on the defensive. He argued that in writing *Native Son* Wright had
written his story; that even if all literature were protest, the obverse was
not necessarily true. The two men argued so furiously and intensely
that a crowd gathered. Most of them, "all of the women and the majority of the men," Himes observed, sided with Baldwin, who seemed so
vulnerable to Wright, who appeared "so secure and condescending and
cruel." The argument continued, and the cocktail party was forgotten.
Later, the three men went to another cafe, and though it was almost
midnight, the discussion went on. "The sons must slay their fathers,"
Baldwin cried out at one time, as the drinks began to take effect.
". . . we managed to throw the whole terrifying subject to the winds,"
Baldwin wrote later of that night, "and Richard, Chester Himes, and
myself went out and got drunk. It was a good night, perhaps the best I
remember in all the time I knew Richard Wright."[9] It was a good night
for Wright, also. He had been able, briefly, to lay aside his concern
about Schine and the American Government's possible interference
with his coming trip to Africa.

He had articulated his intention to visit and to write about Africa,
early in his exile, in his journal recording in 1947. Since that time, the
desire had intensified, primarily due to insistence by Padmore that he
make such a trip. When Padmore was appointed an adviser to Kwame
Nkrumah, the Prime Minister of the Gold Coast, he encouraged
Wright to visit "Ghana," to view for himself the transition of this British colony into independence. The two men had discussed the project
during Wright's stay in London, while Wright worked on *The Outsider*. When the Padmores visited Wright in Paris, in December 1952,
the writer had agreed to undertake the journey, and plans for doing so
were completed.[10] In order to visit Ghana, however, a visa was needed
from the British Home Office, and the "Home Office was loath to have
black American writers visiting Ghana." During April of 1953, Dorothy
Padmore came to Paris to finalize the plans for Wright's trip. On May
4, Nkrumah addressed a letter, "To Whom It May Concern," extending an official invitation in his capacity as Prime Minister. The visa
would certainly now be granted, and Wright made preparations to
leave for the Gold Coast in June. But what about the attitude of his
own government? Theoretically, if the British granted him a visa, there

was little that the United States could do, short of revoking his passport, to prevent him from going. Yet he knew that the government of
England and that of America worked closely together in certain areas.
The Americans could pressure the British. Still, somewhat cautiously,
he continued his preparations. He ushered Himes to a black-market operator so that his friend could change money at a favorable exchange
rate. Near the end of May, he traveled to London in order to be able to
embark from Liverpool.

Presumably, the United States Government had not attempted to
block his trip. But the FBI had manifested concern. On May 27, almost
four days before his departure, a communication requesting "any available information of a security nature concerning Wright" was forwarded
to bureau headquarters.

The government was no more than interested in his forthcoming
trip, and on June 4, Wright set out, aboard the ship *Accra*, for the
Gold Coast.

Even before the journey had commenced, haunting questions had
risen at intervals to plague him, and now, well on his way, they surfaced
again: What would be the effect upon him, an American black man, of
this trip to Africa? Was it possible for him to experience cultural shock,
to have his identity as a Westerner called into question? What, in essence, would Africa mean to him? He was Western, his mind, Cartesian
in structure, rational, trained to seek order, pattern, design. ". . . my
habitual kind of thinking, . . ." he wrote, "had no race in it, a kind
of thinking that was conditioned by the reaction of human beings to a
concrete social environment." What could he possibly have in common
with those black men and women from a different time and place? The
answer was arrived at even before he set foot on African soil for the first
time: except for a common hatred of oppression and a common legacy
of racism and exploitation—nothing!

Twelve days after leaving Liverpool, the ship stopped in Takoradi,
and from a porthole, Wright caught his first glimpse of Africa. The
early-morning mist dampened the air, made it heavy, slightly oppressive. There were a few other ships at the port, but he looked beyond
them, through the mist and fog, at the great abundance of people,
"black life everywhere." Blacks operated the cranes, the tugboats and
fork lifts. He recalled that a South African scholar had declared that
blacks could not operate the machinery of the Western world. Proudly
he surveyed this evidence refuting the racist's assumption. On disembarking, he remained caught up in the spectacle around him: women in
bright garments, carrying their children, papoose-like, on their backs;
the black policemen, black firemen, black engineers, black workmen;
the entire life "that met the eyes" was colored black. Yet, shortly after

this first encounter with the continent, the question of his relationship to Africa and Africans emerged again. A black salesman in a department store asked what part of Africa he came from. When he said he did not know, the salesman stared in disbelief. Surely Wright's mother or grandmother had told him.

They had not. In the African's eyes, he saw the glint of arrogance. He felt humiliated because he did not know the history of his own existence. To soothe his pride, he recalled how the Africans had sold their own people into slavery. He reminded the salesman that neither the Africans who sold blacks to white men, nor the white men, kept records of the transaction. The salesman's question made him wonder, however, whether the key to his identity was really to be found among people whose skin color so nearly resembled his own? There were other incidents, more dramatic than the salesman's questioning, that jolted him. In the African bush, en route to Accra, the sights and scenes brought back visions and remembrances of Mississippi. There was the rich, red alluvial soil of the African earth; there were naked children sitting or squatting near mud-walled huts; there were black women, bare-breasted, washing clothes in soil-darkened rivers; there were men, stripped to the waist, hacking away at grass along the roadside.

He had written of such settings and people in *Twelve Million Black Voices*. Now, confronting them again, he was unnerved. The sea and the jungle, the nakedness of men and women, the densely populated earth teeming with humanity, the market place overflowing with people, and the ever-present poverty induced—the word sprang to his lips— "a conflict" much deeper than he was even cognizant of. "I wanted," he wrote, "irrationally for these fantastic scenes to fade. I had the foolish feeling that I had but turn my head and I'd see the ordered, clothed streets of Paris. . . ."[11] He was being confronted not only with Africa but also with his southern past, and after so many years, he was unable to contend with either. The reality he saw about him, mirroring that of his past, was no longer his reality; the codes of living were antithetical to his own: "There was nothing here that I could predict, anticipate, or rely upon and, in spite of myself, a mild sense of anxiety began to fill me."

The anxiety was far from mild. The life-style of the Africans continued to disturb him. He was affronted by their nudity, their openness about it; their bastardized English—pidgin—affronted his sensibility for language. He was appalled at their religion—mystical, pantheistic, superstitious—and astounded that even African intellectuals believed in juju and "ancestor worship." He was affronted because the Africans regarded him as a European. They did not speak openly and frankly to him, as if he wasn't to be trusted. Nevertheless, he was impressed by

Kwame Nkrumah, Prime Minister of the soon-to-be-independent nation of Ghana, as Nkrumah's militancy and humanism seemed to parallel his own. As a result of his activities for independence, Nkrumah had been jailed by the British, but eventually he had succeeded: Ghana would be the first African state to win independence in the modern era.

Nkrumah had welcomed the suggestion by his ally, adviser, and hero, Padmore, that the Black American writer be allowed to witness and to report upon his tiny nation in transition. He insisted, despite his crowded schedule, on taking Wright on a guided tour of the best and worst of the Gold Coast, through shantytowns and slums, and into neat villages and towns. The tour was impressive: Everywhere the Prime Minister's car arrived, with his entourage of motorcycle escorts, the people broke out in spontaneous celebration. The word "free-dom" was constantly heard. It was loud, thunderous, springing out of emotions of gratitude and hope, as men and women began to dance the moment Nkrumah appeared. People talked, it seemed, with their heads, arms, and legs, expressing joy by using their bodies. Again, an African spectacle brought back remembrances of yesterday: "I'd seen these same snake like veering dances before . . ." in the storefront churches of America, in the "Holy Roller Tabernacles." Now he was seeing them among another group of blacks, separated by geography and time. Was this evidence of lingering African cultural traits, and if not, how could the similarities between what he saw here and what he had seen in America be explained? "The doubt," he later remembered, "lodged firmly in my mind, the riddle complexing and confusing." How had black people in America managed "to retain" despite the passage of time, differing circumstances, and cultural imposition, "such basic and fundamental patterns of behavior and response?"

He had no answer. Africa was more confusing and bewildering than he had imagined it would be. His sense of reality was threatened. With relief, he turned quickly from his personal conflict and directed his attention to the manifestations of European colonialism. The illiteracy of the people was one result; the creation of a small middle class—professionals, businessmen and civil servants who formed the opposition to Nkrumah—was another. The British were responsible also for maintenance of the system of chiefs, whom he considered anachronisms, and for the missionaries, whose allegiance was to colonialism. Overall, British colonialism succeeded in doing to the people of the Gold Coast what American slavery succeeded in doing to American blacks, made them psychological cripples, ashamed of their own culture and denied access to that of their conquerors.

On this common ground of mutual suffering and oppression, he and the Africans could meet as brothers. At a rally held by the Convention

People's Party, Nkrumah invited him to speak from the rostrum. He spoke of the common bond between himself and the Gold Coasters, admitted that he was one of Africa's "long lost sons" come to peruse the land of his ancestors. His human impulses were the same as theirs, his past experiences of oppression, similar. Still, the uneasiness of finding a too close identity in terms of race persisted. He was, he told the rally, a stranger whose ties with them went beyond "race" toward that which was "increasingly human in a world that is rapidly losing its claim to humanity."[12] He thanked the Prime Minister for the tour, but he wanted to be off on his own, to meet "the common people" of Ghana.

He moved to a location near the center of town, a dingy hotel at the edge of a beach. From his hotel balcony, he was able to view Africa in all its squalor, vitality, and fantastic disorder. Yet the same sense of distrust was displayed toward him. He discovered that the village women covered their nakedness when he approached, and he surmised that this was because he wore "western clothes." In the Cape Coast Residential Section, the affluent blacks were also suspicious of him, hiding behind what Wright came to call "the African laugh." His own feelings of distance remained strong. When he encountered two men dancing together, he quickly concluded that the British introduced "homosexuality" into Africa. Upon learning that such activity was part of the culture, he was astounded. In the West, two men dancing with one another was outside of tradition and culture. "Each hour events were driving home to me that Africa was another world, another sphere of being. For it to become natural to me, I'd have to learn to accept without thought a whole new range of assumptions."[13]

He could not do this. But the impact of Africa and its people was causing him to question his assumptions. He looked at Africans as he had looked at American blacks. Here too were illiterates, children, who would have to vault into the literate and industrialized world of the twentieth century. The warm sanctuary of tribal existence had to be discarded, new ways of combating nature and the elements had to be found. He had felt the Africans must escape the enslavement of tradition, push away from innocence, cease to trust in ancient gods and myths. But now the thought, why? It was his desire, not theirs. He was all that he wanted them to be: he was literate, industrialized, and Western. But he was also anxiety-ridden, despondent, pained, without anchor or roots anywhere. "Why, then," he asked himself, "must I advocate dragging these people into my trap?" The reason, he eventually concluded, is that he wanted them "to redeem themselves."

But, redeem themselves for what? And for whom? He does not say. But, in "redeeming" themselves, would they not make the West less ashamed of them? And if this occurred, would he not achieve new status among the men of the West? This was as close to identification on a racial level as he would come on his journey, though the question of race would not cease. He confronted it again in the person of an African intellectual, Dr. J. B. Danquah, one of the founders of the United Gold Coast Party, who told Wright that if he remained on African soil long enough, he would begin to feel anew the knowledge of his race. This, Wright told the scholar, he doubted. In fact, he felt greater affinity in others, like Danquah, who opposed these forces that sought to destroy African tribal life. Here, Wright discovered a new class of men: the tragic elite. They were educated and trained in the culture of the West; still they clung to anachronistic artifacts of the culture that had nourished them. But they were uncomfortable, schizoid, prevented from being fully accepted as part of the West because of racism, and no longer fully acceptable as Africans because of their Western acculturation. They were outsiders, much like American Negroes, who "had one foot in both worlds. . . ."

But, as psychologically depressing as this might be, there was a singular advantage: such people were gifted with a double vision. They knew of these values generated by people who lived simply, close to the earth, nurtured by tradition. Yet they also knew of the rewards to be gained from education, industrialization, and technology, knew something of the benefits to be achieved from Western culture. Thus they were pioneers, able, if allowed, to construct a bridge between man and man, between Africa and the West, between one culture and another. Now, close to the end of his journey, was he seeing in men like Danquah and K. A. Busia, another intellectual, mirror images of himself?

This notion of the tragic elite remained one of the most important discoveries of his trip. In truth, it was more validation than theory. He had offered many explanations for the "rootless" men and women of black America over the years; when he first met the enterprising peoples of the Third World, writers and intellectuals, he saw cultural dualism manifested in them also; now, here, on African soil, the theory took on the clothing of proven fact: The Africans and their descendants, due to their cultural schizophrenia, were granted the opportunity to remake the world. Their history of oppression, coupled with their will to survive and their struggle to rise above their pagan and tribal roots, made them exceptional men and women. More so than any other groupings of individuals, therefore, of Communists and democrats, of Catholics and Protestants, they might humanize the Cartesian world of pragmatism and rationality, make man the beneficiary, not the servant, of technology and industrialization.

After spending almost two months in the Gold Coast, he booked a return to England. Along the way, he stopped to visit the old slave-transportation points: Christianborg Castle, Cape Coast Castle, and Elmina Castle. He found at each stop relics of a brutal past, paraphernalia dating back to the days when people were wrenched violently from one culture and thrust into another. "No one will ever know," he wrote later in some of the most lyrical lines of *Black Power*, "the number or identity of the black men and women and children who passed through these walls. . . . Even today the castle bears marks of a crumbling luxury; there are marble sills at many of the doorways, there are lofty spacious rooms . . . no slaves had ever entered . . . the mere upkeep of such an establishment must have necessitated a staggering turnover in human flesh each year. . . ."[14]

The recounting of this journey to Africa, *Black Power: a Record of Reactions in a Land of Pathos,* was published in September of 1954. To it, he added Nkrumah's letter of introduction, photos of the Prime Minister, and a letter to Nkrumah saying he had felt a oneness, "an odd kind of at homeness" with the people of the Gold Coast. This feeling sprang not from "race" but "from the hard facts of oppression" that were universal. He believed his kinship with the people enabled him to offer council to the Prime Minister concerning his arduous task of projecting his people into the twentieth century. He advocated a program of warfare, a mobilization of people, energy and resources against the forces of irrationality and ignorance. Certain characteristics of the African culture had to be transformed in order to clear the "cloudiness" of the African mentality. The vigorous war waged against colonization must be equaled in intensity by that waged against tribalism, superstition, and against shackling remnants of the colonial past. In this war Nkrumah, he argued, must play the hard, pragmatic game with finesse. One must take from the West and East only that which is needed, and believe completely in neither. The illusions concerning the West must be surrendered, for their "codes, ideals, and conceptions of humanity do not apply to Black men. . . ."

But, somehow, the Gold Coast people, he averred, must "be made to walk, forced draft into the twentieth century. The direction of their lives, the duties they must perform to overcome the stagnancy of tribalism, the sacrifices that must yet be made—all of this must be placed under firm social discipline."[15] And in this warfare, in this great leap forward, he assures Nkrumah, the Gold Coaster does not fight or stand alone.

Black Power was more than a travelogue or a sociological document. It was equally the product of a sophisticated Westerner who, having mastered the discipline of rational and pragmatic thought, emphasized their importance. He discovered that the people of the Gold Coast, like those in black America, were mired under by racism, exploitation, superstition, and mysticism. And he proposed the same Draconian measures for Africans as he had for American blacks. Both, he suggested, had to step outside of history in order to defeat the culture that had nourished and sustained them; in so doing, they would stand forth as examples for the rest of Africa and the world. Was he, however, implying that salvation for Africans lay only in their willingness and ability to transcend their own cultural values and to adopt those of the West? And in this implication there seemed a corollary, that the indigenous cultures contained little of value. It was such implications, perhaps, that led Padmore to tell Himes that, though he personally liked the book, he did not think that many Africans would like it. From an American point of view, Wright's criticism was valid, "but African thinking was different." Himes without even having read the book, thought that Wright had made a mistake in writing it. "In trying to effect his departure from America and its way of life, Dick had become more of an American than he had ever been."[16] At any rate, he could not surrender his belief that the world of the future was the world of industrialization and technology; this new world called for new men and women, those who could merge the best of their own cultures with that of East and West. Such people must, then, be dragged, screaming and protesting "if need be, into the Twentieth Century." On September 24, after dismal advance sales of the book, his agent wired: "You've written a very fine book saying things that Americans don't want to hear and hence won't go into the book stores and buy." But he was probably less concerned at this point with the sales or adverse reviews concerning *Black Power* than he was with his personal situation. Eight days before Reynolds' letter, on September 16, 1954, he interrupted his travels through Spain to hurry back to Paris. He had gone to the Passport Division of the United States Government, situated in the American Embassy, a majestic mansion seemingly superimposed upon the white landscape of the Champs Élysées. There, before Agnes Schneider, "Consul of the United States of America at Paris, France," and, probably, the legal attaché of the Federal Bureau of Investigation, "Richard Wright . . . being duly sworn, furnished a statement consisting of answers to questions annexed to his statement."

CHAPTER SEVENTEEN

The suggestion to write about Spain had come from Gertrude Stein in 1946, during his first visit to Paris. You must go to Spain, she had told him. You will see the past there and find out what the "Western World is made of." Over the years, friends had suggested other areas of interest, and now, with *Black Power* completed, he considered other countries as subjects of study: Israel, Denmark, Egypt, and another country in Africa. He settled on Spain, however, and wrote Reynolds on July 24, 1954, that he thought that he could do a good "job" on a book on Spain. What he would say, he related, would not be simply "antifascist chatter and raving." His interest would encompass the entire country, "its religion and everything else." But was his eagerness to be off on another journey, so soon after returning from Africa, explained by his concern with the culture and people of Spain? He was not yet ready, he wrote his agent, to become involved in fiction again: ". . . there are so many more exciting and interesting things happening now in the world that I feel sort of dodging them if I don't say something about them."[1] But was Spain numbered among the places where exciting and interesting things were happening in the world? Or would Spain satisfy Wright's two desperate immediate needs: the need for solitude and reflection and the need to be involved in a project that might distract him from the fast-occurring events of the past months, allow him time for thought, reflection, perhaps to devise ways of coming to grips with the difficult choices thrust before him by agents of his government?

The CIA, acknowledged by Himes as being interested in Wright because they believed that he had knowledge of the Communist affiliation of important people, was not the only agency with such interests. Other agencies, over the years, had been interested in him for much the same reason. They sought information concerning organizations as well as individuals. In 1953, the National Council of American Soviet Friendship was a prime target of the Justice Department and Attorney General Herbert Brownell and his assistant, Warren Olney III. The organization was founded in 1938 to "promote friendship between the people of the United States and those of the USSR." For a while, the Council enjoyed an era of respectability. In 1942, during celebration of the twenty-fifth anniversary of the Bolshevik Revolution, governors, cabinet officers, mayors, and diplomats were in attendance. The downhill slide began in 1946, when the Council opposed the American Atomic Energy Plan. HUAC subpoenaed the council leaders and their records. The leaders refused to hand over their records and were convicted of contempt and sentenced to three months' imprisonment. They were summarily listed by the Attorney General as subversive, and began to lose "members, sponsors, public support, and revenue."

But the Council went on the offensive. They sued the government for redress and challenged the Attorney General's List, the Internal Security Act, and the Smith Act. "The National Council," stated a memo in 1953, "together with eleven other national organizations, was cited by the Attorney General of the US on April 20 for failure to register as a 'communist front' organization under the Internal Security Act of 1950 (the McCarran Act)." On June 1, 1953, the Council filed a motion for dismissal before the SACB. The motion was denied and the Council was ordered to file answers "to the Attorney General's charges not later than August 20." The attorneys for the Council had expected the hearings to last only for three months. The hearings, however, lasted well into 1954, as the Justice Department, under Olney in concert with the FBI, leaned upon informers and ex-Communists for information concerning the Council and its leaders. In a "Note to SAC's Chicago, Los Angeles, Mobile, and New York": document 88344 advised the agent chiefs: "Bureau files reflect that each of the individuals referred to in the attachment is well known to the office in the area in which he is believed to reside. In the absence of any information in your files which would make such action inadvisable, Bureau authority is granted to conduct the requested interviews." The memorandum stressed urgency, reminding the SAC's that the hearing against the Council would "commence in the near future" and demanding results "no later than December 17, 1953."

In May of 1943, during the intensive research on Wright's activities, an agent had noted in his file that his name "appeared frequently in the Daily Worker during 1941 and 1942." He noted also that in an issue dated "February 28, 1941 Wright was listed as one of the writers who would greet Theodore Dreiser at a testimonial luncheon attended

March 1, 1941 under the auspices of the American Council on Soviet Relations. Others to be present were Jessica Smith, editor of 'Soviet Russia Today,' Clifford Odets, Dr. John A. Kingsbury and others."[2] Was Wright's involvement with the National Council more extensive and, if so, was he in possession of the kind of information sought by the Assistant Attorney General? Moreover, if so, would he divulge it? According to Himes, he had refused to give similar information to David Schine. But had he refused, heretofore, to give such information, when requested by a government agency? And was he in any position to do so? His passport was up for renewal in February 1954. His concern about his possible status, did the State Department revoke it, had already generated concern, as early as 1952. "If the State Department notifies an American citizen living abroad that his passport has been cancelled," he wrote in a letter to the *Yale Law Journal* on May 5, 1952, "and if the passport remains in possession of the owner and is not stamped cancelled, and if the American citizen refuses to surrender said passport, what law is he violating?"[3] They got "Ollie's" passport by a ruse, Ellen Wright told Constance Webb, and they tried the same thing with Wright. Agnes Schneider "took possession of Dick's [passport] and announced she'd have to clear with Washington before issuing a new one." Wright, according to his wife, threatened "to apply to the French authorities for the necessary travelling papers and in general blast it to the press for all it was worth." The threat, she concluded, seemed to work, for, almost immediately, Wright was summoned back to the embassy to retrieve his passport, "with Agnes Schneider oozing with all the charm she could muster for the credit of the State Department."[4] On February 23, 1954, Wright was issued Passport Number 2538, at the American Embassy. In his application, he stated that he was residing with his wife [deletion] and two children [long deletion]. On July 8, however, a "specific request for information reflecting Richard Wright's" defection from the Communist Party was noted by the FBI. "USIA," reads the document, "requesting additional information re [name deleted] and Richard Wright in connection with USIA employee [deletion] specifically requested information re Communist Party defection by Wright [deletion]." A summary of Wright's investigative record follows, with the usual bureau conclusion that the information was furnished as a result of the demand for an FBI check and should not be construed as either clearance or nonclearance "of the individual involved."[5] Sometime between receipt of his passport and the requesting agency's receipt of his file from the FBI, questions had been posed to him and answers were expected. As he traveled alone through the splendor and magnificence of the Iberian Peninsula, undoubtedly his attention veered occasionally to the coming audience with Agnes Schneider. She would not, he knew, be "oozing with all the charm she could muster" this time.

The beauty and charm of Spain was a welcome respite. On August 15, he had piloted the Citroën down the coastline of this country between Africa and Europe. He thought he divined something of the character of the country in the scenery alone. Beside the blue waters of the Mediterranean, under skies darkened by shadows cast by the giant Pyrenees Mountains, there was an ambience of serenity. Yet, beneath the grotesque, commanding presence of the mountains, Spain had undergone the Inquisition, fought a civil war. The show of calm seemed proof positive to Wright of the chasms of fear, insecurity, and tension in the deepest recesses of the "Spanish soul." He moved, in the space of a few hours, from the scenic Costa Brava, where the shimmering blue-green waves of the Mediterranean cascaded thunderously against the sentinel-like gray mountains, to Barcelona. It was another of Spain's cities beside the sea. Along with Madrid, it was Spain's most Europeanized of cities, though it was here, too, that East and West seemed to meet. There were modern ornate architecture and medieval structures; there were wide boulevards that recalled Paris, and unpaved, dirt roads. Sections of the "Roman Wall" still stood, as well as architecture influenced by the African invaders.

Near the waterfront, where ships of all nations dropped anchor, there were the bars and hotels, the pimps and their prostitutes. Farther inland were the mammoth Catholic cathedrals, each valuing its own precious relic of the ancient past. Not far distant from either the churches or the red-light district were the arenas where men pitted their strength against nature, the bull fights, which Wright likened to a ritual of the Church. Yes, he concluded after a few days, this was a strange country. This feeling intensified as he began to meet the people. One of them, Carmen, a schoolgirl, stole a textbook for him: *Formación Política: Lecciones para las Felches*. It was the handbook of the Franco government, "a political catechism for the Spanish masses," required reading for the young of Spain. The book set forth Spain's past and present and its future aims, in simplistic terminology. It linked the history of fascism with the history of the Church: From what time, he scanned a passage, have we known of Spain's destiny? Since the time, he read the answer, when Isabel and Ferdinand, through the universities and Spanish missionaries, sent men to bring civilization to America; "By the conquest made by Charles I in Europe and Africa to defend Christianity."[6]

Was this the reason for the tension he thought he divined? A dualism resulting from the strain of the very human attempt to exist side by side with the Falange? The catechisms from the stolen book and the ceremonies of the Catholic Church convinced him that each survived and endured due to the strength of the other: the glory of God irrevocably yoked to the glory of the fascist government. Caesar and St. Ignatius had achieved a concordat based upon similarity of ends and means, the repressive actions of the former leading to the discipline and obedience demanded by the latter. "I live in a religious Communist state," Carmen's brother, Carlos, tells him. He was drawn to this rebellious and estranged young man who was "alienated from his dark rich earth, from his sea of green, prolific, plants. . . ." His feelings concerning the upper classes, however, were quite the reverse. He hardly could contain his hostility to a duke who told him that Franco was not stern enough and "who found little meaning in the lives of the masses."[7]

Before long, Wright thought he had discovered the vehicle that stifled the desire for freedom and independence in the Spanish and that provided an outlet for their tension. Whether in the raucous city of Madrid or in the sleepy, poetic town of Seville, the congruence of the state function (the bull fight) and the church function (the Mass) was apparent everywhere. The Freudian implications were suddenly apparent to him. Alongside the need of Church and state to repress freedom and individuality was the need of both to symbolize the human proclivity for sex in the secular and religious spheres. The spires of the Catholic Church seemed to reek with symbols of repressed sexuality; the Black Virgin seemingly inspired worship of the female principle, the statue itself embodied the sexual idea: ". . . the most prevalent, powerful, emotional and factual experience in human life."

His observation of the statue occurred when he visited the seat of the famous shrine of the Black Virgin, at Montserrat. On a gigantic mountain, high in the Spanish sky, dwarfing the craggy rock formations nearer the earth and the city of Barcelona, he found in the spiral-shaped boulders surrounding Virgin and child "phallic-looking uprights with oblong, smooth extending heads . . . the complementing male principle of life."[8] "Pedro"—he turned to his astonished companion— "don't you see that conglomeration of erect stone penises?" Here, he concluded, the real and the ideal were symbolized in church trapping: the Virgin symbolized the ideal of purity and grace, "how man likes to feel that he came into the world." But the reality was symbolized in the rock formations he envisioned as "erect penises," the instrument that actually brought man into being, thereby demolishing the ideal of virgin birth. The symbolism was repeated in the offering of the government, the bull fight. Carefully nurtured and groomed, weaned from birth to retain a state of primitive innocence, the bull still possessed the pagan instincts of brutality and murder. He was, for the Spaniards, the object of love and hate; he was a sacrificial offering to the warring instincts of man; he had not only to be "slain but ceremoniously slain."

The matador embodies the people's need and lust for sacrifice. With his driving sword, he "was a kind of lay priest offering up the mass for thirty thousand guilty penitents."

But was it guilt or something more that he saw on that occasion when, after the matador had done his work, hundreds of men and boys, followed by the enormous crowd, rushed to the stadium floor and, finding the dead bull's testicles, "began kicking at them, stomping them, spitting at them, grinding them under their heels. . . . They mutilated the testicles of the dead bull for more than ten minutes. . . ." No, it was not guilt alone, nor simply a reaction to sexual oppression, nor even the tension and anxiety caused by confusions between the real and the ideal. What accounted for such unrelieved passion was the paganism, so close to the surface of the Spanish soul, which, though denied by the Church and the government, obtruded still. This "pagan attitude towards life" was omnipresent, making Spain, the outside nation of Europe, emotional, irrational.

He had gone there, he writes in *Pagan Spain*, the result of his research, to discover, among other things: "How did one live after the death of the hope of freedom?" He thought he had discovered the answer: the people retreated to paganism, to placing their faith and ideals in the irrational. Here was the natural refuge for the powerless who were accosted by tradition, religion, and oppressive governments. All too often, however, his reactions toward Spain border on the very personal. Tradition, religion, and now a hostile government had been and were his bane, even as they were that of the Spaniards. He had somewhat defeated tradition, escaped the religion offered by his family. Now only his government remained as a formidable obstacle. But he could not emulate the Spanish experience. He could not confront his Caesars by escape into emotion and irrationality. He would have to maintain his objectivity, be pragmatic. How much of this was his own anxiety projected in fantasy upon the people and culture of Spain? "I have no religion . . . ," he had told Carmen. "I have no race except that which is forced upon me. I have no country except that to which I'm obligated to belong. I have no traditions. I'm free. I have only the future."[9]

But the future was very uncertain. The questions he had been given by agents of the government dealt primarily with his own status as a Communist. The reports of informants over the years had suggested that he was "still as much a Communist as ever." In April, he had hastily interjected an anti-Communist refutation into the Introduction to *Black Power*. "From 1932 to 1944," he wrote, "I was a member of the Communist Party of the United States of America and, as such, I held consciously in my hands Marxist Communism as an instrumentality to effect . . . political and social changes." He was no longer a member of the Party, he publicly avowed, "or a subscriber to its aims." He had surrendered his membership, because he discovered that "Marxist Communism" was altering the world in a way that would grant him less "freedom" than he had before. When he also discovered that "International Communism" was only "an instrument of Russian foreign policy" he "disassociated" himself from it.[10] But the government desired more from its ex-Communists than public confessions of past error and repentance. On September 16, the picturesque beauty of Spain behind him, he shuffled his notes nervously, kept his eyes away from the American consul and the FBI representative as agents of the United States Government continued to record his statement.

"In that statement, subject identified himself as being the same Richard Wright whose experiences in the Communist movement were included in the book, 'The God That Failed.' Subject stated he could not fix the exact time of his joining the Communist Party because he was a functionary in the Communist Party before he actually joined the Communist Party. He explained that the method used by the Communist Party in recruiting is of such a nature that the time or date of determining the exact membership is very difficult. He stated that to the best of his recollection, the date (about 1933) shown in his book, 'The God That Failed' is correct. Subject stated that he is the Richard Wright who wrote a letter to the League of American Writers expressing his views on the Spanish Civil War, which was published in May, 1938, in the booklet, 'Writers Take Sides.'

"Subject stated at the time of writing the above mentioned letter he was a member of the Communist Party. He stated he is not now a member of the Communist Party of any country in the world."[11]

His break with the Party, he told his interrogators, occurred as the result of "a series of ideological disputes he had with the following Communist officials: Benjamin Davis, James W. Ford, Max Yergan and others." But there were questions to be asked, and his statement was interrupted: "Subject was asked if he was acquainted with [name deleted], who in 1943, was an official in the Office of War Information. Subject stated that he has a slight acquaintanceship with [name deleted] and it dates exactly from the period when he did some voluntary work for the Office of War Information in 1942, and as he recalls was introduced to [name deleted] by [name deleted] who had assisted subject in the producing as a play, subject's novel, 'Native Son,' and that this introduction took place in the presence of [name deleted]. Subject stated that [name deleted] was known to him as a member of the Communist Party, and he described [name deleted] a Negro writer from New Jersey, whose father was a minister.[12]

"In regard to [name deleted] subject stated he was not known to him as having any affiliation with the Communist Party at that time. Subject stated he was somewhat surprised and taken aback when [name deleted] introduced him to [name deleted] because subject had known that [name deleted] was one of the chief political or editorial writers of the 'New York Herald Tribune' and the manner of his being introduced to him implied that [name deleted] understood the subject's political position very well. Subject states that Benjamin Davis, who at that time was a New York City councilman; Max Yergan, who at that time was a prominent official of the Communist Party in the United States, and James Ford, one of the leading Communists of the United States, approached him shortly after his introduction to [name deleted] and asked him to make a formal application to work for the Office of War Information."

The attempt failed and Wright related that he accused Davis and the Party of chicanery, that he told the Communist leader that he would no longer "campaign for him. . . . Subject stated that Davis wanted him to become a member-at-large of the Communist Party, but subject rejected this suggestion of Davis. Subject stated he has had no further contact with Benjamin Davis since that time, nor has he had any contact with the Communist Party or [name deleted] or [name deleted] or [name deleted] or [name deleted]."13

The ordeal over, he made plans to return to Spain, to continue his research. What, however, had it all meant? He had been on the defensive, forced to prove that he was no longer involved with Communist parties "anywhere" in the world. He could not help but be impressed with the information that his interrogators had about him. They knew of activities that he had probably forgotten, of obscure statements made in long-defunct magazines. They knew of conversations held long ago, words and statements whispered supposedly in private. There had long been rumors of informers and agents among the Paris black community, and now he had proof of it. But what about himself? Could the answers that he had given honestly and forthrightly be construed as informing? "I've talked to some," recalled Horace Cayton, "like Ken Kinnamon . . . who wrote his doctor's dissertation on him [Wright] at Harvard. And he advanced the notion that Dick, towards the end, was becoming pretty paranoic. And his preoccupation with this black spy—"

"I don't think that that was any paranoid action . . . ," Sidney Williams replied. "My knowledge of the operation of the CIA, based on my own experience, in Africa in particular, during the war and subsequently, would lead me to believe that this concern that he and I had . . . wasn't something from the excitement of one's imagination. It was real, quite real."14

His fears had been all too palpably real. And he knew now that he was a man with few options. He might return to the United States during this period of McCarthyism and subject not only himself but his family as well to danger. He might become a French citizen. But all of his works were published originally in English; he was an American writer and his audience was American. Cut off from them, he faced the loss of income and, perhaps, his talent as well. But, above all, he stood alone. He had no such support as that enjoyed by others, by Robeson or Ben Davis, for example. Europe was dependent upon the Marshall Plan and other forms of American aid, and he could not expect his European friends to fight for long in his behalf. He was almost as anathema to the French Left as he was to the French Right after the cooling of the relationship between himself and Sartre. His movement toward the Third World was positive, but Africa was relatively weak and its leaders uninfluential. No, he had had no other alternative than to act in his own interests.

"There is no instance," as he had once told an audience, "where a Communist stood up and said 'yes, I am a Communist and I have done what I have done because your system is wrong.'" Given the opportunity to set a precedent, however, he had retreated from his own stance. His interest in the Party, he had told his interrogators, was due to its attitude toward blacks; in time, however, he discovered the hypocrisy of these attitudes: "He stated his decision to break with the Communist Party was predicated upon his disagreement with the Communist Party's position upon the Negro question in the United States." Were his actions prompted as much by a need for vengeance against the Party as self-interest? Both naïveté and vindictiveness may have caused him publicly to label Davis and Winston Communists, during the time when the U. S. Government was hastily preparing for the trial of the Foley Square Eleven, in "Comrade Strong, Don't You Remember?" At that time, the Party's humiliation of him was still fresh in his mind; the rancor and bitterness he bore toward its leaders who had betrayed both him and the people remained strong and vibrant.

But with the American Communist Party in disarray, its top leadership in jail, its effectiveness as an organization rendered useless, what theraupeutic value could an act of such vindictiveness have? He had, according to the FBI files, volunteered little information. He had corroborated information posed in the form of questions. Much of what he had said was public knowledge. None of it was new to the Bureau. Ford was dead. Davis was serving a five-year term in the federal penitentiary at Terre Haute, Indiana. Yergan was, perhaps, a double agent, involved with Du Bois and Robeson, among others, on The Council of African Affairs, now a target of the Justice Department. The status of those individuals whose names were deleted from the files, remain unknown. Yet, none of the Communists whom he had named had ever admitted to being members of the Communist Party, and for good reason. Under the Smith Act, membership in the Communist Party carried a "heavier sentence" than the one received by the Foley Square Eleven, convicted and sentenced to five years for "conspiracy to advocate the overthrow of the United States Government. . . ." Membership in the Communist Party carried a sentence of ten years. Davis and his comrades were to be released in the fall of the coming year. When they were released, in 1955, they were reindicted by the Justice Department and charged with "'joining an organization to conspire to advocate. . . .'" The case was eventually dropped, but other Communists, including an influential black Communist from Chicago whom Wright had known during his years there was arrested in June of 1954 and convicted of being a member of the Communist Party. How much of this did the writer know? "He always struck me," said a friend, "as being naïve about politics." Was it naïveté, therefore, that led him not only to validate information concerning the Communist membership of others but to surrender to the United States Government a signed statement admitting his own past membership in the Party and his association with Communist front organizations? Or was he attempting, still, a dangerous game of walking the middle path? Had he established for himself limits beyond which he would not go? He would not limit his attacks upon American racism, or spy for the government, or volunteer information concerning others. But he would step up his attacks and denunciation of the Communist Party and publicly tilt toward the United States. "God knows," he decides in *Pagan Spain*, "totalitarian governments and ways of life were no mysteries to me. I had been born under an absolutist racist regime in Mississippi; I had lived and worked for twelve years under the political dictatorship of the Communist Party of the United States. . . ."[15]

He returned to Spain on November 8, less than a month after his affair at the American Embassy, and around the middle of December, most of his work completed, he returned to France in order to be with his family for the Christmas holidays. As the New Year approached, he could point with some pride to the accomplishments of the past year, despite the dispiriting confrontation with his government. And despite the negative American reaction to *Black Power*, European interest in it had been good. Even before publication, he had spoken about Africa and his forthcoming book in various lectures. In April he had spoken about the book to "a group of foreign diplomats" at the International Quaker Center.[16] In September, passages from *Black Power* were published in *Encounter* magazine. In October, shortly before his return to

Spain for the second time, he had spoken, under the auspices of the Congress for Cultural Freedom, in Amsterdam. At the reception held after his lecture, which was well received, he met his Dutch translator, Margrit de Sablonière, for the first time. ". . . a handsome woman, tall and large-boned, with a compassionate face and keen blue eyes."[17] Sablonière had earned his affection and gratitude the previous year. His publisher in Holland, after assigning *The Outsider* to the translator, had demanded that "thirty two pages" be cut from the manuscript. Sablonière, interested and well versed in black literature, a writer of some recognition in her own right, refused. Wright was extremely pleased with the translator's action on his behalf. He "demanded that Margrit be named his only translator in Holland. . . . Gradually, they had become intimate friends and Margrit watched over him and his whole family from her house on the canal in Leiden."[18]

During the year, he had also decided to search for a place of refuge, a home away from the hustle and interruptions of Paris. His wife was no longer able almost to stand guard to protect him from the numbers of people who sought him out for favors of one sort or another, as she now was working as a literary agent. Handling Wright's works over the years had given her a certain expertise in dealing with publishers. Along with her friend Helene Bokanowski, she had begun her own literary agency. Among her first clients was Chester Himes. The seclusion that Wright needed could no longer be guaranteed. But his frequent visits to the country home of the Bokanowskis, in the beautiful village of Croisilles, in Normandy, had brought back memories of sprawling fields and open spaces, of rich green countrysides, the earth overflowing with produce. Visits to the Moulin d'Ande had conjured up the same visions.

He had attempted to purchase such a haven in America long before and had met with racism in New England. In Ailly, France, however, he had found a little farm with no difficulty, "not too distant from the Bokanowski estate." He wired Reynolds for five thousand dollars from his dwindling account to purchase the farm and was soon involved in making the place habitable. Repairs were done by contractors. But the writer chipped in with his little family, hanging pictures, sorting out books, arranging furniture, choosing rooms for himself and his wife, the children, and the maid. And choosing also the kind of vegetables he would plant and grow, making plans for his own, homemade garden. Here, in this quiet, peaceful village of Normandy, "beside a tiny dribble" the Normans called the River Eure, he realized, he told Harrington, "that above all he was a man of the country. He needed the smoky, dawn shrouded fields, the ever busy birds and the cattle lowing in the mist." The farm at Ailly, he quipped, was "A place where I can grow me some potatoes."[19]

Later Harrington recalled that he "actually planted his potatoes, and corn." And he spread the largesse around. "There were many writers and artist friends who lived in tiny left bank hotel rooms," Harrington wrote, "who didn't know what in the hell to do with the pile of vegetables Dick dumped proudly on their sloping, linoleum-covered floors. . . ."

His work in Spain was not yet completed, but in January he wrote enthusiastically to Margrit de Sablonière about a conference in Jakarta, Indonesia, that spring: the first international conference of Third World nations. Over a billion people resided in these countries, many recently freed from colonialism. From Japan and Egypt, Ethiopia and the Gold Coast, "the colored people" of the world were planning to assemble to discuss their relationship to East and West. Many of the men who were to lead delegations, among them Jawaharlal Nehru, Ho Chi Minh, Kwame Nkrumah, and Chou En-lai, had been political prisoners. Having "lived lonely lives in exile," they knew the meaning of sacrifice and suffering. He was particularly intrigued because each of the nations was religious, and he concluded that the conference would inevitably deal with the added dimension of "religion and race."

Enthused at the prospect of being involved in such a historic event, Wright set about making plans to attend the conference. He sought financial support from American foundations but was rebuffed, although he was more successful in obtaining aid from the Congress for Cultural Freedom, an organization later revealed as controlled and bankrolled by the Central Intelligence Agency. It was doubtful that he could have been aware of this relationship. Some of the most prestigious and world-renowned intellectuals and writers were and had been members of the Congress. In February, he left again for Spain, intent upon completing his work there and proceeding on to Bandung.

He went almost directly to Madrid, where in addition to visiting cathedrals and being enthralled by the contrast between old Madrid and the newer, more modern city springing up around it, he attended a party given in his honor shortly before his departure. On June 30, when he was already in Bandung, the legal attaché in Madrid fired off a report about the party to the Director of the FBI: "[name deleted] was interviewed by the writer in Madrid, where he had come for a few weeks vacation. . . . He stated . . . that Richard Wright he found to be very anti-American, bitter toward the U.S. role in Asia, and, according to [name deleted], Wright followed the Communist line regarding affairs in Asia. When Wright was in Madrid, he was on his way to Bandung as an observer."[20]

The Madrid legates' attention had been drawn to the party given for Wright by a letter from Military Intelligence sent on March 16. Certain individuals, the letter read, had been following the Communist line in their conversations. Such conversation, the military agent informed the FBI, had been overheard by a writer for the *Reader's Digest*, a guest at the party, which included American employees of American corporations. On April 12, Wright had arrived in Jakarta, Indonesia, site of the Bandung Conference. The legate's report to Washington was dated June 30. On July 27, the FBI answered a request for a name check on Richard Nathaniel Wright. The requesting agency was referred to a similar request it had made and the data it had received on October 25, 1944. The material forwarded on July 27, in response to the request made on July 6, was an up-to-date summary of Wright's record. "Transmitted herewith is an FBI investigative report in the case entitled 'Richard Nathaniel Wright; Security Matter-C' concerning the subject of your name check request." The original plus one copy were sent to (G-2) Military Intelligence.[21]

But the report covered Wright's activities only up until 1951. Reports from agents and informers concerning his association with the Fellowship and various lectures given, plus reports from such agencies as the CIA, are available in the document; missing, however, is reference to the statement given the State Department in September. Was this a case of one intelligence agency refusing to share fully with another? Or had the information been too recent to be fully verified, and assimilated? Or, more likely, was the government reluctant to accept his open confession as proof positive of his break with the past and did it demand more evidence? Despite Yergan's apparent cooperation with the Bureau, he remained suspect. Whatever Wright's own belief concerning the outcome of the meeting on September 16, he was regarded still with suspicion by the intelligence agencies of the government.

By the time the name-check request had been fulfilled, Wright had completed his research in Spain and Bandung as well. He remained in Indonesia after the conference, touring the country and observing the people, leaving finally during the first week of May. On June 9, he wrote De Sablonière telling of his visit to Bandung and that he had put together a book of around a thousand words. The manuscript, on which he confided to having worked night and day, was in New York at the publisher's. His publisher, Harper & Row, however, turned the book down. Since the departure of his first editor, Aswell, to McGraw-Hill, Wright had been having increasing difficulty with his new editors at Harper. His relationship with John Fisher was cordial and polite, but he missed the firm but considerate handling of Aswell. One of Aswell's first acts as editor in chief of McGraw-Hill, however, was to welcome Wright to the company, though McGraw-Hill, on the whole, published little fiction. *The Color Curtain: A Report on the Bandung Conference* was published, with an Introduction by Gunnar Myrdal, by World Publishing Co. in 1956. The book was thus published ahead of *Pagan Spain*, which was released in February 1957.

The Color Curtain differed from *Pagan Spain*, though both were journalistic accounts. The essential difference lay in the risks confronting the writer, risks both political and psychological. The Western powers did business with the Franco regime, but an attack upon the Falangist would likely incur little rancor from the American Government. World Catholicism might and did react to attacks upon the Church of Spain. He was careful in *Pagan Spain*, however, to defend the Spanish Protestants, even making the correlation between the condition of Protestants in Spain and that of blacks in America. Discussions of race are at a minimum in *Pagan Spain*, though race is central to an understanding of the Spanish character, and when such discussions do occur, they are shown in relation to his own, southern experience. More often than not, however, he repeats his theme of racelessness, portrays himself still as a man for whom such categories are anathema. It was a theme that would not be unwelcome among liberals in America.

But the Bandung Conference was sponsored for leaders of the Third World, and considerations of race were unavoidable. Detailed discussion of the explosive topic would bring him into confrontation with his past experiences in America. Could he, however, be as open and frank about those experiences as he had been before? How much of a psychological burden had the meeting of September 16 with the American consul imposed upon him? He could not violate his own personal ethics to the extent of repudiating his past pronouncements concerning American racism. He could not overnight become supportive of a system that destroyed so many men, women, and children. Yet he knew now that whatever he said or wrote was scrutinized even more severely than heretofore. How could he fend off the pressure of the government on the one hand, and maintain his personal sense of integrity on the other?

Again he would walk the middle path. He would censure the West and praise it at the same time. He would suggest ways that the Third World might be saved from being devoured by the Communists. During the first years of his exile, he had attacked the evils of American hegemony as offered via the Marshall Plan; now this same hegemony was viewed as a possible good. Past disavowals of race were soon forgotten, and for this conference at least, he became a man associated with race: ". . . I had one tangible in my favor . . . ," he writes; "I was 'colored.'" The Asians, he discovered, surprisingly hated the white West with "an absoluteness" more extensive than that of black Americans. The hatred of Americans by the black Americans, he now discovers to be limited, partial, centered upon specifics: ". . . he rarely ever criticized or condemned the conditions of life about him as a whole. . . . Once his particular grievances were redressed, the Negro reverted to a normal Western outlook."[22] The Asian, on the other hand, "had a feeling of distance, of perspective, of objectivity toward the West which tempered his most intimate experiences of the West." When Adam Clayton Powell arrives to "defend the position of the United States in relation to the Negro Problem," Wright, in attendance at the congressman's press conferences, notes that he gave America "a cleaner bill of racial health" than it deserved. A few lines later, however, he writes that the problem of blacks in America are "child's play compared to the naked racial tensions gripping Asia and Africa."[23] At the very time when the United States, he avows, was trying to resolve its race problem, the Bandung Conference focused attention upon race and raised the consciousness of the "colored nations" concerning it.

The struggle between East and West, between communism and capitalism, he asserts, must take place on the battlefield not of ideology but of race and religion, and the greatest threat to Western hegemony over Asia and Africa may come from the Chinese, "trained and dedicated Bolsheviks" such as Chou En-lai, "shrewd enough to plow the fertile field of race hatred so richly fertilized by the West." He hoped these former colonialists and exploiters would now be big enough, generous enough, to understand both the bitterness and hope with which the nonaligned looked to the West for Salvation, and in a spirit of cooperation.[24]

Still backward, incapable of solving their many problems on their own, these nationalists had nowhere else to turn. For who but the West can master this new reality, "which has like a volcanic eruption shot up from the ocean floor?" Who but the former masters, who even in oppression accomplished good things: they brought forth the light of civilization, they induced the ideal of freedom, they created an elite more Western than the West? "I know," he writes, "that there are Westerners who will decry my depositing this unwieldy lump of humanity on their moral doorsteps. . . ."[25] But deposit them he did, this onetime antagonist of the Marshall Plan for Africa. Against the beliefs of a liberal Southerner from America who argues that American aid must be given voluntarily on the basis of noninterference, Wright declares: "I think you have a right to interfere, if you feel that the assumptions of your interference are sound."[26] Yet, one year earlier, he had admonished Nkrumah to be wary of the West and cautious in accepting its aid. "I cannot," he had written in Black Power, "as a man of African descent brought up in the West, recommend with good faith the agitated doctrines and promises of the hard-faced men of the West."[27] He had believed that they had no moral, ethical, or human foundation upon which to cement viable relationships with those of dark skins and would, given the opportunity, "pounce at any time upon Africa to solve their own hard-pressing social and political problems. . . ." ". . . I'm convinced," he had written then, "that the cultural conditioning of the Africans will make it difficult for them to adjust quickly to values that are solely Western, values that have mocked and shamed them so much in the past, values that go against the grain of so much in the African heart. . . ."[28]

Since then, the West had undergone transformation to become both benefactor to the Third World and protector against communism, and Wright had discovered a rational basis of "thought and feeling in the Western World" that was broad and secure enough to warrant the West's assumption of a moral right to interfere in the internal affairs of nations of the Third World "sans narrow, selfish, political motive. . . ." One year later, communism represented absolute evil, while the West embodied the principles of both good and evil. Wright quoted the Philippine UN Delegate Carlos Romulo to support his notion: "Yet this white world, which has fostered racism, has done many another thing. A rich mythology of religious thinking and feeling, a rich heritage of art and literature came from them, and, above all, political thought and an astounding advancement of scientific knowledge also came from them . . . just as Western political thought has given us all so many of our basic ideas of political freedom, justice and equality, it is Western science which in this generation has exploded the mythology of race." And Wright interjects much the same sentiment, one year later, at another conference, a gathering of Third World writers: "In the minds of hundreds of millions of Asians and Africans the traditions of their lives have been psychologically condemned beyond recall. Millions live uneasily with beliefs of which they have been made ashamed." I say, "Bravo! for that clumsy and cruel deed. Not to the motives, mind you, behind those deeds, motives which were all too often ignoble and base. But I do say 'Bravo!' to the consequences of Western plundering, a plundering that created the conditions for the possible rise of rational societies for the greater majority of mankind."[29]

It was left to a reviewer writing in the New York *Times* on March 18, 1956, after these sentiments were published in *The Color Curtain*, to view Wright's pronouncements in cold-war-cliché terminology. "He asks," writes the reviewer, "whether the sensitive and resentful people represented there are to be brought out of their present state of poverty, ignorance, and economic backwardness under the aegis of a bloody communist totalitarianism or through wise and generous aid from the West that will link them with our freer democratic system."[30]

However, at that very moment, in America, there were those who were questioning "the freer democratic system" of the United States. None was doing this more forcefully or vigorously than W. E. B. Du Bois. He had been indicted along with other officers of The Peace Information Center for refusal to register the Center, under the Smith Act, as an agent of "a foreign power dedicated to the violent overthrow of the United States Government." Though judged innocent in 1950, Du Bois had felt the full brunt and force of governmental power and vengeance: "My mail was tampered with or withheld. Negro newspapers were warned not to carry my writings nor mention my name. Colleges ceased to invite my lectures or my presence at Commencement exercises. From being a person whom every Negro in the nation knew by name at least and hastened always to entertain or praise, churches and Negro-conferences refused to mention my past or present existence. . . . In fine I was rejected of men, refused the right to travel abroad and classed as a 'controversial figure' even after being acquitted of guilt by a Federal Court of Law. The colored children ceased to hear my name. . . ."[31] The favorable review of Wright's report on the Bandung Conference occurred after the government turned down Du Bois' request for a passport to visit Paris, at the invitation of the Congress of African Writers and Artists sponsored by Présence Africaine, and scheduled for September 14, 1956, a conference at which Wright was destined to play a significant role.

But, in May of 1955, when he returned from Indonesia, he was more concerned about his future role as a writer. He was no longer happy with Harper & Row, and had written his agent from Indonesia that he believed it was time to find a new publisher. The royalty payments for *Black Boy* would end in 1957, and he had already spent most of his savings on the farm at Ailly. What he needed for both financial and personal stability was a long-term contract that would enable him to work on a number of books over a long period of time. He was gratified when Aswell, his former editor at Harper's, suggested that he draw up such a plan, and two months after his return from Indonesia, he secluded himself in the quiet of Ailly to work. "The work I have in mind," he wrote on July 27, 1955, "is a series of novels tied together, not as in the usual case, by plot, but by an attitude. . . ."[32] *Savage Holiday* was to be considered the first, followed by a work he tentatively called "Strange Daughters," and ending the series with a book treating "the psychology of Colonization with the Aztec leader, Montezuma, as the hero," tentatively entitled, "When the World Was Red."[33]

Reynolds' reactions were not encouraging. The plan was not economically sound from a publishing standpoint. The American public would probably not be interested in a figure such as Montezuma; but, beyond this, Reynolds voiced what was becoming his chief worry about his good friend and client. He told Wright frankly of his doubt, that someone who had been away from America for nine years could write "well" about the country, as so much had changed. Wright's most creative period, he suggested, had occurred while he was close to the American scene, but now the creativity seemed muted: "as you have found greater peace as a human being, living in France, and not been made incessantly aware that the pigmentation in your skin sets you apart from other men, you have at the same time lost something as a writer . . . your present situation calls for some serious effort of reassessment, or reevaluation, of discovering where you are and where you are going."[34]

He was not altogether convinced that his agent and his editor, who voiced much the same sentiments, were correct about the changes that had taken place in America. In November he wrote De Sablonière, informing her that murders such as that recently of Emmet Till, occurred daily in the South. Indiscriminate murder of blacks was not so much the policy of the government, but, having waited so long to morally condemn such acts, the government was powerless to stop them. Even now, governmental opposition sprang from the injury such acts did to American foreign policy. Such killings, he believed, would continue until the death of the older generations of whites. "That is why," he added, "I cannot live in America. Such wanton killings fill me with disgust, uneasiness, and a sense of dread."[35]

And as always, personal concern was interchangeable with parental concern. Julia was almost thirteen, Rachel almost six. Julia was one of the leading students in her class at the lycée. She had almost totally forgotten what little she had known of her American experience. Rachel's native language was French. The girls knew nothing of the sense of dread and fear that often made him ruminate long and hard upon his memories of America, and he determined that they never would. He would protect them all, his wife and children, from everything. While at Ailly, Rachel had come down with a fever, alarming him terribly. He insisted on taking her back to Paris, to the family physician, where her condition was in fact diagnosed as scarlet fever. No, he could not live in America again, for his children's sake even more so than for his own. But how long would he be able to walk the tightrope between principle and expediency? How long before the demands of his government became insatiable?

On August 7, 1956, a name check on Richard Wright was requested from the FBI and forwarded on August 22. "[Name deleted]," read the document, "USIA, requested a search for main files (indecipherable)." He advised that only copies of investigative reports of the results of investigation were requested. "Reason for request: Program for People-to-People Partnership (formerly President's Program for World Understanding)." Six reports were included, and, advised the agent, "you are referred to the memorandum entitled, 'Richard Wright,' dated July 8, 1954, which was previously furnished to your agency." The six reports have been deleted from this particular document. The memorandum of July 8 was a summary of investigations of Wright's activities from the thirties to December of 1951.

CHAPTER EIGHTEEN

The fields of Ailly had begun to turn rust brown as Wright arrived for the opening session of the Conference of Negro-African Writers and Artists, sponsored by Présence Africaine. It opened, wrote James Baldwin, on "one of those bright warm days which one likes to think as typical of the atmosphere of the intellectual capital of the Western World. . . . Everyone and everything wore a cheerful aspect, even the houses of Paris which did not show their age."[1] The atmosphere in the Amphithéâtre Descartes, of the Sorbonne, was hectic, as people scrambled to find seats, reporters set up tape recorders, and members of the audience shot pictures of the men seated upon the rostrum. Among the conference leaders was its major organizer, Alioune Diop, described in a State Department memo as "the founder and publisher of the Présence Africaine . . . ," a rather liberal but strongly Catholic Negro, "formerly a resident of Dakar but now living in Paris." The appeal issued in 1955 to black writers and artists to assemble was largely inspired by Diop, and a committee was formed to plan the Conference. On the committee was Aimé Césaire, described by the State Department as a Communist deputy from Martinique and poet, and René Depestre, a Haitian "alleged to be a member of the Communist Party." The American Embassy cabled back to Washington this description of the events preceding the opening session of the Conference:

"The December 1955–January 1956 issue of Présence Africaine carried among its advertisements, an appeal to Black Writers and Artists, printed in both French and English, which constituted an open invitation to the congress of Scholars of the Negro World. . . . The invitation bore the names of eighteen people comprising the executive committee of the Congress. . . . It will be noted that the United States members of the Executive Committee include Louis Armstrong, Josephine Baker and Richard Wright."² The Embassy forwarded copies of the appeal to Washington in its entirety. "For the first time in history, Negro Writers and Artists are going to take the initiative," read the opening sentence of the appeal, "in meeting together and in ascertaining how they are situated and what their specific responsibilities in the world are." Eight of the men chosen to offer suggestions on ways of accomplishing this were seated before the large, overflowing crowd at the amphitheater. They sat before a huge audience that included Césaire; Jacques Alexis, from Haiti; and the Conference president, also Haitian, Dr. Price-Mars. Missing from the rostrum was the American scholar and writer W. E. B. Du Bois.

Although the American Government may have succeeded to some degree in destroying Du Bois' reputation among American blacks, among members of the Third World his reputation was as solid as ever. He was praised and acclaimed in the highest political and intellectual circles of the anti-colonialist world, and his difficulties with the U. S. Government had not prevented the Conference from issuing him one of the first of its invitations. The State Department, however, refused to allow him to attend. In a telegram to the Conference read at the opening session, he cited the reasons: "I am not present at your meeting today because the United States Government will not grant me a passport for travel abroad. Any Negro-American who travels abroad today must either not discuss race conditions in the United States or say the sort of thing which our State Department wishes the world to believe. The government especially objects to me because I am a Socialist and because I believe in peace with Communist States like the Soviet Union and their right to exist in security."³

The reading of Du Bois' message, coming after Diop's opening address, wrote Baldwin, created the greatest stir. The opening lines of the communiqué brought forth applause and cheers, which swelled throughout the reading of the short message. This "extremely ill-conceived communication," wrote Baldwin, "must have compromised whatever effectiveness the five man American delegation then sitting in the hall might have."⁴ But had the American delegation been compromised by Du Bois or by the State Department with assistance from black Americans, both at the Conference and back in America? Was the communication really "ill-conceived" or Du Bois' intuitive grasp of the truth contained in the files of the American State Department? The interest in the Conference was not only American: "Mr. Pignoni," reads the memorandum of May 8, "political adviser in the French Ministry of Overseas Territories, believes the importance of the Congress should not be underestimated and that every attempt should be made to preserve the orientation of the Présence Africaine to the West."⁵

But was there any member of the American delegation more compromised than Wright himself? The Du Bois telegram was a personal bombshell. It was not, he knew better than any member of the large audience, perhaps, except the members of the intelligence communities from throughout the world mingling with the large crowd, an "ill-conceived communication." The message had thrown him on the defensive. Whatever the motivations for his actions in May, knowledge of them could destroy his reputation. And he had been chosen to reply to the Du Bois message on behalf of the American delegation. Again, as in the Anna Strong situation, his own position was ironic. Had he been in America, he undoubtedly could have written Du Bois' telegram in almost exactly the same terms. The government, however, had already seized Du Bois' passport. His struggle was to make sure that it did not seize his. "We had a message today," he remarked during the evening session, "that hurt me and I think my role in this Conference will negate the implication of that message; that the Americans participating here were people who could not speak their minds freely. When my role [is] finished in this conference, I would appreciate it if you would tell me what governments paid me."[6]

But he had not answered Du Bois' charges. Whether intentionally or not, he addressed a charge the black scholar never made. Du Bois did not say that the American delegation was "paid" but that American blacks who traveled abroad must echo the State Department line. Only such blacks, he had intimated, were granted freedom to travel to conferences of such importance, and these were probably chosen with an assist from the government. Wright could vehemently deny that he had been paid or that, as he noted in another reference to the telegram, he was "a fantastic agent of some kind." But could he deny the testimony of his own government, which more than validated Du Bois' assumptions and transformed his "ill-conceived" statement into immediate, frightening truth?

"A Congress of Scholars of the Negro World," the American Embassy in Paris communicated to the State Department in Washington on May 8, 1956, "sponsored by the Leftist *Présence Africaine,* is scheduled to take place in Paris September 19–22. Richard Wright, American Negro on the Executive Committee of the Présence Africaine and former Communist Party member, believes that, through careful selection of the American delegation to the Congress, the Leftist tendencies of the congress can be neutralized. . . . On his own initiative Mr. Wright called at the Embassy to express certain concern over the leftist tendencies of the Executive Committee for the Congress. He believed the members of the Committee were liberal thinkers and he thought there was a distinct danger that the Communists might exploit the

Congress to their own ends. Many members of the *Présence Africaine*, he said, were in search of an ideal they could not obtain and as such would be fertile ground for Communist exploitation. To counteract such a tendency, Mr. Wright wondered if the Embassy could assist him in suggesting possible American delegates who are relatively well known for their cultural achievements and who could combat the leftist tendencies of the Congress. Mr. Wright, the Department will recall, was himself formerly a member of the Communist Party. He indicated that he was originally on the Committee of the *Présence Africaine* but that he had been dropped because of his anti-Communist principles. However, Mr. Wright's name was retained on the list of hosts for the forthcoming Congress."[7]

The government, however, had a list of names of its own. The Minorities Affairs adviser of the Policy and Programs Division of USIA appeared at the Embassy and "submitted the following names of possible delegates to the Congress, names that were subsequently turned over to Mr. Wright." Among those on the government's list were Carl Rowan, Saunders Redding, and Elmer Carter. "Mr. Wright," the document read, "appreciated the suggestions furnished him by the Embassy and added these names to a list of suggested delegates he had himself composed and had already forwarded to Mr. Roy Wilkins, Executive Secretary of the National Association for the Advancement of Colored People. Mr. Wright . . . suggested that Mr. Wilkins might work closely with the Department before sounding out each individual on his willingness to serve as a member of the American delegation.[8] Among the names submitted by Wright were Carl Rowan, Ralph Ellison, and Chester Himes. In addition, Wright encouraged the "American Secretary of the Congress for Cultural Freedom" [the CIA-supported organization], [who] expressed considerable interest in the forthcoming Congress," to go to the Embassy and "to discuss the implications and to offer his collaboration in combatting Communist influence."[9] The final American delegation, however, differed both from those on Wright's list and on the list of the Minorities Affairs adviser of USIA. They included John A. Davis, Horace Mann Bond, James Ivy, Mercer Cook, and William Fontaine. None of the men were known for their "leftist orientation."

Did his activities in consort with the government to secure delegates not likely to be hostile to American interests influence his own lecture despite his disclaimer in responding to the Du Bois telegram? The lecture, "Tradition and Industrialization: the Plight of the Tragic Elite in Africa," was scheduled for delivery at the third session of the Conference. By that time, the American delegation was close to eruption. The Du Bois telegram had thrown them on the defensive. The speeches of

Senghor and Césaire, coming before those of the delegation, had added
to their discomfort. "The American delegates and in particular Mercer
Cook, had been shocked to hear Césaire liken them to a colonized
people."10 Colonization, argued Césaire, had ridden rough-shod over the
indigenous cultures of the colonized. It had bred a subculture in the
place of the indigenous culture, and this subculture, allowed to exist by
the colonizer on his terms, was championed and praised by a few individuals "who find themselves placed in the most artificial conditions,
deprived of any revivifying contact with the masses of people. Under
such conditions this subculture has no chance of growing into an active,
living culture." What the American delegation heard in Césaire's address was the message that they, like all of the colonial elite, were cut
off from the masses. They were not quite Europeans or Americans, but
something in between, having no cultural identity of their own. Du Bois
had not gone so far. He had only called into question who the American delegation was representing. Without direct reference to the Americans, Césaire's answer was that whomever they represented, they did
not represent the people. "We find ourselves," he intoned, "today in a
cultural chaos. . . . We are here to proclaim the right of our people to
speak, to let our people, black people, make their entrance on the great
stage of history." Observed Baldwin: "This speech, which was bril-
liantly delivered . . . wrung from the audience which heard it the most
violent reaction of joy. Césaire had spoken for those who could not
speak. . . ."11

But, for whom would Wright speak? "From beginning to end, deep
in his soul," wrote Himes, "Dick identified with the poor and
oppressed." Undoubtedly, he, too, was touched by Césaire's address.
But there were those looking over his shoulder. The conservative American delegation was dependent upon him to undercut Césaire's "communism." Representatives of the CIA, the Navy, Army, and Air Force
Intelligence, among over twenty intelligence networks, in America and
in Europe as well, had been sent copies of the May document, and
there were undoubtedly a great number of agents present. Despite his
difficulties with some of the African delegates, all regarded him as a
fighter, a spokesman for the poor and oppressed. He had written his
speech at Ailly; after the speeches by Césaire and Senghor, he made
slight emendations. He would like to seek a middle ground, and his
speech sought a synthesis between the ideas of Césaire and the overly
conservative ones of the American delegation. He was, he acknowledged Césaire's contention, a man of dual cultural identity. He was
both black and Western. He was black by accident of birth, Western
by accident of historical circumstances. "What do I mean . . ." he
asked, "when I say I'm Western?" What he meant, he explained, was

that he had been endowed with a rational perspective, a scientific way of looking at and evaluating the world, a system of beliefs hewn out of pragmatism and reason: "I believe in a separation of Church and State. . . . I feel that science exists without any a priori or metaphysical values. . . . I feel that human personality is an end in and for itself. In short, I believe that man, for good or ill, is his own ruler, his own sovereign. I hold freedom as a supreme right and good for all men."[12]

Such beliefs and perceptions, he had expropriated from the West, wrested them, as it were, from those who would deny him access to them. And this was true also for his colleagues in the American delegation, and were the Africans but to open their eyes they would discover that the same was true for them also. They were all products of Western acculturation. They had been stripped of the civilization marked by fetish priests, juju, ancestor religion, irrationality. Theirs was the most glorious of all possible births: They were children of the West, and yet they were not completely Western; they had been educated in the ways of the West, yet they retained the emotional distance that allowed them to view it with objectivity; they were critics of the West, and at the same time, advocates of a Western way of life. They were an elite because of their position, a privileged one between East and West, gained through centuries of immersion in Western culture. They were not separated from the masses, but, like such men as Sukarno, Nkrumah, Gandhi, and Nehru, determined to utilize their Western education and beliefs to lead their people into the twentieth century. How could such people, then, be censured, chastised, for using their Western experience to better the lives of their own people and humankind as well? Who could condemn them for seizing that instrument, Western culture, which offered the best chance of destroying the forces of irrationality and superstition, those forces that had weakened African cultures in the past and allowed the colonization they all deplored?

He had first enunciated this thesis in *Black Power*. Here, however, it was circumspectly amended. The African had been defeated as much by the weakness of his own culture as he had by the powerful weapons of the Europeans. A culture moribund with mysticism and magic had helped defeat him. The forces of animism and emotion had met the forces of science and reason, and Europe had won a decisive victory. If history were not to be repeated on some other battlefield, of the twentieth century, at a time when Western science was even more sophisticated and awesome than before, the Africans had to appropriate the wisdom, science, and technology of the West. . . . To do this meant a reevaluation of the Western role in the past destruction of African cultures. "I have stated publicly," he echoed Romulo, more forceful and insistent than the Filipino had been at Bandung, "on more than one occasion, that the spoils of European imperialism do not bulk so large or important to me. I know that today it is the fashion to list the long and many economic advantages that Europe gained from its brutal and bloody impact upon the hundreds of millions of Asians and Africans. . . . I have no doubt of it. Yet that fact does not impress me as much as still another and more obscure fact . . . an irrational Western world helped, unconsciously and unintentionally, to smash the irrational ties of religion and custom and tradition in Asia and Africa. . . . There was a boon wrapped in that Western gift of brutality."[13]

By launching "vast industrial enterprises" in almost all the lands that they controlled, enterprises that wrought profound alterations in the Asian-African ways of life and thought, "the Europeans set off vast revolutions." They brought freedom and secularization; they imposed new values; they helped to create an "elite" more Western than the West. For all of this, "Today," he writes, "a knowing black, brown, or yellow man can say: Thank you, Mr. White Man, for freeing me from the rot of my irrational traditions and customs, though you are still the victims of your own. . . ." An objective view of history would enable them to believe with him that "What is GOOD FOR EUROPE IS GOOD FOR ALL MANKIND. I SAY: SO BE IT."[14] Wright concluded his speech with an appeal to the West: "You have, however misguidedly, trained and educated an elite in Africa and Asia. Now this elite of yours —your children, one might say—is hard-pressed by hunger, poverty, disease, by stagnant economic conditions, by unbalanced class structures of their societies, by oppressive and irrational tides of tribal religion. You men of Europe made an abortive beginning to solve that problem. You failed. Now I say to you: Men of Europe, give that elite the tools and let it finish the job."

It was the last major speech of the Conference. After heated discussions among the participants, a set of resolutions were drawn up. The resolutions appeared more supportive of Césaire's position than of Wright's. The delegates decided that cultural growth was dependent "upon the termination of . . . colonialism, the oppression of weaker peoples and racialism." It affirmed the right of people to learn their own national cultural values and to enjoy the benefits of education within the framework of their own cultures. It urged black intellectuals and others "to create the practical conditions for the revival and growth of Negro culture" and urged that they "defend, illustrate, and publicize throughout the world the national values of their own people." The Conference regretted the "involuntary absence of a delegation from South Africa," prevented by its government from attending, but due, perhaps, to extensive lobbying by the American delegation, did not further notice the "involuntary absence of Dubois."

On September 29, six days after the Conference, Wright wrote to Daniel Guérin: "The *Présence Africaine* Conference was a success of a sort, but it left me terribly depressed. . . ."[15] Had the Conference managed to walk the tightrope between principle and expediency? And was he in danger of loosing his equilibrium? He had maintained equilibrium thus far because he had been able to adhere to many of his own values and principles. He did believe that communism posed a danger to freedom, that the "darker peoples of the world," through little fault of their own, were socially, politically, and culturally backward. He believed in the ideals and promises of democracy; he believed that what was good for European civilization was good for "all mankind," and he believed that American blacks had benefited as a result of the American experience. Yet, he was not a cold-war advocate. He did not believe, in truth, that America represented absolute good and the Soviet Union absolute evil. He did not believe that the only threat to the Third World came from Russia and China; he did not believe that the Marshall Plan and American hegemony over Europe, Asia, and Africa were good for "all mankind." He did not believe that the racial situation in America had changed appreciably, and he did not believe that government had the right to coerce its citizens into aiding and abetting its policies.

The Du Bois letter had thrown him on the defensive and he was unable to recover. He did not, in his reply, launch an attack upon the black scholar, nor defend the government. But he did not equate the American Government's treatment of Du Bois with that afforded the South African delegation by their government. And this despite his fondness for the valiant old warrior!

Five months after the Conference, in February 1957 (Sidney Williams pinpoints the time), "he was looking upon Dr. Dubois as the real patriarch of the cause, not only of the Black Americans, but of African Independence. . . ."[16] Whatever his true feelings about Du Bois, there is no question of his feelings concerning Padmore. Padmore was more than a friend: he was an example of strength and independence, a man who placed principle above expediency: "The Negro," he had written in a Foreword to Padmore's *Pan-Africanism or Communism* in March 1956, "even when embracing Communism or Western Democracy, is not supporting ideologies; he is seeking to use *instruments* . . . for his own ends. . . . When George discovered that beyond doubt Stalin and his satraps looked upon black men as political pawns of Soviet power politics . . . he broke completely with the Kremlin. . . . BUT HIS BREAKING DID NOT MEAN THAT HE THEN AUTOMATICALLY SUPPORTED THE ENEMIES OF THE SOVIET

UNION. HE CONTINUED HIS WORK ALONE, STRIVING
TO ACHIEVE THROUGH HIS OWN INSTRUMENTALITIES
THAT WHICH HE HAD WORKED FOR WHEN HE WAS IN
THE COMINTERN HIERARCHY, THAT IS FREEDOM FOR
BLACK PEOPLE."[17]

Were these remarks, concerning Padmore, barometers to feelings he
harbored, despite all, concerning himself? Or was he beginning to realize that his own position vis-à-vis the government remained as perilous
as ever? In March 1956, during the period of his negotiations with the
government over the American delegation to the Conference, a cold-
war journal, *The Reporter,* had printed an attack upon him by Ben
Burns, former white associate editor of *Ebony* magazine. *The Reporter's* reputation as a militant progovernment journal was well established, its editor having declared publicly in speaking of Communists, "We cannot take chances with the ringleaders of a conspiracy
that, if successful, would pervert and destroy our institutions. . . ."[18] In
his article, "They're Not Uncle Tom's Children," Burns did not
directly accuse Wright of perverting American institutions, but he did
accuse him of poisoning the minds of Europe in regard to American
race relations: "Wright's venom," he wrote, "plus years of headlines
about Dixie lynching has succeeded in poisoning European thinking
about racial problems in America."[19] Similar sentiments are found in
the remarks of informers concerning Wright. Was his anxiety, as displayed in a letter concerning the article addressed to Reynolds one
month later, due to the fact that he had heard them during his own discussions with the government? But, more important, how many additional requests would he receive from intelligence agencies for information? How many "contact Richard Wright" requests would be
forwarded to the American Embassy? There were no real answers. And
he had dug an even deeper hole for himself with his actions concerning
the Conference. He had aligned himself not only with America but
with the colonial powers, those whose interests lay totally opposed to
those of Padmore—and himself. The pessimism that he expressed to
Guérin was justified, the anxiety that prevented him from working on
his new novel real and palpable. Once again, he faced a conflict of tremendous psychological dimensions. The time for ropedancing, am-
biguity, and contradiction was over. He would have to cross the tightrope to one side or the other. On November 21, 1956, after the
Franco-British invasion of Egypt and the Russian invasion of Hungary,
he wrote De Sablonière that he was being pushed to lend his name and
to join protests against the Russian invasion. He announced to his
friends that he would do so if the protest was directed also against the
Western invasion of Egypt. One morning in 1956, Harrington recalled,

he sat down with Wright to lunch. "Over lunch I realized that he was in quite an emotional state. Never much of a drinker, he seemed to be outdoing himself on the Bordeaux." He wanted to talk about a call he had had from Richard Crossman the night before. Crossman wanted to publish a tenth anniversary edition of *The God That Failed.* "Wright," wrote Harrington, "refused—rather furiously I gathered—and told Crossman to tell them—and he emphasized the word 'them'—that he would write an essay on racism and the cloak and dagger terrorism which was poisoning the climate around the expatriate Paris community. 'They can publish that in their god-damned 10th anniversary issue.' "[20]

Confrontation with problems of similar spiritual and psychological dimensions in the past had sent him to his typewriter. During the forties, pondering his relationship with the Communist Party, he had wrestled with his dilemma in the unpublished essay "There are still men left," broke formally with the organization in "I Tried to Be a Communist," and spiritually, years later, in *The Outsider.* His exile from America had been preceded by private correspondence to friends and notations in his journal, and formalized in the unpublished essay "I Choose Exile." The new novel, with which he was having so much difficulty, was to be part of a series of novels, one, *Islands of Hallucinations,* marking his spiritual exile. ". . . books happen with me," he told Smith in 1950. "I become deeply involved with certain problems. The way I attack them, and think them through, is by writing books." He left immediately after the conclusion of the Conference of Negro-African Writers and Artists for a tour of lectures in Germany. Though he had shied away from lecturing there because, as he wrote De Sablonière, he did not want to be compromised by association with someone who might have taken part in the Nazi holocaust, he spoke in Hamburg "on the publication" of *Black Power* in translation and was the guest of the Congress for Cultural Freedom and the Sociology Department of the University of Hamburg, where he lectured on "The Psychological Reactions of Oppressed People."[21] In October, he went to London for a meeting of the Congress for Cultural Freedom organized by Arthur Koestler, and in November he began his Scandinavian tour.[22]

He spoke in Sweden, Norway, and Denmark. In Sweden, he gave the same lecture he had given in Hamburg, and his Swedish publisher, Bonniers offered to publish this lecture and others related to the same subject. By January, he had compiled a group of essays and written an Introduction to the manuscript.

The four essays are taken from lectures given during the nineteen fifties, revised and amended for publication in book form under the title *White Man, Listen!* It is as much a spiritual and psychological manifesto as an examination of the political and cultural consequences of racism and colonialism. The sense of estrangement, alienation, and its acceptance, runs like a leitmotif throughout the book. "I'm a rootless man," he acknowledges in the Introduction, "but I'm neither psychologically distraught nor in any wise particularly perturbed because of it. Personally, I . . . seem not to need as many emotional attachments, sustaining roots, or idealistic allegiances as most people. . . ."[23] Such disclaimers to the contrary notwithstanding, identification with the men and women of Asia and Africa is here more pronounced, less ambiguous and contradictory. All colonized people have in common their fear and hatred of whites, be they European or American. It is a well-earned and deserved hatred, caused by neurotic, psychologically distraught men, the Westerners; it has created among the oppressed tension, ambivalence concerning identity, and pathological types, but it has created also a revolutionary corps of men and women determined to bring freedom to their nations and people.

These are the tragic elite; they remain, as he had pictured them before, as bridges between East and West. Now, however, he views them as more so than before, as a revolutionary vanguard, bitter at the precarious position they occupy as straddlers between East and West and the treatment of those whose culture the conquerors have destroyed. Césaire had demanded that the elite reunite with the people, cast their lot solidly with those made rootless as a result of Western hegemony. Now, in his revision of past lectures, Wright embraces the position of the "hero" of the *Présence Africaine* Conference. If the old, irrational cultures, steeped in fetish religion, were the indigenous fifth column aiding and abetting European colonization, the tragic elite are the fifth column created by the West but determined to erect barriers of defense against the conqueror, bulwarks against his return. The rationale for industrialization, for attempting the great leap forward therefore is not assimilationism: "The reason for this brutal push of the elite against its own people stems from fear that if they do not quickly modernize their countries, the white man will return."[24] No longer is the white man depicted in the ambiguous terminology of *The Color Curtain* and the unrevised version of "Tradition and Industrialization" rendered at the *Présence Africaine* Conference three months before.

The colonizers brought modernization and progress, to be sure. But they brought also the scourge of inhumanity, the fruits of racial immorality, slavery, greed, and the neurotic habits and practices of the sick, moribund culture of Europe. These "misfits, adventurers, indentured servants, convicts, and freebooters," through acts of racism and oppression, constitute a collective entity: "Whose hands ran the business enterprises? White hands. Whose hands meted out the law? White hands. Whose hands regulated the money? White hands. Whose hands erected the churches? White hands. Thus when the white world is viewed from inside the colored world, that world is a blocked world with little or no division."[25]

Whatever divisions there are, however, occur along ideological, not racial, lines. In *Black Power, Pagan Spain,* and *The Color Curtain,* Wright had portrayed Marxism in terms of absolute evil, written of communism in cold-war terminology. In *White Man, Listen!* he regains his balance, speaks of Marxism sometimes with the idealism of the past. In his attempt to break free of the cultural, social, and political hegemony of the West, the Asian and African will encounter many ideologies. Marxism is among the most powerful. The Marxists are those in the white community who offer to the elite of "Asia, Africa, or black America an interpretation of the world which impels to action, thereby assuaging his feelings of inferiority." It is not a redemptive religion, and for the most part, it is unrelated to the lives of those to whom it is offered. Yet, what other ideology, he asks from remembrances of his own past, offers the oppressed escape from ". . . his black belt? His captured homeland? His racial prison? But that ideology does solve something. It lowers the social and racial barriers and allows the trapped elite of Asia and Africa and Black America the opportunity to climb out of its ghetto."[26]

This very personal note does not signal a return to the past, a remembrance of the ideology that had caused him so much pain. It is an acknowledgment, missing in previous public utterances, of the attraction of a philosophy that professes to care, that ostensibly offers relief to the oppressed who accept it, out of the fear, deceit, brutality, and hypocrisy of the West: "They accept it in order to climb out of their prisons. Many a black boy in America has seized upon the rungs of the Red ladder to climb out of his black belt. And well he may, if there are no other ways out of it." It is language condemned and censured in this area of cold-war politics, and were there not risks in his stating them anew in his attempt to maneuver back to the road of unquestioned principle? Yes, there were! But the choice must be made between keeping silent and winning a "dubious safety," of endorsing "static defensiveness as the price of achieving . . . personal safety" and realizing that "the game isn't worth the candle." He who refuses to veer toward the path of principle will "negate the very conditions of life out of which freedom can spring. . . . In such a situation one's silence implies that one has surrendered one's intellectual faculties to fear, that one has voluntarily abdicated life itself, that one has gratuitously paralyzed one's possibilities of action."[27]

The sentiments are to be found in "Tradition and Industrialization," the lecture first given at the *Présence Africaine* Conference. The lecture has been drastically revised and emended. There are clarifications of the role of the "elite" and that of the West. There is clarification also of his own personal dilemma. Those, like himself, who advocate progressive measures, strong central governments, the necessity of the elite of Asia and Africa to be strong and independent; those who question the values and ethics handed down from the Western world, will be called "Communists" regardless of their true political and ideological perspectives. But the risk of being labeled subversive must also be undertaken, the possible distortion of one's true beliefs accepted: "I cannot . . . ," he writes, "assume that universal good will reign, but I have the elementary right, the bounden duty even, to assume that man, when he has the chance to speak and act without fear, still wishes to be man, . . . harbors the dream of being a free and creative agent." The writer who, at the Conference of Negro-African Writers and Artists, had seemed to tilt toward the West, who had viewed it almost as salutary, a benefactor, now looks at the West in shock and horror, pledges his allegiance to the colonial victims of "their own religious projections and . . . of Western Imperialism . . . being claimed by a negative identification on one side, and being excluded by a feeling of repulsion on the other."[28]

The identification, negative though it must be, is cultural as well as political. In the oft-repeated lecture on "The Literature of the Negro in the United States," the old phrases and sentiments are restated: The horrors that confront blacks remain, in winter and summer, night and day, during times of war and peace: And if those horrors have mitigated somewhat now, it is because Marxism came to invade the black belt, after the emergence of the Soviet Union as a major power: "alien ideologies gripped" alienated intellectuals, among whom "rejected Negroes" were foremost. "Color consciousness lost some of its edge and was replaced in large measure by class-consciousness; with the rise of an integral working-class movement, a new sense of identification came to the American Negro." The anti-Marxist is as opposed to communism as before; like Padmore, however, he is able to articulate once again, without fear and apprehension, the contributions made, negatively by the Soviet threat, which forced Americans to attempt to "set their racial house somewhat in order in the face of world criticism." He has made the same point privately in correspondence with De Sablonière concerning the Emmet Till murder; now he makes it in the public arena.

White Man, Listen! was a courageous book, in light of his difficulties with his government. There was passionate caring in the book, pathos, sentimentality, even romanticism; at bottom, however, it was a spiritual and personal manifesto, much like "I Tried to Be a Communist" and "I Choose Exile," marking off the perimeters beyond which the maintenance of individual security must give way under the totalitarian assault upon individual freedom. It was not a new step in his evolutionary development, but a return to steps previously covered by the drifting sands of political coercion.

Aswell, who had moved from McGraw-Hill to Doubleday, in addition to offering Wright a contract for his new novel, accepted *White Man, Listen!* for publication. The book was released on October 15, 1957, and for the first time since *The God That Failed* the FBI added to its files a clipping of a review of one of Wright's works. The review, written by an associate of the Brookings Institution, was published, in the Washington *Post*, under the title "White Man Is Intrusive." "Those who need to read this book," the review reads in part, "will probably not do so, because it is written by a Negro. Those who do read it may not like it, especially if they are inclined to feel that everything said about social problems must be constructive. For this is a bitter and vituperative book, 'explosive and blatantly unacademic.' " In October, however, Wright wrote De Sablonière commenting that the book more or less was not well received in America. The book was truthful and still the Americans hated it. He confessed to feeling depressed, asking his friends why he should continue writing books that people would not read.

But *White Man, Listen!* was now behind him. The year 1956 had been fairly good in terms of work, economically, and his personal growth and liberation, though depressing incidents had somewhat marred it. He had learned that Aunt Maggie was dying from cancer, and quickly forwarded money for an operation. His favorite aunt, with whom he had begun the trek from South to North, died on January 20, 1957. There had been his embarrassing position at the Conference and overtures from the investigative agencies of the United States Government. And there had been attacks such as those leveled by Ben Burns in *The Reporter*. ". . . it is only important . . . ," writes Fabre, "to note that such abuse had started to preoccupy him and disturb his peace of mind just when he was embarking upon his first novel since *The Outsider*. . . . Although these tensions made the composition of it proportionately more difficult, they also inspired him to be explicit about his militant anti-colonialism, and uncompromising in his condemnation of both American and Western policy in general."[29]

From 1956 onward, writes Harrington, "Wright seemed obsessed with the idea that the F.B.I. and the C.I.A. were running amuck in Paris. He was thoroughly convinced that Blacks were special targets of their cloak and dagger activities and that several of his African friends

. . . were being eliminated. At about the same time, [he] became co-organizer and Chairman of a Franco-American group of artists and intellectuals in a movement to free Communist Party leader Henry Winston from federal prison and planned to tour Europe in that role. For him it was a period of feverish activity; a period in which Richard Wright, the mature man, was trying to square accounts with Richard Wright the mature artist."[30] He had made a mistake, he told Himes one day on the corner of crowded Boulevard St. Germain, in writing "only political books," such as *Black Power, The Bandung Conference,* and *Pagan Spain.* He was going to pick up the black oppression theme again. His first book on this subject would involve "an ignorant black undertaker in the backwoods of Mississippi who had made a fortune burying ignorant blacks and kowtowing to ignorant white politicians. . . . Dick said he would carry forward his story with Fishbelly [son of Tyree, the funeral parlor owner] who got involved with many white women in Paris."[31] He was envisioning a series of novels centered around one major protagonist, Fishbelly Tucker. On May 5, 1957, he wrote De Sablonière that he was working "very hard" on his new novel, which dealt with the racial situation in the American South. And four months later, he wrote to announce that the novel had been sent to his publishers in America and that it was "over 200,000 words long." The first novel of what was to become a trilogy was eventually published under the title *The Long Dream.*

Tyree Tucker and his son, Fishbelly, are the central characters of the novel. The action takes place in Mississippi, where the unwritten law of the South has cut the southern town Clintonville into fiefdoms. Tyree, owner of a funeral parlor and a house of prostitution, rules over the black part of town. Because of his color, however, his rule is not absolute. He shares power with the white authorities and is in direct collusion with Hadley, the white chief of police, who allows the illegal operation of the house of prostitution. Within his fiefdom, Tyree operates exceedingly well. His ability to adapt readily to the codes of racism has made him wealthy and respected among the town's blacks. Through cajoling, playing upon the sympathies of whites, accepting his own inferiority, he has managed to manipulate the white community all his life. These stratagems of success, he wishes to leave as a legacy to his son.

Fishbelly, however, is disdainful of his father's method of dealing with whites. He views his father as "a castrated man." He has earned his money and power at the expense of his self-respect. Tyree's attempt to convince him of the possibility of safety if one plays the racial game is aborted when Fishbelly learns of the lynching of a friend. The lynching is a signal event: he learns that he must immunize himself against the cruelty and brutality of the white world. When he comes upon a dead dog, he immediately thinks of his murdered friend. He cuts the dog open, hacking through bone, blood, gristle; pulls out the dog's entrails, slices away its privates: ". . . now . . . when the whites came at him, he would know what death was."

However, the whites eventually come after Tyree. The house of prostitution burns down, killing numbers of people. Hadley fears that the public investigation demanded by the authorities will reveal his association with Tyree and his role as part owner of the house. He demands that Tyree turn over the canceled checks, evidence of his complicity, of payments he had received through the years. Tyree, however, has secreted some of the checks with his mistress. In the event that something happens to him, the checks are to be handed over to Fishbelly. Unable to convince Hadley that he does not possess the remaining checks, Tyree is killed. Fishbelly thus inherits the funeral home, the rebuilt house of prostitution, the remainder of the canceled checks, and Tyree's code of dealing with white people.

He is no Tyree! He cannot scrape and bow with sincerity. He cannot pay the proper obeisance to whites. Hadley is well aware of the fact that Fishbelly is a dissimulator. Years of dealing with Tyree has taught him how "sincere" blacks act. Fishbelly's unease in his role of "Tom" marks him out for the chief as an imposter, "a new Negro." Fearful that he might yet be implicated in the house of prostitution fire, the chief has Fishbelly framed. A white woman is sent to his apartment. Her screams and cries of rape bring the police, secreted nearby. Fishbelly is sentenced to jail. Attempts to force him to reveal the secret of the missing checks fail. Finally, he is released and ordered to leave town. Before going into voluntary exile in Europe, he hands the missing canceled checks over to a reform group.

In each of his previous novels, *Native Son, Lawd Today, The Outsider, Savage Holiday*, Wright interjected nuances of his own personal psychological conflicts, and he would do so again in *Islands of Hallucinations*. Did this pattern hold true also for *The Long Dream?* He had written De Sablonière about his plans for the novel, telling her that he would demonstrate the extent to which "racial conditioning" remained strong among blacks even after they had left the environment that engendered it. His book would be predominantly psychological. The model for Fishbelly was a Mississippi-born black expatriate, Ish Kelley —a good-looking lad, noted Himes, expelled from France because of his illicit relationships with a number of women. Books Two and Three of the projected novel would belong to Fishbelly, but book One, *The Long Dream*, is dominated by Tyree Tucker. Is there in Wright's attempt to explain Tyree to Fishbelly, an attempt to explain this master manipulator of white people also to himself? How closely can he identify with Tyree's perilous situation, with his attempt to straddle the tightrope between principle and safety? "I ain't corrupt," Tyree thunders at a white reformer, "I'm a nigger. Niggers ain't corrupt. Niggers ain't got no rights but them they buy . . . don't call me corrupt when I live the only way I can live. Sure, I did wrong. But my kind of wrong is right; when you have to do wrong to live, wrong is right. . . ."

Given Wright's own actions in relation to the government, in what amounted, at least, to cooperation, no matter how forced, between himself and governmental investigatory agencies, did the words of this character strike a responding chord in his own breast? Had he, like Tyree, attempted to safeguard his hard-won achievements by attempting to manipulate his antagonists? And had he prepared a safety valve for himself, as Tyree had done by secreting portions of the canceled checks from his business dealings with Hadley, with his mistress? "I have papers, documents," a very close friend wrote in 1976; "he left them with me."[32] Another friend spoke of the letter writer: "She knows a lot about what happened with Dick. She's scared to talk." And did the words of rebellion placed in Tyree's mouth on that day when disaster loomed echo now the new spiritual awakening occasioned, among other things, by the incessant demands of the United States Government and enunciated first in *White Man, Listen!* and accord with his new stance? "You see me crying and begging," said Tyree, "well that's a way of fighting. And when that way don't get me nothing, I have to do something else."[33]

Tyree managed to assimilate both identities without psychological distress. Fishbelly was unable to do so. Neither, it seemed, was Richard Wright! And was this inability to do so mirrored in his actions toward old friends? Himes considered himself to be one of the few black writers with whom Wright did not fall out sooner or later, and, he remarks, "near his end he accused me of attacking him in *A Case of Rape*. . . . he had managed to estrange himself from almost all of the younger American Negro writers in Paris." Wrote James Baldwin, ". . . Gone were the days when he had only to enter a cafe to be greeted with the American equivalent of 'cher maitre.' . . ." I had come to the Café Tournon, wrote Himes, in company with three women. Two were Germans. They sat beside Wright in the cafe. When the women left, Himes remembered, "Dick said to me, 'Those are nothing girls, they shouldn't be alive.' "[34] But, on September 28, 1957, he wrote De Sablonière about his concern for France, of the possibility of France becoming fascist, ending with the depressing note, "Poor mankind. All for now. Am kind of tired."

He *was* exhausted. And it was due in part to his having completed his new novel, and to his growing concern about political events in Paris concerning the Algerian question. But it was probably due also to the estrangement of which Baldwin and Himes wrote, between himself and the black expatriate community. The estrangement was not all attributable, as Baldwin suggests, to his exaggerated sense of importance, nor was he simply imagining various attacks upon him. There was always a small bank of Americans, wrote Harrington, "who never tried to cloak their outright hatred of the great Negro writer. They would often attack Wright in the most insulting manner, referring to his books and his opinions with contempt. They hurled the term 'expatriate' at Wright with a venom which shocked the listening French and other European intellectuals."[35] But they also hurled the term "FBI agent" at him, mostly out of earshot. "There were certainly those rumors," said a friend, "that he was working with the CIA and the FBI."

Were the FBI and the State Department the sources of these rumors? Were they attempting to curb his new truculence as evidenced in *White Man, Listen!*, in public lectures and perhaps in rejecting the government overtures, by discrediting him among the black expatriate community? On February 13, 1958, he appeared once again before Agnes Schneider, for renewal of his passport. Again he was forced to submit a "sworn statement." "On February 13," reads the document of April 4, 1958, "Richard Wright appeared before Agnes Schneider, Consul of the United States of America, Paris, France, being duly sworn, stated he was submitting the following statement as part of his application for a passport which he executed on February 13, 1958. In that statement, subject stated he was not then a member of the Communist Party, but had been a member of the Communist Party from 1932 to 1942, and called attention to the statement he had executed at the American Embassy, Paris, France, on September 16, 1954 for further details in that regard."

Data from the document imply that there were two separate meetings, one concerning the statement, the other his passport. Under "Synopsis of Facts," the document reads: "On 2/13/58 . . . subject executed a sworn statement in which he stated he had been a member of the Communist Party from 1932 to 1942. . . . On 2/13/58, subject executed application for Passport at Paris, France, in which he stated he has resided outside the United States since September, 1949 and that his return to the United States is indefinite."[36] Were the two meetings interrelated, and if so, what questions were posed to him on this occasion? If questions there were, the document of April 4 does not, like that of September 16, 1954, show any response from Wright. Was he intent, against the wishes of his interrogators, on not going beyond the statement and answers he had given in 1954? Was the government now placed in the position of having to prove that his new attitude stemmed from renewed Communist ties, rather than knowledge damning to their methods of operation? His passport was renewed on February 21, 1958. But the compilation of the April 4 document began on March 18 and is the most extensive document in the files made available. Copies were forwarded to the CIA and to the Paris Legat. Wright's passport history is detailed from 1939 to 1958. The statement issued in 1954 is recorded. "On March 18," begins the paragraph under 'Details,' [name deleted] Legal Section, Passport Office, Department of State, made available [deletion] the passport file of Richard Wright. . . ." Was the CIA, the State Department, the FBI, the Foreign Service, or all collectively, searching for new ways of exerting pressure or of forcing the exile back to America, or was the extensive request for passport information linked to the explosive "Gibson Case" which rocked the black expatriate community in the spring of 1958? Wright's own apprehensions and anxieties were pronounced. Six days after appearing before Agnes Schneider, in a long letter to De Sablonière, he expressed concern as to when his passport might be taken and he would be "faced with semistatelessness."

His anxieties concerning the Gibson affair, therefore, and his efforts to protect himself were well founded. In 1956, Harrington had rented his apartment to a fellow black American, Richard Gibson. When Harrington returned to repossess his apartment, Gibson refused to give it up. Moreover, he laid claim to all of Harrington's personal property. Several fights erupted between the two, in which Harrington thrashed Gibson very soundly. Himes wrote of the second fight: "I was thinking about going over to Ollie's to retrieve my kitchen utensils when he and Gibson had their second fight. . . . Ollie beat up Gibson so bad that time the police arrested him. . . ." Harrington, however, was reluctant to press charges, due to his expatriate status and his reputation as a Communist sympathizer. The black community began choosing sides in the conflict. Himes and Wright supported Harrington. Gibson had the support of William Gardner Smith. In 1957, a letter attacking French policy was printed in *Life* magazine under Harrington's signature. The letter was later proved to have been a forgery, written by Gibson. Another altercation between Gibson and Harrington occurred soon after, and this time Gibson was beaten so badly that he was taken to the hospital. He later signed a confession, "but the American Embassy possibly intervened with the Sûreté Nationale to hush up the affair."[37] Wright was involved as a friend of Harrington's and because he was called, in the spring of 1958, to testify on Harrington's behalf. His interest in the affair did not stop there. He kept documents of the investigation, wrote a letter to Gibson demanding answers "to a list of thirty questions," and made a drawing of Harrington's apartment, in order to demonstrate how forged letters might have been written on his friend's typewriter.

He was as preoccupied with the role of Smith as with that of Gibson. Were both Smith and Gibson in the service of the FBI? And if so, how much did they know about his statements to various agencies? The increasing rumors concerning his status as an agent were being repeated with more regularity, and he believed that agents of the government were keeping such rumors alive. And in defending Harrington, whose Communist sympathies were well known, was he not fueling even further the government's attitude toward him? And if Smith and Gibson were providing information to the government, was he not most certainly the subject of a great deal of that information? The extensive research that he conducted in a case that seemed of relatively little threat to his own security, was warranted. On April 4, 1958, a memorandum was forwarded to the Director of the FBI from SAC, WFO. "Being forwarded herewith to the Bureau are four copies and to New York three copies of the report of SA [deletion] WFO. . . . Copies of passport application photo of subject and his wife will be forwarded to New York via routing slip. . . . This case was called to the attention of WFO by [name deleted] Chief, Legal Section, Passport Office, Department of State."

And on May 26, 1958, the FBI coveted his cooperation once again. The letter was sent from the Special Agent in Charge, Chicago, to Washington, with reference "Rebulet dated May 2, entitled [long deletion] and New York letter to bureau May 13, 1958 [deletion] and my airtel of May 22, 1958. On May 21, 1958 [deletion] Chicago, former wife of [deletion] telephonically advised that [name deleted] in 1936 or 1937, had been extremely close to a Negro believed by [name deleted] to be Richard Wright . . . the individual believed to be Richard Wright . . . was connected in someway with the Abraham Lincoln School of Chicago . . . [name deleted] stated that . . . Wright was highly regarded by [name deleted] and could possibly furnish information concerning discussions he had with [name deleted] regarding [name deleted] trip to Russia and in particular the 6th World Congress of the Young Communist International held in Moscow, Russia in late 1935."[38]

The Bureau in return requested ". . . the New York Division be permitted to contact Richard Wright concerning his possible knowledge of [deletion] and in particular to develop any recollection of any discussion had with [name deleted] concerning the 6th World Congress of the Young Communist International held in Moscow. . . . It is particularly desired that information be developed of Wright concerning any statements made by [name deleted] concerning his speech at the

Congress or any recollection Wright may have concerning any publications in which the proceedings of the 6th World Congress and the
speech of [name deleted] may have been reported."[39] On May 29, however, Washington Headquarters, after researching its own bureau files,
discovered that Wright had already applied for and received a passport
on February 28. Undoubtedly, the situation was now complicated. "In
the absence of a specific request from Department attorneys handling
[deletion] the Bureau will not authorize an interview with Wright
by its representatives in Paris."[40] By June, in a document dated the
twenty-sixth of that month, a memorandum, under the letterhead of
The Foreign Service of the United States of America, was sent from the
legal attaché, Paris, to Washington Headquarters. The memo calls attention to "Washington Field Office let to Bureau 4/4/58." The message itself has been completely deleted. But did a letter accompany
Wright's complete passport files, mailed to various agencies on May 4?
And did this letter suggest the writer's new attitude regarding any semblance of cooperation with the agency? Wright's infractions, of whatever nature, had spurred a new concern with his activities: Dominated
by the influence of the McCarthy Committee and HUAC, the Foreign
Service operated under the authority of the Department of State. It
maintained close ties with the Attorney General, who was charged with
enforcing the provisions of the Smith Act. The Subversive Activities
Control Board remained among the chief weapons utilized by the Attorney General in action against individuals suspected of subversion or
those who failed to cooperate with the government. Du Bois had already
fallen victim to the "registration provision" of the Board. Now, suddenly, documents forwarded to Washington bearing the heading of the
Foreign Service were stamped, ominously, "Subversive Control."[41]

By this time, however, Wright was back in Ailly, working long hours
on a book that would fictionalize the Gibson affair and the machinations of the American investigative agencies abroad. His hero was Fishbelly, transported from Mississippi to Paris, from an environment of
corrupt county officials to an environment populated by agents, counteragents, and informers. The new novel was entitled *Islands of
Hallucinations*.[42]

CHAPTER NINETEEN

By the end of the summer, he had written over three hundred pages of his odyssey of Fishbelly Tucker, and returned to Paris. On September 20, 1958, he wrote De Sablonière informing her that *The Long Dream* was scheduled for publication in October. He was working on another novel that he had not yet titled, he wrote, and not nearly finished. And he expressed his despondency about the coming school year, when black children would attempt to integrate southern schools again. He expected violence, he confided, and expressed happiness that his daughters were not in America; such an atmosphere would cripple their minds and emotions. Again he wrote of tiredness and confessed that he sweated whenever he tried to type.

He received the advance reviews of *The Long Dream*. They were not encouraging. The novel was published in mid-October, and the unfavorable reviews continued. The same theme ran through most of the reviews like a leitmotif: he had been away from America too long and had lost touch with a changing racial situation. It was a theme that he heard all too often now, in public and private. He did not think that the criticism was valid. But even if it were, he would not take his family back to America. His girls were emotionally and physically healthy, his wife doing well in her new profession. No, he could not go back to America—he could not subject his family to American racism; he could not subject himself to the vengeance of the United States Government.

As if preparing for such vengeance, the government continued to add to its personal file. Copies of the FBI memorandum dated July 7 were sent to the Department of State, the CIA, and ACSI. "On July 2, 1958," reads the memo, "a source abroad furnished the following information concerning Richard Wright, U.S. citizen, born September 4, 1908, at Natchez." The source told the Bureau of Wright's association with the Franco-American Fellowship, and noted that he had made several trips to Belgium, England, and Italy, in connection with his work. In addition, reported the source: "He reportedly belonged to the Carry Davis movement. Subject is known to have been in contact with one [name deleted] born April 8, 1924, at Chicago, who from [deletion] was employed at [deletion] in Paris and in [deletion] was working at the [deletion] in Orleans, France." On August 21, under the heading Foreign Service, the legal attaché forwarded a censored report to Washington. Three other memoranda, July 21, 1958, September 28, 1958, and November 21, 1958, up until February 1959, are forwarded to the Department, each referring to a letter based upon the July memo. All of the documents are censored and all bear the stamp "Subversive Control."[1]

And if not for motives of revenge, why the sudden accelerated activity, undertaken almost exclusively by the government's foreign units, the Paris Legat, the CIA, the Foreign Service? "The C.I.A. was . . . interested in Wright," said Himes, ". . . because of the fact that . . . he might be conceivably having a dialogue, not a conspiracy or anything, but just a dialogue with people they considered dangerous such as Nkrumah or Frantz Fanon."[2] "He was being followed," said a friend, "how much I don't know, but in the last two years. He came into the restaurant one day, called me over, said, _____ give that sonofabitch over there a drink; he's with the Government and he's been on my ass for months." The consistency with which the letters of 1958 appear, indicate a feverish attempt to make a decisive case against him. That all of the memos are censored, indicates the extreme sensitivity of the contents. At least one segment of the governmental apparatus, the FBI Headquarters, in Washington, expressed doubt that any such case could be made, and demanded in a communiqué that evidence be provided for continuing the investigation.[3]

Closer to the American scene, did the Bureau realize that now, with Wright's passport secure, there was little that could be done toward bringing him back to America? Indeed, it was the government that was on the defensive now. American liberalism, though still slightly, had begun to raise its head and find its voice. McCarthy's attacks upon the Army had led to censure by the Senate on November 11, 1954. By the end of the year, his enormous power and prestige were dissipated. During the years between 1954 and 1958, "In seven separate decisions, the Warren Court threatened to dismember the octopus of repression. . . ."[4] The court found for the defendants in cases involving "Fifth Amendment dismissals," "state sedition laws," "investigation of beliefs, utterances and affiliations," and "the Smith Act." Black discontent had overflowed into the streets of American cities and brought

forth new organizations and new leaders. Though *The Long Dream*
was attacked by a wide spectrum of reviewers, liberal and black included, had Wright come back to America he might have had support
against any arbitrary action of the government, support he had not enjoyed previously. But the government could orchestrate, still, as it had
done in the cases of Du Bois and Robeson, acts designed to impair his
reputation and curtail his chances of making a living.

Was this the intent of an interview accredited to him, which he
never gave, in a magazine whose representative he had turned down
only a week before the supposed publication, titled "Amid the Alien
Corn"? *Time* magazine published the article, on November 12, and
quoted Wright as having declared: "'. . . I like to live in France because it is a free country. Then, there are my daughters. They are receiving an excellent education in France.' 'What of the danger of getting out of touch with U.S. life?' Snaps Wright: 'The Negro problem
in America has not changed in three hundred years.' "⁵ He had made
such statements before, both in private and in interviews, but he had
not made them to the *Time* representative. Why this outright fabrica-
tion by a magazine known to be sympathetic to the American right?
The words attributed to him are analogous to those uttered by Robeson
during his triumphant appearance before HUAC in 1956: "In Russia,"
said Robeson, "I felt for the first time like a full human being. No color
prejudice like in Washington. . . ."⁶ Was this an attempt to sabotage
further his reputation as Robeson's and Du Bois' had been? The three
men, differing in temperament and ideology, had been the leading
black voices against American policies at home and abroad in Africa
and Europe. Wright's voice, tempered for a while, had now gained new
vigor and emphasis. In an interview in 1957, on which he spoke about
the racial situation in Little Rock, Arkansas, he declared that "The
Negro in the United States may very well suffer the fate of the Jew in
Germany."⁷ Du Bois and Robeson had all but been rendered ineffec-
tive, though both continued to speak out against American actions.
Now Wright was alone, the one credible, unequivocable black voice, attacking American policies not only on the racist home front but on the
international stage. Were the sentiments that he expressed to De Sablonière in March of 1960 not as applicable in November of 1958? The
government, he had avowed, was hard after him because his work fell
"like a black shadow" upon their activities in Asia and Africa. They
wanted to force him back to the United States, he declared. He would
give up his citizenship first, "for they would shut me up and physically
destroy me."

As 1958 drew to a close, there were other concerns plaguing him, all
no doubt heightened by the persistent campaign of the Foreign Service

against him. Aswell died on November 6, and he lost a trusted friend as well as a devoted editor. His mother became seriously ill, and he "immediately cabled $100, but he had to borrow it from Reynolds. He no longer had any savings, and it did not look as if the sales of *White Man, Listen!* and *The Long Dream* would provide much income." And on November 20, in London, during a debate in Parliament, John Strachey, former member of the Labour Cabinet, now representative from Dundee, West, arose to extract a public statement from Home Secretary Reginald Butler to honor his recent commitment and allow Richard Wright to immigrate to England.

Wright's decision to leave Paris was given added impetus by the events taking place in the city's streets regarding the Algerian war, events to which he had alluded in the letters to De Sablonière in August and September of 1957. Visions of the Paris he had encountered on his arrival in 1947 came back to haunt him. Chaos seemed to be everywhere: Armed militia patrolled the banks of the Seine and moved menacingly through the narrow streets of the Algerian quarter. Clashes between left and right occurred with some regularity. A fascist dictatorship, he believed, was a definite possibility. But there were other factors. The atmosphere of the Paris of the early years had been polluted. The agents of the United States Government had done their work well. The Afro-American community was in turmoil, black artists and writers looking askance at old friends and associates, attempting to divine the CIA agent behind every cordial smile and greeting. Wright had long since given up frequenting some of the more famous black-expatriate cafes, the Monaco and the Tournon.

More important, however, was the success of his daughter, Julia. In 1958, Julia had received overtures from both Cambridge and Oxford universities. He was proud of his daughter, and reluctant to allow her to go off to England alone. He did not want to be separated from his family. The decision was made that Ellen would accompany Julia and set up residence. Wright would follow. In preparation for the move, he appealed to John Strachey. Strachey agreed to help and sounded out Reginald Butler, who issued one contradictory statement after another. On November 20, during a debate on the Expiring Laws Continuance Bill, Strachey sought to pin down the Secretary to a definite commitment. In defending the Alien Restriction Act, Butler announced that it was British policy to grant asylum to those whose lives were threatened for political reasons, those who were financially solvent and would not be wards of the British State, and those of good character and reference. "But we should not," the Home Secretary averred, "grant asylum except in cases where the record is genuine."[8]

Wright's case, Strachey believed, was genuine. ". . . I want to remind the Home Secretary"—he rose to join the debate—"of an example. . . . It is a case which I put before him a little time ago—the case of Mr. Richard Wright, a well known American author, who wanted to come and write his books in this country. . . . It is true that in his case there were considerations which may or may not . . . have prejudiced his case. There is the fact that he is a Negro. . . . It is also true that he is an ex-Communist . . . there is no doubt about the 'ex' because he is very vocal ex Communist. He made a notable contribution to . . . *The God That Failed.* . . . Anyone who had written that could certainly no longer be a Communist, even if he wished to be one. . . . The Home Secretary assured me that . . . he was refused permission to live here simply on the ground that this was not a country of immigration. . . . When [the Home Secretary] says that the ruling under which, quite clearly and overtly—I have his letter on the subject—Mr. Wright was excluded is to be altered in the future, I hope we may be assured that he will . . . consider the old cases. . . ."[9] Strachey received such assurances during the evening session, and Wright, with renewed vigor, continued to execute his plan to leave Paris. Ellen secured a small house in London, Julia enrolled in Cambridge, and eleven-year-old Rachel was enrolled in a French school in London. Wright sold both his farm in Ailly and the apartment at 14 rue Monsieur le Prince and moved into a two-room flat on the rue Régis, in the Sèvres-Babylone district of Paris. He was preparing to join his family in London, to await the final outcome of his efforts to secure admission to England, when the tiredness and sweating he had previously complained of in his correspondence to De Sablonière gave way to serious illness. In February of 1960, he wrote to inform her that he had been ill since the previous July. It was an amoebic condition that he had contracted probably in Africa or Asia. By that time, he announced also, he had already gone to a specialist and hoped that the worst was over.

The attack caused postponement of his trip in the summer of 1959, and he spent the months undergoing "treatments and numerous examinations" at the American Hospital in Paris. By November he was able to travel, and he was granted a three-month visitor's visa to join his family in London. Again he saw Padmore and contacted friends about his application. The Home Secretary had not honored his commitment. The Home Office refused to alter its previous decision. "After much red tape," Harrington sums up the affair, "the application of Richard Wright for a residence visa was rejected! . . . Wright was greatly shocked by the unexpected refusal. . . . Telephone calls were made, important names were discreetly dropped. . . . In the end there was a final, heated discussion in the Home Office, where, according to Wright, . . . [an] official told him that he could expect an extension of

30 days and not one day more. . . ."[10] Exhausted, somewhat weak from his recent illness, Wright returned to resume his life in Paris. What factors lay behind the equivocation of Butler and the British Government? Were they racial, as Wright suspected and related to Harrington? Were the British still smarting from his attacks on their colonial policy in *Black Power*? Or had the Foreign Service intervened to keep Wright in Paris, where its apparatus of agents and informers were already in place? As late as 1977, the British Government refused even to discuss the case. "We don't give out that kind of information," snapped a harassed functionary of the Home Office in July of 1977. Persistent requests to speak to higher officials were finally met with the suggestion that the researcher write a letter to the Home Office. The letter was written and mailed "Return Receipt Requested."

The letter, dated September 15, 1978, was answered on March 9, 1979. "The Home Office personal file of Mr. Wright," wrote a departmental record officer, "falls within a category of records which is closed to public inspection for up to 100 years. . . . Access to such papers may . . . be given to persons engaged in scholarly research, and your application has been very carefully considered on that basis . . . however, it has been decided that Mr. Wright's file cannot be made available to you whilst it has such a long period of closure still to run.

"I would, however, like to assure you that the question of Mr. Wright's permanent residence in this country was dealt with under the normal policy which applied to all foreign nationals at that time."[11] British contacts, however, believed otherwise. They were sure that racism was not the reason. "If they did not let him in," remarked a reporter, "it was politics, not race." "In the nineteen fifties," said a London political observer, "the government couldn't blow its nose without asking the United States."

In 1954, the FBI legal attaché in London had requested and received an extensive document detailing Wright's history from the nineteen thirties to 1954. The FBI maintained a "Foreign Liaison Unit abroad in 16 countries," and many of the documents relating to Wright had been forwarded to the unit over the years. The close relationship between the FBI and the secret police of other countries involved sharing "certain types of information with . . . law enforcement and intelligence agencies in many countries on a reciprocal basis."[12] On November 21, 1958, the Legat, Paris, forwarded another censored letter to Washington, under the heading of the Foreign Service, but whether this memo or the follow-up, sent on February 13, 1959, related to Wright's experience with the British Government is unknown. In fact, the number of censored documents during these last, most troublesome years of Wright's life make it difficult to know just what areas of his life or activities were targeted. On February 19, 1959, even the Washington Office was uncertain. "Relet stated that no additional information had been received from your source regarding the subject," Washington wrote the legal attaché in Paris, "and there was no indication that he was participating in any subversive activities in Paris. . . . According to records you submitted to the Bureau, this case was being carried as pending at Paris as of the end of January. Bureau file does not show that there is any outstanding investigation pending at Paris in this case. Advise the Bureau as to why this case is pending."

The reply was sent on February 26, 1959, and referred to the memos of February 19 and 13. Again the contents of the memos were censored. The foreign units, however, had no intention of dropping their investigation of Wright. On February 11, 1960, another, partially censored document was forwarded to Washington: "The following information was set forth in the above referenced U. S. Army report: In December 1951, a U.S. citizen, a Negro woman who was at that time a night club singer in Paris, stated that Richard Wright is active in the French Communist Party and has been engaged in spreading communist doctrine through the Franco-American Fellowship Group."[18] Was there not some justification for Wright's assuming that somewhere behind his difficulties of 1959 was the fine hand of the intelligence agencies of the United States? And not being able to pinpoint their exact area of interest, was he not justified also in seeing forms of their harassment everywhere?

Did the American Society for African Culture reject his proposal to do a study of French West Africa, similar to the one he had done on Ghana, on orders from its sponsor, the CIA? On May 11, he wrote John A. Davis, Executive Secretary of AMSAC, outlining the details of his proposal. He wanted to investigate and to write about the frightened and tragic elite, in such countries as the French Sudan, the Ivory Coast, Upper Volta, and Niger, to examine relationships between the colonial masters (the French) and the colonized. He wanted to assess the impact of Western values and influence upon the elite, to discover if these, too, were psychologically distraught men, torn between obedience to the demands of their own, indigenous cultures and the attraction of those of the West. And he wanted to ascertain an answer to the major question posed by his proposed study: What basis is there now in French West Africa for the erection of independent stable governments?

Davis presented the proposal to the New York committee. He summarized the various avenues of research detailed by Wright. He mentioned Wright's assertion that to aid him in his study, he could count on support from a number of sources, among them contacts in the De

Gaulle government. They had offered to place certain facilities at his disposal, though he believed that to accept such an offer would compromise his independence as a writer. If he went to French West Africa, he would do so only as an independent journalist and not allow himself to be placed in a position where he would feel obligated to "slant" the facts as he found them. Davis concluded the summary: "Mr. W. is concerned that Black Africa, during the next fifty years will astonish the Western World. The African, unlike the Asian, has little or no past and his traditions are fragile. For this reason he is free to face the future."

In a letter of May 23, replying to Wright's proposal, Davis implied that AMSAC would reject the plan. Wright had received assurances from Doubleday and World Publishing Company that his findings would be published in book form. It may be, the secretary pointed out, that the organization may not wish to associate itself with the book that might result from his studies. Censorship was not mentioned, but to Wright the message seemed clear. In reply, he told Davis that there were no guarantees as to what he would find and thus no certainty of what he would write. In that event he could not guarantee that AMSAC would not be compromised. All that he could guarantee were his own principles, and perhaps he could best do this by forgoing the project. In doing this, he wrote, he was personally accountable for whatever he wrote and for public reaction. Equally as distressing as his rejection, however, was the knowledge that he had helped to found the American Society for African Culture. Now undoubtedly, the intelligence agencies of the government had influenced them against him. Was this, too, part of a strategy, one aimed at isolating him abroad while sabotaging his reputation at home, and thus rendering him, once again, extremely vulnerable? If so, he was convinced that, on both fronts, the strategy was working well. In the spring of 1959 plans were initiated to adapt his novel *The Long Dream* to the Broadway stage. Anthony Quinn was to produce the play and to play the role of Tyree. Lloyd Richards, whose credits included *Raisin in the Sun*, was to direct it.[14] The play opened on February 17, minus Quinn, who had turned over his producer's role to Cheryl Crawford and his acting role to Lawrence Winters. The play was canceled two days later, after a succession of bad reviews. ". . . (Cleveland Amory had gone so far as to chastise Wright for his exile on a radio program). . . . Ketti Frings, in her indignation, had decided to withdraw the play from the bill of the Ambassador."[15]

The question of his exile had also occurred in an interview granted to Kenneth Faris in April of 1959. "I think that your removal from your own people and country," Faris, one of the last visitors to the apartment on rue Monsieur le Prince had told him, "is part of the reason why you've largely stopped creating characters and chosen to make statements in non-fiction form." Wright listened attentively. He refrained from informing his visitor that his latest fictional venture, *Islands of Hallucinations*, was receiving negative commentary from Doubleday. He told him instead that he saw no relationship between his work and his being abroad. Again he reiterated the major reason why he remained in exile: "I wouldn't want to expose my daughters to the conditions I object to in America. There's nothing there for me. I have what I want in Paris." During the course of the interview, he told his American guest that his play *Daddy Goodness* was then in rehearsal for a Paris opening, and jokingly, relates Faris, he said that "They'd put some grease paint on me and use me in the play since they were short of males." *Daddy Goodness* was slated to meet the same fate as the stage adaptation of *The Long Dream*.

The play, centering upon a religious charlatan not unlike some famous American "divines" was adapted by Wright in 1956 from a manuscript, *Papa Bon Dieu*, by Louis Sapin and Georges Vidalie. "Attempts to bring the play to the stage had failed, but on February 19, the English version was presented at the American Theatre Association in Paris." The rehearsals that Wright alluded to in his talk with Faris were occasioned by a projected spring production by ATA, based upon the director's favorable impression of the February production. The venture, however, was unsuccessful, and producers shied away from making necessary investments. Again a project that, years before, might have been sustained by his enormous reputation alone, was aborted. After the failure of *The Long Dream*, he wrote Reynolds attributing the closing of the play to his exile and the American hostility toward him, both "occasioned by the fact that he was the only uncontrolled Negro alive today."[16] But he also considered himself one of the most alienated. "I am alone," he wrote a friend on July 7, 1959. "I belong to no gang or clique or party or organization. If I'm attacked there is nobody to come to my aid or defense. . . ."[17]

The sense of alienation, of being a man under siege, intensified during 1960, the year of his fifty-second birthday. The year opened with chill and dampness to the streets of Paris. The sometimes arctic winds were modified by the Seine and the stone parapets that enclosed it on both sides. The raw weather failed to prevent the fishermen—old men, women, and sometimes young boys—from searching the waters for the tiny, minnowlike fish that helped to substantiate a meager diet. The magnificent gardens were chilled, dazed by the winter cold. There were no roses, chrysanthemums, or geraniums to be seen. Where once there had been sparkling green grass and the laughter and banter of many children, there was now hard, frozen ground, and only an occasional traveler, pausing briefly in the Tuileries or the Luxembourg Gardens, en route to some other destination. The Paris of the night remained the Paris it had been for centuries. The lights still flickered like beacons from the Eiffel Tower and Notre Dame, and the Arc de Triomphe still lighted up vast areas of the Champs-Élysées. And in his tiny, two-room apartment on rue Régis, Wright lived in virtual seclusion with daily bouts of despair and tension. He was used to living alone and this did not bother him, he wrote to De Sablonière on March 22, but the "tension" was killing. And, he related, he did not want tension at this time.

Part of the anxiety was due to the forced separation between himself and his family. For the first time, they would be apart for an indeterminate length of time. He had not wanted to interrupt the schooling of his daughters again, after his failure to gain permission to live in London. His wife would remain there with them, while he sought to buy the apartment above his in order to make larger living arrangements in preparation for their eventual return to Paris. There was another reason for wanting the apartment upstairs, he jokingly told Himes and Harrington: he would build a spiraling stairway that reached through the ceiling, spiraled all the way to London, through the Houses of Parliament, and end at the foot of Reginald Butler. But the sense of loss of old friends and loved ones added to his moments of depression. Over the past eight months, first Aswell, then his mother, and then Padmore had died. Each death saddened him and caused him to think about his own mortality, his own failing health. Recovery was slow, uncertain; relapses occurred frequently; there were profuse sweating, near-total exhaustion, and spasms of the body and the muscles. On February 2, he had written De Sablonière that he had found a "good doctor," one who specialized in stomach disorders. The doctor was a fan of his and would not accept payment for the treatment. His major difficulty, he wrote, still remained; he was weak most of the time, deprived of "50% of my old energy."

On his first visit to Dr. Victor Schwarzmann, Wright was surprised to find a copy of *White Man, Listen!* on the doctor's desk. The doctor was interested in the affairs and culture of the Third World, and before long, he had become both physician and friend to the writer. He prescribed a rigid diet, vitamins, doses of bismuth, and rest. For a time, Wright underwent a slow but steady recovery. But the aftereffects of the treatment, combined with renewed tension, brought on a relapse diagnosed by Schwarzmann as the colic. At the beginning of spring, Wright was confined for long hours at a time to his bed, saddled with illness and concern for his future.

Despite his assurances of the contrary to De Sablonière, his financial situation was dire indeed. To this day, Himes observed in 1976, no one knows what happened to the enormous sums that Wright earned from *Black Boy*. The sums were nowhere near as enormous as Himes and others supposed. "Dick," noted a friend, "was tight as hell with a buck. He just never had it the way the white writers had it. Faulkner, Hemingway, Steinbeck—Dick was in that league—literally; but when it came to real bread, it was always a white boy's thing." Wright's dashed hopes for the success of the stage adaptation of *The Long Dream* and *Daddy Goodness*, coupled with the indecisiveness of Doubleday concerning *Islands of Hallucinations*, had led him to seek other means of bolstering his income. He now had to support two households. He wrote offering his services to the prime ministers of African countries with whom he was familiar. The letters were not answered. He considered and then rejected an offer to work in India. He began writing blurbs for a record company, but the protests of black artists caused him to discontinue. Was this another instance of governmental harassment? Musicians, according to the FBI files, had been among the major informants supplying information on him. Who was the "Eddie Wiggins" who threatened to lead a boycott of the record company unless Wright's services were terminated?[18]

Again the magnitude of the government's operation against Wright and the undefined perimeters of the Foreign Service's activities made every action and individual justifiably suspect. A Dutch journalist whom he had met at the Bandung Conference attributed statements to him that he had never made: derogatory statements about Africans and Asians. The situation was all too similar to the actions of *Time* magazine, some months before, in connection with the article "Amid the Alien Corn." Could not this attack also be laid at the doorstep of the American Government? The forged letter that he had supposedly received from Sartre attacking him, reminded him of the Gibson affair, and he wrote De Sablonière that he knew the source of the letter, that it was only one of such letters mailed to blacks in Paris. But was he on firmer ground in laying the incident at the University of Nancy to French, British, and American intelligence? The invitation to give the lecture had come from an American professor, Ernest Pick. Wright had agreed to talk on "The Psychological Reactions of Oppressed Peoples." Upon returning from Leiden, where he had gone with Schwarzmann and his father, he discovered that the lecture had been canceled. The reason given was that another lecture to be held the same night would cut into his audience.

But did the evidence supporting his suspiciousness of government-inspired attacks against him and his guilt concerning his own past actions combine to force him to see conspiracy everywhere, even among his old friends? ". . . Dick learned," wrote Himes, "that he had a prominent role in [my] book and classified me as one of his enemies."[19] The book referred to was *A Case of Rape*, which included a character who was modeled upon Wright. His role in the book was that of a detective. When six black Americans are arrested and sentenced for the rape of a white woman who died in a room in which the men sat playing cards, Wright, "the great black writer," comes into the story to protest the innocence of the blacks and to set about trying to prove it. His thesis is that such a charge against blacks abroad must be based not on actuality but on politics. Himes, Wright told De Sablonière, had received his information from agents of the CIA.

Again, when the publishers of *Black Metropolis* wrote asking him to write an introduction for a new edition that would assess the changes made in race relations since his last introduction, over fifteen years before, he agreed. But repeated attempts to contact either Cayton or Drake failed. Neither of the writer's old friends would answer his communications. He dropped the project and noted that the nonresponse of the two was most assuredly attributable to American racism, which forced blacks to hate one another. If old friends might be numbered among his enemies, what was he to make of new ones, like Schwarzmann? His feelings concerning the doctor were mixed. He considered him a strange man. He sometimes attributed the doctor's empathy toward blacks as the kind of condescension one discerned in "emotionally disturbed whites" who sought a sense of themselves in association with a deprived minority. On the other hand, he regarded the doctor as a good and generous friend, who had helped him immensely during his period of crisis. Though vastly improved, his financial state was still precarious. He was a little moody now, he confessed to his friend, and constantly preoccupied. On July 23, he wrote to De Sablonière that he had been depressed. He was coming out of it, however. These "black periods" occurred without warning, he noted, and one just had to see them through. Back in Paris in September, Arnaldo Palacios, a friend, found him often sitting in the apartment on rue Régis, shades drawn, listening to the sonorous, melodious chords of Negro spirituals.

Shortly after his return, he fell seriously ill again. In letters to De Sablonière he reflected on his inability to force his body to move to its natural rhythm. Schwarzmann eliminated the daily doses of bismuth, and prescribed antibiotics, rest, and relaxation. Over time, the fierce spasms that wrenched his body and the almost daily convulsions ceased. The high fever, which often drenched him in perspiration, subsided. His elder daughter arrived from London, and discovering him in his weakened state, made plans to continue her education at the Sorbonne, in order to be near him. Dorothy Padmore arrived from Ghana, where she had been staying since the death of her husband, and he told her about a plot against him, implicating "the French security, the American FBI (perhaps CIA) and ex-Trotskyites."[20] He had evidence also, he told her, of a plot against Nkrumah and asked her to pass on the information to the Prime Minister. Arna Bontemps also arrived, and Wright showed his friend from the old days about the city of Paris. He continued to discuss plans for his "publishing company," and he worked on a speech he was to deliver at the American church. And from somewhere, he purchased a revolver, kept it on his person, loaded, at the ready.[21] To De Sablonière, he confided on November 23, five days before his death, that he had again been attacking the United States in writing, the broadcast media, and public speeches. One of the public speeches to which he probably referred was his last, delivered on November 8 and entitled "The Negro Intellectual and Artist in the United States Today."

He was still weakened from his last attack, but he had come down to the American church to lecture at the request of his old friend Rev. Clayton Williams. Somewhat weak and unsteady, he moved purposefully to the rostrum, looked out at the crowd of people, and began to speak in his somewhat high-pitched voice. The speech was rambling and discursive, indicating that he was veering away from his notes, interjecting thoughts and ideas as he moved along. It was a dire speech, angry, highly personal and subjective in nature. He spoke warmly of his friend Aswell; he spoke of other black writers in negative terms; he spoke of the campaign by *Time* magazine directed against him, and he told of his attempt to enlist Ethel Waters in a venture, and of her refusal to do so out of fear of whites. If there was a major metaphor in this lecture, it was himself, the black intellectual and writer besieged by American racism and black bourgeois compliance.

Men like himself had always, historically, been the enemies and targets of these two forces. Christianity and philanthropy, both weapons wielded by whites to keep blacks subjugated, were early introduced into the black belt. The black bourgeoisie, accepting the money and education offered by whites, wielded these weapons in their stead, and succeeded in stilling the discontent and rebelliousness of those who remained in the ghetto in poverty and silent fury. Marcus Garvey was born of this silent fury and discontent, and his movement galvanized the masses, offered them new hope, threatened the control of the whites and their black surrogates. Fearing revolution that would end their cheap supply of labor, the whites and blacks, acting out of a mutual fear, moved to stifle the Garvey rebellion. Out of this action, the black agent was born. His objective was to guard against the possibility of another Garvey.

But new men were waiting to be born, nevertheless, and they brought an ideology more influential than Garveyism. Pan-Africanism was their religion, one that provoked the ire of Communist and capitalist alike. Du Bois had heralded the new religion, and it had been taken up by such men as George Padmore. Today it was looked upon as a threat to American hypocrisy and pretensions across the globe. Thus, once again, the whites and their surrogates, in fear, have declared war. "It is a war of deadly proportions, one in which brother is set against brother, in which threats of mystical violence are hurled by one black against the other, where vows to cut or kill are voiced."[22] And it is a war that multiplies the number of counteragents and black spies, who seek to do the impossible, to control this ideology "in the black belt." To counteract Pan-Africanism, these agents spread a false gospel of "Communism": "Indeed, I'd say that there is more Communism being talked among Negroes today than ever in American history, but it is a false Communism, the language of the informer, the spy. . . ." Most revolutionary movements in the West, he informed his audience, are sponsored by the government and initiated by agents provocateurs. These government-inspired movements serve to organize the dejected masses in order that the government can more carefully scrutinize the emergence of true revolutionary movements, such as Pan-Africanism.

How, then, did one combat this hypocrisy? How did one engage himself to the fullest in this war? The answer was by "describing various forms of moral corruption—corruption which has its roots in fear and greed." This was the job of the committed intellectual and writer, the alienated, the men and women who must pay a terrible price for their willingness to fight on behalf of the oppressed. He told the audience of a recent visit by Martin Luther King. King had come to Paris shortly after an attempt on his life. "He had stayed at my house," Wright related, "and did not want to go out and meet other Negroes. Such caution for those who are seriously committed, he believed, was well justified."[23]

It was an effective speech. "The audience," writes Constance Webb, "was stunned. It had been his intention to speak boldly; he had reached the point in life where he felt it was not worthwhile to hint at information he had gathered. He named names, dates, places. . . ."[24]

But it was a speech also of vindication. He saw himself in the image of such fearless, courageous men as Du Bois, Padmore, King, Garvey—even Robeson—though he did not share their ideologies. All were part of the American "tragic elite," men thrust by the circumstances of race and history into the role of warriors. Men like these were always in grave danger, as were other such men throughout the world, from whites and blacks as well. Yet, their courage was marked by their fierce determination to pursue their course in the face of all dangers, to walk the lonely world of alienation and exile. The audience, he wrote De Sablonière, was "shocked" at what he had to say, and he thought of turning the lecture into a book. He could then expand upon his initial theses, offer more details of the problems confronting the black artist and intellectual in America.

Immediately after his address, he once again fell violently ill. This time he was bedridden for twelve days. His daughter and friends kept a steady vigil by his bedside. In addition to high temperature, he underwent intense spells of dizziness. After the crisis was over and he felt somewhat better, his doctor advised him to go to the Eugene Gibenz Clinic for "extensive examinations." On the day he was scheduled to check into the clinic, Langston Hughes arrived at his apartment. When he had seen him on that day, Hughes later wrote, "he did not look ill. . . . Periodically, he said, he needed routine treatment for an old stomach ailment he had picked up in Paris." He felt fine, he told Hughes, except that he had not eaten very much in the past few days. "The medicine he had taken," he said, "upset him worse than the ailment." He said good-by to his old friend, and after depositing his revolver with another close friend, he checked into the clinic on November 26. Extensive examinations revealed no sign of serious illness, and he was scheduled for release on November 29. On the night of the twenty-eighth, he talked by telephone with his wife, and made plans to meet Palacios the next day for further discussions concerning the creation of a publishing company. And he tried to call Harrington, who was away from Paris, in Normandy, at the time. He forwarded a telegram instead, which, wrote Harrington, ". . . simply said, OLLIE PLEASE COME TO SEE ME AS SOON AS YOU GET THIS." He had never heard of the clinic, wrote Harrington, but when he returned and found Wright's telegram, he put through a call to the clinic. ". . . I asked to speak with Monsieur Richard Wright. I was told that it would not be possible. 'Monsieur Wright died last night.'" Harrington concluded: ". . . It was the first time in more than 10 years that he'd not gone to the American Hospital. And it was the only time he'd failed to call either me or Chester Himes."[25]

The FBI attaché in Paris noted his passing by sending two obituary clippings to Washington on December 7. One was from an unnamed paper, the other from the Paris edition of the *Herald Tribune*. The document referred the Bureau to the censored letter of February 11. The message was short, cryptic: "Enclosed is a clipping from the 11/30/60 issue of the 'New York Herald Tribune,' European edition, Paris, reflecting the death of the subject at Paris on 11/28/60." Not even his death had completely stilled the government's interest: On May 9, 1963, four copies of a memorandum were sent to various agencies, including one to the Foreign Liaison Unit. The document read: "Reference is made to your communication dated April 26, which inquired as to whether we had any information confirming the death of Richard Nathaniel Wright and any adverse record of [name deleted]. According to newspaper articles, Richard Wright, who appears to be identical with Richard Nathaniel Wright, born September 4, 1908, a renowned American Negro author, died as a result of a heart attack in Paris, France, on November 29, 1960." Several passages and names are deleted before the document concludes, cryptically, "Regarding Wright he was the author of *Black Boy* and *The Outsider* dealing with problems of the Negro in American Society. . . . Since [deletion] is in possession of all information concerning Wright's Communist Party affiliation there is no need to reiterate such data."[26]

London, Paris, Madrid, N.Y.C.,
1979

SELECTED
BIBLIOGRAPHY

Abcarian, Richard. *Richard Wright's* Native Son. Belmont, Calif.: Wadsworth Publishing Co., Inc., 1970.

Adams, Phoebe. "The Outsider," *The Atlantic*, Vol. CXCI, May 1953.

Awoonor, Kofi. *The Breast of the Earth*. Garden City, N.Y.: Doubleday & Co., Inc., 1975.

Baldwin, James. *Nobody Knows My Name*. New York: Dell Publishing Co., Inc., 1961.

———. *Notes of a Native Son*. New York: Dial Press, 1963.

———. *The Devil Finds Work*. New York: Dial Press, 1976.

Barnett, A. N. "Long Dream," *Library Journal*, Oct. 15, 1958.

Barry, Joseph A. "Americans in Paris," New York *Times Magazine*, Aug. 15, 1948.

Bogle, Donald. *Toms, Coons, Mulattoes, Mammies, and Bucks*. New York: Viking Press, 1973.

Bone, Robert. *The Negro Novel in America*. New Haven, Conn.: Yale University Press, 1958.

Brignano, Russell Carl. *Richard Wright: an Introduction to the Man and His Works*. Pittsburgh, Pa.: University of Pittsburgh Press, 1970.

Byam, M. S. "*White Man, Listen!* by Richard Wright," *Library Journal*, Vol. 82, Sept. 15, 1957.

Cameron, May. "Prize Winning Novelist Talks of Communism and Importance of Felt Life," New York *Post*, Mar. 12, 1939.

Camus, Albert. *The Rebel*. New York: Alfred A. Knopf, Inc., and Random House, Inc., 1956.

Cannon, Terry. "Was Richard Wright Assassinated?" *Daily World*, Dec. 10, 1977.

Carr, Virginia Spencer. *The Lonely Hunter*. Garden City, N.Y.: Doubleday & Co., Inc., 1976.

Caute, David. *The Great Fear!* New York: Simon & Schuster, 1978.

Conroy, Jack; and Johnson, Curt; eds. *Writers in Revolt: The Anvil Anthology*. New York: Lawrence Hill & Co., Inc., 1973.

Cook, Fred J. *The Muckrakers*. Garden City, N.Y.: Doubleday & Co., Inc., 1972.

Cowley, Malcolm; and Piper, Henry Dan; eds. *Think Back on Us . . . the Literary Record*. Part II. Southern Illinois University Press, 1967.

Cowley, Malcolm. *Think Back on Us . . . the Social Record*. Part I. Southern Illinois University Press, 1967.

Cruse, Harold. *The Crisis of the Negro Intellectual*. New York: William Morrow & Co., Inc., 1967.

Curti, Merle; Shryock, Richard H.; Cochran, Thomas C.; and Harrington, Fred Harvey. *An American History*. New York: Harper & Bros., 1950.

Davis, A. P. "'Outsider' as a novel of race," *Midwest Journal*, VII, 1955–56.

Dickstein, Morris. *Gates of Eden*. New York: Basic Books, Inc., 1977.

Drake, St. Clair; and Cayton, Horace R. *Black Metropolis*. New York: Harcourt, Brace & Co., 1945.

Du Bois, W. E. B. *The Autobiography of W. E. B. Du Bois*. New York: International Publishers Co., Inc., 1968.

Dunlea, William. "Long Dream," *Commonweal*, LXIX, Oct. 31, 1958.

Eckman, Fern Marja. *The Furious Passage of James Baldwin*. New York: M. Evans & Co., Inc., 1966.

Ellison, Ralph. *Shadow and Act*. New York: The New American Library, Inc., 1966.

Fabre, Michel. "Interview with Simone de Beauvoir," *Studies in Black Literature*, I, Autumn 1970.

——. *The Unfinished Quest of Richard Wright*. New York: William Morrow & Co., Inc., 1973.

——; and Wright, Ellen; eds. *Richard Wright Reader*. New York: Harper & Row, 1978.

Fanon, Frantz. *The Wretched of the Earth*. New York: Grove Press, Inc., 1963.

Files from the Central Intelligence Agency (two documents).

Files from the Federal Bureau of Investigation (1938–63) (Approx. fifteen documents).

Files from the United States Department of State, May 8, 1956 (one document).

Franklin, John Hope. *From Slavery to Freedom*. New York: Alfred A. Knopf, Inc., 1967.

Frazier, E. Franklin. *The Negro in the United States*. New York: The Macmillan Co., 1957.

Fuller, Hoyt. "On the Death of Richard Wright," *Southwest Review*, No. 46 (Autumn 1961), pp. 334–42.

Gayle, Addison, ed. *The Black Aesthetic*. Garden City, N.Y.: Doubleday & Co., Inc., 1971.

Giles, Louise. "Lawd Today," *Library Journal*, p. 1549, 1963.

Gilman, Richard. "Eight Men," *Commonweal*, p. 130, 1961.

Graham, Gladys P. "Richard Wright Returns to America," *Atlantic Daily World*, Aug. 27, 1950.

Haiman, Franklyn S. *Freedom of Speech*. New York: Random House, Inc., 1965.

Harrington, Ollie. "The Last Days of Richard Wright," *Ebony* magazine, Vol. 16, Feb. 1961.

——. "The Mysterious Death of Richard Wright," *Daily World*, Dec. 17, 1977.

Hill, Herbert. *Anger and Beyond*. New York: Harper & Row, 1966.
———. *Soon, One Morning*. New York: Alfred A. Knopf, Inc., 1966.
Himes, Chester. *My Life of Absurdity*. Garden City, N.Y.: Doubleday & Co., Inc., 1976.
———. *The Quality of Hurt*, Vol. 1. Garden City, N.Y.: Doubleday & Co., Inc., 1972.
House of Commons debate, Hansard, Vol. 595, No. 18, Nov. 20, 1957.
Howe, Irving. "Eight Men," *New Republic*, CXLIV, p. 17, 1961.
Hughes, M. C. "The Outsider," *Commonweal*, Vol. LVIII, Apr. 10, 1953.
Hunt, Carew R. N. *The Theory and Practice of Communism*. New York: The Macmillan Co., 1951.
James, C. L. R. *Nkrumah and the Ghana Revolution*. Westport, Conn.: Lawrence Hill & Co., 1977.
Katznelson, Ira; and Kesselman, Mark; eds. *The Politics of Power*. New York: Harcourt Brace Jovanovich, Inc., 1975.
Kennedy, Ellen Conroy, ed. *The Negritude Poet*. New York: Viking Press, 1975.
Klotman, Phyllis Rauch. *Another Man Gone*. New York: Kennikat Press, 1977.
Koestler, Arthur; and others. *The God That Failed*. New York: Harper & Row, 1963.
Lamming, George. *In the Castle of My Skin*. New York: The Macmillan Co., 1970.
Loewen, James W.; and Sallis, Charles; eds. *Mississippi: Conflict & Change*. New York: Random House, Inc., 1974.
Lynd, Staughton. "Lawd Today," *Commentary*, XXXVI, p. 255, 1963.
Macebuh, Stanley. *James Baldwin—a Critical Study*. New York: Joseph Okpaku Publishing Co., Inc., 1973.
Marcuse, Herbert. *Eros and Civilization*. Boston: Beacon Press, 1966.
McCall, Dan. *The Example of Richard Wright*. New York: Harcourt, Brace & World, 1969.
"Native Son Author Backs Ford, Browder," *Daily Worker*, Sept. 30, 1940.
Negro Digest, "Richard Wright, His Life and His Work," Johnson Publishing, December 1968.
Nevins, Allan; and Commager, Henry Steele. *The Pocket History of the United States*. New York: Pocket Books, Inc., 1956.
Nkrumah, Kwame. *Revolutionary Warfare*. New York: International Publishers, 1969.
North, Joseph. *New Masses*. New York: International Publishers, 1969.
Patterson, William L. *Ben Davis*. New York: New Outlook Publishers, 1967.
———. *The Man Who Cried Genocide*. New York: International Publishers Co., Inc., 1971.
Proceedings and Debates of the 79th Congress: First Session, Vol. 95, No. 218, June 27, 1945, 128:91.
Raleigh, J. H. "The Outsider," *The New Republic*, Vol. CXXVIII, p. 19, 1953.
Rascoe, Burton. "Rascoe Baiting," *American Mercury*, #50, July 1940.
Ray, David, ed. *New Letters*. Kansas City: University of Missouri Press, 1971.

Record, Wilson. *The Negro and the Communist Party.* New York: Athe-
    neum, 1971.
———. *Race and Radicalism.* Ithaca, N.Y.: Cornell University Press, 1964.
Redding, J. Saunders. *Long Dream.* New York *Times,* 1958.
———. *No Day of Triumph.* New York: Harper & Bros., 1942.
———. *They Came in Chains.* New York: J. B. Lippincott Co., 1950.
Reed, John. *Ten Days That Shook the World.* New York: International
    Publishers, 1934.
Rogge, Heinz. "Die Amerikanische Negerfrage ein Lichte der Literation von
    Richard Wright und Ralph Ellison," Die Neuem Sprachen, 1958;
    Wright: p. 56, Ellison: p. 103.
Rosenblatt, Roger. *Black Fiction.* Cambridge, Mass.: Harvard University
    Press, 1974.
Shapiro, Charles. "Long Dream," *The New Republic,* Nov. 24, 1958.
Silver, James W. *Mississippi the Closed Society.* New York: Harcourt,
    Brace & World, Inc., 1963.
Smith, William Gardner. "Black Boy in France," *Ebony* magazine, Vol. 8,
    July 1953.
Solomon, Maynard. *Marxism and Art.* New York: Alfred A. Knopf, 1973.
Steinfield, Melvin. *Our Racist Presidents.* San Ramon, Calif.: Consensus
    Publishers, Inc., 1972.
Stockwell, John. *In Search of Enemies.* New York: W. W. Norton & Co.,
    Inc., 1978.
Swanberg, W. A. *Dreiser.* New York: Charles Scribner's Sons, 1965.
Turner, Darwin T., ed. *Afro-American Writers.* New York: Meredith Cor-
    poration, 1970.
Tuttle, William M., ed. *W. E. B. Du Bois—Great Lives Observed.* Engle-
    wood Cliffs, N.J.: Prentice-Hall, Inc., 1973.
Ungar, Sanford J. *FBI.* Boston: Little, Brown & Company, 1975.
Watch Tower Bible and Tract Society of Pennsylvania. *One World, One
    Government, Under God's Sovereignty.*
Webb, Constance. *Richard Wright.* New York: G. P. Putnam's Sons,
    1968.
Wertham, Frederic, M.D. "An Unconscious Determinant in *Native Son,*"
    Journal of Clinical and Experimental Psychology, Vol. 6, July 1944,
    p. 111–15.
"Why Richard Wright Came Back From France," *P.M. Magazine,* Feb. 16,
    1947.
Williams, John A.; and Harris, Charles F.; eds. *Amistad I.* New York: Ran-
    dom House, Inc., 1970.
Wilson, Edmund. *The Shock of Recognition.* New York: Grosset & Dun-
    lap, 1955.
———. *The Triple Thinkers.* New York: Oxford University Press, 1963.
Wright, Ellen; and Fabre, Michel; eds. *Richard Wright Reader.* New York:
    Harper & Row, 1978.
Wright, Richard. "Ah Feels It in Mah Bones," *International Literature,*
    No. 4, April 1935.
———. *American Hunger.* New York: Harper & Row, 1977.
———. "Between Laughter and Tears," *New Masses,* XXV, Oct. 5, 1937.
———. "Between the World and Me," *Partisan Review,* No. 2 (July–August
    1935).

——. *Black Boy.* New York: Harper & Row, 1945.
——. *Black Boy.* New York: World Publishing Co., 1950.
——. *Black Power.* New York: Harper & Bros., 1954.
——. "Born a slave, she recruits 5 members for Communist Party," *Daily Worker*, Aug. 30, 1937.
——. *The Color Curtain.* New York: The World Publishing Co., 1956.
——. "Comrade Strong, Don't You Remember?" New York *Herald Tribune*, European ed., Apr. 4, 1949.
——. *Eight Men.* New York: World Publishing Co., 1961.
——. "Everywhere Burning Waters Rise," *Left Front*, No. 4 (May–June 1934).
——. "Gertrude Stein's Story Is Drenched in Hitler's Horrors," *P.M. Magazine*, Mar. 11, 1945.
——. "Haikus," *Studies in Black Literature*, I (Summer 1970).
——. "How He Did It and Oh! Where Were Hitler's Pagan Gods?" *Daily Worker*, June 24, 1938.
——. "How Jim Crow Feels," *True* magazine, Nov. 1946.
——. "How Richard Wright Looks at Black Boy," *P.M. Magazine*, Apr. 15, 1945.
——. "Huddie Ledbetter, Famous Negro Folk Artist," *Daily Worker*, Aug. 12, 1937.
——. "I Am a Red Slogan," *International Literature*, No. 4 (April 1935).
——. "I Have Seen Black Hands," *New Masses*, No. 11 (June 26, 1934).
——. "Is America Solving Its Race Problem?" *America's Town Meeting of the Air Bulletin*, #11 (May 24, 1945).
——. "Joe Louis Uncovers Dynamite," *New Masses*, No. 17 (Oct. 8, 1935).
——. *Lawd Today.* New York: Walker & Co., 1963.
——. Letter to the editor, *Partisan Review*, June 1936.
——. *Native Son.* New York: Harper & Bros., 1940.
——. "Negro Author Criticizes Reds as Intolerant," New York *Herald Tribune*, Jan. 28, 1944.
——. "Negro Tradition in the Theatre," *Daily Worker*, Oct. 15, 1937.
——. "New Negro Pamphlet Stresses Need for U.S. Peoples Front," *Daily Worker*, Oct. 25, 1937.
——. "Not My People's War," *New Masses*, No. 39 (June 17, 1941).
——. "Obsession," *Midland Left*, #2 (Feb. 1935).
——. *The Outsider.* New York: Harper & Row, 1953.
——. *Pagan Spain.* New York: Harper & Bros., 1957.
——. "A Red Love Note," *Left Front*, No. 3 (Jan.–Feb. 1934).
——. "Rest for the Weary," *Left Front*, No. 3 (Jan.–Feb. 1934).
——. *Savage Holiday.* New York: Universal Publishers & Distributing Corporation, 1965.
——. "The Shame of Chicago," *Ebony* magazine, VII (Dec. 1951).
——. "Ten Haiku," *New Letters*, No. 38 (Winter 1971).
——. "Two Million Black Voices," *New Masses*, XVIII, No. 9 (Feb. 25, 1936).
——; and Rosskam, Edwin. *Twelve Million Black Voices.* New York: Viking Press, 1941.
Wright, Richard. *Uncle Tom's Children.* New York: Harper & Bros., 1936.

———. "Urban Misery in an American City: Juvenile Delinquency in Harlem," *Twice a Year*, Nos. 14–15 (Fall 1946–Winter 1947).

———. "U.S. Negroes Greet You," *Daily Worker*, Sept. 1, 1941.

———. "Walter Garland Tells what Spain's fight against Fascism means to the Negro People," *Daily Worker*, Nov. 29, 1937.

———. "What Happens at a Communist Party Meeting," *Daily Worker*, Aug. 16, 1937.

———. *White Man, Listen!* Garden City, N.Y.: Doubleday & Co., Inc., 1964.

———. "A World View of the American Negro," *Twice a Year*, Nos. 14–15 (Fall 1946–Winter 1947).

NOTES

CHAPTER ONE

1. James W. Loewen and Charles Sallis, *Mississippi: Conflict and Change* (New York: Random House, 1974), p. 2.
2. Richard Wright and Edwin Rosskam, *Twelve Million Black Voices: A Folk History of the Negro in the United States* (New York: The Viking Press, 1941), p. 34.
3. Michel Fabre, *The Unfinished Quest of Richard Wright* (New York: William Morrow & Company, 1973), p. 1.
4. Ibid., p. 2.
5. Richard Wright, *Black Boy: A Record of Childhood and Youth* (New York: Harper & Row, 1945), p. 154.
6. Ibid., p. 9.
7. Richard Wright's private papers.
8. *Black Boy*, p. 17.
9. Ibid., p. 34.
10. Ibid., p. 42.

CHAPTER TWO

1. *Black Boy*, p. 55.
2. Ibid., p. 118.
3. Ibid., pp. 127–28.
4. Ibid., p. 159.
5. Ibid., p. 165.

CHAPTER THREE

1. Fabre, op. cit., p. 46.
2. Conversations between the author and past associates of Wright.
3. Frederic Wertham, "An Unconscious Determinant in *Native Son*,"

Journal of Clinical & Experimental Psychology, Vol. 6, July 1944, pp. 111–15.
4. *Black Boy,* p. 45.
5. Ibid., p. 215.

CHAPTER FOUR

1. Grace McSpadden White, "Wright's Memphis," *New Letters,* Vol. 38, No. 2 (Winter 1971), p. 106.
2. *Black Boy,* p. 235.
3. Ibid., p. 253.
4. Ibid., p. 251.
5. Ibid., p. 270.
6. Ibid., p. 274.
7. Ibid., p. 280.
8. Ibid., p. 284.

CHAPTER FIVE

1. Richard Wright, *American Hunger* (New York: Harper & Row, 1977), p. 1.
2. Constance Webb, "Interview with Ellen Wright," Sept. 1963 (New York, Richard Wright Collection, Schomburg library).
3. *American Hunger,* p. 27.
4. Fabre, op. cit., p. 79.
5. *American Hunger,* p. 26.
6. Ibid., pp. 27–28.
7. Ibid., p. 29.

CHAPTER SIX

1. *American Hunger,* pp. 44–45.
2. Ibid., p. 48.
3. Fabre, op. cit., pp. 82–83.
4. *American Hunger,* p. 62.
5. Fabre, op. cit., pp. 96–97.
6. *American Hunger,* pp. 62–63.
7. Wilson Record, *The Negro and the Communist Party* (New York: Atheneum, 1971), p. 58.
8. *American Hunger,* p. 63.
9. Richard Wright, *I Have Seen Black Hands,* in Maxwell Geismar, ed., *New Masses: An Anthology of the Rebel Thirties* (New York: International Publishers, 1969), pp. 49–51.
10. Fabre, op. cit., p. 101.
11. *American Hunger,* pp. 69–70.
12. Richard Wright, "What Happens in ACP Branch Meeting in the Harlem Section," New York *Daily Worker,* Aug. 16, 1937, p. 6.
13. *American Hunger,* p. 66.

14. Fabre, op. cit., p. 115.
15. Ibid., p. 110.
16. Henrietta Weigel, "Personal Impression," in *New Letters*, p. 20.
17. Ibid.
18. Margaret Walker Alexander, "Richard Wright," in *New Letters*, p. 189.
19. Richard Wright, "How Bigger Was Born," a Foreword to *Native Son* (New York: Harper & Row, 1940), p. xxvii.
20. *American Hunger*, p. 92.

CHAPTER SEVEN

1. Eugene Lyons, *The Red Decade*, quoted from the Federal Bureau of Investigation Files on Subject Richard Wright, May 14, 1943, p. 2.
2. *American Hunger*, p. 95.
3. Ibid., p. 98.
4. Margaret Walker, *New Letters*, p. 200.
5. Wright, *Black Boy*, p. 45.
6. FBI Files, May 14, 1943, pp. 1–2.
7. Walker, *New Masses*, p. 200.
8. Richard Wright, *Lawd Today* (New York: Walker and Company, 1963), p. 101.
9. Walker, *New Masses*, p. 185.
10. Weigel, *New Letters*, p. 18.
11. William L. Patterson, *The Man Who Cried Genocide: an Autobiography* (New York: International Publishers, 1971), p. 149.
12. Wilson Record, op. cit., p. 153.
13. Ibid.
14. *American Hunger*, pp. 104–5.
15. Fabre, op. cit., p. 126.
16. Record, op. cit., p. 157.
17. Richard Wright, "A Tale of Folk Courage," *Partisan Review*, Vol. 3, April 1936, p. 31.
18. Ibid., p. 183.
19. Ibid., p. 195.
20. *American Hunger*, p. 109.
21. Walker, *New Letters*, pp. 198–99.
22. Patterson, op. cit., p. 149.
23. *American Hunger*, p. 110.
24. Ibid., p. 125.
25. Fabre, op. cit., p. 138.

CHAPTER EIGHT

1. Richard Wright, *The Outsider* (New York: Harper & Row, 1953), p. 17.
2. Walker, *New Letters*, p. 192.
3. Weigel, *New Letters*, p. 17.
4. Ibid., p. 19.

5. Malcolm Cowley, *Think Back on Us: A Contemporary Chronicle of the 1930's* (Carbondale, Ill.: Southern Illinois University Press, 1967), p. 168.
6. Jerry Mangione, *The Dream and the Deal*, p. 245.
7. Ibid., p. 103.
8. Ibid., p. 245.
9. Ibid., p. 256.
10. William L. Patterson, *Ben Davis: Crusader for Negro Freedom & Socialism* (New York: New Outlook Publishers, 1967), p. 21.
11. Richard Wright, "How He Did It and Oh! Where Were Hitler's Pagan Gods?" *Daily Worker*, June 24, 1938, p. 8.
12. Ben Davis, Jr., *Daily Worker*, June 24, 1938, p. 1.
13. Ibid.
14. Richard Wright, "Silt," *New Masses*, Vol. XXIV, Aug. 24, 1937.
15. Walker, *New Letters*, p. 193.
16. Document, FBI File, April 18, 1943.
17. Constance Webb, op. cit., p. 211.
18. Richard Wright, *Uncle Tom's Children* (New York: Harper & Row, 1938), p. 35.
19. Ibid., p. 102.
20. Ibid., p. 106.
21. Richard Wright Archives, Beinecke Library. See also Webb, op. cit., p. 230.
22. Walker, *New Letters*, p. 194.
23. Weigel, *New Letters*, p. 19.
24. Constance Webb, "Interview with Ellen Wright," Richard Wright Collection (Schomburg).
25. Wertham, "An Unconscious Determinant . . . ," p. 111.
26. Richard Wright, "How Bigger Was Born," p. xxiii.
27. Ibid., p. xiv.

CHAPTER NINE

1. Document, FBI Files, August 20, 1940.
2. David L. Cohn, review reprinted in Richard Abcarian, *Richard Wright's* Native Son: *A Critical Handbook* (Wadsworth Publishing Company, Inc., 1970), p. 80.
3. Richard Wright, "I Bite the Hand That Feeds Me," in Abcarian, op. cit., p. 81.
4. ———. "A Symposium on an Exiled Native Son," in Herbert Hill (ed.), *Anger and Beyond* (New York: Harper & Row, 1966), p. 198.
5. Ben Davis, review, reprinted in Abcarian, op. cit., pp. 73–74.
6. Fabre, op. cit., pp. 185–86.
7. Unpublished essay, "There are still men left," p. 1. See also Webb, op. cit., pp. 149–50.
8. Davis, in Abcarian, op. cit., p. 74.
9. Wilson Record, op. cit., p. 184.
10. Malcolm Cowley, op. cit., p. 189.
11. Richard Wright, "There are still men left," pp. 1–2.

12. Richard Wright, "Richard Wright's Statement supporting Browder, Ford," *Daily Worker*, Sept. 30, 1940, p. 1.
13. Margaret Walker, interview with Nikki Giovanni, p. 96.
14. Jerry Mangione, op. cit., p. 324.
15. Constance Webb, "Interview with Ralph Ellison," (Richard Wright Collection, Schomburg).
16. Ibid.
17. Fabre, op. cit., p. 203.
18. Ibid., p. 202.
19. Ibid., p. 204.
20. Document: FBI Files, April 6, 1958, p. 6.
21. John Houseman, "Native Son on Stage," in *New Letters*, p. 72.
22. Wright, *Black Boy*, p. 43.
23. Houseman, op. cit., p. 70.
24. Ibid., p. 72.
25. Ibid., p. 71.
26. Ibid., p. 74.
27. Document: FBI Files, June 9, 1944, p. 1.
28. Webb, *Richard Wright: a Biography*, p. 193.
29. FBI Files, April 4, 1958, p. 6.
30. Fabre, op. cit., p. 226.
31. Wright, *Twelve Million Black Voices*, p. 145.
32. FBI Files, Oct. 13, 1942, p. 1.
33. Ibid., Dec. 9, 1942, p. 3.

CHAPTER TEN

1. Wilson Record, op. cit., p. 213.
2. FBI File, May 28, 1943, pp. 4–5.
3. Webb, *Richard Wright: a Biography*, p. 154.
4. Ibid.
5. Benjamin Appel, "Personal Impressions," in *New Letters*, p. 22.
6. Ibid.
7. Virginia Spencer Carr, *The Lonely Hunter: a Biography of Carson McCullers* (Garden City, N.Y.: Doubleday & Co., 1976), p. 127.
8. Ibid.
9. Ibid., p. 129.
10. FBI File, May 28, 1943, p. 5.
11. Ibid., April 4, 1958, p. 4.
12. Ibid.
13. Ibid.
14. Ibid., pp. 4–5.
15. Ibid., p. 5.
16. Ibid., Feb. 9, 1943, p. 2.
17. Ibid., July 8, 1944, p. 2.
18. Horace Cayton, "The Curtain," *Negro Digest*, Dec. 1968, p. 12.
19. Ibid., p. 14.
20. Richard Wright, "Richard Wright Describes the Birth of *Black Boy*," *New York Post*, Nov. 30, 1944, p. 6.
21. Ibid.

22. Richard Wright, "Comrade Strong, Don't You Remember?" New York *Herald Tribune*, European edition, April 4, 1949, p. 4.
23. Ibid.

CHAPTER ELEVEN

1. FBI Files, p. 1.
2. Ibid., p. 7.
3. FBI Files, Aug. 29, 1943, p. 1.
4. FBI Files, Sept. 14, 1943, p. 1.
5. FBI Files, June 9, 1944, p. 2.
6. Sanford J. Ungar, *F.B.I.: an Uncensored Look Behind the Walls* (Boston: Little, Brown & Co., 1975), p. 131.
7. Ibid., p. 124.
8. Ibid.
9. David Caute, *The Great Fear! The Anti-Communist Purge* (New York: Simon & Schuster, 1978), p. 115.
10. Ibid., p. 168.
11. FBI Files, July 8, 1944, p. 1.
12. "Richard Wright Describes the Birth of *Black Boy*," New York *Post*, Nov. 30, 1944, p. 6.
13. Fabre, op. cit., p. 253.
14. Wright spoke of the details of his first meeting with Aswell in his last untitled lecture, unpublished, delivered Nov. 8, 1960, in American Church, Paris.
15. Fabre, op. cit., p. 254.
16. Ibid.
17. Harry Birdoff, "Personal Impressions," *New Letters*, p. 26.
18. Fabre, op. cit., p. 253.
19. FBI Files, July 8, 1944, pp. 2–3.
20. Richard Wright, "Melody Limited" (unpublished), p. 1.
21. W. A. Swanberg, *Dreiser* (New York: Charles Scribner's Sons, 1965), p. 502.
22. FBI Files, July 8, 1944, p. 1.
23. Ungar, op. cit., p. 129.
24. FBI Files, Aug. 5, 1944, p. 3.
25. FBI Files, Aug. 8, 1944, p. 3.
26. Ibid., p. 4.
27. Ibid., p. 5.
28. Ibid., p. 3.
29. FBI Files, Aug. 4, 1944, p. 1.

CHAPTER TWELVE

1. Fabre, op. cit., p. 266.
2. Ibid.
3. Robert Minor, "Mr. Wright Didn't Discover It," *Daily Worker*, Aug. 15, 1944, p. 6.
4. FBI Files, Sept. 5, 1944, p. 1.

5. Ibid., p. 8.
6. Ibid., p. 9.
7. *American Hunger*, p. 133.
8. Fabre, op. cit., p. 271.
9. Richard Wright and Antonio Frasconi: "An Exchange of Letters," *Twice a Year*, Nov. 1944, p. 259.
10. Fabre, op. cit., pp. 273–74.
11. Richard Wright Archives (Beinecke).
12. Constance Webb, "Interview with Ralph Ellison," Richard Wright Collection (Schomburg).
13. Benjamin J. Davis, Jr., "Some Impressions of *Black Boy*," *Daily Worker*, April 1, 1945, p. 9.
14. Orville Prescott, New York *Times*, Feb. 28, 1945, p. 2.
15. Congressional Record, June 7, 1945.
16. FBI Files, Feb. 26, 1945, p. 1.
17. Wright, Journal, 1945, Richard Wright Archives (Beinecke).
18. Fabre, op. cit., p. 275.
19. Ibid., p. 276.
20. Ibid., p. 286.
21. Journal, Richard Wright Archives (Beinecke).
22. Richard Wright, Introduction to *Black Metropolis: a Study of Negro Life in a Northern City* (New York: Harcourt, Brace & Co., 1945), p. xxi.
23. Richard Wright Archives (Beinecke).
24. Ibid., Journal, 1945. See also Webb, *Richard Wright: a Biography*, p. 262.
25. Richard Wright Archives (Beinecke), Journal, 1945.
26. Fabre, op. cit., p. 586.

CHAPTER THIRTEEN

1. Fabre, op. cit., p. 289.
2. Chester Himes, *The Quality of Hurt* (New York: Doubleday & Co., 1971), p. 116.
3. Fern Marja Eckman, *The Furious Passage of James Baldwin* (New York: M. Evans & Co., 1966), p. 102.
4. Ibid., p. 104.
5. Fabre, op. cit., pp. 292–93.
6. Ibid., p. 579.
7. Journal, 1945; see also Fabre, op. cit., p. 587.
8. David Caute, op. cit., p. 28.
9. Ibid., p. 90.
10. Ibid., p. 89.
11. Wilson Record, op. cit., p. 227.
12. Ibid., pp. 228–29.
13. Ibid., p. 229.
14. Ibid., p. 230.
15. Webb, *Richard Wright: a Biography*, p. 245.
16. FBI Files, April 4, 1958, p. 7.

17. See Caute, op. cit., Chapter 12, "The Golden Curtain: Passports and Immigration."
18. Richard Wright, "I Choose Exile" (unpublished Ms, Richard Wright Archives).
19. "Why Richard Wright Came Back from France," *P.M. Magazine*, Feb. 16, 1947, p. 5.
20. Ibid.
21. Fabre, op. cit., p. 285.
22. Ibid., p. 306.
23. Ibid.
24. FBI Files, June 18, 1946, pp. 1–3.
25. Caute, op. cit., p. 191.
26. C. L. R. James, *Nkrumah and the Ghana Revolution* (Westport, Conn.: Lawrence Hill & Co., 1977), p. 63.
27. *P.M. Magazine*, p. 5.
28. Dodson, *New Letters*, p. 31.
29. Ibid., p. 492.
30. John A. Williams and Charles F. Harris, *Amistad I: Writings on Black History and Culture* (New York: Random House, 1970), p. 87.
31. Michel Fabre, "Wright's Exile," *New Letters*, p. 154.
32. William Gardner Smith, "Black Boy in France," *Ebony* magazine, Vol. 8, July 1953, p. 39.
33. Webb, op. cit., p. 257.
34. Ibid., p. 259.
35. Journal, 1947, Richard Wright Archives.
36. Caroline Caro-Delvaille, *L'Amérique sans Hollywood*, Paris, 1959.
37. Richard Wright Archives (Beinecke), Journal, 1947.

CHAPTER FOURTEEN

1. Smith, op. cit., p. 39.
2. Journal, also see Webb, op. cit., p. 277.
3. Richard Wright, "The Shame of Chicago," *Ebony* magazine, December 1951.
4. Journal, 1947.
5. Caute, op. cit., p. 90.
6. Ibid., p. 164.
7. Richard Wright, "Two Letters to Dorothy Norman," (*Art and Action*, 1948), pp. 69–70.
8. Wright, "I Choose Exile."
9. FBI Files, March 3, 1952, p. 2.
10. Chester Himes, *Amistad*, p. 86.
11. Fabre, op. cit., p. 331.
12. Richard Wright, "Comrade Strong . . . ," p. 4.
13. Caute, op. cit., p. 190.
14. Wright, "Comrade Strong . . . ," p. 4.
15. Paul S. Nathan, "Books into Films," *Publishers Weekly*, Vol. 156, No. 14 (October 1, 1969), p. 1586.
16. Comments concerning the film are made in relation to the screenplay

by Pierre Chenal and Richard Wright, in the Richard Wright Collection. I was unable to obtain a copy of the film.

17. FBI Files, Jan. 8, 1952, p. 2.
18. Fabre, op. cit., p. 351.
19. Ibid., p. 352.
20. Ibid., p. 354.
21. Caute, op. cit., p. 48.
22. Ibid., p. 170.
23. Caute, op. cit., p. 245.
24. Patrick J. McGarvey, C.I.A.: the Myth and the Madness (Maryland, Penguin Books, 1972), p. 118.

CHAPTER FIFTEEN

1. FBI Files, May 12, 1950, p. 1.
2. Ibid., p. 11.
3. Chester Himes, My Life of Absurdity: the Autobiography of Chester Himes, Vol. 2 (Garden City, N.Y.: Doubleday & Co., 1976), p. 75.
4. Central Intelligence Agency, June 20, 1951, p. 5.
5. Ibid., p. 1.
6. Ibid., pp. 2–6.
7. Ibid., p. 3.
8. Fabre, op. cit., p. 360.
9. FBI Files, Jan. 3, 1952, p. 1.
10. FBI Files, pp. 4–5. Jan. 3, 1952.
11. James Baldwin, Nobody Knows My Name (New York: Dell Publishing Co., 1961), p. 156.
12. Ibid., p. 158.
13. Ibid., p. 167.
14. William Gardner Smith, "Black Boy in France," Ebony magazine, Vol. 8, July 1953, p. 40.
15. Ibid., p. 41.
16. Richard Wright, The Outsider (New York: Harper & Row, 1953), p. 230.
17. Ibid., p. 282.
18. Walker, New Letters, p. 200.
19. Fabre, op. cit., p. 367.
20. Richard Wright, Savage Holiday (New York: Universal Publishers and Distributing Corporation, 1965); published initially by Avon, 1954; p. 215.
21. Fabre, op. cit., p. 375.

CHAPTER SIXTEEN

1. Chester Himes, The Quality of Hurt, p. 177.
2. Ibid., p. 184.
3. Ibid., p. 203.
4. Passim.
5. Caute, op. cit., p. 106.

6. Himes, op. cit., p. 198.
7. Ibid., p. 198.
8. Ibid., p. 196.
9. Baldwin, *Nobody Knows My Name*, p. 158.
10. Fabre, op. cit., p. 387.
11. Richard Wright, *Black Power: a Record of Reactions in a Land of Pathos* (New York: Harper & Bros., 1954), p. 36.
12. Ibid., p. 77.
13. Ibid., p. 111.
14. Ibid., p. 341.
15. Ibid., pp. 345–46.
16. Himes, *My Life of Absurdity*, p. 8.

CHAPTER SEVENTEEN

1. Fabre, op. cit., p. 407.
2. FBI Files, Dec. 3, 1953, p. 3.
3. Quoted in "Wright's Exile," by Michel Fabre, *New Letters*, p. 142.
4. Webb, p. 419.
5. FBI Files, July 8, 1954, pp. 1–3.
6. Richard Wright, *Pagan Spain* (New York: Harper & Bros., 1957), p. 24.
7. Ibid., p. 69.
8. Ibid., p. 62.
9. Ibid., p. 17.
10. Wright, *Black Power*, pp. xi–xii.
11. FBI Files, April 4, 1958, p. 2.
12. Ibid., p. 3.
13. Ibid., pp. 3–4.
14. Horace Cayton and Sidney Williams, "Personal Impressions," *New Letters*, p. 39.
15. Wright, *Pagan Spain*, p. 1.
16. Fabre, op. cit., p. 405.
17. Webb, p. 392.
18. Ibid.
19. Ollie Harrington, "The Last Days of Richard Wright," *Ebony* magazine, Vol. 16, Feb. 1961, p. 84.
20. FBI Files, June 30, 1955, p. 1.
21. Ibid., July 27, 1955, p. 1.
22. Richard Wright, *The Color Curtain: A Report on the Bandung Conference* (New York: World Publishing Co., 1956), pp. 25–26.
23. Ibid., p. 178.
24. Ibid., p. 201.
25. Ibid., p. 209.
26. Ibid., p. 211.
27. Wright, *Black Power*, p. 345.
28. Ibid.
29. Richard Wright, "Tradition and Industrialization," *Présence Africaine*, No. 8–9–10 (June–November 1956), p. 356.
30. Fabre, op. cit., p. 424.

31. W. E. B. Du Bois, *The Autobiography of W. E. B. Du Bois* (New York: International Publishers Co., Inc., 1968), p. 394.
32. Fabre, op. cit., p. 427.
33. Ibid., p. 430.
34. Ibid., p. 432.
35. "Correspondence," Richard Wright Collection (Schomburg).

CHAPTER EIGHTEEN

1. Baldwin, *Nobody Knows My Name*, p. 24.
2. State Department Files, May 8, 1956, p. 1.
3. Du Bois, *Présence Africaine*, p. 383.
4. Baldwin, op. cit., p. 27.
5. State Department Files, p. 1.
6. Wright, *Présence Africaine*, p. 67.
7. State Department Files, pp. 1–2.
8. Ibid., pp. 2–3.
9. Fabre, p. 437.
10. Fabre, p. 437.
11. Baldwin, *Nobody Knows My Name*, p. 40; see also Aimé Césaire, "Culture et Colonisation," *Présence Africaine*, pp. 190–205.
12. Wright, "Tradition and Industrialization," *Présence Africaine*, p. 350.
13. Ibid., pp. 354–55.
14. Ibid., p. 357.
15. Fabre, op. cit., pp. 440–41.
16. Williams, *New Letters*, p. 38.
17. Richard Wright, Foreword in George Padmore's *Pan-Africanism or Communism* (London: Dodson, 1956), pp. 13–14.
18. David Caute, op. cit., p. 52.
19. Fabre, op. cit., p. 448.
20. Ollie Harrington, "The Mysterious Death of Richard Wright," *Daily World*, Vol. X, No. 110 (Dec. 17, 1977), p. 35.
21. Fabre, op. cit., p. 441.
22. Ibid., p. 442.
23. Richard Wright, *White Man, Listen!* (Garden City, N.Y.: Doubleday & Co., Inc., 1957), p. xvi.
24. Ibid., p. 31.
25. Ibid., p. 8.
26. Ibid., pp. 19–20.
27. Ibid., p. 45.
28. Ibid., p. 49.
29. Fabre, op. cit., p. 450.
30. Harrington, p. 5.
31. Himes, *My Life of Absurdity*, pp. 215–16.
32. Correspondence from an intimate friend of Wright's, 1976.
33. Richard Wright, *The Long Dream* (New York: Ace Publishing Corporation, 1958), p. 228.
34. Himes, *My Life of Absurdity*, p. 75.
35. Harrington, *Ebony* magazine, p. 90.

36. FBI Files, April 4, 1958, p. 1.
37. Fabre, op. cit., p. 462.
38. FBI Files, May 26, 1958, p. 1.
39. Ibid., p. 2.
40. FBI Files, May 29, 1958, p. 1.
41. FBI Files, July 7, 1958, p. 1.
42. Request by the writer to read this novel was denied by the staff of the Beinecke Library.

CHAPTER NINETEEN

1. FBI Files, July 7, 1958, p. 1, Aug. 21, 1958, p. 1, Feb. 13, 1959, p. 1.
2. Himes, *Amistad*, p. 87.
3. FBI Files, Feb. 19, 1959, p. 1.
4. Caute, op. cit., p. 156.
5. Fabre, op. cit., p. 471.
6. Caute, op. cit., p. 167.
7. Fabre, op. cit., p. 458.
8. Debate in the House of Commons on the Expiring Laws Continuance Bill (London, Hansard, Vol. 595, Nov. 20, 1958), pp. 1342–43.
9. Ibid., pp. 1353–54.
10. Harrington, *Ebony* magazine, p. 88.
11. Letter from the Home Office, London, Mar. 9, 1979.
12. Ungar, *FBI*, p. 234.
13. FBI Files, Feb. 11, 1960, p. 2.
14. Fabre, op. cit., p. 497.
15. Ibid.
16. Ibid., p. 500.
17. Ibid., p. 492.
18. Ibid., p. 623.
19. Himes, *My Life of Absurdity*, p. 216.
20. Fabre, op. cit., p. 622.
21. From conversations between the writer and a friend of Wright's.
22. Richard Wright, "The Negro Intellectual and Artist in the United States Today." (Delivered at the American Church, Nov. 8, 1960), p. 5.
23. Ibid., p. 19.
24. Webb, op. cit., p. 377.
25. Harrington, "The Mysterious Death of Richard Wright," p. 5.
26. FBI Files, May 9, 1963, p. 1.

GLOSSARY

This is a partial list of terms found in the documents used in this book. The list was compiled from *FBI: an Uncensored Look Behind the Walls*, by Sanford J. Ungar, and from a list supplied this writer by the Federal Bureau of Investigation.

1. ACSI—Department of the Army.
2. ASAC—Assistant Special Agent in Charge.
3. Bureau—Usually Refers to the Washington Headquarters.
3b. CIA—Central Intelligence Agency.
4. CIC—Central file, Department of the Army.
5. CID—Criminal Investigation Division.
6. CPUSA—Communist Party of the U.S.A.
7. Field division—Territory covered by a field office.
8. Field office—one of fifty-nine regional units of the FBI.
9. Foreign Liaison Unit—unit at FBI Headquarters.
10. G2—Department of the Army.
11. GID—General Intelligence Division.
12. HISC—House Internal Security Committee.
13. HUAC—House Un-American Activities Committee.
14. INS—Immigration and Naturalization Service.
15. Legal attaché—Overseas agent of the FBI, usually based in an American embassy or consulate.
16. Legat—Shorthand term for legal attaché.
17. NIA—Naval Intelligence Agency.
18. NEA—State Department.
19. M-5—British Security Service.
20. M-6—British Intelligence Service.
21. OIC—State Department.

22. OLI—State Department.
23. ONI—Office of Naval Intelligence.
24. OCB—State Department.
25. OO—Office of origin, field office that did the initial Investigation on any Bureau case.
26. OSS—Office of Strategic Services; forerunner of the CIA.
27. Rebulet—"Regarding Bureau letter."
28. Region IX File—Department of the Army.
29. SAC—Special Agent in Charge.
30. SACB—Subversive Activities Control Board, established by the Internal Security Act of 1950.
31. USIA—United States Information Agency.
32. WFO—Washington Field Office.

INDEX

WITHDRAWN

ALBERTSON COLLEGE OF IDAHO
PS3545.R815.Z664
Richard Wright :ordeal of a native son /

3 5556 00057754 4

DATE DUE

PRINTED IN U.S.A.